Everton

The Official
Autobiography

Everton

The Official
Autobiography

'Once Everton has touched you,
nothing will be the same'.

Alex Ball

'Once Everton has touched you,
nothing will be the same'

- Alan Ball

The Official Everton Autobiography
Compiled by James Cleary.

Everton FC Publications Editor: Darren Griffiths.

Editing and Production: Alan Jewell and Adam Oldfield.
Design (jacket and endpapers): Graeme Helliwell.

Published by Trinity Mirror Sport Media,
official publishing partners of Everton Football Club.
Executive Editor: Ken Rogers.
Senior Editor: Steve Hanrahan.
Editor: Paul Dove.
Senior Art Editor: Rick Cooke.

Compiled from archives of Liverpool Post & Echo, Everton FC archive.
Images (jacket and endpapers): Trinity Mirror, Press Association Images.

First Edition
Published in Great Britain in hardback form in 2012.
Published and produced by: Trinity Mirror Sport Media,
PO Box 48, Old Hall Street, Liverpool L69 3EB.

ISBN: 978-1-908695-20-8

Printed and bound by CPI Group (UK) Ltd, Croydon, CR0 4YY

Contents

Introduction		8
David Moyes		11
1892-1901	*Goodison Grand Opening; First FA Cup Final; Inaugural Merseyside Derby; More Cup Agony*	13
1902-1911	*Sandy Four-midable; Championship Contenders; Cup Finally Ours; Turner Prize; Taylor Trauma;*	33
1912-1921	*Fiery Cup Clash; League Champions; Double A Step Too Far; Post-War Blues*	51
1922-1931	*Signing William Ralph Dean; Title Triumph; Dixie's 60-Goal Record; A Brief Relegation*	67
1932-1941	*The Road To Wembley; A Second Cup Success; Goodison's Greatest Game; Dean Out, Lawton In*	91
1942-1951	*Eight-Goal Derby Thriller; Lemons And Lawton; Record Crowd; Dropping Down A Division*	105
1952-1961	*Hickson's Finest Hour; Top Flight Return; Pitch Pioneers; A Golden Vision; Catterick Takes Reins*	121
1962-1971	*Champions Again; Euro Quest; TV Cup First; Cup Heroes; Building Bellefield; Holy Trinity*	165
1972-1981	*Catterick Departs; Latchford For Kendall; Chairman Carter; Kendall Appointed*	251
1982-1991	*Kendall Delivers Silverware; All-Merseyside Cup Final; Euro Ecstasy; League Titles Eight & Nine*	307
1992-2001	*Kendall Quits; The Great Escape; Royle Ascent; Cup Conquerors; Southall Exit; Kenwright Era*	395
2002-2012	*Rooney Emerges; Moyes And The People's Club; Big Dunc's Farewell; Super Tim; A Bright Future*	437

Introduction

There have been many comprehensive history books written about the remarkable football institution that is Everton Football Club.

These include Thomas Keates' 1928 classic . . . penned 50 years after the formation of the club. This title provides a fascinating insight into those pioneering St. Domingo's days and the emergence of Everton FC as powerhouse founder members of the Football League.

Experienced national newspaper journalist John Roberts fulfilled his remit in 1978 to write Everton's Official Centenary history, exactly 100 years after the formation of the original St Domingo's.

I was hugely proud to be asked to research and write the official centenary history of the club's famous stadium in 1992: '100 years of Goodison Glory'. The title was updated and re-published in 2000 under the banner of: 'Goodison Glory: Everton's Millennium Giants Edition.'

In 2006, one hundred years after Everton's first FA Cup Final victory, 'Everton's FA Cup 100' carried the last interview with legendary and much-loved captain Brian Labone. Now Everton have taken the ultimate step and commissioned the most comprehensive publication ever about one of the greatest clubs in the world.

This 'Official Autobiography of Everton Football Club' is not one author's work, but rather an encyclopaedia of happenings and events that come together in one remarkable volume to bring to life every relevant moment in the club's history, told by the people who were there at the time.

It was the Reverend Ben Swift Chambers who was the acknowledged founding father of St Domingo's football team and therefore Everton FC. Chambers' unkempt, lost grave was discovered in the Yorkshire village of Shepley, and then restored thanks to the investigative work of author Peter Lupson and the full support of Everton FC. The fascinating and comprehensive publication 'Across The Park' followed.

As a true blue Evertonian, you will fully understand the unbridled ambition of those early pioneers and why they changed the name of the club from St. Domingo to Everton. You will feel proud of the confidence and defiant nature of George Mahon who, in 1892, took Everton from Anfield and walked them the short distance across Stanley Park to a new home where dreams would now become reality.

In this book, you will listen to the illustrious Dixie Dean talking about his legendary 60 goal Football League scoring record that will never be beaten; you will get inside the secretive head of famous 1960s manager Harry Catterick ; you will know instinctively why Alex Young was truly the 'Golden Vision; you will feel a glow just thinking about Everton's holy trinity of Ball, Harvey and Kendall; and stride forward with your head held high into Howard's unmatchable 1980s era and the supremely organised world of David Moyes.

Reading the 'Official Everton Autobiography' will be like sitting in a room full of legends and journalists whose news stories and reports would ultimately become Everton history.

I am proud to be one of those dedicated Everton followers, both as a boyhood fan and a lifetime journalist. I reported on the golden Catterick era, sat in Alan Ball's blue E-Type Jag and listened in awe as he laid out his royal blue ambitions, and survived the challenging Seventies to emerge as the Liverpool Echo's Everton correspondent in the supremely successful 1980s era of the great Howard Kendall and Colin Harvey.

Having been in the fortunate position to have read the 'Official Everton Autobiography' in advance of publication and felt inspired by and captivated by every page, I have no doubt that this is a book you will not be able to put down, from the first mention of Ben Swift Chambers to the remarkable episode that has been David Moyes and the age of the People's club.

Every Evertonian has a grasp of the glory and passion of one of the world's greatest football institutions. But when you've finished this book, you will truly be able to proudly declare: "I really do know my history!"

And the Z-Cars theme will ring in your head all day as you say: 'Blue Nose . . . and proud of it!'

Ken Rogers, Executive Editor,
Trinity Mirror Sport Media

Welcome to Everton

"*T*he people made me come here. I am from a city not unlike Liverpool myself. I have been brought up with Glasgow Celtic and Glasgow Rangers and I am now in a city where football means as much as it does up there. I think I am joining a football club which is probably the people's football club in Liverpool.

The people in the street support Everton and I hope to give them something over the next few years that they can be very proud of.

You don't get jobs in football management when things are easy and I think we would all be lying here if we said that we didn't think it was a big job.

It's been a big job for all the previous managers and it will be no different for me, but it's one which I'm really positive about."

David Moyes,
March 14, 2002

1892-1901

It rivals the greater American baseball pitches
(Out Of Doors, August 24, 1892)

How a popular sporting publication of the day viewed the birth of Goodison Park, which opened its gates to the public on the 24th of the month.

$\mathcal{B}$EHOLD Goodison Park. No single picture could take in the entire scene the ground presents, for it rivals the greater American baseball pitches.

On three sides there are covered stands and on the fourth side the ground has been so well banked up with thousands of loads of cinders that a complete view of the game can be held from any position.

The spectators are divided from the playing piece by a neat, low hoarding and the touchline is far enough from it to prevent those accidents which used to be predicted at Anfield Road, but never happened.

Grandstand start to the season
(Liverpool Courier, August 30, 1892)

$\mathcal{T}$HERE is one huge covered stand, and it is contemplated covering those at either end, a shield from the rain or cold winds that will be much appreciated by those who patronise the more "popular" places, whilst those who prefer to view the play from the sloping banks will find the survey of the field of action free and uninterrupted. The offices and dressing rooms provided on the ground will be gratifying to the players and officials and if the turf, which at present appears on the whole well, there will be less liability of injury to players when reaching "mother earth," as they inevitably do in the course of spirited play. The programme of Everton is a good one, consisting of 30 league fixtures in addition to cup-ties. The second team will be chiefly occupied in maintaining the high position they secured last year in the Combination.

Shareholders' grounds for optimism
(The Liverpool Courier, August 30, 1892)

An early shareholders meeting of the club, reflecting the financial impact of the move to Goodison Park.

A MEETING of the shareholders of the Everton Football Club Company Limited was held last evening in the schoolroom of the Presbyterian Church Royal-Street. Mr G. Mahon occupied the chair, and there was a good attendance. Mr R. Molyneux (secretary) read the notice convening the meeting, explaining that it was called for the purpose of electing directors.

The chairman gave an account of the progress of the company. He said they had now arrived at that stage in the history of the club when they were determined that no secret should be held from the general body of the shareholders. There were now 431 shareholders, and this was considered very satisfactory when they remembered that the total membership of the club was 490.

These shareholders held 1,730 shares, and he would like to explain that it was thought advisable not to give out the shares in blocks, by which means they would have had the whole of the capital subscribed, but rather to have a number of applications, so that there would be more supporters of the club.

The number of old members belonging to the company was 304, and there was 40 old members who had taken season tickets. Of the 431 shareholders there were 338 holding season tickets, and as applications were coming in daily he expected there would be another hundred. Showing the confidence that the public had in the club, he might point out that there was 40 more season-ticket holders up to the present time in excess of the total number applied for on the old ground. *(Applause.)* They had a profit on the first athletic festival of £150, and he expected there would be a profit of about £100 on the second. The total new ground expenditure amounted to £2,700, being £700 in excess of the estimate, but he thought that as they had obtained double the accommodation which was provided on the old ground there was no cause to grumble. *(Hear Hear.)*

It was moved and seconded that the following be re-elected to act as directors: Mr G.Mahon (chairman), Dr. Baxter, Messrs. J Atkinson J.Griffiths A.T.Coates, W.E.Leyland, J.Davies, W.R.Clayton, F Currier, and W Jackson. Mr. Swan moved an amendment: "that the board of directors shall consist of six directors, two of whom shall retire by rotation at the close of each financial year, and that all vacancies on the directorate shall be filled by shareholders at the annual meeting, at which retiring directors shall be eligible for re-election."

He was of opinion that six directors would be quite sufficient. On the amendment being seconded and put, only three votes were recorded for it, and the original proposition was then enthusiastically carried.

The meeting closed with a vote of thanks to the directors for their work during the summer.

Goodison gates open for the first time

(Liverpool Courier, September 3, 1892)

Edited extracts from the match report of two of the earliest recorded Goodison fixtures: an exhibition game with Bolton Wanderers and an impressive victory over Newton Heath, the club that would later change its name to Manchester United.

*T*HE new Everton Football Ground, Goodison Park, Anfield (the new ground was in Walton but old habits clearly prevailed amongst the

Courier journalists) was opened for practical use last evening, when the Bolton Wanderers came down to play a friendly. There was a splendid crowd of spectators, fully ten thousand people being present. Punctual to time, the teams entered the ground from the covered stands, the Wanderers first, both having a most cordial reception by the huge crowd already present. Mr Mahon, the president of the club, kicked off for Everton and Somerville effected a return.

As darkness was creeping over the ground, the final result was: Everton, four goals, Wanderers, two goals.

Newton Heath hit for six

(Liverpool Mercury, September 26, 1892)

It's fascinating to see how newspaper football reporting has changed over the years. The language used is very different to what we are familiar with today.

*T*HE league attraction at Goodison Park was the visit of Newton Heath, one of the newly-promoted clubs, the weather, fortunately proving very enjoyable. A large crowd numbering between 10,000 and 12,000 assembled, who must have been delighted with the exhibition given by the home XI but who would naturally anticipate a much closer contest than that which ensued.

Everton facing the sun and wind, kicked off and went at once in goal and within a minute Latta scored from passing by Chadwick and Geary. Loud and long was the cheer which greeted the smart piece of play.

Soon Everton were assuming the aggressive, when Geary following a free-kick, scored with a grounder. Two goals had thus been scored when the game had been in existence but a quarter of an hour. Newton Heath were not demoralised by them, reverses, and for a time had as much of the play as their opponents, but they were never threatening, and by degrees, Everton took up their attack, and severely taxed the defensive qualities of Mitchell and Brown, who were safe at this period.

Howarth effectually arrested a raid, as had Holt just previously and then Geary came in for applause for a brilliant run, but he had outpaced his colleagues and as he could not shoot himself, the sprint was of no avail. Then Chadwick improved the position of his club by completely baffling Warner with an oblique shot, the ball passing through near the far post.

Maxwell and Geary seemed so dangerous that a corner was conceded in clearing which another corner was forced. This was also rendered nugatory, but the visitors' lines were out cleared, and Latta sent in a very hard shot, which struck the bar and the ball rebounding into the field of play, Chadwick drove it into the net.

Warner stopped many a trackless shot, but he had to strike his flag to both Maxwell and Milward and when the end came, Everton had won deservedly by six goals to nil.

Bumper crowd treated to Blues master class
(Liverpool Mercury, February 13, 1893)

Arguably the greatest result in the club's history to that point occurred against Preston North End, Double winners in 1888/89 and champions again the following season, Preston were outclassed at Goodison in front of (officially) 27,500, a record Goodison gate. The date of publication would also see the side secure a 2-0 victory at Sheffield Wednesday, the sixth of eight successive wins in league and cup.

*E*VERTON scored their greatest triumph in their whole career on Saturday, and are to be congratulated on the splendid achievement of defeating Preston North End by six goals to nil. Interest centred in the combat and never was such a large gathering of spectators seen at a league match as that which crowded Goodison Park. Hundreds could not obtain admission, whilst others found accommodation inside the fence which skirts the field of play and on the roof of the stands. The adjacent housetops were also brought into requisition, and together the scene was an imposing and animating one. The spectacle quickened the pulse of all present and, the sun shining brightly during the greater part of the time, the crowd enjoyed their sport under the most happy auspices. The "gate" realised £725 10s 9d., upwards of 28,000 spectators passing through the turnstiles. In addition to these there were the members subscribers, and "complimentaries", and there would thus be quite 30,000 people present. North End were ever popular, and have always drawn "big houses" but it was not their fame alone that served as the magnet. It was the recent strong play of Everton that gave so much seat to the event, on the strength of which the match was generally conceded to be a very open one, with Preston North End slightly the most fancied as winners with the exception of N. J. Ross on the one side and Geary on the other, the teams were at full strength, and so they met on pretty equal terms.

Everton had the good fortune of choice of ends and turned their backs to the sun and the wind during the first half. They got into a remarkably fine and firm stride from the kick-off and when Latta opened the scoring account within a few minutes of the start it was the result of some clever dashing all-round play that at once gave assurance that North End had at length met their match. Everton even improved as the game went on, asserting their superiority in every department, and at the end of the intensely interesting and spirited game a vociferous cheer signalled their emphatic victory, not a show of fluke characterising one of the six goals scored. Everton were compelled to put up with 10 men with Kelso retiring hurt for the last quarter of an hour of the first half, but even when short-handed they more than held their own.

The home side were conscious that Drummond was a vulnerable spot in the North End defence, and aided by the somewhat cross wind, they brought special pressure to bear on the left-back during the first half. N. J. Ross was certainly missed, but his presence could not have altered the issue.

The Everton half-backs were seen at their best, good as they have been in the proceeding matches and the ease with which they beat the Preston giants created immense enthusiasm. Howarth and Kelso got though their work so effectively that Williams was never hard pushed and only had about four shots to attend to, none of which had much power behind them. Geary was absent through injury to a thigh received in the Notts Forest match, but his inclusion could scarcely have improved the Everton' vanguard. They combined splendidly, their passing being well timed, whilst they infused surprising dash in the work and shot with great keenest and accuracy.

The condition of the men was an important factor in their favour, their staying powers speaking eloquently of the advantage of exercise at Hoylake and the attention paid them by their popular and efficient training.

Long-kicking indulged in by both sides
(Liverpool Mercury, March 21, 1893)

A first FA Cup final appearance was achieved at the third time of asking in East Lancashire. The semi-final match report extracts included reference to the level of Evertonian following and the adoption of the long-ball game by both sides. Clearly the School of Science had yet to take hold.

*T*HE teams had met twice at Bramall Lane, Sheffield, a draw ensuing on each occasion. Two goals each were scored in the first game, and nothing in the second. The capacious ground was packed long before the time of starting, and there must have been quite 30,000 within the enclosure. Many hundreds failed to obtain admission, and crowds of disappointed ones took advantage of the hill beyond the ground, where they had a distant view of the play. The conditions were favourable for a true and skill exhibition of the Association code.

North End were first to appear, and were well received but a more flattering reception was accorded Everton a few minutes later, and they evidently had most partisans. Trainor won the toss and Everton attacked the Darwen goal.

Maxwell receiving from the left, dribbled and scored with a terrific high shot opening the scoring after just a half-hour's play. Everton at once returned to goal, but were held in check, and then survived a remarkable tussle right in the goalmouth of a protracted character. A delay now occurred and on resuming, long kicking was indulged in by both sides, and momentarily play was desultory. This culminated in favour of Everton, and first Maxwell and then Chadwick, had good shots. The game was more spirited than ever, and amidst the wildest demonstrations, the players flitted up and down with great gusto, neither defences having any respite. Twenty minutes before time North End equalised on J. Ross shooting across towards Gordon who, though seeming to be offside, shot into the net at the further end of goal.

Milward got away, compelling N. J. Ross to concede a corner. This was placed by Chadwick so well that Gordon headed into the net, Everton thus assuming the lead five minutes from "time". North End immediately afterwards swooped down on goal, but Williams got the ball round the post, or North End might have equalised.

A throw-in to North End was the last item, and the whistle sounded whilst Preston were attacking with the result Everton 2 goals; Preston North End 1. It must be admitted that on the whole Everton were in luck's way. The attack of the losers was better sustained than that of the winners, but this fact only demonstrates that Everton were grand in defence, Kelso and Williams especially so. On arriving at the Liverpool Exchange Station a large crowd awaited the team, who had a most beauty [sic] reception, Williams being carried shoulder high. To be well prepared for the final tie next Saturday, the Everton players leave for the country today. The gate amounted to £790.

Solo strike ends Blues' Cup dream

(Liverpool Mercury, March 27, 1893)

Everton's first FA Cup final ends in disappointment at a Fallowfield (Manchester) venue that struggled to contain the crowd.

*A*T one time on Saturday there were serious doubts as to whether the final tie for the trophy between these clubs would come off. This question arose from the fact that the weather was beautifully fine and summer-like – and a crowd estimated at from 40,000 to 50,000 present, had been attracted to the Manchester Athletic club ground at Fallowfield in the expectation of seeing an exciting contest.

Early in the day it was seen the crowd would be an enormous one, and that some difficulty would be experienced in keeping the field clear of action. During the progress of the match between boys from Sheffield and Manchester, the barriers were severely tried and at last one near the pavilion gave way, the result being a general stampede to obtain a better view of the more important match when it should start.

It had been generally stated that ample provision had been made to maintain order, but the idea was soon routed, as the eager spectators quickly caused the larger number of members of the fourth estate, skated immediately in front, to make a shift for their personal safety. In fact, the police present seemed altogether disinclined to handle the crowd, and reinforcements were sent for.

The Everton men made their appearance in the pavilion, but it was left for the "Wolves" to be first in the field, the men from Wolverhampton who had numerous supporters, entering the enclosure from the large stand at exactly 3-30. Howarth led the Everton men on to the enclosure at 3-34, the scene then being a very lively one indeed.

When the competition was entered upon, few people would have credited the assertion that it would be left for Wolverhampton Wanderers and Everton to contest the final.

The Liverpool club on Saturday made its first appearance in the final, in fact, they have never previously been past the last four. They have taken the Liverpool Cup several times, but though also taking part in the Lancashire Cup ties have failed. Everton's stay at Buxton, however, appeared to have worked wonders and one and all turned out apparently in the best of condition.

Weather of a more delightful character could not have been desired and, but for the untoward circumstances already alluded to, the affair would have proved a gigantic success. As it is the gate will no doubt be found to be a record.

Throughout the game, Wolverhampton played with more dash than their rivals and it is to this they owe their victory as the appended will show:

Wolverhampton Wanderers entered the field from the Whitworth Lane end in amber and black jerseys, with black knickers, and five minutes later Everton were led on the enclosure by their captain, the players wearing blue jerseys and white pants. At this time there would be quite 40,000 people present.

The Liverpool contingent having lost the toss played with the sun in their eyes, and Maxwell kicking off for them.

From a throw-in at midfield, Butcher passed to Wykes, who ran down the field but finished up by shooting just outside. Milward at the other end beat the "Wolves" custodian, but the goal was disallowed owing to some previous infringement of the rules.

Hands against Holt caused the representatives from the banks of the Mersey to fall back. Milward and Chadwick on the left, showed a fine display of passing, and the latter sending in a good shot, Rose saved his charge by pulling the crossing down and allowing the ball to go just over. The half-time period arrived with a blank sheet, and longer rest than usual was taken by the players until the crowd had been got outside the touch line.

A free-kick for hands against Allan came to nothing and both teams, considering the hot weather, played up splendidly, and proved that their respective trainers had done their duties well. Eventually Allen sent in a long shot from the right wing for the "Wolves" and although Williams ought to have stopped it, he let it go though his hands and the first blood was drawn against Everton amidst tremendous cheer. The second portion of the game had been in progress about 10 minutes when this reverse to the Liverpool men took place, and, as it afterwards proved, was the only score of the match. Wykes shortly afterwards sent exactly a similar shot, but this time Williams was successful, in preventing the leather from going through.

Everton had a look in for a short time. Holt and Howarth doing yeoman service. Swift, however, played a grand defensive game at full-back, and prevented these efforts on the part of the Evertonians from taking effect. Once again Everton in their endeavour to equalise got the leather up the left wing, but the "Wolves" were defending in such grand manner that the "boys" in blue could not score. Midst the cheers of the spectators Wolverhampton won by one goal to Everton nil.

Wolverhampton Wanderers: Rose (W. C.), goal, Swift (G) and Baugh (R), backs, Kinsley (G), Allen (H) and Malpass (J. W.), half-backs, Griffins (A), Wood (H), Butcher (J. H.), Wykes (D) and Topham (R), forwards.

Everton: Williams (R) goal, Kelso (R) and Howarth (R. H.) (captain), backs, Boyle (R), Holt (J) and Stewart (A), half-backs, Latta (A), Gordon (P), Maxwell (A), Chadwick (E) and Milward (A), forwards.

Referee: Mr. C. J. Hughes (Cheshire), Messrs, T. Gumley (London) and Roberts (Derby).

Vast crowd watches first Mersey derby win

(Liverpool Mercury, October 15, 1894)

Match report extracts from the first Merseyside derby in the Football League, which provided a welcome outcome for the home side against the fledgling club in residence at their former home. The game would also see a record crowd of 44,000, and more than £1,000 in gate receipts

*T*HE long looked-for meeting of these local rivals took place at Goodison Park, and excited all the interested. A great game, from a scientific point of view, was not expected, but the public appetite was whetted by the fact that Everton and Liverpool were to oppose each other at full strength for the first time in their history. The event recalled recollection of those keen games in which Everton and Bootle, some six or seven years ago, used to take part; but the parallel ends with keen local rivalry.

The entertainment of Saturday surpassed in attractiveness every great that had occurred before, and Everton, who held the record of gates for the league matches, which was that of £735 taken the season before last, when Preston North End were beaten so easily, have broken their own record, the money taken on Saturday being £1,026.

This would show that the attendance must have been something like 40,000 included in which number were several leading citizens. Whilst the vast crowds were assembling a capital exhibition of football was given by picked teams of schoolboys of Liverpool and Nottingham, but the visitors were no match for the local lads, who won easily by three goals to nil.

A few minutes before time fixed for starting, the teams appeared within the area, and met with a hearty reception. Many had been the rumours during the week of men that could not play owing to injuries or other causes, but Chadwick was the only conspicuous absentee, he having received injury to a leg at Bolton. The clubs were accordingly represented in their full strengths with the exception named, though Hartley ably filled the position of inside-left.

Everton lost the toss, and prompt to time Holt kicked off against the wind. Two free-kicks fell to Liverpool of no avail, and then Bell forced to leave the ground momentarily. In the meantime, Kerr received from Ross, and made a running shot into the people. Parry was next hard pressed, but cleared, and kicked onto the stand. McLean was next in request, and put into touch four times in quick succession in grappling with Latta and McInnes, and from pressure on the left Hannah gave hands near in. Stewart took the place, and McInnes headed a goal in 10 minutes from the start.

Liverpool then attacked strongly. Both Parry and Stewart gave fouls, and a hot scrimmage ensued, when Cain and Parry checked keen shots. Southworth was next going strongly, but Hannah checked him, and the heading work looked well for Everton, but the movement was gamely required. The home forwards improved in their combination, severely harassing the visitors defence. At this exciting period, McInnes hurt his leg, apparently a twist and had to leave the field.

Everton responded quickly and scrimmaged near the post. This was tided over, and on Boyle essaying a wild shot, the whistle sounded for the interval, with Everton in command by a goal to nil, the rest of very even play.

Liverpool held out during a renewed severe tussle and rushed up the right, and when Kerr shot accurately a goal seemed certain, but Cain pushed the ball straight to Ross, who lifted over the bar with a wretched shot. The Liverpool right wing again beat Parry, and another opening was at hand but, to the relief of Evertonians, Bradshaw put just over the bar. The latter at the same time received an injury, but did not leave the field.

The home team were more fortunate when their turn at attack soon came, as on Bell centre-ing Latta sent into the net, after an hour of the game had arrived. Both sides improved in their play at this advanced time, a grand movement finished off with a splendid shot by McQueen and a brilliant saved by Cain. McCann was also called upon, and he too saved splendidly.

A free-kick by Boyle enabled Bell to penetrate goal, but offside was awarded. A little later however, Everton attacked with the desired effect, on the right wing making ground, Bell breasted into the net. The home team were now in a safe position. The play continued to be spirited, and McCartney was reprimanded for badly fouling Southworth. Everton had the best of exchanges, but could not score again, thus winning by 3 goals to nil.

Liverpool people are the greatest supporters

(Liverpool Mercury)

First Merseyside derby match comment piece, with the locals attracting warm praise for their support of the fledgling sport.

*W*ELL it's a record £1,026. The phenomenal sum indicates that there must have been something near 40,000 spectators, and yet the attraction was purely local. Probably 99 of every hundred were Liverpoolians. If so, to what great extend the Association game of football has caught on in the district within the space of about 12 years. The game is new to Liverpool compared with some other towns, and Mr. R. Wilson demonstrated the rapid growth when he informed a circle of friends that, as treasurer of Everton, he had the unique experience of having been the custodian of Everton's smallest "gates" (2s 1d) and of their largest. From a couple of shillings to a thousand pounds is a big jump to accomplish within a decade, but Liverpool people have accomplished it and can boast that they are the greatest supporters of the good old game of football, as remodelled and perfected into an up-to date science.

The game itself turned out to be a much better exhibition of play than one dared to hope. Excitement of course ran high but considering the dimensions of the crowd the behaviour of the spectators was admirable. Fouls were numbers, certainly, but were of a light kind, with perhaps one exception, and were all through. Mr J. Lewis, the referee, had the men well in hand, and promptly and impartially exercised his authority.

Everton won solidly, but their superior staying power carried them triumphantly, as it had done so consistently this season. For the first hour it was anybody's game. The fouls and corner-kicks were about equally distributed, and so there can be no charge of undue roughness or claim of greater pressure of one team over another. Everton were in addition to their superior stamina, more compact in front of goal, following up quickly and shooting more accurately than their opponents.

The half-backs were a strong feature of the Everton team. Holt was in the thick of the fray, scoring repeated successes. Boyle checked Bradshaw and McQueen in his usual quiet and effective way, feeding his forwards also with taste. Stewart had the most active wing to grapple with in Kerr and Ross, and he rendered his old club mate very impotent in the later stages of the game.

The forwards were in good formation, notwithstanding that Bell and McInnes had to retire for a time. Hartley made a good inside-left in the place of Chadwick, and thus gave further proof of his usefulness, as a utility man. Either on the left, the right or centre, and with McInnes, Latta, Southworth and Bell up to their standard, notwithstanding that the latter was a bit lame, the Everton forwards gave much satisfaction.

The purchase of Goodison Park
(August 1895)

Goodison Park's Everton future was ensured three years after the club moved in. Finances were rarely a straightforward matter in football, even in the late 19th century.

*T*HE Liverpool football public generally will be delighted to learn that the directors of Everton Football Club have successfully negotiated the purchase of the ground at Goodison Park, the completion of the business being finally arranged at noon yesterday. For some time past rumours have been cast about that the directors had been unable to raise money by mortgage on the ground, or at any rate that they had approached several financiers for that purpose and that they could not effect a deal at all serviceable to their requirements. Be that as it may, we are able to inform those who circulated the silly reports that a mortgage of £6,000 has been obtained and signed, sealed and delivered most satisfactorily for the club. Furthermore, the directors have paid down in cash an additional £1,000 to the one previously made by the old board of directors when negotiations were first arranged for the purchase of Goodison Park by the club, and that the whole business has now been completed.

Blues edged out in Crystal Palace thriller
(Liverpool Mercury, April 10, 1897)

A second FA Cup final, but unfortunately a second disappointment, this time at Crystal Palace. Runaway champions Aston Villa completed the Double, only the second team to achieve the feat after Preston North End.

*T*HE central parts of London were literally alive with provincials from an early hour on Saturday. As the heavily-laden excursion trains arrived at the different terminals in the Metropolis, seeming to swarm more and more with visitors from the country, and by nine o'clock hosts of familiar Liverpool faces were visible in the Strand and other noted metropolitan thoroughfares.

Liverpool apparently supplied an even bigger contingent of spectators than the nearer city of Birmingham.

Then railway companies [who had] made elaborate arrangements for the conveyance of people from Liverpool and Lime Street presented an extraordinary spectacle. By ten o'clock the inlet to Crystal Palace had fairly began, special trains departed from the Victoria and other stations as frequent intervals, but the crowds were too vast at first to be subsequently coped with, and several blocks occurred.

At midday at least 20,000 persons must have congregated in the Palace ground and increased at an emirates rate. The supporters of the clubs freely sported their respected colours, and whenever opposing parties met noisy but in good manner.

Both teams arrived at Crystal Palace at three o'clock, and immediately made for the dressing rooms, which by the way were splendidly appointed, each of the players had a room and a bath to himself.

They quickly dressed and proposed themselves for the fray, and at 10 minutes to four a tremendous shouts vented the air as Stewart stepped on to the field and led his companions to the arena. The Villa players were somewhat later in arriving, but another enthusiastic cheer greeted them when they made their appearances.

A strong wind was blowing from goal to goal, and Devey winning the toss, won for his side this tangible advantage. Two minutes to four o'clock Hartley set the ball in motion, and some vigorous play by Milward and Chadwick carried play into the Villa's quarters, Spencer brought relief, and the ball was rapidly transferred to the Everton and when Storrier effected a clearance with a free-kick in a twinkling the ball was carried to the Villa half again but Evans proved a great stumbling block, and for a few moments the play raised with the Villa forwards.

At this stage the hearts of the Everton supporters went into their mouths, in consequence of Athersmith kicking Holt, and the little centre-half dropping heavily on the field. A brief stoppage was therefore made, but amidst cheers, Holt was able to resume.

The Villa forwards resumed the aggressive. An unfortunate shakiness in the Everton defence was now observable, and the Villa men were not long in taking the advantage of it. Athersmith steadied himself as if for a shot but decided to pass to Devey, who with a long oblique shot scored the first goal for the Villa, the ball just passing inside the post out of the reach of Menham. This success coming after 16 minutes' play was naturally cheered.

The Everton forwards were eventually rewarded with the anxiously-desired equalising point. Half an hour from the start the Everton right wing together with the centre dashed the ball along, Bell, using his speed to splendid effect, got past the Villa backs almost before they knew where they were. Whitehouse seeing a goal inevitable ran out, but just before he could reach the ball, Bell with fine judgement tipped it past him and then having nobody to face easily put the ball into the net, the success being greeted with vociferous cheering.

Everton now had decidedly the best of matters as their success seemed to infuse new life into them. Only a few minutes later Hartley got nicely away and passed over to the right wing, Taylor then shooting high over the bar. At the same time a foul was awarded against one of the Villa men, the ball was scrimmaged into the net, thus giving Everton the lead.

Then Storrier was so hard put he had to concede a corner. This led to nothing tangible, but from a free-kick shortly afterwards awarded against Taylor John Cowan, with a quick shot from short range, equalised.

The game now was far more evenly contested, both sides of singularly level terms. Storrier conceded a corner in attempting to head the ball away, and though Menham first cleverly cleared the ball, it was quickly returned into the goalmouth and Wheldon headed it into the net, thus giving Villa the lead once more, the score being three to two in their favour.

The game was certainly very stubbornly contested and it would be difficult at this stage to say that either team was superior to the other. Play was in the centre of the field when the whistle sounded for the interval. Half-time result, Aston Villa 3 goals Everton 2.

The sun now shone brilliantly and bothered the Evertonians in their efforts as it was right in their faces. Bell got clean away, and was preparing to centre when Spencer tripped him badly, and from the free kick the ball was sent beautifully into goal. It was then headed an inch or two over the bar.

A grand rush on the part of Chadwick, Hartley and Bell made the Villa partisans look exceedingly glum, but just when the final touch was necessary for the equalising goal. Spencer stopped them and saved an apparently certain goal.

The Liverpoolians showed tremendous and praiseworthy determination although they were still in a minority. Meechan added to the other good points a great inclination to score goals. He grandly tricked a couple of men and finished up with a lightning shot which would have put the team on even terms had it only been a few inches lower.

As the end approached the Everton men played splendidly and raised the crowd to a tremendous pitch of excitement by their grand efforts to equalise. Chadwick put in a fine ground shot, and Taylor followed this up with another shot, which Whitehouse saved just on the line.

It was a magnificent finish, and nobody would have grumbled had Everton's gallant efforts to equalise been rewarded.

The match was admitted to be the best final tie ever played in the English cup competition. It must be confessed that the Villa were slightly superior in the first half, and possibly deserved the advantage of a goal. At the same time, the magnificent fashion in which Everton forwards backed to their work after being twice in the rare was heartily recognised by the crowd.

Aston Villa: Whitehouse, goal, Evans and Spencer, backs, Crabtree, Jas Cowan and Reynolds, half-backs, Cowan, Weldon, Campbell, Devey (captain) and Athersmith, forwards.
Everton: Menham, goal, Storrier and Meechan, backs, Boyle, Holt and Stewart (captain), half-backs, Taylor, Bell, Hartley, Chadwick and Milward, forwards.
Referee: J. Lewis, Messrs J. Nowetch (Redcar) and A. Scagg (Crewe).

Grand opening of a new Goodison stand
(Liverpool Daily Post, September 1897)

A new season, and a new development at Goodison on Bullens Road for the 1897/98 campaign.

*O*N Saturday afternoon, the immense new structure erected during the close season was formally opened to the public, the ceremony being performed by Dr. Morley of Blackburn, one of the vice-presidents of the Football Association. An effort had been made by the directors to get Prince Ranjitsinhji to officiate, but that gentleman was unable to come to Liverpool in consequence of indisposition.

Dr. Morley was met in the afternoon at the Adelphi Hotel by a number of the directors and other gentlemen, and the party afterwards drove to Goodison Park in several open carriages. There was a large gathering of the public present awaiting the arrival of the party at the entrance to the stand in Bullens Road, and the ceremony was at once performed. In the evening the company sat down to dinner at the Adelphi Hotel, under the chairmanship of Mr W.R. Clayton.

Club directors treat the players
(Liverpool Mercury, September 18, 1900)

An official club function, with the club trainer part of the entertainment.

*T*HE directors of the Everton Club entertained to dinner at the Alexandra Hotel, last evening, the players associated with both the first, and second team of the club. It was one of a series of pleasant gatherings held during the season. All the Everton directors and also the players were present, and Mr W. R. Clayton occupied the chair. During the evening an interesting musical programme was presented by Messrs. G. Hill, A. Dean, F. Girvan, M. Govener, J. C. Clinton, J. Elliott, trainer of the club, and G. Gregson, who accompanied.

1902-1911

Pride of the city

(Liverpool Mercury, January 11, 1902)

A 4-0 Goodison victory over Liverpool signalled Everton's championship intent. These extracts are notable for mention of the impressive showing of Alex "Sandy" Young and Liverpool's inexperienced goalkeeper Marshall.

*U*NFORTUNATELY for the complete success of the great match at Goodison Park, the weather broke down about an hour before the time appointed for the kick-off, and though there was a satisfactory gate, the attendance would have been considerably augmented had the conditions been more enticing. Those who did attend witnessed an almost one-sided game, in which one team displayed form worthy of the championship, whilst the other never got above the dull level of mediocrity.

Liverpool were not simply beaten; they were routed, completely overplayed, and overwhelmed by the superior methods of their rivals. On one side was noticed a well-marked plan of campaign, evidently thoroughly understood by each Everton player; the method of attack was carried out on excellently-designed principles with the half-back line as the base of every movement.

Lying well on to the opposing backs, Young was the pivot on which most incursions devolved, and the ball was deftly lodged with him from right and left halves and backs.

Thence the whole attacking machinery was set in motion and with wide sweeping movements the Everton forward line bore down with merciless persistency on the Liverpool defence, like wolves on a fold.

The Everton centre fairly surpassed himself for not only was his footwork tricky, thus enabling him to baffle Raisbeck with repeated frequency, but he placed to the wings most judiciously, and fulfilled his part in the game with consummate skill. His display was far ahead of anything seen from him since he came into the team, and must have opened the eyes of many.

At half-back, Everton were seen at their best; for not a single weakness was noticeable in this line during the whole course of the game. The trio were most aggressive in their tactics, not only breaking up with ease the Liverpool forward movements, but being beautiful in touch with their own quintet, whom they most assiduously and judiciously kept ever on the advance.

This was a granite wall of defence to the visitors and whereas Abbott completely swamped Robertson and McGuigan, Booth attended to right and left with equal efficiency and Wolstenholme, to the delight of the home section of the crowd, shadowed Cox most persistently, and what is more, kept going to the final blowing of the whistle.

Further behind, Balmer played a capital game and Sharp, after a most inauspicious quarter of an hour at the start, steadied down and shaped remarkably well. His timing of the ball, and well-judged returns were alike worthy of praise, and he appeared to be under some hypnotic influence with Abbott, for the pair worked together with almost mechanical accuracy.

Marshall could not be blamed for the big debit account against him, but there is this difference between the class custodian and the novice: the former anticipates a shot and is in the position for receiving when the ball does come goalwards, thereby saving many a well meant effort from the invaders; the less experienced player only makes a start for the ball when it is too late to prevent it reaching the net.

On Saturday's form, Everton appear to possess a rare chance of securing final honours in the league journey for the team are keen on the accomplishment of this desirable object, and Sunderland have to come to Goodison Park yet.

Four he's a jolly good fellow

(Liverpool Courier, April 2, 1904)

Alex "Sandy" Young hit four goals on April Fool's Day in a convincing derby victory in front of a season-high 40,000. Just two years after winning the league, Liverpool would be relegated at the end of the month.

HE outstanding event locally in the Association football yesterday was the return league match between Everton and Liverpool at Goodison Park. Apart from the interest in the meeting of local rivals, the game was of the utmost importance to Liverpool, who have a hard struggle to maintain their position in the First Division of the league.

Though the weather was somewhat uncertain, rain fortunately held off during the progress of the game, and a holiday crowd of at least 40,000 people witnessed the match. Liverpool were at full strength, while Everton played Young centre-forward in place of Settle.

Liverpool kicked-off against the sun, and at once made progress. Goddard was in evidence, but Raisbeck missed his kick when danger threatened the Everton goal. Then Hardman got away and after the ball had been transferred from player to player Wolstenholme opened the score for Everton with a long shot, which Cotton might easily have saved.

There was a determination about the work of the Liverpool attack, which deserved to be awarded, and the equalising goal was not long delayed. Hewitt cleverly beat the home backs and passing to Cox, that player centred, with the result that Robinson headed into the net. It was a good goal, and deserved the applause with which it was received.

So far the game had been contested in the best spirit, and unfair tactics were rare. At the same time the wind was of great assistance to Everton. Suddenly Hardman broke away, and although protests were made on the ground of offside he centred the ball, the result being that Young shot past Cotton and gave Everton the lead.

Some pretty touches were recognised by the crowd, and following a free-kick against Parry the ball was placed to Young, who headed in, Cotton apparently was over the line when he handled the ball. A goal was allowed, and this gave Everton a lead of three goals to one.

Stung by this reverse the Liverpool players strenuously attacked, and after a free-kick against Taylor, the ball was sent into the goalmouth by West. A scrimmage ensued, and during an exciting encounter the ball was sent into the net, Parry as far as could be seen from the press box being the executant.

Liverpool were now going great guns but a raid by the Everton front line brought no tangible result, but a moment later Taylor ran down, and a weak clearance by West presented an open goal to Young, who had no difficulty in putting in a fourth for Everton.

Hughes was hooted for tripping Sharp, and the infraction of the rules proved of use to Everton, for from the free-kick, taken by Wolstenholme, Young added a fifth goal for his side.

Liverpool were awarded a penalty-kick in the closing stages, but to the chagrin of Liverpool supporters, Raybould failed miserably, sending the ball high over the bar. The end came immediately afterwards.

Pulsating Cup derby sets up final encounter

(By Citizen, Daily Mirror, April 2, 1906)

Landing derby honours in an FA Cup semi-final, something denied in 2012, was at least achieved over a century ago. Everton prevailed 2-0 to secure a first final in nine years, and hopefully now the elusive silverware could be obtained.

 *E*VERTON beat Liverpool at Birmingham on Saturday, by two goals to nil, and were, perhaps, a trifle lucky in winning by so great a margin – a goal would have represented the difference in the teams.

It was a case of science beating force, superior tactics overcoming vigour, and it was one of the most thrillingly exciting games I ever remember seeing in connection with the cup. Never a dull minute, desperately fast, he would, indeed, have been a cold-blooded mortal who did not find his pulses quicken as he looked on at the stirring incidents of the momentous struggle.

Half of the second half had elapsed before a goal was scored, but in that hour and a quarter there had been enough thrilling incidents for a half-a-dozen matches.

Then the first goal, which went to Everton, after Liverpool had been attacking in most resolute style for a long time, was just one of those commonplace affairs, which support my oft-expressed theory that "goals are the accidents of the game".

There was a dash on Liverpool's goal, and Abbott, one of the half-backs, sent in a ground shot. Dunlop, Liverpool's left-back, tried to kick the ball away. He reached it, but failed to get hold of it and, slithering off his toe, it rolled softly over the line, well out of the reach of Hardy.

Then was a scene equalling pandemonium. Blue favours were waved. Hats, sticks and caps flew wildly up into the air, and a mighty roar burst from that section of the great crowd whose pent-up enthusiasm had waited so long for a chance to let itself loose in a shriek of triumph.

This was a rather lucky goal, but in less than a minute Everton were swarming round the Liverpool goal again, and this time H. P. Hardman got his head to a fine centre from Sharp, and this time there was no luck about the goal. Thus, in the space of one minute, the decisive points of the struggle were gained, and the other eighty-nine minutes were filled in with quick-change kaleidoscopic work delightful to watch. It always promised goals, but the defence was the feature of the match, and for the most part it prevailed.

Both goalkeepers were superb. Hardy, of Liverpool, was more orthodox in his methods, and he made many brilliant saves. Scott took one's breath away by his very daring, but he made no mistakes, and justified his methods by the success which attended them.

The red favours of Liverpool and the blue of Everton dominated the streets of the Midland capital all day, and in the evening crowds of excursionists filled the streets, cheering for their respective sides. Liverpool were "not downhearted", and Everton were naturally "cock-a-hoop."

Cup is finally ours

(Liverpool Football Echo, April 21, 1906)

The 1906 FA Cup final, and finally success was achieved after previously finishing as runners-up twice. It was an apparently drab encounter against Newcastle United, who had also lost the previous year's final. However, the fact that Everton were the victors remains enough to shout about even today as the barren run was ended.

The below extracts are from the Football Echo Saturday evening match report, with Alex "Sandy" Young the 77th-minute match winner – although the Daily Mirror was more critical of the match as a spectacle.

*K*ICKING-OFF at 3.29pm, the game failed to ignite with both sides cancelling each other out. Settle went closest with a header in a drab first half, while Rutherford had what proved to be Newcastle's best chance before the break, his shot cannoning off Balmer for a corner.

Eight minutes into the second half, Sandy Young had a goal ruled out for offside from Settle's pass – Jack Sharp's cross having been fumbled by United keeper James Lawrence. But Everton remained the better side with Newcastle needing to be warned by the referee for their 'ungentlemanly conduct'.

Young started the leather on the eventful journey, and Old Sol smiled on the efforts of the Blues.

Young smartly followed after the leather, and finished up by doing the trick in fine style.

Needless to say, the pent-up feelings of the vast multitude broke forth in such a volume of sound, that it was a wonder the threatening rain clouds overhead did not discharge their deluge.

(Daily Mirror)

*T*HE tamest final for many years. (Everton) would have done better even had Young, the centre forward, not marred his dashing display with a good many petty tricks, which Mr Kirkham (the referee) generally noticed and always promptly penalised.

(Liverpool Football Echo)

Jay CKK kept tabs on the clock during the match, with some of his comments on the match recorded in the Liverpool Football Echo that night. Here is how they appeared:

3.35 – Everton all over the other people. Bolton shoots. His idea is good; his execution rotten.

3.38 – Everton forwards having a field-day, but they seldom shoot – the importance of the occasion too great, I suppose.

3.41 – Young is giving great satisfaction.

3.43 – Poor play in midfield.

3.44 – The same.

3.45 – Worse.

3.57 – Goals are mighty scarce.

4.05 – Pressure by the Blues hot and strong.

4.06 – More pressure.

4.07 – And still more.

4.14 – Half-time, no score.

4.25 – Off again.

4.30 – Everton still top dog, and visions of the precious bauble loomed in my eye.

4.34 – Linesman Whittaker stops the game and examines the ball. He thinks it has gone soft, but it is all right.

4.35 – Everton press like demons.

4.36 – Young scores, but Kirkham declares him offside. Great snakes! No matter. Our withers are unwrung.

4.39 – Only one team in it just now. The other team is Newcastle.

4.55 – At last a goal, Sandy Young. Fireworks and miniature earthquakes galore.

4.56 – The big glasshouse still shaking to its foundations.

5.11 – The Cup is ours. Haroo!

Heroes' welcome awaits Blues

(Liverpool Echo, April 23, 1906)

*A*FTER playing their league match at Sheffield this afternoon, the Everton team will arrive home via Central Station, Ranelegh Street. A procession will be formed headed by a brass band, which will receive the victors by playing 'The Conquering Heroes'. Afterwards the team will journey to Goodison Park via Church Street, Whitechapel, Scotland Road, Walton Road thence to the club offices.

The 'special Grand Central train' was due to leave Sheffield at 6.05pm, due into Liverpool at 8.20pm.

The engine will be specially decorated with the colours of the Everton Club. Only a limited number of people were to be allowed on the Central Station platform, with admittance 'ticket only' – while the Lord Mayor was also set to be present to 'add his congratulations on behalf of the city'.

Booth's Cup final reflections

(Liverpool Echo, April 23, 1906)

Injured Everton skipper Tom Booth was interviewed by the Echo.

*W*HEN we left the Forest Hotel, Chingford, which had been our training quarters, there was a jovial feeling amongst the little party of us which made one feel that we were going to be on the right side at last.

What a sight to see the crowd of people, the dimensions of which were estimated at between 70,000 and 80,000.

The Newcastle forwards never got into their stride, for our half-backs gave them no time to settle on the ball.

Some good play by the right wing ended in a goal being scored, which the referee disallowed for offside. I thought it a very near thing, though I must confess I was not in as good a position as the referee to judge, and therefore, I should not like to say but that the referee's decision was right.

Everton deservedly won. I say deservedly, for they were without doubt the better team in every department save goal, where Scott, owing to lack of opportunity, had not the chance to show comparison with Lawrence.

Thus I conclude my version of the match by complementing Jack Taylor (as captain of the team) and all the other members for the manner in which they have played during the Cup-ties, and for having won matches when every outsider seemed to think they had no chance of success.

Echoing the fans' sentiments

(Liverpool Echo, April 23, 1906)

Page 3 of the Liverpool Echo offered its congratulations with an open letter to the team, "containing Cup congratulations and criticisms"

*D*EAR Jack Taylor – Your hand! All Liverpool has respected you for your honourable career, and as you captained the successful side on Saturday in the time-honoured final of the Football Association Cup, may we offer you our warmest congratulations.

The letter continued in this vain, complementing each member of the team with individual comments ('To W. Balmer – One of your best games, William. You had Gosnell in your pocket, and Orr was at least under the flap of the pocket.' 'To Makepeace – Thought you weren't going to play? Glad you did.')

Tame final, claims hard-hitting report

(Liverpool Echo, April 23, 1906)

Monday's Liverpool Echo report.

*T*HE tamest final for many years. That was the general and freely-expressed opinion of those who visited the Crystal Palace on Saturday to see Everton win the English cup by a goal to none. The football was not worthy of the occasion; there was a listlessness about the crowd, and the players – or at least the Newcastle side – seemed stale. There was none of that sprightliness one expected from them. To tell the truth, they failed once more to rise to a great occasion, and just as they did last year, when beaten by the Villa, they lost to a better side on the day's play. But had the game been a league match on neutral ground I am disposed to think that the United would easily reverse the decision.

It is always unfortunate when the great match of the years ends up in a game which arouses no enthusiasm. The London section of the crowd on Saturday was clearly apathetic, and as they provided the bulk of the spectators, the enthusiasts who had travelled from Northumberland and Lancashire were not helped in their endeavours to make the scene compare with those previously enacted on the historic arena.

I was surprised to hear that the crowd numbered over 75,000, and more surprised still to see thousands vacate their seats before the finish and leave the ground. The rush to the rails to see the cup and medals presented was less eager than ever before.

In a few words afterwards, Aitken admitted that his men played nervously, and said that there was not much good football in the match. Taylor was naturally pleased, but blamed the light ball and hard ground for the scrambling play.

Carr and Sharp had many tussles, and for the most part when they came in conflict Carr was the victor.

I had just remarked on this to my neighbour when the incident of the match happened. Sharp was sent speeding down the wing by Makepeace. Carr gave the first-named just a trifle too much rope and the Lancashire cricketer was off and away like a flash. Carr never caught him, and his centre, beautifully placed, went unerringly to Young, who popped the ball in the net well out of reach of Lawrence.

Then we had the one enthusiastic show of the afternoon, and blue-and-white umbrellas and other favours of the same colours were waved vigorously and some hundreds of hats came to grief.

Everton deserved to win. Quicker on the ball, faster and more intelligent, they were the ones to sum up the situation.

Grand show is talk of the Toon

(By Citizen, Daily Mirror, January 21, 1907)

A Goodison highest crowd up to that point in the 1906/07 season, as the league-leaders outclassed their main title rivals.

*T*HE match of the day was Everton v Newcastle and there were 45,000 spectators present at Goodison Park to see last season's cup finalists and this season's leading competitors for league honours, opposed. Newcastle started well but fell away to nothing. Pretty all the time, they were ineffective in front of goal, just as they were last April in the final at the Palace. On the other hand, Everton showed admirable form throughout.

Just before half-time Young, the Everton centre, who had previously missed an open goal, scored for Everton, and in the second half put the cup holders two-up. After this there was only one team in it, and Sharp, the Lancashire cricketer and Everton outside-right, shot a third goal. At all points of the game, particularly at half and back, Everton played grandly.

Young and foolish but Blues prosper handsomely

(By Citizen, Daily Mirror, March 14, 1907)

Everton were also taken to a replay in the quarter-finals – but the FA Cup holders duly took one closer step to retaining the trophy, despite the apparent bad-boy antics of their final goal hero the previous year.

*E*VERTON won their cup tie with the Crystal Palace by four goals to nil, and won it well, but there was nothing like four goals between the sides on the day's play. Indeed, during the second half, when the winners had much the better of the exchanges, they only scored once. They were, however, always the better side.

With one exception, it was a delightful game to watch, full of incident and clever play. The exception was supplied by Young, the Everton centre-forward. I make no hesitation in saying that Mr J. T. Ibbetson, the referee, neglected his duty in allowing him to remain on the field. Young started badly by arguing with the referee over a decision, and got worse when he foully-charged Hewitson, the Palace goalkeeper, after he had cleared the ball.

He added to his delinquencies when he kicked Innerd and earned a caution, and finished up by kicking Ryan. Yet he was allowed to remain on the field. He is the cleverest forward in the team – I was going to say in England, and I think I should be correct.

All the Everton forwards played fine football, and in spite of Young's delinquencies, one cannot overlook his genius. He is wonderful.

Now we're motoring

(March 23, 1907)

*I*N search of a second successive FA Cup final appearance, the Blues faced West Brom at Burnden Park, Bolton.

The papers made great play of the "shock news" that the sizeable army even included a 15-strong group who were going by "motor-car", which was chartered by the Fruiterers Association. The group expected the 60-mile journey to take two-and-a-half hours, a trip that would be achieved in less than half that time these days. Most fans went by train.

Skipper Jack Taylor, who played despite a stomach complaint, was "tackled" by an over-enthusiastic Evertonian on the pitch before the game.

The fan caught the defender round the neck – and was promptly tripped up by the annoyed captain. The subsequent Echo match report noted that the incident didn't overly affect the team, although Taylor struggled throughout the match.

Everton ran out 2-1 winners thanks to George Wilson and Jack Sharp goals either side of the break.

Player power yet to take hold

(April 20, 1907)

*F*A Cup holders Everton would lose 2-1 to Sheffield Wednesday, who they had beaten on the way to winning the trophy. The Blues had dropped semi-final scorer George Wilson after he had hit out at the club's directors.

It was suggested the directors' shock selection decision was based on a contract dispute. The rumours were that the board would not play Wilson unless he put pen to paper. The player's anger clearly increased when they refused his demand for a bonus. An early example of when the clubs held all the aces.

When a Liverpool Echo reporter visited Wilson's terraced home in Bardsay Road, Walton, he found the house empty and the furniture on its way back to Scotland. Wilson was eventually traced and found to have a cup medal in his possession, even though he did not play in the final. Asked where it came from, he said one of the Everton players had given it to him, saying: "Here, George, take it. If anybody deserves it, you do." Wilson revealed he had been offered a final chance to sign on the morning of the match, but refused because of his wife's health. He would have done so had he been able to live in Southport or Hoylake. Clearly a player who knew his own mind – the directors would likely have seen him as a trouble-maker.

Cup hopes crumble in unlikely fashion

(By Citizen, Daily Mirror, April 22, 1907)

1907 cup final reflections, concerned with day-trippers' fashions and an admittance that Everton had been below par.

*A*T the Crystal Palace on Saturday, Sheffield Wednesday beat Everton in the final tie of the English cup by two goals to one after a keen, hard game. We had "cup-tie weather", and once again the annual carnival which brings thousands upon thousands of provincials to town was favoured by delightful sunshine.

The hordes of Yorkshire, Lancashire, Midland and Northern enthusiasts have apparently resented the "cup-tie weather" statement, in many London papers, that they all wear caps and chokers. On Saturday many wore white bowlers or shiny black bowlers with the long fur smoothly ironed and brushed, a type of hat largely worn in the North; and well-cut jacket suits. Altogether they were a smart provincial crowd in their best clothes, and on their best behaviour.

Between twelve and one o'clock they began to go to the Palace. A jolly, good-tempered crowd, all keen on the game. All Lancashire saying how many goals Everton would win by – 3-1 was the popular tip – and all Yorkshire, especially the "mon fra Sheffield", forecasting quite another ending to the game and, as it turned out, the correct one.

Everton were apparently a trifle stale. They were not the great side that beat Bolton and West Bromwich. They only played their game for about a quarter of an hour. Sharp was splendid and "Jock" Taylor, at centre-half, was splendid indeed. Neither Makepeace or Abbott did so well as usual, and the Balmers both kicked badly, and were bustled many times. Scott kept goal well, but should have saved the last goal, and that was the one that counted.

Turner signing about to pay off

(Liverpool Echo, April 5, 1909)

The announcement of a new signing is generally always welcomed by supporters, and Robert Frewen Turner's move, "Bob" to the football fraternity, would boost Everton immediately. That said, his wish for a decent pay-day fell on deaf ears in the mind of the writer, with Turner being duly reminded of the maximum wage in force. Just days after signing, Turner would be among the goals in a memorable derby debut.

*A*FTER weeks of waiting and some anxious moments, Everton have signed up Robert Frewen Turner, a young fellow, who is 21 years, and great football possibilities. Turner was loath to leave his own fireside, as it were, and, as is known fully now, said he would only do so if paid well, ignoring all the rules of the Football Association, as to the £10 limitation. We all make mistakes, Turner has made one which has, unlike the hundreds previously committed by seasoned players, been discovered. That is Turner's misfortune. This penalty is a heavy one, when he makes his appearance at Walton he can be assured, as all players can, of a hearty welcome. In fact, the crowd will look upon him with such generosity of heart in view of recent happenings. He weighs 11st and stands 5ft 8ins in height.

On Saturday, Mr W. C. Cuff informed me he was at Leicester, and duly obtained the signature, and he adds that Turner, was again the outstanding man on the side. If selected he will of course play in the great local "Derby" between Everton and Liverpool on Friday next. Turner is a winger of class, too good a man to play in second League football, and of course the Fosse are going back to the Second Division.

Turner might attain absolute brilliance. He is not of big build, but is just the size which full-backs find so worrying. He is fast, and centres very accurately. That he knows where the goal lies is shown by the fact that he has three times found the net this season, and it must be remembered that a winger as a rule is not guilty of shaking the rigging. Nevertheless Turner's sterling point is his centring.

Sportsmanlike conduct cannot be overdone
(January 19, 1910)

An FA Cup first-round replay against Middlesbrough at Goodison Park produced an inspired display from visiting goalkeeper Tim Williamson – despite the Blues still progressing 5-3.

*T*HE Echo noted how, at the end of the first half, the "cheers for Williamson were very loud and long and this sportsmanlike conduct cannot be overdone".

Indeed, Liverpool Echo headline summed up the match: 'WILLIAMSON AND THE POSTS AGAINST ATTACK'.

An eventful opening in front of an initial 5,000 crowd saw chances at both ends, ('Barlow finished tamely with a shot that was ridiculously wide') before Cail netted for the visitors ('Scott touched the leather, and should certainly have saved'). Everton continued to press and Taylor gave Williamson no chance before Freeman gave the Blues a half-time lead.

The Everton pressure continued after the break, with Sharp striking the post before Young struck the third. 'Loose play on the part of Maconnachie' let in Common to pull a goal back and with Everton forced back, Cail set-up Bloomer for the equaliser.

Boro hitting back seemed to inspire Everton though, who lay siege on Williamson's goal in the final 15 minutes. Young, Freeman and White went close and Sharp struck the post. before Makepeace, with a powerful drive, and White finally put the tie beyond doubt.

Tim Williamson was given generous applause by the home crowd with an inspired display for Boro ('Cheers for Williamson at the end of the first half were very loud and long and this sportsmanlike conduct cannot be overdone. Let us be jealous of the crowd's good name in the Mersey city').

Taylor trauma ends Cup chase

(March, 1910)

*T*HE FA Cup semi-finals of 1910 saw Second Division Barnsley standing in the way of Everton's path to a third final in five seasons. The first tie ended goalless at Elland Road, but hopes were high for the replay at Old Trafford, Manchester – described by the Press as 'Cottonopolis'.

But after a lively opening, in which both sides missed spot-kicks, the turning point occurred:

Out of the blue Jack Taylor, the Everton centre-half, took a kick to the neck. Doubled up in agony, his team-mate White approached him, but Taylor was breathless. His pain was only eased when two spectators, who appeared to be 'medical men', came to assist. They turned out to be Doctors Whitford and Baxter. It's highly likely that the latter was actually Dr. James Clement Baxter who, in 1892, gave Everton an interest free loan to help them build the build new Goodison Park. Baxter would become a board member. Medical examination later revealed that Taylor had sustained severe damage to the larynx, an injury which forced him to quit the game. It was reported that the player could hardly speak after the match.

The eventual 3-0 defeat was inevitable – not least because goalkeeper William Scott was forced off for a spell after tearing the webbing of his second and third finger, a truly nasty and painful injury.

Matchday traffic

(February 6, 1911)

The following observation came from a Liverpool Echo reporter in his 'Casual Comments' column in the wake of Everton's 2-1 FA Cup defeat of Liverpool. Prophetic words from the Echo scribe. If only he could see County Road before and after a match these days!

*M*AKING one's way quietly to Goodison Park today the first thing that struck one was the alarming growth of taxi-cabs and motor-cars. They have become a positive epidemic and unfortunately there seems no likelihood of the disease being stamped out.

1912-1921

Blues win 'away' at Goodison

(Daily Mirror, February 9, 1912)

A 1-1 FA Cup draw with lower division Bury at snow-bound Goodison Park produced a replay at Gigg Lane, or so the fans thought. In an echo of future meetings between top-flight clubs and traditionally 'smaller' sides, the tie was switched to Goodison, being played on a Thursday. As a result the Shakers received £750 for keeping the game at Everton, with the Blues losing £100 as a result from lost gate receipts. And the outcome? A 6-0 'away' win for Everton (Thomas Browell netting four goals), although they were helped by Bury being without key players Currie and Duffy for the replay. The former was injured, but his team-mate was ruled out because he was 'unable to get away through scholastic duties'. Incidentally, there was no three-day wait for another game. Two days later Everton saw off Sheffield United 3-2 at Goodison

NOTHING could have been more convincing than the form shown by Everton at Goodison Park, Liverpool, yesterday, in their replayed tie with Bury. On Saturday Bury, on the same ground, adapted themselves better than their rivals to the adverse conditions of a snow-covered turf, but yesterday they were routed, Everton winning in decisive fashion by six goals to none.

From start to finish there was practically only one team in it, and at no time was success for Everton in the slightest doubt. Readily surmounting the difficulties presented by the heavy state of the ground, Everton gave a sterling display and outplayed their opponents at all points.

Makeshift side hit for six on home turf

(Daily Mirror, October 28, 1912)

A third successive defeat was suffered, at the hands of Newcastle United, although it was a "strangely unfamiliar side" who fell to a 6-0 home reverse, a match "too one-sided to be interesting".

OWING to injuries to several of their players, Everton had a strangely unfamiliar side against Newcastle. Simpson, a junior back from Redcar, and Wareing, the big old Preston North End half-back, were included in the team and Gourlay, a forward, filled another of the half-back places. And the result was not happy, Newcastle United simply swamping the defence opposed to them.

In the first half Low and McTavish got through it and subsequently the Everton men were completely played to a standstill. Stewart quickly got a couple of goals, and before the end Low and McTavish added further points and completed the downfall. The match was really too one-sided to be interesting.

Victory over rock-bottom United

(Daily Mirror, January 5, 1914)

Newcastle United's struggles appeared of more concern than the fate of the victors.

$\mathcal{I}$N a keenly-contested game at Everton, Newcastle United were beaten by two goals to nothing. The opening half was fast and even, with the forwards on both sides playing well. Parker scored for Everton after fifteen minutes and despite United's efforts to get back on terms, the interval came with Everton leading by a goal. Jefferis scored another ten minutes after the interval. Wilson had a good chance for Newcastle, but he failed badly. Newcastle are now in one of the last places in the table, a peculiar position for a side with such great resources.

Seven men finish fiery cup clash

(January 9, 1915)

A busy afternoon for the referee in a match which made history for the wrong reasons.

$\mathcal{F}$IVE years after their semi-final defeat to Barnsley, Everton had their chance of revenge at Goodison. A Jimmy Galt header put the home side ahead but soon after George Harrison, who had taken the corner to set-up Galt, became the first Everton player to be sent off in an FA Cup tie.

The reason was unclear – Ernest Edwards in the Liverpool Echo claimed to have not seen the incident which also saw Barson dismissed for the Tykes.

Edwards viewed how Barson lay injured outside the goalline near the Bullens Road. He then stated: 'The players concerned shook hands as they left the field.' It was later noted that Barson had swept away Harrison's feet, with Harrison retaliating.

Bobby Parker netted to give Everton a 2-0 advantage at the break before he was also sent off in the second half – the only occasion Everton have had two men dismissed in an FA Cup tie.

Around the hour mark, Tykes keeper Cooper smothered the ball in a goalmouth scramble. This did not deter Parker, who became the third player to take an early bath for trying to "rush the goalkeeper". Cooper then pushed Parker, who retaliated by kicking him back.

Despite this, Jimmy Galt struck a third goal soon after and Barnsley failed to break through – despite Everton finishing the game with seven men. Joe Clennell – who had been injured for some time, came off five minutes from time, 'having been indisposed' while Tom Fleetwood went off with a problem just before the final whistle.

The Barnsley tie also saw an early show of 'hooliganism' at Goodison Park although it wouldn't have raised an eyebrow in the modern game. At 3-0 up a spectator threw an orange onto the pitch, which hit a Barnsley player.

The Echo reported that the referee called Everton captain Jimmy Galt to address the crowd and, 'Ask them to be sportsmen.' Galt did so, and possibly because they feared the Scottish brogue would not be understood, team-mates Makepeace and Maconnachie assisted in the lecture.

Double a step too far

(Liverpool Echo, March 27, 1915)

Chelsea were the underdogs going into the 1915 FA Cup semi-final at Villa Park, and it was Everton who were pursuing success in both league and cup. However, it was a feat that seemed impossible to a Liverpool Echo reporter of the day, who made the following observations.

I HAVE thought all along that Everton would win the cup this season, but I didn't fancy them for the league as well. It is too much to ask any club nowadays to bring off the Double.

Has it ever been done?

The scribe went on to highlight Double achievements.

Oh yes. First to do it was Preston North End, but it wasn't such a feat then, because at that time the Prestonians were in a class by themselves, and had nobody to beat. In 1897 it was accomplished by Aston Villa. Of course, that, as you can understand, was more of a performance, because there was a lot of football talent knocking around in 1897, and among other things, the Villans had to beat Everton in the final of the Cup.

In the end, those fears that the Double might be beyond Everton proved correct with Croal and Halse on target for Chelsea, who wore white while Everton sported blue and white striped shirts. Controversy raged regarding the continuation of the domestic season despite the beginning of what proved to be World War I Although some, including an Echo reporter, were grateful that football continued, offering a much-needed mental diversion to the anxieties of war. He wrote:

It is good to think that some professions are not having their lot made harder by cranks who would bar everything taking place, as though this were the time to shut up the shop and call for an undertaker.

Having a 'hard go' at the league

(Liverpool Echo, April 1, 1915)

There was still the league title to play for.

$\mathcal{T}$HERE are those who think Everton have no chance for league honours. That's a silly attitude to take up. Slips at holiday periods are part and parcel of football's history. Everton may slip, it is true – equally Oldham, the Sheffield clubs, Blackburn and Manchester City may slip. It's a toss-up which club will win the league.

One thing is certain. Everton's players have made up their mind to have a hard "go" at the league honours, and thus recompense for the blow they received and gave to their supporters last Saturday. The display Everton gave was unlike anything Evertonians as one could imagine. However, the cup-tie is but a memory. There's more work to be done, and the league is showing to be worth going for.

1906 Cup heroes to take on boxers

(By Bee, Liverpool Football Echo, April 3, 1915)

Two defeats in two days appeared to have put the skids on Everton's Championship ambitions. The home defeat to Sheffield Wednesday came on Easter Saturday, with 5,000 fewer fans in attendance than on Good Friday, who witnessed a 2-0 home defeat to Burnley. The Wednesday game also saw some unwanted fan interaction involving a popular fruit! Still, the reporter who wrote under the pen-name 'Bee' had other things on his mind – a charity game involving local boxers and footballers from the 1906 FA Cup-winning side.

$\mathcal{B}$EFORE dealing with Everton's match with Wednesday of Sheffield, let me introduce you to a fixture that must interest you. Thanks to the enterprise of Messrs J. A. Wilson and Jack Sharp, a match is to be played on a Wednesday night at Goodison Park – kindly lent for the occasion – for the War Funds. The teams will set old followers of the game talking of the good old times we spent together. Read this eleven – all booked bar Parry, who is training with the Montgomery "sojers", and is expected to play – and be assured that if the team's reappearance does not draw you, the view of the boxers' team will certainly make you attend:

Cup team – William Scott; W. and R. Balmer; Parry; Booth; Crelley; Sharp; Jack Taylor; Parkinson; W. Abbott and H. P. Hardman.

Boxers – Gordon Simms; J. A. Wilson; Bandsman Rice; Tancy Law; Matt Wells; Jerry Delaney; Bombardier Billy Wells; Jimmy Wilde; Kid Doyle; Sergeant Basham and Owen Moran.

Is that collective good enough? Rather! Some of the boxers have football form that you do not know of. Their captain, Mr J. A. Wilson, of the Liverpool Stadium, is well-known in local football circles as the Orrell player. A year ago today he was helping the North-East club to win the cup offered at Bruges. Then Bombardier Wells has played for Tottenham, and more frequently for Fulham. Kid Doyle is the Boldon (Newcastle) centre-forward Gordon Simms, the reserve goalkeeper for Portsmouth, and Bandsman Rice has played in many of the Army's representative games.

Everton's Cup team of 1906 – or the nearest possible approach to it – is sure to find favour. The defence would be worth watching, and the added attraction of seeing Jack Sharp trip down the wing with John D. Taylor as partner – Taylor's first-love might call it – and Walter Abbott making his bow again as a forward, would be a big delight to Everton folk. Harold Hardman has recently taken up football training again, and is playing for Manchester United Reserves – he is a director of that club, you know.

Now to the Everton match. The ground was in a shocking condition and it was very necessary that the ball should be hit hard. When a quarter of an hour had gone Wednesday's forwards had a bit of luck – not that the goal was not a good one, but that its origination was due to a fluke. Fleetwood, after neat defence, being unlucky in not preventing the ball going to touch. The throw-in led to a centre by Robertson being snapped up by Kirkman, who had cut in towards goal. A surprise goal, and one-all against the run of play. Still, it confirmed the deadliness of Sheffield's attack.

A left-foot drive from Wilson took effect, the ball grazing the crossbar. Brittleton complained to the referee of the remarks of a certain section of the crowd, and when Mr Taylor addressed the spectators he was struck in the eye with what appeared to be a piece of orange peel.

One of the greatest treats of the past few years

(Liverpool Echo, April 8, 1915)

Bee's charity match update.

*J*ACK Sharp is making himself responsible for the 1906 cup team, and, while it is impossible to get the full team, he has certainly "broken the back" of that side, as shown by the team I published in Saturday's paper. He cannot get Maurice Parry's address, and I am asked to request the old Liverpool half-back to communicate with Sharp. The date of the match has been fixed for April 28. This is the Wednesday after the cup final. This kick-off is timed for four o'clock, and this time will permit businessmen getting there. A later kick-off was aimed at, but was found impossible, owing to some of the players wishing to travel back home the night of the match.

'Evertonian' writes: There is a name missing from the team, and if the man I refer to – Jimmy Settle – could be secured to play alongside

H. P. Hardman with Walter Abbott in his old place, at left half-back, it would be one of the greatest treats of the past few years, and a truly pleasant renewal of the acquaintance of old favourites. Now see what can be done regarding "Jimmy".

James Settle is getable. He's in Bolton nowadays; but I cannot do more than throw out the correspondent's suggestions.

A succession of thrills leaves Blues in hunt

(By F.E.H, Liverpool Football Echo, April 10, 1915)

A second successive win, both away from home (Sunderland had been defeated four days previous), left Everton in fourth with three matches to play

*I*T was a very depleted team which Everton took to West Bromwich today to meet the Throstles. Within the past few weeks injuries have played havoc with the wearers of the blue jersey, and this afternoon there were no fewer than six of the regular first league team absent.

The men left Lime Street early this morning, and a somewhat improved train service landed them in Birmingham shortly after twelve o'clock. The finishing stage of the journey was made by motor, and on arrival at the Hawthorns the weather was eminently fitted for a fast game.

A clever movement resulted in a well-contrived goal. Harrison got clear away, and centred strongly. The ball struck Reed, the home centre-half, and Fleetwood being then onside, passed back to Harrison, who ran the ball into the net.

Everton were not long in again putting themselves ahead. They moved along smartly on the left, and Harrison put in a difficult oblique shot, which Pearson ran out to reach. Unfortunately for himself, he completely missed it, and Fleetwood improved the shining hour by crashing it into the net.

The struggle was a ding-dong one in every department, and thanks to the lively ball there was quite a succession of thrills.

Kirsopp followed suit with a wild shot, which went ridiculously wide, and the game eventually fizzled out in tame fashion.

'Beastly' blizzard to the rescue
(Liverpool Echo, April 14, 1915)

Note was made of Everton moving for Harry Chambers, although it would be Anfield which would be his destination, going on to become a hero for Liverpool following WWI. There was also mention of that day's trip to Bradford Park Avenue, a re-arranged game in which Everton were losing in the original fixture before its abandonment. Maybe fates were with the club in 1914/15.

MR Tom Watson may secure the signature of a smart young inside-left named Harry Chambers. He is only 18 years of age, and has earned his reputation in North-Eastern league circles, as a member of North Shields Athletic.

Everton have visited Bradford today to play off the "thawed match". It will be recalled that when they were losing 3-0 at Park Avenue the referee stopped the game through the beastly weather. The winning of the toss meant everything that day, as the snowstorm carried from goal to goal. Bradford won the toss, and some of the Everton players never saw their partners during the game, the blizzard preventing their looking up to see how their passes had gone. Some spectators regularly take up their positions at the back of the goal believing in seeing some of the important points of the day without hindrance. However, at Bradford on the snow day there was not a soul behind Fern's goal and when the ball was put very wide and into the spectators' portion, it was some time before the ball was returned, as the players were too cold to attempt to scale the hoarding. Finally, the man in the programme box left his perch and obliged. Several players collapsed through the bitter wind and the biting storm of snow and the game was abandoned.

Today's team showed a novelty on the lines of last Saturday's game at West Bromwich, Grenyer this time taking the Fleetwood role and leaving the half-back line for the forward line. This was a change caused through the illness of Clennell, who, like Parker, is laid down with a cold. A lot of comment was created by the non-appearance of the Everton captain at West Bromwich when it was found that he had played for the reserves. It appears that late-on changes necessary in the first team, left Everton Reserves short-handed and Gault, unfit as he was, offered to fill a gap in the Walton match.

Bradford victory sets up title tilt

(Liverpool Echo, April 15, 1915)

Everton secured a vital 2-1 victory at Bradford Park Avenue, who had not been beaten at home since the previous October. The Blues moved up to second, with Alan Grenyer scoring his first goal for the club, while the Echo writer couldn't help but have a dig at other news sources.

$\mathcal{E}$VERTON'S away form received a top-stone yesterday, when Bradford were beaten at Park Avenue. The score was given incorrectly in one Liverpool quarter last night, but that corner was not the "Echo", of course. To beat Bradford at Park Avenue IS a performance. The stiff-built Yorkshiremen have not failed before their own supporters for months – early October – and they could not grumble at their downfall yesterday, because Everton were full value for their win, and, considering the formation of their team, they must have surprised themselves. With Maconnachie, Makepeace, Parker and Clennell unable to play, Fern going to goal with a finger that looked angry and must have given him pain when he made three fine punches, and Chedgzoy breaking down again, it will be seen that Everton did not have a rosy time.

Bradford did not like yielding their ground to any visiting team, and right to the end they fought for the full points possible. Maybe the idea of the former game between the clubs being replayed rankled in their mind. That game was abandoned at half-time through a snowstorm, Bradford leading at that point by 3-0. However, the game was replayed, and Everton won the day through their ability to stay the distance and by employing the better methods of attack.

It was a capital match for a midweek game, and the attendance was satisfactory, although Everton will not share much in the way of gate receipts, because there are so many season-ticket holders at Park Avenue.

Manchester triumph sees Blues go top
(By F.E.H, Liverpool Football Echo, April 17, 1915)

It was to be third v second in Everton's penultimate game of the season. A victory – a fourth on the spin, all away from Goodison – would lift them to top spot.

*I*N view of the fact that both the contestants held a running chance for championship honours, extraordinary interest centred on the meeting of Manchester and Everton at Hyde Road this afternoon.

This was reflected in the attendance, for there were about 30,000 people present.

Happy days on the road
(Liverpool Echo, April 19, 1915)

Joe Clennell was the man on target with the only goal. The title was within reach.

*F*OR the first time this season Everton have topped the League Division 1. That's a great performance, considering the losses sustained at Goodison Park during Easter. Had Everton won their cup match with Chelsea, it is a possibility that they would not have lost one of the games at home at Easter-time. Truly they have been at home when away. Home has not been sweet to them. I do not recall any club taking so many points from other grounds in previous seasons, and 27 points out of 36 will take a deal of beating. On Saturday the club collected two points at Hyde Road against one of the best defences in the league, and now we are certain that the destination of the league honours will not be settled till the very last week of the season, an even struggle that will be awaited in Liverpool and Oldham with the greatest of interest.

English champions through War years

(Liverpool Echo, April 27, 1915)

At home to relegation-threatened Chelsea on the final Monday in April, the Blues were fortunate to earn a point – which was enough to secure a second league title, and first since the move to Goodison, after Liverpool defeated the Blues' nearest rivals Oldham Athletic. It was to be the final official league game played for over four years, due to WWI. The 1914/15 season was completed despite the spectre of the War, with critics divided on whether the campaign should have been abandoned. As proved, Everton would be English champions by default throughout the War years.

*H*AD you or I faked this football season we could not have made a more startling finish than the ordinary course of events is producing. Last night the value of Liverpool's win at Oldham was made evident. Liverpool have reason to be proud of their share in making Everton's position secure. Chelsea showed yesterday they can play real football when allowed. Everton until yesterday had not got a point or a goal out of the Chelsea men, although they had met twice before.

It was for a long time a wretchedly one-sided game. Everton were penned in for 20 minutes at a stretch. Then there came fluctuations that kept us attentive the whole time. Somehow there was not the enthusiasm that one expected would be seen.

First, the league champions received a reception that was not too hearty, Chelsea, in truth, having a heartier reception from the crowd. Not until Everton became fiery did the crowd warm up to Everton's cause, and then Fleetwood gave them something to "hum" about. It was a typical Fleetwood dribble – zig-zag his course and low and crosswise his shot – that led to the enthusiasm among Evertonians. Parker, as was fit and proper, also completed the season with a great goal.

Gault hat-trick makes up for absent friends

(By Vulcan, Daily Mirror, February 24, 1919)

The 1918/19 season was the final war-time football campaign, with clubs often fielding guest players.

$\mathcal{D}$ESPITE the absence of three regular players, Everton proved themselves much too good for Bolton at Goodison Park, and won by four to one. At the outset the Wanderers shone, Vizard being particularly prominent with clever foot work. He opened the scoring after Pickup had missed. Rigsby might have equalised had he made a first-time shot. Shortly afterwards the same player gave Mitchell a teaser. Everton improved and clever play by Kirsopp, and bungling by Nuttall, allowed Gault to score with a shot which cannoned off the upright.

Gault gained the lead from the penalty against Davies, who fouled Kirsopp. Woods stopped the place kick, but the rebound was safely netted. Gault completed his hat-trick, after the defence had been hard pressed. Bolton rarely got within range, and the fourth goal arrived when Donnachie snapped up an opportunity, after a free-kick close in. Everton fully deserved their big win if only by reason of the fact that they made the most of their opportunities.

Misfiring Blues concede title to Forest

(Daily Mirror, May 19, 1919)

Everton as Lancashire section winners met Midland champions Nottingham Forest to decide the overall champions. Unfortunately, the home side left their shooting boots anywhere but Goodison.

$\mathcal{N}$OTTINGHAM Forest won the league championship on Saturday by defeating Everton by one goal to nil at Goodison Park.

It was a rather fortunate win, for the shot from Burton which won the match, halfway through the second half, was the only one directed at the Everton goal. But the Lancashire section winners have only themselves to blame, for their shooting was poor.

Hardy, in the Forest goal, affected some fine saves in each half, which saw Everton doing everything but score goals.

60,000 at Bridge see visitors hit back

(By J.W.H, Daily Mirror, September 8, 1919)

Competitive football returned at the end of August, with Chelsea coming out on top in a five-goal clash. Everton recovered to win at Bradford Park Avenue in midweek, before hitting back at Stamford Bridge seven days after the Goodison clash, in front of 60,000 spectators.

CHELSEA lost their first match on Saturday when Everton visited Stamford Bridge and won by a goal to nil. Thus the Lancashire side avenged the defeat inflicted upon them at Goodison Park by Chelsea on the opening Saturday. It was a peculiar game, for in the first half the play was of the highest order, yet for nearly half an hour of the second half the football was poor.

Everton deserved their victory. Their forwards and halves were superior, and once they had settled down they gave a sparkling exhibition. Harrison, on the Everton left wing, was too fast and clever.

With Rigsby, Harrison formed the best wing on the field. Chedgzoy and Kirsopp were not far behind them, and Gault was a skilful leader.

The Everton side was splendidly balanced. The half-backs found time to look after their own forwards as well as stop the Chelsea front line, and the backs – Maconnachie and Thompson – were great.

The only goal came a little less than 20 minutes from the end, and was cleverly obtained. The Everton forwards indulged in some clever passing, and for some minutes the Chelsea defence was nonplussed. Chedgzoy sent across a square low centre, and although Gault had his back to goal he turned sharply and with a "first-time" shot left Molyneux helpless.

Forwards out-think 'famous Magpies'

(Daily Mirror, February 21, 1921)

An 'official' crowd of 54,205 witnessed a comfortable FA Cup third-round victory, and a masterclass in thinking football.

$\mathcal{E}$VERTON v Newcastle United drew 58,000 people to Goodison Park, where the receipts amounted to £4,961. Newcastle tried their famous "offside game" but it did not come off. The Everton forwards used their brains, and circumvented the tactics. Crossley scored for the Lancastrians in the first half, and Crossley and Davies got further goals afterwards, with the result that the famous Magpies said goodbye to the competition for 1920/21.

Defiant Everton douse Reds' fire

(Daily Mirror, November 7, 1921)

A Bonfire Day derby saw the spoils shared in front of 52,000. A week later, the sides would draw again 1-1, both decent results for an Everton side who would struggle in 1921/22. Liverpool, meanwhile, would run away with the league.

$\mathcal{F}$IFTY thousand people saw the "Derby" between Everton and Liverpool, and everybody was satisfied except possibly the Liverpool players, who had the best of the game and had to be content with one point.

1922-1931

Hit for six by underdogs

(January 9, 1922)

Struggling in the First Division, Everton wouldn't have relished a visit from mid-table Second Division side Crystal Palace. Indeed, the Liverpool Echo match preview was of the view that 'Everton is one of the last teams to regard Second Division opponents lightly,' having lost to such opponents the previous two seasons. Unfortunately an unwanted hat-trick was achieved at Goodison Park although surely even the most optimistic Palace fan could never have imagined a scoreline of: Everton 0, Crystal Palace 6. How such a result in the Press would be met these days is anyone's guess, although radio phone-ins would surely go into meltdown. The result remains Everton's biggest-ever FA Cup defeat

*T*HE sensation of the day was the complete and humiliating overthrow of Everton. It was known that the Londoners were a sturdy lot, but few can have anticipated that they would sweep the Evertonians off their feet in the way they did. To be defeated at all was bad enough, but to go under by six clear goals may well give the supporters of the Merseyside club pause.

Eyeing up the Tranmere boy wonder

(Liverpool Echo, March 16, 1925)

A certain Tranmere Rovers goalscoring sensation was attracting interest.

*E*VERTON went out boldly at the weekend for a number of big deals. At the time I write, Saturday night, nothing has been sent through the wires, but I think we can take it as certain that Everton, by their policy of re-creating the team, will make some bold moves. People are asking why they don't get boys in the locality such as Dixie Dean. Well, many a club is hanging up its hat to Tranmere, and I think that the time is ripe for the transfer of the boy.

Price is everything, and Tranmere won't part with such a money-producer for a mere song. He ought not to go far from our doors, seeing that he is to all intents and purposes a local. He is, to my mind, the most promising centre-forward I have seen for years.

That does not mean that I would be content to pay a foolish price. He might get hurt or go "back". Who knows?

The signing of Dixie Dean

(Liverpool Echo, March 17, 1925)

A certain new signing was pictured in action.

$\mathcal{D}$IXIE Dean, who has had no rest from the attentions of other clubs since he began scoring goals for Tranmere Rovers, has at last been "placed". Everton signed him on yesterday, and have certainly got one of the most noted centre-forwards of the day.

Give the kid a chance

(The 'Echo' Hive, Liverpool Echo, March 17, 1925)

Evertonians were urged to give their new boy-wonder time to settle in...

$\mathcal{I}$T is impossible on the score of time and money to write to every Everton spectator a very necessary postcard on a very important point. So I will print the postcard here and let the spectator digest it at his leisure:

Dear Spectator – Pardon my intrusion, but you may have heard per

6LV, or through the columns of the "Daily Post" that Dixie Dean has been transferred by Tranmere Rovers to Everton. It is not a world-making move; it is just the movement of a local boy from Prenton to Goodison Park. The boy has good chances of doing well out of football, but in view of the way another young boy was spoiled at Goodison Park, I thought I would write you to ask that the boy shall not be spoiled by sickly adulation. At Tranmere, there has been too much of Dixie-this and Dixie-that; if it continues the boy – he is but 18 years old – may easily lose his balance and his football form. He is a very human being. Do not imagine that I am intruding or that I am not going to take a firm hold on my own writings about the boy. I promise you I will; but it is the crowd that has the spoiling of this boy. Do be normal – and let him be likewise.

Sincerely yours, "Bee".

Not what he does, but the way he does it

Bee also offered more background to the signing, including other clubs who were chasing Dean and the record fee.

*N*EVER has a boy been so seriously sought as Dean. He had the makings of a footballer, he had the shape of a player, the height, weight, temperament and the latent skill. Every scout who came to see him play asked my verdict, and each of them said, "A real good footballer in the making. It is not what he does, but the way he does that opens out the prospect for future years."

That was the reason they were so keen on his transfer. He is a very good boy off the field as well as on, being rational and reasonable, and it is good to know that Mr Secretary Cooke took him in hand early on, and the boy was thus able to make use of his wages, rather than live up to fabulous heights, and then be brought to earth so soon as his football career was clinched by injury, or what not. Manchester United, per Mr Dale, Villa, Birmingham, Albion, through Dan Nurse, director and ex-player, Huddersfield, through the canny manager and good friend, Mr Herbert Chapman, also an ex-player, and a host of other members got busy pulling the strings and working the wires.

It is probably the heaviest transfer fee that has ever been paid for a mere boy. It is impossible to state the figure with any degree of accuracy but we can state definitely that Tranmere were asking £2,500 and a gift of other players from the club that obtained his signature. Whether Everton paid that is another matter – it is highly improbable – but that was Tranmere's original claim for their treasure.

He is a natural footballer with a stout heart, a willing pair of feet and a constitution that will stand him in good stead. He has not appeared in all the matches this season through injury and so on, but he scored 29 goals, and he seems to have "more in his locker".

Everton are determined to sweep away the tradition of a year ago and aim at young men with a push and go that has been missing from some of the ranks of the side. Everton have been very pretty; they have been tantalisingly so. Now the club directors are showing a stern hand, and are in effect stating that the side has not been nearly good enough and must be amended so that the new Everton shall be a forceful, enterprising Everton.

Let the fans have their voice

(Liverpool Football Echo, March 28, 1925)

Complaints about the attitude of the Everton Board towards the fans.

I HAD a chat with a fairly large shareholder this week, and picked out one definite opinion that I could not accept – to the effect that the question of the position of the club was the sole concern of the directors and shareholders.

I grant that they have the power, but no business firm that caters for the entertainment of the public can afford to ignore the feelings and expressions of opinions of its customers with regard to the style and quality of the programme provided. The patrons of Goodison have been extremely patient, and have trudged a long road without murmuring, looking for the turn which appears to be as far off as ever.

In my opinion there has been a woeful want of consistency in the selection of the team. This quick-change business provides bullets for the snipers who are already well provided with ammunition without the directors handing out an extra stock.

Everton's responsible officials have secured excellent material, and no club in the country has a finer set of players on its books, yet they do not weld together as a team.

I have no doubt the club will scrape through from relegation this season, but those that have the right should see to it that fighting to escape the drop is not consistent with the wealth and standing of the Everton club.

Villa victory heralds a promising future

(Liverpool Echo, March 30, 1925)

Dean's first goal for the club on his home debut, in a victory over Aston Villa, although Everton would remain in 20th place despite picking up two points – just a place above the drop with seven games left.

*E*VERTON beat the Villa, but not the real Villa, and for that reason I would ask the Everton supporters to stay their hand and not settle themselves to the idea that all Everton's troubles are over. There was still some weaknesses in the side, and until these are righted I would ask you to "wait and see", writes "Stork":

Kennedy was to my mind the "star" man of the line, for he schemed, shot and used his speed to the best advantage. The first goal was due to his scheming. Most of the onlookers thought he would allow the ball to go over for a corner, but in the twinkling of an eye he changed his ideas and from almost off the line he hooked the ball back to the middle, where Dean met the ball before it touched earth and slammed it into the net. This was not the only thing Dean did. I liked the way he directed his passes to the wing. They were not square, but just far enough forward to enable his wing colleagues to take them on the run.

Eye on the prize

(Daily Mirror, April 24, 1928)

Dixie Dean was closing in on an English goalscoring record as his Everton side looked to close in on the league title. However, the writer appears to have counted his FA Cup goals that season in his total, which at this point was 53.

$\mathscr{D}$IXIE Dean, of Everton and England, has recently been scoring with great freedom, though, in the excitement of the Cup final and promotion and relegation questions, the fact has escaped notice. At the moment he has scored 56 league goals this season, so he has to find the net four times in Everton's last two games in order to beat the English record of 59 goals set up by Camsell, of Middlesbrough, last season. Dean's 56 goals is, of course, easily a record in First Division football.

Heading for a Turf battle

(By Stork, Liverpool Echo, April 27, 1928)

All roads led to Burnley as the leaders headed to Turf Moor in their penultimate game looking for two more points towards the First Division crown – while Dean chased an individual accolade.

$\mathscr{E}$VERTON'S endeavour to win against a side still in the throes of relegation makes the game one further cup final! Burnley's ground has not been a kind one to Everton and, candidly, I make this out to be Everton's greatest test this back-end of the season.

Dean has undoubtedly been playing in spite of injury, and it would be a thousand pities if the big man could not indulge in the last two games of this his most memorable season.

Record run keeps title dream alive

(Liverpool Football Echo, April 28, 1928)

Four goals for the "whippet"-like Dean and five for Everton; a fourth league title was all but secured.

$\mathscr{D}$EAN startled Burnley by a cunningly contrived goal in 30 seconds. But the Turf Moor team quickly regained their senses, and Page and Beel by clever goals altered the complexion of the game. Dean, however, soon put Everton on level terms, and then clinched the position by completing the hat-trick. After the interval Beel equalised. But Martin and Dean put Everton ahead by five goals to three.

With the score standing at 4-3, Everton's prospects were undoubtedly rosy, and when Hill made an error and failed to clear, Critchley smashed the ball into the centre, and Dean went after it like a whippet and, getting the better of Waterfield drove a tremendous ball into the Burnley net, Down standing there quite unable to do anything with it.

Dean now requires three goals to beat Camsell's record of 59 goals.

Hot on the championship trail

(Liverpool Echo, April 29, 1928)

Further post-match reflections, this time in Bee's regular Echo column. Huddersfield Town, with games in hand, were the only side who could stop Everton taking the championship.

$\mathscr{E}$VERTON are hot on the trail for the championship cup. It is not yet won, but Everton's slashing victory over Burnley at Turf Moor has put them right in the firing line, and Huddersfield have only to make the slightest slip and the honour will come to Liverpool. It has been a magnificent fight, but no better than the fight Everton put up against Burnley, who wiped out a 30 seconds' goal, and actually took the lead in a game that was chockfull of thrills and good football.

League win and history in the making

(Liverpool Echo, May 4, 1928)

The calm before the storm – the eve of Everton's final game of the 1927/28 season. Huddersfield Town had lost to Sheffield United and Aston Villa, so the league had now been secured. But could Dixie Dean hit the three goals against Arsenal to break George Camsell's record of 59 league goals in season – a mark set the previous season?

*T*HIS is the final day. This is the championship day. At Goodison Park tomorrow, the sting of the league game would, ordinarily, have left the game, but the bonus and the natural desire of Everton to wind up with a victory and, more than all, to see Dean pass all existing English league records, make the day a gala day in the history of the city's football marks. Goodison Park, many years ago, had a scene in connection with their cup-winning episode. The officials and players stood in the grandstand and no one could tell what was being said.

Today other arrangements are made, and it is up to the spectators to take note of their part in the proceedings and make the final act a joyous one. Amplifiers have been spread around the ground, just as they are spread at Wembley, with the result that if spectators kept their positions, and do not race across the field of play, every one of the expected record gate will be able to hear every word of the presentation by Mr John McKenna, the English League president, of the cup – it is a cup, not a shield as many believe – that goes with the marathon result.

In many clubs, success such as one man (Dean) has won would have been fatal; there would have been petty jealousies, but at Everton that is not the case; they all recognise Dean's worth and his great help, and naturally they are as keen as Dean to see Camsell's record go by. It is an alluring prospect, and with the presentation to follow, the game becomes an historic one in the history of the Everton club.

Dean's record 60th

(By Bee, Liverpool Football Echo, May 5, 1928)

He's done it, to the delight of all concerned, even on the Arsenal team.

*T*HERE was an electric start.

Shaw scored for Arsenal in one minute.

After five minutes' play, Dean had scored twice, equalling the Camsell record of 59 goals.

O'Donnell headed a ball back into his own goal at the 35th minute.

Dean created the record of sixty individual goals in a season at the eighty-second minute. With nine minutes to go, the crowd yearned for a goal to Dean or anyone, and nearly got their voices working when Martin shot and Paterson punched away over the bar for a corner-kick.

This was the beginning of Dean's historic record goal in English football. Troup took the corner-kick and out of a ruck of probably fourteen players, Dean, with unerring accuracy, nodded the ball to the extreme right hand side of the goal.

There has never been such a joyful shout at Everton. It was prolonged for minutes and went on to the end of the game. The crowd never stopped cheering for eight solid minutes, and Dean was hugged by all his comrades, and indeed there was a threat of the crowd breaking on to the field of play.

In fact, two men rushed across through the barrier of police, and the referee had to bundle one man off, and out of the way of trouble.

There were some curious interludes before the finish, Paterson, the Arsenal goalkeeper, making a catch at the top of the bar, and when the referee gave a corner-kick he protested loud and long that the referee had erred.

The goalkeeper went back to his place accepting the referee's decision, and giving Dean a shake of the hand, a sporting act fitly recognised by the crowd. A moment later, while the corner-kick was being taken, Butler took the opportunity of congratulating Dean.

In a minute the whistle had gone for the final, O'Donnell had carried off the ball, and the crowd settled themselves down to listen to the speech of Mr John McKenna, English League president, who presented the trophy to Cresswell, amid roisterous cheers.

The amplifiers did their best to make the speech of the presenter heard, but it could not be said they were very successful. And that's how Everton wound up the season and ended their memorable year of office.

Final: EVERTON 3, ARSENAL 3

At the end of the match, Mr W. C. Cuff, chairman of the club, whose voice carried well over the microphone, congratulated the side upon its victory, in what he described as the most wonderful season the game of football has ever known.

Head and shoulders above the rest

(Liverpool Football Echo, May 5, 1928)

*N*EVER has a football player caught the public imagination as "Dixie" Dean has done. The man that broke his head in a motor-cycle accident so recently as the summer of 1925, is leading league scorer today, and has got most of his goals with that same head.

Fine behaviour of champions

(By Bee, Liverpool Echo, May 7, 1928)

Bee tells of the post-match celebrations, a far more cordial affair than one might suspect in modern times.

*E*VERTON FC held what they termed "a domestic gathering" on Saturday night after winning the league championship, at the North Western Hotel, under the chairmanship of Mr W. C. Cuff. All the players except Taylor were present, and near the league trophy was a plan of the Everton football field in sweetmeat, this being the work of the manager, Mr Newburn.

I am here to record the fine behaviour of the team, and to say that the Everton players have just earned the term "champions" in the greatest season the game has ever known. No club in England, Scotland, Ireland or Wales had been able to celebrate its jubilee with championship honours until now.

Mr Cuff spoke of the loyalty of the players, and the particular aim of the club to play good class football – a type that should appeal to friend and foe. They might have their rebuffs in the results column, but at least their supporters would be able to say we have seen good football (applause).

Mr Ernest Green, vice-chairman, made two special points. The first the captaincy of Cresswell, in whom, he said, we have had a wise leader, who never obtruded himself at the wrong time. Yet at other times made himself scarce (laughter). Mr Green said he did not wish to make odious comparisons, especially as Hunter Hart had done such good work, and was captain of the side in the time of trouble. Mr Green's second points bore reference to the marvellous performance of Dean. The speaker suggested that if anyone could beat the amazing figure of sixty goals, that it could only be Dean himself.

Mr Jack Sharp, claiming to be one of you, when he addressed the players, recalled a period when Everton should have won the league, for they were leading against the Arsenal when fog stopped play. At the replay of this game, they were beaten, thus a championship was lost to the club. It was a happy thought that they had wound up a successful season against the Arsenal that day.

It was announced that today the winners of the league will visit the White Star liner in Gladstone Dock, visit the Empire tonight, Shakespeare tomorrow night and then proceed to Switzerland, leaving Liverpool on Wednesday morning.

The Everton directors and officials desire to thank and congratulate the spectators for their magnificent conduct after the match had ended. The answer to their appeal, for the sake of the condition of the turf, was unanimous there was no breakthrough.

The club have received congratulations from all over the country.

They are unable to answer them personally and desire to do so through the medium of these notes. Clubs, players, personal friends and one from Switzerland sent messages of congratulations.

On a Swiss roll

(Daily Mirror, May 9, 1928)

Dean's goalscoring feats were set to spread beyond these shores, as a post-season tour was about to begin, presumably ruining the players' chances of a week in Magaluf

*A*PARTY of Everton football players, accompanied by several of the directors, will leave for their Switzerland tour today. Games will be played at Basle on May 12, Berne May 13, Geneva May 17 and Zurich May 20, the team returning home on May 23. As Dixie Dean will be one of the party, the Swiss are in for a great treat, and the financial returns from the matches should be considerable.

Lack of heart spells trouble

(Liverpool Echo, March 31, 1930)

Only two seasons later, and a 4-2 home defeat to Birmingham City, a fourth in succession, sounded alarm bells ringing

*H*OME matches had to be won; they could have been won if the players had been good enough; they were not good enough and the price must be paid. There has been a definite lack of heart in the side and there have been innumerable changes of plans and formations of sides till the players have lost their nerve and their confidence – but they have never lost the Everton habit of holding a ball needlessly, nor yet the habit of forsaking the first-time drive. A Briggs drive such as took the scores to 4-2 would never be found in the Everton category – you may say because the player would fear missing it and getting the crowd's goat. I disagree.

There has been a very prolonged and persistent grub in the attack which for weeks led me to say to myself: "Who, then, will shoot, if the present good chances are not accepted at once!" And I answered myself, "Nobody." And the natural sequel to that is – there can be no goals.

I had been a super-optimist till Saturday. Now I can see the shutters indicative of Division II. Pity 'tis true: true 'tis pity. Yet we shall be able to survey some new avenues of football and maybe out of the Second Division fire we may find moulded a side that shall be a shade more biting in front of goal and not be a slave to the whirring wheel that seems to be their lot as they gather the ball. I am not one to shout, "Get shut!" but I do say that no Everton player today seems to think of a wise pass after drawing or beating a man – they want to do it all over again.

Stunned by four-goal defeat

(By Stork, Liverpool Football Echo, April 12, 1930)

Over 47,000 witnessed rock-bottom Everton stunned by Joe Robson's four goals, for a Grimsby side just a place above them. A sixth successive defeat meant that with five games to go, the club's unbroken top-flight run was likely to be ended.

GRIFFITHS was Everton's "big man". His tackling was great, his heading was likewise, and he was the chief shooter of the Everton team. Everton were rewarded with a corner, and this brought a tremendous fight under the Grimsby crossbar. It ended when the ball was cleared, and four or five men lay prone on the ground.

The Grimsby defence gave nothing away, but I must say that there was little shooting done by the Everton forwards. They made many attacks, but they ended when they got close to goal.

Robson took the free-kick, and with a smashing drive registered his hat-trick. Even the most staunch Evertonian had to admit they were three grand goals. Such shooting has not been seen for some time.

Money is no guarantee against relegation
(Liverpool Echo, April 29, 1930)

After a run of three wins and a draw, Everton had given themselves an outside chance of survival. They would need to defeat Sunderland and hope for the best elsewhere.

I EXPECT there will be 60,000 spectators at Goodison Park to see Sunderland's final game here and to learn the verdicts from Newcastle, Manchester and Burnley. It will be a remarkable curtain to football's wonderful season. Meantime, let me say that when the protestors gather together it would be considerate if they saw to it that those present were shareholders. One of the longest speakers at last night's protest was a man who has not a share. Then I am rather perturbed to know some of their principles.

For instance, four years ago a protest meeting was held, and the chairman slammed the officials for their supposed poverty of football ideas. Later on the same gentleman congratulated Everton upon the championship, and frankly admitted that these same gentlemen merited his warm thanks. Now the team has gone back he is nominated for a seat on the board, and the same board of directors is said to be useless. Maybe it is. I am not expressing an opinion; I merely want to know if the shareholders realise that two teams must go out; that money alone is not a guarantee against relegation; that if the elections are to be made according to the position of the club, then this gentleman who desires to go to the board must, by such a rule, move off at a very early date!

The chairman (Mr W.C. Cuff) was not able to be at the game, but he sent his ambassadors, Mrs Cuff, who, after a lapse of 20 odd years, has forsaken the garden of roses and comes in to be the best mascot the club has got. She has not seen Everton lose a game since she resumed her "innings" a few weeks ago. The club has picked up seven points out of the last eight possible.

All bets are off

(Liverpool Echo, May 1, 1930)

The build-up included tales of potential foul play – a blackmail scandal no less.

*T*HERE was a sensational incident today in connection with Everton's vital match with Sunderland at Goodison Park, on Saturday.

As a result of an anonymous letter received from the Liverpool district, the Sunderland FC directors called to a conference the players selected to appear against Everton. The letter alleged that the writer was in a position to say that efforts had been made to square the game, and that he had been asked to lay bets on Friday evening on Everton winning by two clear goals.

The Sunderland management informed the players that while they did not believe for one moment that any such arrangement had been arrived at between them and any other party, it was their duty to inform the players of the seriousness of the position if such did take place.

While the Sunderland club sympathised very much with a club like Everton faced by relegation, they had an honourable duty to perform to the rest of the clubs in the Football League.

'Their regret is ours'

(Liverpool Football Echo, May 3, 1930)

A dark day at Goodison.

*E*VERTON relegated! There is a sad ring about the words. Everton stood for the real football. Throughout 38 seasons and 42 years of League football they have carried, it must be, millions of people to heights of admiration uncommon for all but a few fortunate clubs. Of those millions, many will regret that even a classic club like Everton must go the way of the worst in the Football League, and be relegated to Division II. Their regret is ours.

Anxious wait on a bittersweet day

(By Stork, Liverpool Football Echo, May 3, 1930)

A 4-1 victory failed to save the Blues

ODAY saw Goodison's biggest gate of the season. It was difficult even to get into the Press box, such was the jam at the top of the stairs.

The interest was enormous; it had been the topic all week; so it was small wonder there was a huge crowd. The weather was nice for the onlooker's part, but, I should imagine, would be a shade too sultry for the playing members. However, it was their day today and as I looked round I saw many anxious faces.

The Everton mascot was busy shooting the ball into the net. I only hope that the Everton forwards will put it there half as many times. Then a win, and we must have that, will be practically assured.

The Blues received a tremendous ovation when they made their appearance. During the interval all eyes were turned on the scoreboard, and when the Burnley score was put up there was a big sigh, for it showed Burnley winning 1-0.

However, there was some relief when Grimsby and Newcastle's affairs were "published", as not having scored.

When Everton got their fourth goal, it was due to White's persistency, for he had to shake off Shaw before he could get an opportunity to shoot. Now Shaw is not a small man, but White bundled him over quite easily, and then shot a great goal.

There was not nearly so much interest in the game as there was in the doings on and when it was seen that Sheffield United had beaten Manchester United to the tune of 5-1 it was not at all a satisfactory bit of news.

Critchley, after making a rousing run made a bad finish. This was practically the concluding incident, but there was not a move from the mighty crowd which waited on anxiously to hear the news from other quarters.

Case of mistaken identity

(Liverpool Football Echo, May 3, 1930)

Potential confusion averted as plans are made to change things at Board level – as if Liverpool fans would ever be allowed.

*A*T the Everton protest meeting on Monday three names were offered as possible directors, Messrs. Wright, F.W. Lake and R. Williams.

It has been pointed out to me that the last-named may be confused with Mr Ronald Williams, son of the late chairman of the Liverpool Football Club, and I am asked to state that Mr Ronnie Williams has no intention of changing the colours he has worn since birth. Those who know him as well as I do, will know that like his dear father, he has followed Liverpool from the word "go", and that he has a great heart for the club's good; in fact, he is one of their most persistent followers at the away matches.

Make it a year – and a year only

(Liverpool Echo, May 5, 1930)

Fans are invited to look at the positives of relegation – and the potential recovery of Dixie Dean.

*T*HE agenda is full; the annual stock-taking is due, and the main feature is the descent of Everton. One may ask: "Why should not Everton go to Division II?" To which friends ask: "Why should they?" The answer is that they have played a style of game that is not suited to the changed offside rule.

Football has become more even in the last four years than ever before in the course of its long football stays; never mind bothering your head today why they have gone to Division II; who is to blame; theorising, etc. More important is it that the sentence be one of "one year's punishment."

Let the slogan be: "Make it a year – and a year only." As the chairman has already said: "If the same spirit is shown next season as has been shown during the last seven matches the stay of one year may bring in its course some good results. After all the rally in the last series of matches was remarkably fine and is appreciated.

The club has at least found a side that appears to be a fighting force, and perhaps we can hope that Dean's "cold muscle" – they tell me that is the result of his foot operation – will warm up to a considerable extent. I wish Dean a return to his glorious form; I wish the team a return to their proper sphere.

An axe to grind

(By Stork, Liverpool Echo, May 5, 1930)

Trust Everton not to get a favour from other clubs in the relegation dogfight! It's just as well the Blues have managed just fine since.

*I*T never does to rely on others for anything you want. If you can do it yourself get on with it, and then you know it is done.

Everton had to rely upon others if they were to retain their First Division status. They had to reckon on some team's failure, what time they were registering a victory.

Unfortunately for the Merseysiders the others had their own axe to grind, and each team included in the relegation problem brought off startling wins, so Everton, after their long and glorious career, join up with Burnley in a descent to the Second Division.

Interviewed after the match, Mr W.C. Cuff, the chairman of the club, said: "We have fought well. Fate was against us; but we accept the position with a good heart and I feel confident that if the team shows the same determination and spirit as it has done in the past few weeks we will soon return to the premier League."

The verdict is out

(May 5, 1930)

How the scores elsewhere were relayed – 1930s edition.

 *T*HE fleeting minutes of the match with Sunderland will remain in my memory, for I have never seen anything like it. Everton's victory had been won.

What of the others? We knew that Sheffield United had scored a big success at Old Trafford, and so cramped Everton's prospects, but the Grimsby, Burnley and Newcastle finals were desired.

They were Everton's only hope, and every man and woman stood patiently waiting the verdict.

If you have ever seen a murder trial, and the waiting of the foreman juryman's decision you have got some sort of idea as to the feeling of the huge crowd (50,000).

I scanned the many faces, and found them drawn tense with anxiety, and it would have been possible to have heard a pin drop. Then all of a sudden a murmur went round the ground. The indicator man was about to put the numbers in the frame. What would they tell us? "Guilty or not guilty?"

Grimsby Town had won and despite the fact that it meant everything to Everton, there was a cheer, for the "Mariners" had become popular because of their great fight.

We were still short of two scores, and Everton's fate was as yet unknown. Men were pencilling their programmes, but they had no need to have done so, for both Newcastle and Burnley had won, and Everton had lost – lost their proud record, of being one of the few teams which had never before been in danger of relegation, at least not on the last day of the season.

It was undoubtedly a historical finish, and the spectators left the ground silently, and full of sorrow for the famous old club.

Act of revenge for a famous defeat

(Liverpool Post & Mercury, January 24, 1931)

Revenge was sweet from the humbling in the same competition nine years previously. The Crystal Palace v Everton tie also saw the occasion of Everton goalkeeper Billy Coggins being joined between the posts by a spectator. The reporter made note of the following occurrence in the second half, with Everton at this stage 4-0 ahead.

*E*VERTON came through their test with flying colours, and the shattering of the Palace by exactly the same score on the reverse sides to that at Goodison Park in 1922 gives supreme satisfaction to Merseyside. Dean played a prominent part in his side's victory, four goals rewarding his dashing efforts. The hundreds who went from Liverpool were able to say they had taken part in the act of revenge for a famous defeat sustained by Everton at their own ground in 1922, when Crystal Palace pranced around the Everton stars and went home with the joy of a 6-0 victory. The result nearly wrecked the Everton board of directors, and some of the players caught the blow in the signing-on season.

(In the second half), a spectator took off his coat and hat and went from the back of the goal and coolly joined Coggins as a goalkeeper and he would not take his leave. The game was stopped. The referee ordered the man off, but he expressed a desire to stay, and finally the police took him out of the ground.

Beautiful footwork against Palace

(Liverpool Football Echo, January 31, 1931)

The performance prompted this letter from a Mr. D. Morris of 1 Gillingham Street, Victoria, London, S.W. in the following Saturday's Football Echo:

I AM taking the liberty of writing you to thank the Everton team for the brilliant football served up on Saturday. I have seen many First

League matches in London this season, but it is many a day since I saw such beautiful footwork as that served up against the Palace.

The name of Everton has always stood high in the football world, for the class of football they play, and the clean, sporting way they play it. They added to their reputation.

The will to win and the confidence to do it

(By Blackstaff, Liverpool Echo, January 31, 1931)

Reflections on the progress made by the side since relegation.

*H*OWEVER sore a point it may be to people who have proudly admired and boasted of Everton's 40 years in the First Division, I think relegation has been a blessing in disguise for the club.

Is it really a new Everton? A practically non-losing Everton is something we have not had for years. In championship years Everton lost 31 points in 1927/28, 30 points in 1914/15 and 15 points in 1890/91 – in the latter case when there were only 12 clubs in the league. So far Everton has lost 10 points in 25 games. This Everton has gained the will to win and the confidence to do it.

Would this Everton be any use in the First Division? I should say certainly, but only by reason of the confidence and experience they have gained in the Second Division. Here's the secret, cribbed from another critic for short. "With First Division skill Everton have blended Second Division thrust, speed and first-time shooting."

Everton were relegated full of latent good football – better football, perhaps, than was being played generally in the First Division just then, but as so often happens to good craftsmanship, it was smothered by the rougher, readier, more practical football of rivals.

This new Everton in its new sphere has learned to watch and weigh an opposing side, then play upon its weaknesses. For years Everton had dazzled and dallied with the ball without realising the necessity of putting it between the sticks – barring, if you like, Dean's 60-goal season. Something rigorous has come into Everton's play and attitude towards play – a psychological change in team spirit which is not the gaining of a superiority complex, but the losing of an unsuspected inferiority complex, a fading of the team feeling that "My football's better than theirs, why don't they let us beat them, and stop trying to score their silly tell-tale goals."

Searching for the icing on the cake

(Liverpool Echo, February 26, 1931)

How transfer deals were done.

*W*HEN there is a midweek game the scouts gather at the fountain of tea with cake and take their meal while they consider ways and means of broaching the subject of a possible transfer deal. There was such a case yesterday at Goodison Park when Mr Huntbach and a Blackpool director were in the act of stocktaking. Everton have not been idle – they have been searching for a back, have considered a Scottish deal, but are not enamoured of it, and now are settling their minds about the cup-tie of Saturday and future days.

Hitting a high note

(Liverpool Echo, February 27, 1931)

Pre-match entertainment treats announced for supporters ahead of the Southport FA Cup quarter-final tie.

*T*HE programme of music for Goodison Park tomorrow, by the Aigburth Silver Prize Band (conductor, Mr Harry Wearing) will be as follows: March, "The Elephant" (Ord Hume); overture "The Bohemian Girl" (Balfe); foxtrot "Wasn't It Nice" (Feldman); foxtrot "All the King's Horses" (Lawrence Wright); two-step "The Stein Song" (Keith Prowse); march "B. B. & C. F." (Old Hume).

Shrimps net bursts

(Liverpool Echo, February 28, 1931)

*The fans rallied behind the Blues as they secured a 9-1 victory against the 'Shrimps',
thanks to a stunning forward line performance*

*A*LOCAL derby against Southport was the barrier to Everton
reaching an FA Cup semi-final for the first time in 16 years. Interest
was high among supporters, with £2,000 worth of tickets being sold
by the Thursday before the Saturday game, while a broadcast of the
game was also to be heard from Liverpool (Lime Street) Station at 6pm
that night.

On a snow-covered mud bath that was the Goodison Park pitch,
Everton romped into a 7-0 half-time lead – a club record – before
the "Shrimps", as they were called then, kept the score down in the
second half. The Blues eventually ran out 9-1 winners, with Dixie
Dean scoring four of them. Incidentally, former player Frank Jefferis'
post-match verdict claimed that the Blues' front five was 'probably the
best forward line that ever represented Everton.

300 injured in cup crush

(March 28, 1931)

*A record gate for the FA Cup semi-final and pandemonium as some fans were
injured. Everton dominated the first half but ended up losing 1-0.*

*S*ECOND Division champions-elect Everton were drawn to face
fellow title-contenders West Brom in the 1931 FA Cup semi-final at
Old Trafford. A crowd of 70,000 yielded record semi-final gate receipts
of £7,629 while more than 20,000 fans packed the Old Trafford
concourse. In the confusion, over 300 people were injured. The crowd
was such that the match was stopped on several occasions due to the
crowd spilling onto the pitch.

1932-1941

Dean's goal decides

(By Bee, Liverpool Post & Mercury, May 2, 1932)

Division Two champions in 1931, to First Division winners the following year – although the manner of the clinching 1-0 victory over Bolton Wanderers raised a host of contradictions in the writer's mind.

*F*ROM the head of Division Two, to the same position in the premier league is a long and arduous journey, but Everton managed it in successive seasons. When they were reaching out for the top rung they showed more "nerves" than at any other stage. Far from being a triumphal march to victory at the expense of Bolton Wanderers, Everton scraped home in the kind of match one generally associates with relegation problems rather than winning league championships.

Ten minutes from the end, when Everton realised that they were within 10 minutes of becoming champions, they took stage fright. The minutes lagged; the game had a will-it-ever-end fervour and Everton forsook their policy of attack for a what-we-have-we-hold attitude. It looked bad coming from the leading club in the country, but when the boredom of seeing the ball continually out of play, of seeing players sauntering up to take throws-in had passed, one began to appreciate how Everton felt about things.

A season's play might have been jeopardized by other tactics. Gee, who had been injured early and who had finally left the field in the second half, was off the field and the 10 men versus 11 theory must have been uppermost in the players' minds. They had to risk losing the match or play safety. Whichever course they took they would have been criticised. Yet who can blame a team for playing for safety when the efforts might go for nought through losing a game of this kind.

The goal which meant Everton's success was not a brilliant one, but it served its purpose. Dean's header was worthy of so good a player in this department and Jones could not save the effort, although he flung himself at the ball. The point came 33 minutes after the start.

It is my belief that if Cresswell had not been the coolest player on the field Everton might have caved in to this over-dribbling Bolton team of bits and pieces. While Everton's display was not up to their usual standard, they are worthy of commendation for they recovery.

Figures speak for themselves

(By Bee, Liverpool Post & Mercury, March 6, 1933)

FA Cup sixth-round opponents Luton Town of Division Three South appeared straightforward opposition at Goodison. Train-loads of "straw-hatted" Luton fans arrived at Lime Street on the morning of the match, reportedly singing: "We'll get Dixie down." The outcome? 6-0 to the home side, with Dean among the scorers.

 $\mathcal{E}$ VERTON passed to the semi-final for the second time in two years by their defeat of Luton Town before a big gate and a handsome financial yield – 55,431 spectators made a haul of £4,143 6s 4d. Everton won by six goals, and the figures speak for themselves.

Jack's in the driving seat

(By Bee, Liverpool Post & Mercury, April 22, 1933)

West Ham were defeated 2-1 in the semi-final at Molineux, with Ted Critchley the hero. Manchester City, who beat Everton 3-0 in February, were to be the opponents in what was the club's fifth Cup final. Mr Jack Pagenham, of Seaforth, who drove the coach through the streets of Liverpool 27 years previous to carry the victorious 1906 side, expressed his wish to do the same should Everton be victorious.

 $\mathcal{I}$ T was getting dark when we neared Spellow Lane and here we were joined by a torch-light procession which remained with us until Goodison Park was reached.

Would he again like to drive the present Everton team should they succeed next Saturday? Would he? He would jump at the opportunity. Quaint though his idea may at first seem in these days of changed locomotion, it is quite good and may bear fruit. It is this.

A Liverpool firm has the replica of the coach he used. He would seek permission to use it and the horses could be supplied by Messrs. Thompsons Ltd of County Road, with whom he is now employed.

Final fit for a king

(Liverpool Echo, April 25, 1933)

The 1933 FA Cup final was unique for several reasons.

IT will be novel because:

Neither team will wear its proper colours.

Every player, for the first time, will have a huge distinguishing number on his back.

Both teams – Everton and Manchester City – come from Lancashire.

There will be more foreign soccer enthusiasts than ever before.

The King (a regular Cup final visitor and understands football with the knowledge of an expert) and the Queen were to be in attendance, along with West Indian cricketers, 'who are in this country'.

Singing in the rain

(By Bee, Liverpool Echo, April 25, 1933)

Some people were pleased with the April showers ahead of the final.

"OH it's damp down here" – this is the song of the Everton footballers. And they are charmed with the beautiful rain. It suits their purpose; they feel that every drop of rain adds to their chance of victory over Manchester City in the final tie of the Cup, because there is not one member of the Everton side who does not prefer the "steady" ball rather than "the bounder" such as was experienced in recent weeks. Mr W.C. Cuff, the Everton chairman, tells me that Lord Derby has a prior engagement but "hopes to call in during the evening at the hotel when the dancing is in progress". Lord Derby made a similar entry at the Everton jubilee meeting at the Philharmonic Hall, and made one of his lordship's characteristic speeches. Mr Cuff is improving in health at a happy rate; the nasty boil at the side of his head was dangerous-looking during the weekend, but it is now mending speedily.

Dogs have had their day

(Liverpool Echo, April 26, 1933)

Last-minute preparations are underway at Wembley.

*W*HEN the greyhound racing meeting at Wembley Stadium ends tonight, the concluding preparations for the Cup Final on Saturday between Everton and Manchester City will be set in hand. The great lights in the stands will be ablaze all night while workmen tackle the task of installing an extra 20,000 seats. Tomorrow morning the goal posts will be erected and all the greyhound racing equipment, including the trap, the hurdles, hundreds of electric light globes, miles of cables, and an eight-ton steel girder bridge over the hare escape, will be removed and the pitch will be cut and rolled for the last time.

Hey-ho for the South

(Liverpool Echo, April 26, 1933)

Everton's secretary-manager Theo Kelly was confident things were going to plan.

*W*E have never had such a nice time as this week at Buxton. You would not have thought it was Cup Final week – just a nice breather, the weather is perfect. We will have a sprint or two, then some golf. We leave tomorrow, and the boys are going to make this afternoon their last hit with the sticks (golf) before they strike out for the Cup.

Good luck gifts

(Liverpool Echo, April 27, 1933)

Everton set off with the best wishes of the Mayor of Buxton and the people of the town behind them. Mayor Councillor J. Brindley issued a speech at Buxton Station, announcing: "If you bring back the FA Cup, it will be a credit not only to Merseyside but also Buxton". There was also a good luck present for the team.

MR J. Hewlitt, the manager of the hotel where the players have been staying, presented each of the team with a blue and white trumpet, while they also wore blue and white enamelled badges which had been sent to them by a firm in Liverpool last night. Other presents they have received are flannel trousers and raincoats.

Dixie Dean, their captain, was carrying a toy dog mascot wearing the Everton colours, which had been presented to him by the hotel staff. He declined to discuss his team's chances or to pose for photographers.

Now putt it into practice

(Liverpool Echo, April 28, 1933)

THE Cup Final is likely to be played in typical April weather.

"There will probably be showers, with a good deal of cloud and some sunshine tomorrow", an Air Ministry expert told the Echo today.

'There is now no need for further intensive training, and we are taking things easily,' it was stated at the hotel at Dorking where Everton are staying. 'The boys are having a quiet, restful day. They are out on the putting green of the hotel. It's a nice, mild, restful amusement in preparation for the big event. Some of them are very expert at it, too. They can drop the ball like clockwork. If they shoot the way they putt, then the Manchester goalkeeper will be in for a warm time tomorrow.'

Be on your best behaviour

(Liverpool Echo, April 28, 1933)

A warning to the fans the day before the final.

AND to those who make the journey I would just ask one thing – the railway companies have told me of the wanton destruction that occurred to the railway carriages on a recent trip, and they beg the people to be sporting and behave! It will be a spirited final tie, but that should not make anyone forget the good name of the best game of all, whose government has been an object lesson to all other sports.

Dixie Dean: "I want one for game, just one more trophy to 'make the set. It is going to be a great game, and with the changed conditions and our boys in perfect harmony and condition we shall, I feel sure, be successful. We have waited long for this – we made our vow last November – and I am confident we are going to put the world record on the books – First Division championship, Second Division championship, and the Cup in successive years."

Mugs from the North, they call us

There were an estimated 20,000 Everton fans at Wembley, with 'two hundred thousand Cup-tie trippers from the provinces, it was estimated added to London's millions today.' A Liverpool Echo reporter who travelled on the first of the Cup-tie special trains, made the following comments.

SHORTLY after 5am the shock troops from Liverpool and Manchester poured into the Metropolis. The invaders were accompanied by a gang of audacious camp followers, who having stowed away on a train, left it near Wembley. Thousands disappointed at being unable to go to Wembley, seemed to derive a kind of pained pleasure in watching others depart.

Those lucky folk who had tickets started queuing up before 10pm in order to be sure of getting on the 12.30am train. The numbered ticket system ensured that every passenger to the capital – there were nearly 700 counted on each train – was provided with a seat.

More enthusiasts joined us at Allerton and Runcorn and then we 'rattled' along with community singing, and the strumming of ukeleles, guitars, banjos, mouth organs and whistles. As the first exuberance died down a pair of enterprising 'buskers' did good business.

A few minutes after passing Wembley we were entertained to a new thrill. The train, with the signal against it, halted and in the twinkling of an eye a carriage door flew open and our friends the buskers were speeding it away. They were followed by a gang of youngsters, and before the train officials, or most of the passengers had realised what was happening some nine or ten stowaways – most of them youths in their teens – had made their getaway over a wall bounding the railway.

"Mugs from the North they call us," said one patriotic Liverpudlian. "Why, those kids could buy and sell these fly Cockney blokes."

The many women folk who accompanied their men folk, true to their sex, could be heard over their early morning refreshments planning a round of the shops – for them these are the sights of London.

It was in a café that one heard the inevitable word "gradely". It was used by a waitress to a party of Liverpudlians to show she knew the speech of these Lancashire folk; and she wondered at the withering look that greeted her friendly efforts.

Dixie's Cup

(By Bee, Liverpool Echo, April 29, 1933)

An almost perfect day for the club, as a unique treble of Second Division, First Division and now FA Cup success in three successive seasons. From this extract it appears Manchester City were never in it, as Everton produced an impressive display to secure a second cup success

*F*ROM the wretched angle of the Press box one pictured the ball passing over his head into goal, but what actually happened was that it sliced out towards Stein, who tried to head in and was baulked by force of numbers.

Langford brought the ball to the notice of the referee, owing to a lace protruding. This would be dangerous to the eye if a player tried to head the ball. Manchester fought back and a shot by Brook was high, strong and angled so that when Sagar leapt into the air he performed a fine goalkeeping feat. It was clean catch worthy of any cricketer.

Other observations:

The Everton captain was always getting the ball with his head, in spite of the crush of the opposition.

Dean's goal:

As the ball winged its way towards Langford's outstretched right hand, we had this position. Langford with an upraised right arm was actually touching the ball when Dean charged him flat to the ground and being practically on the goalline, the ball was breasted in and might have gone in if Dean had not touched it.

Court out

(Liverpool Echo, May 1, 1933)

*S*EVEN young men who stowed away on excursion trains in London after a desperate effort – fruitless in some cases – to see the Cup Final, appeared at Liverpool Police Court today.

They were all charged with travelling from Euston to Lime Street, Liverpool, without paying their fare – and with no intention of paying.

The magistrates dealt leniently with the offenders, but the chairman (Mr Harold Lee) gave them a serious warning.

The chairman stated: "We are in a difficulty about you young men. It is no use fining you because probably you have no money. We don't want to send you to prison, lest you have swindled the railway company. They offer cheap fares, and you take advantage of the rush and travel without any intention of paying, just on the chance of being able to scramble through. It is a shabby and mean thing to do."

The first was Philip Morgan (18), Byrom Street, Liverpool, who arrived at Lime Street early yesterday. He told the ticket collector that he had no ticket, it was stated, and tried to bolt through the luggage gate. He was caught. Morgan then said: "I got through the barriers at Euston when there was a rush by the crowd." Morgan told the bench that he had walked to London. Mr G Clarke (prosecuting): "I am afraid that he got to London the same way as he came back – rushing the barrier with the crowd." Morgan was placed on probation for a year.

Everton fans, apparently, have been modest in their celebrations of the Cup victory, for there was no perceptible increase in the number of "third court" drunk cases in Liverpool today.

One man, who had been seen shouting and waving his arms, denied that his behaviour was the result of stronger beer, and quietly explained: "I was celebrating Everton's success."

Everton's bogey is buried forever!

(Daily Mirror, May 2, 1933)

Jack gets his wish after all on the victorious homecoming

 IXIE Dean and his men of Everton received a wonderful welcome last night when they arrived in Liverpool with the FA Cup.

Tremendous crowds assembled at Lime Street Station and in the main streets, all traffic was brought to a standstill on the route of the triumphal procession to the Town Hall, where the team was welcomed and congratulated by the Lord Mayor. The drive round the city was made in an old coach driven by Mr Jack Pagendam – the same coach that carried the victorious Everton Cup team in 1906.

As the coach left the station, Dixie Dean, the captain, standing in front beside the driver, waved the Cup in the air, and was greeted with deafening cheers. After the civic reception the procession made its way to the Everton ground, where the Cup was seen by thousands of people. Half a dozen youths created amusement by conducting a mock funeral for the vanquished finalists. They carried a coffin and a banner bearing the words: "Everton's bogey is buried forever!"

Before the team left London, Dean said: "I think that the better team won. It was a great game which we all enjoyed, and although at the same time some of us might have regretted any bits of bad luck that we might have had, we have forgotten all about it, for the Cup is ours."

Alec James and Alec Jackson, those great exponents of the game, were at Euston to give their congratulations to Everton, as was Sir Frederick Wall, secretary of the FA. Probably the happiest carriage was that occupied by the wives, sweethearts and friends of the players.

Six in the fishermen's net

(By Stork, Liverpool Echo, January 12, 1935)

Cup progress is made at the expense of Grimsby Town 6-3, as the Mariners' fishing links are utilised by joyous sub-editors – this headline (above) was the one that appeared in the newspapers. A week later Everton would defeat the same opposition 3-1 in the league, with Jimmy Cunliffe scoring in both games.

*A*GREAT game. Everton had many anxious moments against an excellent forward line, but Geldard, with three goals and many gift offerings, put paid to the account of a gallant Grimsby.

Sunderland get shorts shrift

(By Stork, Liverpool Daily Post, January 28, 1935)

Everton's equaliser had apparently arrived with Dixie Dean off the pitch to get another pair of 'pants' as Johnson, the Sunderland back, had torn them.

*E*VERTON sprang one of the surprises of the round by holding the great Sunderland team to a draw and earning a replay, each side scoring a goal, and with the slightest bit of luck they might have won. For had not Thorpe made two amazing saves in the last few minutes Sunderland would have figured among the fallen.

Match of a lifetime

(By Bee, Liverpool Daily Post, January 31, 1935)

Interest was high in the replay, set for the Wednesday afternoon. Other noticeable points beforehand were that a change of referee had been made, a Mr Pinckston of Birmingham, appointed by the FA due to the rough tactics employed by Sunderland in the first game. The tie would be dubbed "the greatest ever at Goodison". At the end of 90 minutes with the score at 3-3 Sunderland manager Johnny Cochrane (later stories state his surname was spelt 'Cockrane') was ordered off, although it is suggested he may have entered the pitch to help give his weary side an extended break before the resumption (he had gone to the middle of the field against the rules to talk to his players). The extra-time period yielded four more goals including the completion of Jackie Coulter's hat-trick as Everton ran out 6-4 winners (the Liverpool Daily Post reported how 'the Everton players had difficulty in retracing their steps to the dressing room because the crowd surged on and mobbed the players, who had hardly sufficient strength to make their way through any more opposition'). It was reported that Cunliffe had played through the last half-hour in a state of semi-consciousness, having headed a ball and thus played on through instinct. The Liverpool Echo's Ernest Edwards summed up the match: "I would like to ask whether there has ever been a greater display of skill in the mud in any league or cup match?"

The tie also yielded some instances of crowd control, which perhaps sums up the lack of attention paid to crowd safety in the 1930s.

*E*VERTON passed to the next round by beating Sunderland before 59,213 spectators (a gate of £4,382 5s 6d), the score of 6-4 being an uncommon figure and a just one, obtained only after the greatest amount of effort on the part of the Everton team after extra time.

It was a match of a lifetime; one international player of years gone by told me he had never seen anything to approach this historic struggle. Thrill packed on thrill; incident upon incident; goal upon goal; a home victory seemingly settled a quarter of an hour from the finish of the 90 minutes; only for a rallying force by Sunderland (shocked by the two goals margin) fighting back to accomplish the seemingly impossible –

two goals in the closing stages – the equaliser to bring the score to 3-3 being the most spectacular and strange-looking goal of the 10.

A first half occurrence: The crowd broke in at the edge of the goal double-decker, and the scene was without parallel since Newcastle and Barnsley refought a final tie here. They surged across the pitch while the game was in progress, and the police were well-nigh powerless to stop their inroads around the playing space.

The police allowed them to cross the field to the far side of the ground and sit down. This eased the position, as the playing pitch was clear.

Lawton for Everton

(By John Peel, Liverpool Daily Post, January 1, 1937)

A new striking prospect was brought in, with Everton hoping he would prove to be as successful as one of their previous teenager buys from another local club

*E*VERTON yesterday made an important capture from Burnley the transfer of T. Lawton, their much-sought centre-forward, who is only seventeen years of age. Lawton, who first played for Burnley last March at the age of sixteen, has scored eleven goals in eighteen matches this season. He stands 6 feet and weighs 12st, 5lbs. The fee paid by Everton is stated to be in the region of £3,000. Lawton may appear for Everton in a Central League match tomorrow.

Everton have been fortunate in their choice of boy centre-forwards. First was "Boy Browell" who created a stir when he joined Everton from Hull City. Then Dean came along to eclipse all records and it is stated that Lawton has the making of another Dean. The boy has certainly made a good start. Everton and other clubs have been showing an interest in Lawton for some weeks, but the Burnley directors have been holding on in the hope that home gates would improve and that they would be spared having to realise on this valuable young player.

Despite his youth Lawton has been a member of Burnley's Lancashire Cricket League team. He is a hard hitter, and has figured as a match winner on several occasions.

Permission to play, sir

(Daily Mirror, February 6, 1940)

Footballers often had to get leave from the army to get a game during WWII.

*T*OMMY Lawton, Everton and England centre-forward, may play for Charlton on Saturday against Chelsea in the first of the Regional games. Charlton's right-half, George Green, recently re-signed from the police to enter the R.A.F. instructional course at Aldershot.

Yesterday he wrote to his manager, Jimmy Seed, saying he would be available for next Saturday. A postscript said: "Tommy Lawton is here with me and is dying for a game. What about it?"

Jimmy is wasting no time. He wrote to Everton last night asking permission for Lawton to play at the Valley.

Saxophone gifts at turnstile

(Daily Mirror, February 21, 1940)

Supporters did their bit to keep soldiers' minds off the ongoing conflict.

*P*ASSING through the turnstile at the ground of a famous league club, the supporter paid his shilling...and handed the official a saxophone. He was one of hundreds of fans who have given the club gifts to pass on to the troops.

Supporters of this club alone have provided enough musical instruments to start several jazz bands, literature to equip several libraries, stacks of playing cards, cigarettes and sports equipment. The presents have been given to Everton in response to an appeal by secretary Theo Kelly. It took two lorries to carry one consignment from Goodison.

"One unit has been furnished with a complete library," said Mr Kelly. "All types of readers were catered for, but the popular fancy was for Wild West yarns. The appeal has met with a tremendous response... but there's still need for more."

1942-1951

Football in the offing

(Ranger's Notes, Liverpool Echo, August 10, 1942)

While war raged, regional football continued, although the normal league programme was suspended.

*E*VERTON are getting down to business this week, though in their case no public practices are being held. Activities will be confined to private trials of the many youngsters who have had their names submitted to the club. Several of these were up at the ground last week, where they went through the capable hands of trainer Harry Cooke and indulged in sprinting and general loosening up exercises. Mr Theo Kelly has plenty of promising talent from which to choose to fill any possible vacancies during the coming season.

A great struggle

(By Stork, Liverpool Echo, September 21, 1942)

Eight-goal derby entertainment – did the best team draw?

*T*HE "Liverton" Derby was better than many pre-war games between these two old rivals. And what a finish – a finish which sent people away bubbling over with excitement. Liverpool equalised almost in the last minute of the game. Some folk are sceptical as to whether football will come back into its own. With such games as that on Saturday, who dare say it has ever left us? There was not a dull moment. There was something in it every minute – excellent rounds of combination, hefty drives and goals, stubborn defences, scintillating attacks – aye, everything that football can produce.

Everton were bound for a convincing victory, for their first-half display was good enough for League days. They undoubtedly seemed to be riding to victory by their clever footwork, accurate rounds of passing, and the shot, but Liverpool are famed for their fighting quality. A game is not won until it is lost with the Anfielders, and they proved the axiom to be right.

Two goals in 12 minutes was a nasty blow to Liverpool but they hit back and reduced the lead, only to find Everton regain their two-goal advantage by half-time. It is not comforting to resume with such a heavy list, but the Anfielders fought on trying to get themselves into something like their true shape, but Everton were playing with the confidence which a nicely-sized lead can give. Few imagined that Liverpool could catch up, not even when the score read Everton three Liverpool two. You see, Everton were going great guns, whereas Liverpool were stressing and straining and were not a united whole, and when Everton got two goals ahead again, there appeared little possibility of them losing their grip on things.

It was then that Billy Liddell struck his international form. Watson and J. E. Jones had taken good care of him up to then, and in doing so had run themselves out. Liddell saw his chance and utilised it to the full. He bounced past them with intricate close control, offered chances to colleagues – took one himself in fact. I would say this was Liddell's match so far as Liverpool was concerned. He lit the flame which set Liverpool alight and so the match which promised to be in Everton's safe-keeping ended all square.

It was a grand fare, boys, and each and every player deserved a pat on the back for an afternoon's splendid entertainment. Everton were the more polished team, their artistry was without compare but Liverpool got the same return from their more direct methods. The last goal came from the penalty spot, when Done was nudged off the ball. Two minutes remained when Dorsett strode forward to take the spot-kick. Would he fail? No! The ball went into the net like a rocket to the accompaniment of a roar such as I have not heard for an age.

Egyptian Everton

(Daily Mirror, February 13, 1943)

Everton in Egypt.

$\mathcal{C}$ORINTHIANS v Aston Villa; Sheffield United v Arsenal; Everton v Manchester City. Matches to be played on Saturday, February 13. Yes, today.

Fixtures such as these have the ring of a peacetime English Cup draw. But these games are being played far from the Homeland.

Men of the Eighth Army stationed in Cairo have formed their own football league – and all the teams have been named after famous English or Scottish clubs. On dusty pitches around the Egyptian capital, General Montgomery's men fight out their championships with all the ardour of their famous namesakes.

The comeback kid

(Daily Mirror, February 13, 1943)

A young goalkeeper defied medical predictions to return from injury.

$\mathcal{W}$ATCHING Wilf Birkett, young amateur goalkeeper, make a brilliant first appearance for Everton, the crowd little realised that he had walked straight out of hospital. But he had!

A year ago, playing for Haydock, his amateur club, Birkett was badly hurt. "He'll never play again," was the gloomy prediction of the first doctor who examined him.

"He may get better, but he must not kick a football again for two seasons," said the bone specialist, more optimistically.

Well, Wilf went into the local Providence Hospital, made a first-class recovery – and was invited to play for Everton. But before he went off to the match, he went to the hospital to tell the sisters and nurses that he was playing again, and to thank them and the doctors for all they had done.

Jones treble sees off United

(By Stork, Liverpool Daily Post, February 25, 1943)

*M*UCH of Everton's Cup tension was reduced when they defeated Manchester United by four goals to one at Maine Road (Between 1941 and 1949 United played most of their homes fixtures at Manchester City's old ground because Old Trafford had suffered bomb damage).

Points were vital to Everton and they got on top of the United almost from the outset, and having scored two goals in 20 minutes they had the United on the collar for most of the first half.

In the second half the United did show some improvement, but there was still that lack of finish and an uncertainty that prevented them from taking goals, despite the fine work of Birkett in the Everton goal.

The first half had been all Everton, and after Bentham had led off with a goal at 14 minutes, Jones obtained a second at 20 minutes and a third at 35 minutes.

With such a lead they could have rested on their oars, but this might have been folly, for when the United resumed they did so in a manner which encouraged the home crowd.

Nevertheless Everton had one or two breakaways, and from one of them, Jones got his hat-trick and it was not until three minutes from the end that United got a consolation goal through Smith.

Much of Everton's success was due to Mercer, Humphreys and Curwen in the half-back line, although one could not help but give praise to Bentham, Mutch, Jones and Stevenson.

But it was an all-round victory, and these two points will be of immense value to Everton in their efforts to quality for the cup competition proper.

One of the first 'educated' Everton Blues?

(Daily Mirror, March 17, 1943)

*F*ROM school team to a First Division club and a University "Blue" – all within two seasons. It reads like the life story of the hero of some schoolboy magazine.

It is, in fact, the record of Frank Finch, brilliant 19-year-old Everton amateur outside-left. Finch comes from Bryn, near Garswood, Lancs, and last season was playing in the Ashton-in-Makerfield Grammar School team.

Everton noticed him: asked him to help them as an amateur. Finch this year went up to Cambridge – and within a few months was given a war-time Blue against Oxford.

He is playing so brilliantly in the Everton team now, that the club's officials say he would have been a certainty for an amateur international cap – but for the war.

The Garswood district seems to have been a happy hunting ground for Everton in recent months for besides Finch, the club has found two other promising lads there – Wilf Birkett, goalkeeper, and Martin McDonald, centre-half.

Soccer under the African sun

(Daily Mirror, December 24, 1943)

A pre-Christmas work-out attracts interest.

*E*VEN under the boiling African sun, the Englishman does not lose his hero worship of the soccer stars.

A match had been arranged between two teams in the British North African Forces. An RAF side was to meet an Army XI. A good "gate" was assured.

But when word went round that several famous League players would be taking part, the crowd literally stormed the turnstiles – or whatever it is they use for turnstiles in that part of the world.

Bryn Jones, of Arsenal, was playing inside-right for the Army; Andy Beattie, of Preston, left-back and Geldard (Everton) centre-forward.

Everyone returned to camp satisfied with the final score at 1-1.

Injured soccer player toughens up

(Daily Mirror, January 8, 1944)

Everton utilised some war training methods in a bid to help one player rediscover "his nerve".

$\mathcal{B}$ILLY Lowe, young Everton outside-right of high promise, is to be put through a special toughening course to ensure than an accident has not broken his nerve.

Billy fractured a leg playing against Tranmere Rovers some time ago. A major setback for a boy still in his teens, on the threshold of his senior career. Everton were worried in case the accident should cause him to lose his zest for the game.

So that there shall be no possibility of young Lowe's career being ruined that way, Everton manager Kelly and trainer Cooke are to put him through a miniature Commando course. Not until all psychological effects of the accident have been eliminated will young Lowe be allowed to take the field again.

War-time football topsy-turvy? Ask Davies, the Everton player. Davies went to the Valley ground at Charlton expecting to play for Millwall against Fulham. But he found this match was being played at Selhurst Park – Crystal Palace's ground – several miles away, and there was no time to make the extra journey.

Instead, Charlton were meeting Southampton at the Valley. Did he go without a game? Not on your life. Charlton were short of a player. They rang up Millwall asking for permission to play Davies and everything ended happily.

Soccer fans threw lemons to players

(Daily Mirror, April 17, 1944)

Local hooligans or appreciation at the need to build up vitamin C reserves for the players?

$\mathscr{A}$S the Liverpool and Everton teams took the field for their league match at Anfield on Saturday about two dozen lemons were tossed to the players by spectators. They were stacked in the back of the goals until half-time.

FA stops match

(Daily Mirror, April 19, 1944)

So straight to pens it is then?

$\mathscr{T}$HE Football Association have refused permission for Everton and Liverpool to replay their Lancashire Cup match at Liverpool this evening. They point out this fixture would run counter to a Home Office desire that no senior competitive match is to be played in midweek.

Sporting gossip

(Daily Mirror, June 4, 1945)

The Everton board were keen to keep hold of the club's star man amidst rumours of a potential move south.

$\mathscr{W}$HEN Everton FC directors meet tomorrow the question of Tommy Lawton's request to be placed on the transfer list will be discussed, but it is already apparent for economic reasons, that the answer will be an emphatic "No".

League lift ban on three-match star

(Daily Mirror, October 11, 1945)

Londoner "Alfred" Wally Fielding was allowed to return to action for the club having been banned for apparently asking for "more money" when moving to Goodison the previous month.

*A*LFRED Fielding, Everton's three-match star, will be back in League football on Saturday when his club meets Manchester United at Goodison Park.

Fielding was suspended by a committee of the Football League on September 27 following an inquiry in London.

It was understood that Fielding's offence was in the process of signing for Everton, he asked for more money than a new professional was entitled to.

His case was considered again at Monday's meeting of the Management Committee – who conveyed the news of the suspension to the club yesterday.

Fielding, signed by Everton as a professional on September 7, rose to stardom in Middle East Services football after his release following capture at Tobruk.

He had been an amateur on Charlton's books, and, when he signed for Everton, Charlton asked the League to hold an inquiry into the circumstances of his joining Everton.

Invited to comment on the Management Committee's decision, Mr F. Howarth, Football League secretary, said:

"The Management Committee confirmed the sub-committee's decision of the suspension of Fielding, but after taking into account that the player had come from overseas, and that perhaps he acted in ignorance of the rules following his long absence abroad, together with the fact that he is at the start of his career, the committee decided to lift the suspension forthwith."

Lawton goes to Chelsea today

(Daily Mirror, November 8, 1945)

Chelsea get Everton's star man.

$\mathcal{E}$NGLAND centre-forward Tommy Lawton will be transferred from Everton to Chelsea this morning.

Chelsea manager Willie Birrell went to Lawton's military depot in Cheshire last night to complete the transfer.

The agreed fee is understood to be between £10,000-£12,000 – much less than was at one time expected and nowhere near the record (£14,500) paid by Arsenal for Bryn Jones.

Lawton was placed on the transfer list at his own request because, for health reasons, his wife, who is at present ill in bed at Liverpool, has been advised to live in the south.

Lawton, a C.S.M I., is not due to be demobilised till next June.

The FA Cup returns

(January 10, 1946)

$\mathcal{W}$ITH league matters not set to resume until August 1946, the 1945/46 season saw the introduction of two-legged FA Cup ties – an experiment which was to prove unsuccessful as it was scrapped for the following season.

Everton were paired with Preston. They lost 2-1 in the first leg at Deepdale with Harry Catterick scoring on his FA Cup debut for the Blues. In the return, the Blues equalised to take the tie into extra time. A goal apiece in the extra period (Everton had led 2-0 for only one minute in the first half of extra time) saw the tie still level on aggregate after 110 minutes (two periods of 10 minutes were played).

The solution? Sudden death, or what has been more commonly known as the "golden goal". In what would be a precursor of future occasions, one Bill Shankly proved Everton's nemesis, scoring a penalty nine minutes in after Everton captain Norman Greenhalgh had fisted a Livesey effort off the line. The Liverpool Echo carried the headline: PENALTY IN THE DARK.

The reporter said: "There was an exciting finish when after the nine minutes of extra time, Preston were awarded a penalty for an offence which, in the failing light, I could not see."

Ironically, Shankly had been set to miss the first leg, which highlighted the selection problems clubs had in the months after WWII. As the Liverpool Echo noted beforehand: "Bill Shankly has written saying that he will do his best to get down from Glasgow, where he is stationed with the RAF. Preston's board meet tonight to choose the side.

"Their hopes that either Bob Beattie or Tom Finney might be home from abroad in time seem doomed to disappointment."

Football League resumes
(Daily Mirror, September 2, 1946)

Football officially returned – along with grey skies – on the final day of August. Unfortunately the Blues suffered a 2-0 home defeat.

$\mathcal{S}$OCCER kicked off after seven years in pelting rain, on slippery grounds – and with sensations in plenty. Brentford took away points from Everton. Newport v Southampton was postponed through floods.

Crowds of close on a million saw the league games. Everton drew 55,000. The total for league matches was 847,000. Add the few smart ones who dodged through the turnstiles.

They see a future in the past
(Daily Mirror, January 1, 1947)

The management sought new blood.

$\mathcal{N}$AMES which insist on cropping up whenever and wherever soccer is discussed, Dixie Dean, Joe Mercer, Eddie Wainwright. Names which you automatically associate with one club, Everton, even though Mercer is now an Arsenal player and Dixie saw service with other clubs before finishing his first-class career.

Three of the outstanding names in years of football, all found in junior soccer by the same club.

And now Everton, fallen away from their former glory, are to go back to the old hunting grounds, the parks and the recreation grounds, in a bid to put the club back on its old pinnacle.

Club chief Mr Theo Kelly, always a greater believer in encouraging the youngsters, plans to run 10 junior sides. A large spare ground owned by the club is to be modernised. Dressing rooms, a clubhouse and showers will be built.

"From these teams," says Mr Kelly, "we should find enough players to meet demands. It is obvious that with the prices being asked for ready-made stars, we cannot afford to buy. So we will make our own.

"The cost will be high, but in return we should pick up some players as great as those who have worn our jerseys in the past."

Record crowd at Goodison

(By Stork, Liverpool Echo, September 18, 1948)

The record crowd – later confirmed as 78,299 – see a derby draw.

*E*VERTON confounded the critics. Not only had they played grand football but the "old guard" lasted it out to the bitter end. Perhaps not as good as some "Derby" games we have seen, because mainly the defences were in command.

Record for the ground is 74,721 in last season's fourth round FA Cup tie between Manchester United and Liverpool (Old Trafford had yet to reopen after bomb damage and Maine Road was unavailable), but it was quite possible that these figures would go by the board today, as each section of the ground looked to be well and truly packed, and there were many thousands outside.

There were many casualties and some swaying in parts of the paddock. As is usual in "Derby" games, the players came out in pairs, and it was seen that Stevenson was the Everton captain.

There was great cheering as the players made their appearance. Stevenson won the toss, and elected to kick towards the Gwladys Street. He took a corner himself but it was speedily cleared, and Liverpool were soon down in Everton territory, where they found Jones solid as a rock. Not only that he was as cool as a cucumber, extricating himself from difficulties with a classical touch to a better-placed colleague.

Sagar had to save from Fagan and Shannon in quick succession. He took both balls in cricket fashion. It was a good "Derby" game, not perhaps up to the standard of some we have seen, perhaps because it needed a goal to bring it to real life. The football had been uncommonly good. But the supporter wants something more than that.

Then came one of the most thrilling moments of the match. Fagan took a ball which came across field without allowing it to touch mother earth. He hooked it with terrific power, and it seemed the ball would just go inside the upright, but Sagar pounced down on it as it was passing over the line near the upright. It was a glorious shot and an equally fine save.

The game was stopped while Tommy Jones came over to speak to Harry Cooke, the Everton trainer, no doubt to explain that he was injured. Cooke later came up to the touchline with a bandage, and Jones left the field and had his injury bandaged. He was only off a few minutes, but during that time Liverpool had scored a goal. Fagan was right in the spot, and he shot hard and true to the far side of the goal.

A corner against Liverpool proved fatal. Boyes swung the ball into the goalmouth where it was bandied about for a time until it finally came out to Boyes who shot with all the power at his command, and with Sidlow well and truly beaten Shepherd took over the role of goalkeeper and tipped the ball over the bar with his hand.

Dodds took the spot-kick and although Sidlow got his hands to the fierce drive he could not keep it out of his net. Time: 84 minutes.

New Everton FC manager

(Liverpool Echo, September 20, 1948)

The following Monday, attention turned to a potential managerial appointment.

*T*HE Echo understands that Mr Clifford S. Britton, a former Everton FC star player, may be appointed manager of the Everton Football Club. He would take over his duties almost immediately.

Britton was one of the greatest half-backs Everton have had, and since he went to Turf Moor has brought the Burnley club many triumphs.

Britton is a student of football. He knows what he wants and, what is more, how to impart his knowledge to his players. He brought Burnley up from the Second Division, and then took his club to Wembley after they had beaten Liverpool in the semi-final at Manchester. The chapter of triumph was spoiled by Charlton's 1-0 victory in extra time.

Mr Britton will not have to ask a player to do something he cannot, for even now he takes the field with his colleagues in training. There is no more popular figure than this quietly spoken but efficient manager.

Britton was in Everton's cup-winning team of 1933, and many will recall his lob, which enabled Dixie Dean to score the second goal against Manchester City. The Britton lob became traditional, and many of Dean's goals came from that source. Britton had to rely on skill, rather than brawn, for he was on the slim side, but there can be no aspect of the game, in play or management, he does not know.

National and semi-final clash

(Daily Mirror, March 15, 1950)

The Grand National/Merseyside FA Cup semi-final weekend caused concern; Mirror readers were given a geography lesson.

*A*N appeal is to be made to the Home Secretary to have him use his influence to prevent the clashing of the Grand National and the

Liverpool-Everton Cup semi-final. Both are fixed for Saturday week.

Alternatively, Tophams, managers of the Aintree racecourse, want the football match played at some ground other than Manchester so as not to interfere with traffic to Liverpool.

A representative of Tophams said yesterday they had a letter from the FA declining to change the date of the match or the venue.

"This is going to be a Grand National on an unprecedented scale," he said.

Note: Manchester is about 35 miles from Liverpool.

Catterick at the double in cup win
(January 30, 1950)

*H*ARRY Catterick, later to become one of the club's greatest-ever managers, was the Everton hero in January 1950, as his two goals booked Everton a last 16 berth at the expense of West Ham. In a "thrilling match on an icy surface" McGowan had put the home side ahead before Catterick made his mark in a six-minute spell midway through the first half.

The omens appeared to indicate that this could be Everton's year – as the previous two wins against the Hammers (all 2-1 outcomes) in the competition had seen the Blues reach the final (in 1907 and 1933).

Relegation – the dreaded blow
(By Ranger, Liverpool Echo, May 5, 1951)

The team had struggled since the end of hostilities, and were on a downward curve. Relegation had looked a possibility in previous seasons, and it was no surprise when the inevitable came after a run of only one win in the last 10 games prior to the capitulation at Sheffield Wednesday – who would also go down.

*T*HE dreaded blow has fallen on Everton. After holding their own for the first 25 minutes, they were badly blitzed during an overwhelming spell of superiority which brought three goals to the home side in eight minutes before the interval, two of them due to slips by Everton defenders.

Sheffield went further ahead in the second half, and also missed a penalty. An injury to Fielding early in the first half may have been responsible for the winger losing much of his effectiveness, but it had nothing to do with Sheffield's overwhelming victory.

The Wednesday were more like a championship than a possible relegation side, and only brilliant saves by Burnett in the second half prevented the score being much greater.

'Unknowns' earn places

(Daily Mirror, September 3, 1951)

A couple of Everton new-boys made an impression in a victory over Leeds United – including an energetic centre-forward.

*A*LTHOUGH Tommy Eglington, Everton's Irish international outside-left, shot both goals in his side's 2-0 defeat of Leeds United, the Goodison Park stars were two unknown youngsters making their league debut.

Tony McNamara, 21, a Merseyside product, is a long-legged outside-right with a shot well above the average. Dave Hickson, 21, is a menacing centre-forward who chases every loose pass.

1952-1961

Cannonball Kid's finest hour

(February 14, 1953)

*E*VERTON took on Manchester United in the FA Cup fifth round, with the Second Division Blues expected to roll over. With Arthur Rowley netting for the visitors midway through the first half all appeared to be going to the script. However, United should have known more about the fighting qualities of Dave Hickson. With nearly 78,000 packed in, the No. 9 inspired the Blues to a famous win.

Tommy Eglington soon levelled soon and close to half-time, Hickson launched himself headlong in among flying boots as he tried to get on the end of a Jock Lindsay cross. He emerged with blood streaming from an eyebrow, having "connected" with a defender's boot.

Hickson emerged minutes after the second half had begun, dabbing the wound with a handkerchief, although it would soon open up after heading an effort against the post. Although the referee wanted him to go off again, the "Cannonball Kid" would have none of it and the Goodison hero stayed on and tormented the United defence. Fittingly, he fired home the winner just after the hour mark.

Everton paint the town green

(Liverpool Daily Post, February 16, 1953)

The Goodison win had seen fans struggling to get in due to crushing. This led to royal blue taking a backseat...while there was also a nod to the supporters.

*S*OME people sought refuge in the Gwladys Street school

playground. On Saturday morning the railings had been newly-painted green; on Saturday night they were almost cleared of paint, and there were unorthodox green decorations on hundreds of overcoats in Liverpool.

So, said the wags, Everton, by winning one of the greatest cup-ties ever seen in Liverpool, had painted the town red – and green.

Mrs Matt Busby, wife of the Manchester United manager, gave her own reason for the victory. "It must have been those spectators," she said. "I have never heard such sustained roars of encouragement – it even surpassed the Hampden roar."

FA Cup semi-final heartache
(March 21, 1953)

*T*HE Blues faced First Division Bolton Wanderers in the FA Cup semi-final, three years after suffering defeat to Liverpool in their first post-war last-four clash. The Trotters showed their class by racing into a 4-0 lead at the break with the Blues in complete disarray.

Dave Hickson was off the field for 15 minutes – again with a head injury – and Tommy Clinton missed a penalty on the stroke of half-time which did not help Everton's cause.

But the Blues stormed back, with two goals from John Willie Parker and another from Peter Farrell. Parker's second, Everton's third, came six minutes from time to set up a pulsating finale.

However, Bolton clung on as Maine Road proved unlucky again.

Wasp-like Blues win 25 corners, but crash out
(February 20, 1954)

*E*VERTON, on their way to promotion from the Second Division, were drawn to face top-flight Sheffield Wednesday at Hillsborough in a tough FA Cup clash. Both sides sported their blue home strips. To make them stand out, Everton wore wasp-like yellow and black hooped stockings.

The visitors, backed by 10,000 fans, some of whom who had boarded 15 special trains, suffered an early blow when Shaw gave Wednesday the lead, but from then on Everton dominated.

Tommy Eglington, making his 300th appearance for the club, was among a host of players who went close before Dave Hickson equalised before the hour mark.

There appeared to be only one winner – with Everton forcing 25 corners – but unfortunately it did not prove to be the Merseysiders. Breakaway goals from Sewell and O'Neill in the last five minutes saw Everton bow out and the home side progress to the quarter-finals.

According to the Echo, there was to be further disappointment for over 500 Everton fans. Having been too late for the specials arranged for them, they were brought back by a later train although it did not get to the city centre until 2.30am. The fans then faced a long walk home as all the buses had stopped running.

Soccer's Don Quixote with a dash of Captain Blood

(By Ranger, Liverpool Daily Post, May 3, 1954)

Everton's stay in the second tier lasted three years, with a dramatic end to the season culminating in a 4-0 victory at Oldham Athletic.

*C*ONGRATULATIONS to Everton upon a splendid achievement and another milestone in their long and distinguished history. Pleasure at their return to the First Division is not limited to Merseyside. All the senior clubs in the country are delighted that once again they will be visiting Everton's palatial home. The only folk sorry to see the Blues leave the Second Division are those humbler clubs who have shared the tremendous gates Everton have enjoyed this season.

As the Blues went up, the Merseyside Reds went down. Everton skipper Peter Farrell saluted the splendid work of manager Cliff Britton and all the players, with special mention of that wonderfully keen but sometimes over-impetuous lad in the middle, who, perhaps more than any other single player, ensured that Everton achieved their heart's desire, namely, energetic, determined and tearaway Davie Hickson, soccer's modern Don Quixote with a dash of Captain Blood.

This is not the place to go into all the pros and cons of Hickson's style, ability or provocative displays. Suffice it to say that I firmly believe that without Hickson Everton would not have gained promotion. He has embodied in his strong and resolute body and pugnacious temperament more fighting spirit than the rest of the forward line put together.

Three years ago Everton set their face against dabbling in the transfer market. The board reaffirmed its belief that the Britton policy of producing his own stars by coaching and training the younger members of the staff would prove Everton's salvation.

Perhaps that was a gamble, but at least it was bold and ensured that the club would not be placed in an embarrassing position financially.

The first part of that policy has proved successful. Promotion has been granted without the purchase of a single player of note. Some of the younger professionals, such as O'Neill, Donovan and Jones have shown that the home-produced article can be as good as anything available at a reasonable figure in the transfer market.

Given a fair share of fortune, we can count on the promoted Blues to consolidate their position next winter, and as time goes on build further upon the solid foundations laid during the past few years, so that their future will be assured for a lengthy period.

Goodison events that live in the memory

(By Leslie Edwards, Liverpool Echo, March 10, 1955)

Memories of Goodison Park.

*E*VENTS at Goodison Park which come easily to mind are almost invariably those not connected with Association Football.

We are so sated with league and cup matches it is hard to recall one match in particular, yet non-footballing occasions on the famous

Everton ground have been so few that one's recollection of them is almost immediate.

My earliest Everton visit was in 1911, a year which produced the visit of the King and Queen to Liverpool for the inauguration of the Gladstone Dock. I remember thousands of schoolchildren, decked in red, white or blue, who formed a human Union Jack on the pitch that sunny day for the Royal visitors.

My next big memory was the rugby league visit of the Australians to Goodison. They played a team representing Lancashire and Yorkshire – virtually an England RL side – and great was the soccer spectator's wonderment at the way these iron men flung each other about.

Since the Second World War we have reason to remember the soccer visit of the Portuguese national team. That was a fine match.

Television has given the soccer man a new appetite for continental football and we clearly want to see more of it at Goodison Park.

A word in the ear of the slow handclappers!
(By Leslie Edwards, Liverpool Echo, September 5, 1955)

A disappointing home defeat leads to frustration for the fans.

A WORD in the ear of the slow-clapping spectator. In the bitter cold of mid-winter it would serve a useful hand, if not heart-warming purpose; in the sunny serenity of Goodison Park and with your team carrying three young men trying hard to justify themselves (and some older ones equally trying to justify themselves) slow clapping has nothing to commend it. Do the stupid who create this bane of all events sporting think their derision helps to snap a team into renewed endeavour? If they do they have a poor knowledge of psychology. No, slow-clapping can only do harm. How can one expect a player to give his utmost when people treat them so shamefully.

Fans have their means of redress – they can stay away. No one wants them to, but better that than to cheer first-half effort and stay to deride merely because the other team has taken the only goal of the match. None will convince me that Everton's eleven against Luton were not doing their utmost before the epidemic of slow-clapping broke out; none can convince me that men trying to play football to the accompaniment of this disgraceful background of sound will be jerked into higher standards of play.

Given a goal the Everton crowd might have gone away happy. Denied one, many went away with the name of transferred hero Hickson on the lips. Yet in one half – the first – young "Bomber" Harris had done as much as any centre-forward could, short of scoring.

Times change in football. Years ago if players had used the waiting moments before kick-off to indulge themselves in jugglery of the ball people would have thought them affected. Now Luton players were early on the scene and demonstrating, as did the Hungarians at Wembley, in the foot-and-head control of the ball, which is the basis of a footballer's ability.

Everton fans ask, "Has Mr Britton any more at home like the Harrises?" Much depends on the answer.

Everton are not going to spend their £25,000 cheque for Hickson wastefully, if they spend it at all.

They believe that the day when a club could go into the market and buy the player they wanted has gone.

They believe that even if they bought John Charles they would not have bought a player who has what they believe to be "everything" a player must have.

Visiting fans help clear the pitch

(February 18, 1956)

*H*AVING taken five attempts to see off Burnley in the FA Cup, champions Chelsea visited Everton on February 18, 1956.

The 'Pensioners' hardly relished the opportunity to visit Goodison because there had been little opportunity to rest their players. Indeed, their manager Ted Drake was reportedly quoted as stating that

"Everton would not be happy to beat one of the two fine but tired sides which played at Highbury on Monday and at White Hart Lane yesterday, and that there could be little satisfaction for them if they win on Saturday" (Liverpool Echo, 16/2/56).

Everton were lying ninth in the First Division while Chelsea were 13th. One special train carried 600 Chelsea fans although with doubts concerning the state of the pitch (heavy snowfall had been forecast), two fans of the Londoners did their best to make sure the tie went ahead.

The Liverpool Echo reported: 'Among those who volunteered to spray sand on the Everton pitch were Reg Parris of Sutton Dwellings, Chelsea and Charlie Vass of Holborn Place, Chelsea. They travelled from London on the midnight train and arrived at the ground at about 6.30am.

"We were in a cafe later when we heard that the ground would have to be sanded so we offered to give a hand," said Reg as he wheeled a barrow load of sand onto the pitch. We didn't want to come all the way from London after losing a night's sleep and then find the game postponed."

The sand spraying began at 7.30am with the temperature at minus 3C, with the referee Mr. R.H. Mann deeming the pitch playable shortly before noon.

Peter Farrell's 400th appearance
(February 18, 1956)

*T*HANKFULLY for Everton, the Chelsea tie did go ahead. Making his 400th appearance for the Blues, it was fitting that Peter Farrell should net the only goal that put Everton into the last eight of the FA Cup – his first goal since Good Friday two years previous. It seemed luck had been with the home side, as Chelsea saw a late goal disallowed after Leyland, "harassed by two opponents, had thrown it out to the feet of Bentley".

Indeed, it could have been due to a female fan, as the Liverpool

Football Echo reported:

"The first woman to start queuing was Mrs Esther Howard of Harris Drive, Bootle. She arrived at Gwladys Street five hours before the game. In her handbag she carried a crushed rosette, which had been bought at Wembley when Everton last won the Cup in 1933. She said: "I have got it with me today just for luck.""

Another footnote was that it was the last tie that Cliff Britton took charge of.

Britton's departure came about after the Everton board announced they would like to appoint a caretaker manager while he was abroad with the team, although Britton himself stated on his departure: "I want managers to have the freedom to do the job for which they were appointed, which is to manage their clubs."

Following his departure the players were run by a three-man committee until the appointment of former Scottish amateur international Ian Buchan as team coach.

Blues stars complain at £17 a week!

(By Leslie Edwards, Liverpool Echo, July 29, 1957)

A wage row threatened to disrupt Everton's plans ahead of the 1957/58 season. The abolishment of the maximum wage wasn't too far away.

*E*VERTON FC's proposal not to pay top-ranking players the new League maximum of £17 per week during the playing season, but to give them £15 a week with an extra £2 only when they appear in the first team, has caused some dissension in the dressing room. The players concerned asked the board to reconsider the matter and at the directors' next meeting tomorrow the decision is likely to be taken that the men of first-team status will be paid top money whether they are in the first team or not.

The idea of the proposal to pay £15 with the extra £2 contingent on a player being in the first team stemmed from the club's desire to give their players some form of incentive to reach first-team status.

Reports that the 12 players concerned in the protest threatened to ask to be put on the transfer list if their demand for top money were not met is, says an Everton official, not true. The players concerned are goalkeepers Dunlop and O'Neill; backs Tansey and Donovan; half-backs Peter Farrell, Birch, Jones, Rea and forwards Fielding, Gauld, Jimmy Harris and McNamara.

There is little doubt that Everton will reverse their decision and that the players will get their demands. So, with Dave Hickson, newly-signed from Huddersfield, Town reporting today, Everton should be a happy place again when the players attend for training this morning.

Board bow to players demands

(By Leslie Edwards, Liverpool Echo, July 31, 1957)

There was defence for the players who were to be given their extra £2 a week – while there was support for the re-signing of Dave Hickson, perceived by some to have been a backward step by the club.

*I*T did not take last night's Everton board meeting long to change their proposal not to treat the £2 per week increase authorised by the Football League as a general increase. So now all Everton players who were on top money last season will get £17 per week, irrespective of whether they play in the first team or not. Everton describe as grossly exaggerated the report that senior players threatened a mass walk-out unless the increase was paid. There is now no need for players' grouses. The seniors are on £17 per week; any reserve or even 'A' team player who plays for the first team automatically draws £17.

Even on the new rate professional soccer offers a not very lucrative living. The arrival in this city of first-class floodlighting should help players here to supplement their wages, but many who might have become full-time professional footballers are tempted to play part-time with a well paid job in industry on the side, as it were. Some Third

Division players for whom football is not a full-time occupation are drawing more money per week than leading players with star Football League teams.

Though a minority of Everton followers think re-signing Dave Hickson was a retrograde step, everyone seems agreed that the day of his return to Everton colours on August 24 will produce a memorable moment. Everton's opponents on the opening day of the season, at Goodison Park, will be Wolverhampton Wanderers.

It is clear that Everton are going to get back in the first half-dozen matches much of the fee they paid Huddersfield Town for Hickson. The Wolves gate may well be a near-capacity one. In other circumstances one could have hoped for an attendance of 40,000. Hickson has set Everton tongues wagging. He has given Everton followers new hope.

Hickson's second chapter at Goodison Park should be a happier one. He knows that referees are primed to take special note of his play; that players are prepared to 'mix it' on the slightest provocation. Hickson must start a fresh page to his new chapter. He must forget that old propensity for anticipating trouble; that old propensity for talking to referees. Both have produced trouble for him in the past.

Hickson must get on with the game and with delivering to either flank those unselfish passes which characterised his play seasons ago. It might not be a bad thing, either, if players benefitting from these passes remembered where they came from.

What a start for revitalised Blues

(Liverpool Echo, September 12, 1957)

It was the club's best start to the a post-war top-flight season, a 3-2 victory at Arsenal two days before having moved Everton up to third after six games.

*T*HE Everton team which has given the Goodison Park club its best-ever start to any post-war First Division season has not only not cost a penny in transfer fees, but actually shows them a profit, which must be a record in modern football.

True, Dave Hickson involved them in an outlay of around £6,500 when they signed him for the second time – he was without fee on the first occasion – but against that they received £20,000 when he was transferred to Aston Villa two years ago, so that they are in on the double deal to the tune of £13,500.

Everton are, therefore, very much in pocket, financially, so far as their present team is concerned, after allowing for the very moderate sum they paid Bradford City for Graham Williams, who played in the first two games, and the donations they have subsequently handed over to the amateur clubs from whom some of the other players were recruited.

Never before since the last war have Everton taken nine points from their first six games in the First Division, and only once during their three-year spell in the Second Division did they equal this return. That was in 1953/54, when they also had nine in the kitty after six games had been played.

Naturally everybody connected with the club is well pleased at this excellent start, and particularly Mr Ian Buchan, the chief coach. Though not carrying the title of manager, Mr Buchan in certain respects has more responsibility than officials who do carry that label.

He has unfettered scope in choosing the team, has the courage of his convictions and has adopted the wise though not so easy policy of not being swayed by past reputations.

He is doing a first-class job and those who prophesied that sooner or later Everton would have to employ an ex-professional player as manager are beginning to revise their ideas.

Climbing over the walls to get in

(Liverpool Echo, January 30, 1958)

Everton's FA Cup fourth-round tie with Blackburn Rovers was played on a Wednesday night, having been postponed the previous Saturday due to the state of the Goodison pitch.

Rovers, managed by future Everton boss Johnny Carey, were worthy 2-1 winners with a certain Roy Vernon catching the eye of Liverpool Echo reporter Leslie Edwards who noted: 'This young Rhyl boy showed what a great potential he has.' Any chances Everton had were all but extinguished by a first-half injury to Derek Temple, who was forced to hobble through the rest of the game.

The attendance was predicted to have been nearer 80,000 (the official figure given was 75,818, with receipts of £10,575). The crush was such that spectators were allowed to leave the pens and exit via the side of the pitch. Having been allowed to leave they were then allowed to return although as Edwards noted: 'Thousands of people who had been in the ground when the game started were on their way home long before the interval.'

It later transpired that two crush barriers had broken as a result of the crowd's swaying. Extracts from the match report are noted here.

JOHNNY Carey's Blackburn team, including two former Everton players, Leyland and Woods, avenged themselves for cup defeat a year ago at Goodison Park. They won deservedly because in the first half-hour they showed us, and Everton, football of such brilliance one might have supposed one was looking at a Manchester United in one of Carey's vintage seasons.

The attendance was some three thousand fewer than the record one which saw the Everton v Liverpool game in 1948. I do not doubt that many who suffered severe crushing at Goodison Park imagined some 175,000 people were present. I never saw Everton enclosures so tightly packed; so prone to sway like a field of corn. The vast number of terrace spectators must have felt like sardines in some huge tin with a football match taking place on the label.

From time to time hundreds of spectators, many of them boys, were allowed to ease the pressure by coming over the barrier and on to the surround of the pitch. First the police shepherded them down the players' subway to exit doors. Then remote authority ruled that they could come back and see the match to the finish. Not all elected to do this and I was told at the interval that thousands of people who had been in the ground when the game started were on their way home long before the interval.

Doors were shut once enclosures became full, but I heard talk – how true I cannot say – that spectators were seen climbing over the high wall at the Church corner of the ground. There looked to be 80,000 present and rarely have the police and the excellent St John Ambulance been kept busier giving aid.

Fans anger at Goodison crush

(Liverpool Echo, January 30, 1958)

Fans recall the crush in various parts of the ground.

$\mathcal{S}$CORES of people telephoned the Echo today to complain about the packing of the ground which resulted in such great discomfort that thousands of spectators who had queued to get into the ground were queuing to get out again even before the kick-off.

Two crush barriers were broken, and about 100 spectators required treatment from the St John Ambulance men on duty. While there were no serious injuries, all the people treated were suffering from the effects of being crushed in a crowd which swayed violently when the game was most exciting.

Thousands of spectators saw very little of the game. They were too busy looking after their personal safety to gain a vantage point.

Ken Thomas of Wallasey queued for two hours for a place in the paddock but only got to within 20 yards of the turnstiles when they were shut. He queued again and managed to get on the terraces behind the goal.

"It was murder," he said. "I had an apple in my pocket and when I got out of the ground I discovered it had been mashed to a pulp. I've never experienced anything like it. At one stage I put my hand up to attract a mate who was being carried away in the ebb and flow of the crowd. It was so packed I couldn't get my arm down again for 20 minutes."

Other spectators who saw Everton's game with Liverpool on

September 18, 1948, when the ground record of 78,299 was set up, said that they were more comfortable then than they were last night, when 75,818 were present.

Scouting revolution at Goodison

(By Ranger, Liverpool Echo, March 31, 1958)

Innovations in Everton's player recruitment drive attracted attention – and not one mention of an agent sending a dodgy YouTube compilation of their star's best moments.

*E*VERTON FC have decided to completely reorganise their scouting system in readiness for next season, and are doing it in a comprehensive fashion that will make them one of the best equipped clubs in the country in this direction.

They are to appoint not only a full-time chief scout, but also five full-time area scouts who will cover the whole of the British Isles. Hitherto the club has relied for its player scouting activities on part-time officials, plus certain stipendiary officials, who have had to dovetail scouting with their other duties, and the efforts of directors.

The new scheme is devised to put the scouting system on a firmer and more business-like basis. It will be a fairly expensive scheme, for the chief scout's salary will be substantial and that of the area scouts will be very good. But the club believes that if the idea produces one or two really star players per season it will pay for itself in the long run.It will be the first occasion Everton have had full-time scouting officials.

Warney throws his hat in

(Liverpool Echo, April 3, 1958)

A 1920s/1930s Blues legend puts his hat in the ring for a job at Goodison.

*T*HE Everton decision to appoint a chief scout is an important one. I know of one famous old Everton player – Warney Cresswell – who wants his name to go down among the possibles. He is a hotelier in Sunderland, but still hankers after living and working on Merseyside.

Hickson doesn't need Dutch courage

(By Ian Hargraves, Liverpool Echo, April 17, 1958)

Played amidst a run of five successive defeats (they would make it six, against Manchester City, on the following Saturday), Everton hosted Dutch opposition in a late-season friendly. It appears that even in a non-competitive match, Dave Hickson only knew how to play one way.

*A*FTER a depressing stream of defeats Everton must have been delighted to score six goals against even such a relatively undistinguished side as Fortuna at Goodison Park last night. For once they met opponents whose finishing was as inadequate as their own, and since right winger Jimmy Harris seized the opportunity presented by slack defensive marking to score five times they finished victors by a rather flattering margin.

Dave Hickson, the other goalscorer, with Everton's first goal after eight minutes, seems unable to avoid physical clashes even in a friendly game, but otherwise did fairly well!

Blues turn up the heat

(Liverpool Echo, May 8, 1958)

The club were pioneers of undersoil heating, installed in the close season ahead of the 1958/59 season. It was arguably the beginning of the club's change towards investing on and off the pitch.

*S*OCCER history is being laid below the surface of Everton Football Club's ground. For Goodison Park is probably the first sports field in the world – certainly the first in Britain – to be provided with a built-in heating system under the turf.

The whole job, including the complete re-laying and re-seeding of the pitch, is costing Everton something like £13,000, of which the total cost of the electrical turf warming installation is about £7,000.

Woeful start and questions asked

(By Horace Yates, Liverpool Echo, September 8, 1958)

A woeful start to the campaign – a 6-1 home defeat to Arsenal being their fifth in a row – meant solutions were being sort amidst criticism of the team's preparation.

*M*R RE Searle, chairman of Everton FC, who have failed to gain a single point from their first five matches, declared last night that he was dissatisfied with the training of the team.

"Our players are three yards slower than the opponents we have met," said Mr Searle.

The club's chief coach, Mr Ian Buchan, when asked about the statement, confirmed that the position would be discussed and added: "I have no comment to make on the chairman's statement."

Everton, the only club in the four English leagues without a point to their name, have conceded 17 goals and scored only three in reply.

Many supporters will argue that Everton's failings go deeper than a difference of opinion about the effectiveness of the training, for they consider that only the infusion of new blood, the importation of really first-class players in key positions, will be an effective remedy against the slide in club fortunes.

Fans were aghast to learn that a player of the experience and strength of Tommy Docherty, who was at Goodison as a member of the Arsenal team which whipped Everton 6-1 on Saturday, was allowed to go to London when he was so badly needed by the Goodison club because, according to report, Everton were unwilling to find the extra thousands pounds or two which Preston demanded.

This is one of the worst moments in Everton history for them to stand on ceremony and to miss their goal because of a so-called principle.

We have everything but a winning team

(Liverpool Echo, September 8, 1958)

*M*OST followers of the club, it seems, are more dissatisfied with the competence of the board to tackle the enormous task of rescuing the club from the position into which it has drifted. Everton have the finest ground in the North; a lovely pitch; magnificent floodlighting; money to spend; a soil-warming system which means that they can play in frost when others can't, but they haven't a team, and that, for such as the loyal 40,000 who saw them beaten 6-1 by Arsenal, is unforgivable.

After the Britton era, when Everton were said to be all-out to make Goodison the Arsenal of the North (doubly ironic in view of Saturday's opposition) it was said that the board would never again make a managerial appointment. If they are strong they will think again. In the most successful clubs directors direct and managers manage.

The club may pin blame for defeat on Ian Buchan, but surely the blame is not wholly his. Everton fans will ask: "Who was responsible for letting so many good players go elsewhere when their careers were far from finished?" The need of such players at Goodison Park – many of them very experienced – was never greater; yet these men are absent; most of them are highly successful with new clubs.

The names of Walter Gailbraith, one-time New Brighton player and Accrington Stanley manager, and Arthur Turner, who resigned recently from joint-managership of Birmingham City, are linked. But first the board have to decide whether a manager is necessary.

Six losses and trainer loses his job

(By Leslie Edwards, Liverpool Echo, September 10, 1958)

In the wake of a 3-1 defeat at Burnley, the club's sixth successive loss – news also included note of Stan Bentham being promoted to reserve-team trainer.

*T*HE mystery of the non-appearance last night at Burnley of the

Everton first-team trainer, Mr Harry Wright, was solved today by a statement issued at midday by the club. It ran: "Mr H. Wright has been relieved of his duties as first-team trainer and Mr T. G. Watson has been appointed first-team trainer in his place. Mr Wright remains a member of the training staff of the club.

The news will surprise all Everton fans, since Mr Wright, once a first-class goalkeeper with Charlton and Derby County and later the head coach at Luton, is so well qualified in every way to do his job.

At Everton, a club he joined in September 1956, at the time Everton appointed Mr Ian Buchan as chief coach, Mr Wright has been instrumental in implementing the training schedules of his chief.

As recently as last season, Everton had a run of success in which they were acclaimed as one of the fittest, if not the fittest, team in the First Division.

A point about certain Everton players which has escaped notice is that not a few of them are in the Forces and they therefore come little under the training system by Everton for their playing staff.

The club has preserved a complete silence on the possibility of their appointing someone with full authority to manage the team.

Bring on pocket dynamo Bobby Collins

(By Horace Yates, Liverpool Echo, September 13, 1958)

Changes were needed – and it was hoped the signing of Bobby Collins would be the catalyst. Everton duly won 3-1 at Manchester City later that day, with Collins on target.

 *E*VERTON have taken the plunge and their record £24,000 splash has not only brought Scottish international inside-forward Bobby Collins to Goodison, but has created a heart-warming enthusiasm among supporters whose spirits were at their lowest ebb.

By this one stroke Everton have set the crowd hoping afresh and because the former Celtic star will be at inside-right in the team to play Manchester City today, there will be very many more Everton fans among the Maine Road crowd than would otherwise have been the case.

Collins is a ball player of the highest class, a clever strategist right in the Alex Stevenson and Jimmy Dunn tradition.

If his usefulness measures up to either of these diminutive "giants" of the past, the signing might well prove to be the turning in the lane, which was beginning to look so depressingly straight.

It is no secret that Everton have admired this player, 27 years old and 5ft 3ins tall, for many years for in 1949 he was within an ace of signing while still a junior player with Pollock, but chose Celtic instead.

Buchan out, Carey in

(By Horace Yates, Liverpool Echo, September 23, 1958)

Ian Buchan was relieved of his duties despite a 3-2 victory over Leeds United the previous Saturday. Everton knew who they wanted as his replacement.

$\mathcal{E}$VERTON Football Club yesterday took the first step towards appointing a manager to help them out of their mounting difficulties when they offered the post to Mr John Carey, the present manager of Blackburn Rovers.

Everton's determination to spare no expense is shown by the fact that since the end of last season Everton have bought Collins, Parker, Harburn and O'Hara, installed a floodlighting scheme at a cost of about £45,000, had their ground electrically heated as a safeguard against frost and turned Goodison Park into the finest stadium in the country.

It is a conservative estimate that over £120,000 has been expended and though there may be now a temporary shortage of ready cash, Everton's assets are tremendous, so Mr Carey can be assured of strong financial backing.

When the taxi brought Johnny in!

(By Horace Yates, Liverpool Echo, September 24, 1958)

It was thought Carey would sign a five-year deal having accepted Everton's offer, believing his prospects to be greater than at Blackburn, who had agreed to offer Everton's terms. He was expected to take charge on October 20.

$\mathcal{M}$R John Carey, manager of Blackburn Rovers FC, last night accepted an invitation to become manager of Everton FC.

The Blackburn board of directors, who had been kept informed of developments since the first Everton approach, were expecting the announcement although it was news they would very much have preferred not to have heard. His resignation was accepted and they wished Mr Carey good fortune.

Although not under contract to Blackburn, Mr Carey will stay on at Ewood for about a month before moving to take over at Goodison.

75,000 for a night match!

(By Leslie Edwards, Liverpool Echo, January 29, 1959)

The previous weekend Everton had earned an FA Cup fourth-round replay with Charlton after the Blues had hit back from 2-0 down with 15 minutes left at The Valley to earn a replay – the equaliser even prompting a mini pitch invasion from some joyous travelling fans.

Dubbed as "the most fantastic game never seen" due to fog, the Goodison tie saw the Blues leading 1-0. Dave Hickson was the scorer and many in the 75,000-crowd left near the end of the game thinking this was to be the final scoreline.

Only one of the five goals was scored at the Gwladys Street End where fans were unaware of the other goalscorers due to the conditions. Visibility was passable at ground level although even Liverpool Echo & Evening Express reporter Michael Charters confessed to a lack of visibility.

He stated: 'The odd thing is that when people come to recall it they will never be able to say they saw it, but merely that they saw a little of it and heard the rest. And I don't mind confessing that too.'

He added: 'Later the linesmen took to running two yards inside the pitch confines and that the 90 minutes could be completed, much less an additional 30 minutes, was little short of a miracle.'

*S*HOULD 75,000 spectators be allowed to pack the Everton ground at Goodison Park for a night match?

This is the question everyone is asking after the fantastic fourth-round cup replay last night in which Everton beat Charlton Athletic 4-1 after extra-time. Never have I seen more ominous swaying on the huge terracing immediately below the main stand.

Never have police and ambulance men had such difficulty in tugging – yes, literally tugging – to the touchlines unfortunates overcome or injured by the crush of bodies.

This despite Everton's close-season introduction of many more crush barriers placed at right angles to those which already existed.

Why did 75,000 spectators create so much difficulty for authority and for themselves? The answer is force of circumstances.

Because of the mist which nearly obliterated all sight of the match, the gates were not opened until an hour and a quarter before kick-off at 7pm, many must have gone to this pay-at-the-turnstiles game convinced that the fog would have cut the attendance by 10,000. Instead, the whole of the football-following public of Liverpool tried to get into the ground.

The rush of people in the hour before the kick-off was so great that police had the utmost difficulty in controlling queues to the turnstiles.

An Everton official said: "These fans were fighting mad to see the match, and I fear some of them got a little out of hand.

"Also, the fact that so little could be seen from the rear terraces, owing to mist, meant that everyone was determined to get as near the pitch as possible."

Everton's dramatic 4-1 win, seen by so few, heard by so many, sent everyone home in good humour, though some of the spectators at the Gwladys Street end did not even know the final score!

Supreme pride in loyal fans

(By Horace Yates, Liverpool Echo, May 8, 1959)

Crowds were at their collective peak on Merseyside.

*I*F Everton and Liverpool have nothing else to boast about in a season which has produced little real achievement and plenty of disappointments, they can certainly point with pride to the loyalty of their tremendous following.

Season 1958/59 saw 820,958 spectators pass through their turnstiles to see their league games, which gives an average of 39,093, compared with the previous season's return of 821,875 and an average of 39,136, and there is a story of consistent and solid support that will be the envy of clubs all over the country. In addition, their four cup matches produced a gross total of 234,264 and an average of 59,566. If we deduct 44,094, which was the gate at Charlton in round four, we find that a grand total of 1,015,128 spectators saw the cup and league games at Goodison Park this season, which is a terrific and encouraging number by any standards.

If we add the figures for the two clubs it will be seen that no fewer than 1,774,251 saw cup and league football at Goodison and Anfield.

No wonder it is said so often and so widely that a city like Liverpool should never be without two First Division clubs. Certainly the support warrants it.

In addition to the figures we might add a further 97,783, who saw the three cup (Floodlight and Lancashire Senior) meetings between the two clubs, and the grand total then soars to the magical figure of 1,872,034. For good measure there could be added another 31,780, who saw the friendly games with Newcastle at Anfield and the South Africans at Goodison.

I should say that reflection on these returns is the greatest possible urge to the clubs to see that nothing but the best is good enough for the Liverpool sporting public.

Goodison a goldmine - to other clubs!

(By Michael Charters, Liverpool Echo, May 27, 1959)

Losses were reported – while there is an example of how other teams could benefit from a share of gate receipts when they visit popular clubs.

*E*VERTON'S balance sheet reveals that the club lost £16,712 last season, compared with a profit of £35,122 the previous year. Transfer fees make the most striking comparison between the two years, for the club paid out £35,350 last season and nothing at all in the preceding 12 months. Similarly, scouting expenses last season amounted to £5,954 as against nothing the year before. The payment of transfer fees is the net figure on both comings and goings. The club signed Collins, Parker, O'Hara, Harburn and Laverick but were able to set against that cost the fees for the sale of Williams, Harburn, Kirby and Fielding.

Visiting teams were paid £20,998, compared with £22,332, but Everton received only £10,700 from their share of away gates. Goodison Park is indeed a goldmine to other league clubs.

Everton remain pitch pioneers

(By Michael Charters, Liverpool Echo, January 20, 1960)

Under-soil heating required tweaking.

*I*N the summer of 1958, Everton spent some £16,000 in ripping up the Goodison Park pitch to install under-soil heating wires and the consequent re-laying of the turf. Although many clubs have been interested in the results, not one has followed Everton's pioneering lead.

There are two reasons for this, I believe. First, the cost of the operation; secondly, and more important, Everton have had serious trouble with the pitch ever since the electrical system has been installed and until now drainage has become a major headache.

Now, however, a new beat-the-snow plan has been found for £7,000 – less than half the Everton cost – with little disturbance to the ground.

Vernon signs at the second time of asking

(By Leslie Edwards, Liverpool Echo, February 11, 1960)

The Echo newspaper picture caption showed Roy Vernon sitting with his wife in Johnny Carey's office. The Everton manager and Vernon's wife were standing over Vernon, Carey with pipe in mouth. Vernon made his debut – with Ring and Collins also in the side – at home to Wolves on the Saturday. The biggest crowd of the season, 51,135, witnessed a 2-0 home defeat to a side who would finish as league runners-up, an increase of nearly 20,000 on the previous home attendance. Vernon would score his first Everton goal the following week in a 2-1 defeat at Arsenal, going on to score doubles in the next two games – a 4-0 home victory over Preston and a 2-2 draw at West Ham. Gates at Goodison until the end of the season were 50,000 plus with a high of 65,719 attending a 4-0 Good Friday victory over Blackpool. This trend only ended for the final home game of the season, 37,885 attending a 1-0 win over Leeds.

$\mathcal{T}$HIS was the scene a month ago in Everton manager John Carey's office when Roy Vernon came to Goodison Park with his wife, inspected club houses and the ground, and then refused to move from Blackburn Rovers. Mr Carey took "no" for an answer then, but never gave up hope that Vernon would change his mind. It proved so yesterday when the deal went through, with Eddie Thomas moving to Ewood Park in part exchange, at a secret signing spot midway between Liverpool and Blackburn.

The incoming of Tommy Ring and Roy Vernon is not the end of the story. On the contrary. But none will expect the club to strengthen their playing hand further until another Mr Right comes along.

Mr Carey's quiet persistence has impressed Everton supporters as it has done me.

He's persistence personified and the soul of discretion but that does not mean that his intentions are leak-proof!

Vernon's appearance at Goodison Park on Saturday means that the attendance will be jacked up to 60,000 and more. The further appearance of Ring would have ensured a 40,000 gate. Thus Vernon will have helped to pay off a thousand or two of the money Everton have spent on him. And the fact that Ring, Collins and Vernon are now up front in the Everton eleven means that big attendances will patronise them home and away.

There never was a city like ours for reacting quickly and enthusiastically to the attraction of new faces and more important, new feet.

Club reveal how big deals faltered

(Liverpool Daily Post, June 24, 1960)

Everton admitted they had been chasing two of the stars of the game during the club AGM.

*H*OW Everton Football Club's willingness to pay almost unlimited sums to lure such players as Joe Baker and Denis Law to Goodison had broken down was revealed to shareholders at the club's annual meeting last night by Mr Fred Micklesfield (chairman).

Shareholders also heard from Mr John Moores – to whom they gave an enthusiastic reception – some of his hopes for the future as a recently co-opted member of the board.

It was stated during the meeting that Mr Moores had loaned the club £56,000 free of interest to enable star players to be secured.

Describing the negotiations in Scotland in an effort to secure England international centre-forward Joe Baker, of Hibernian, Mr Micklesfield said the board had given unlimited power to the negotiators to get their man.

"We went to Edinburgh with virtually a blank cheque," he said. "We made offers many thousands of pounds above sums previously paid for a player in Scotland.

"I filled in the sum of £45,000 on the cheque, but their chairman told us that even if we could have added another £5,000 they still wanted to keep their player."

Everton met a similar reply in their quest for Denis Law, of Huddersfield. Again the negotiators had gone prepared to pay a very high figure, but because Huddersfield thought that they had a chance of promotion they wanted to keep Law.

"Some may think that having decided on a man, all that is necessary is to go in with a substantial cheque," said Mr Micklesfield. "We found that that was not the case."

Mr Moores also spoke. He admitted to being a "tyro" in football directorship but he had been very disappointed at the poor teams Everton had had for the past 20 years. "I encouraged the directors to spend heavily," he said. "We still need more players and we will have the money to buy the right ones.

"But it is no use people telling us to go out and buy world-class players like Real Madrid can do. The League rules will not allow it. If I had offered Puskas a £15,000 signing-on fee when he left Hungary, and made him a director of Littlewoods at £10,000 a year, I still could not have signed him for Everton because the Home Office would not have admitted him into the country as an alien, the Players' Union would have objected and the League would have vetoed it too. We must live within the rules and I am sure the shareholders would not want the Everton directors to do otherwise."

The era of 'Millionaires' beckons

(By Leslie Edwards, Liverpool Echo, July 6, 1960)

A new era at Everton, as John Moores rallies the squad ahead of the 1960/61 season.

*M*ULTI-MILLIONAIRE former Pools chief, Mr John Moores, the new Everton chairman, met the club's players when they reported for training at Goodison Park this morning. In a speech which must have left the players in no doubt about his enthusiasm for the cause, he said: "The main thing here is that we all want the same thing – a winning team and with that go bonuses, medals and international honours for you.

"I want Everton where they should be and I shall do everything I can to put them there. I ask you to help me. If we all do our best we should succeed. I am new to football, but I have long experience in business. I want you to put your backs into it and I will give you all the help I can. Do your best to make a successful 'do' of it."

Mr Moores is anxious to implement his wish that one director or other should attend each training session and he plans to visit Bellefield himself tomorrow. He wants players to feel that directors are taking a personal interest in them. No big signings are anticipated for the time being, but the Moores' enthusiasm for a winning team is such that decisive moves will be made, and quickly, if they are necessary.

Fans clock a new opportunity

(Liverpool Echo, July 25, 1960)

Littlewoods were quick to make an impact at Goodison – with a big clock.

$\mathcal{E}$VERTON FC, whose policy for so many years has been broadly against displaying advertisements at Goodison Park, plan to start the new season by installing a huge clock, like the one at the Arsenal ground. The clock will, I understand, form part of an advertisement for a pools firm (Littlewoods). The income received each week from such a concession is considerable.

The club clearly believe that the new clock will be an eye-catcher rather than an eyesore, and that it will supplement the normal size clocks whose faces have been a feature of the two main stands for as long as I can remember. The only advertisement Everton has countenanced in the past was the billboard carried round the ground before a match and during the interval detailing forthcoming Stadium boxing programmes.

New League Cup and it's Accrington Stanley

(By Leslie Edwards, Liverpool Echo, August 3, 1960)

A new cup competition makes its debut.

*E*VERTON are drawn at home to Accrington Stanley in the first round of the new Football League Cup competition, the draw for which was made in Manchester. Never in Everton's long history have these two clubs been paired together in the FA Cup. The remaining 41 clubs were given byes.

At last, Everton's Golden Vision pays off

(By Horace Yates, Liverpool Echo, November 24, 1960)

George Thomson's signing was overshadowed somewhat by the arrival of the Golden Vision.

*T*HE great chase is over. After weeks of patient endeavour Everton last night signed Scottish international centre-forward Alex Young and his team-mate from Hearts (the Scottish First Division club), left-back George Thomson for a fee of £55,000 to complete the biggest deal in the Goodison club's history.

They were taken to the home of Scottish international Bobby Collins, where they had a meal and then accompanied Bobby and his wife to last night's League Cup match against Bury.

The signing of the two Scots brings Everton's outlay on signings in the last two years, beginning with the combined O'Hara-Parker deal, to more than £220,000.

This makes Everton, who now have a total of six Scots available for their team, the costliest side in current British football.

Everton have had a centre-forward problem ever since Hickson was transferred to Liverpool.

Though Jimmy Harris has filled the gap since then it was obvious that if Everton were to achieve the greatness which has been mapped out for them in boardroom planning, a centre-forward of the highest quality was essential.

They have looked in many directions for a solution and included in their efforts have been offers to Hibernian for Joe Baker and to Middlesbrough for Brian Clough.

Police action thwarts Goodison disaster

(Liverpool Daily Post, December 28, 1960)

It seemed safety concerns remained at Goodison despite the warnings of recent years. Hundreds were turned away before kick-off in this home game against Burnley and the St John Ambulancemen on duty had a busy afternoon.

PROMPT action by policemen saved hundreds of people from injury yesterday as parts of the huge 75,667 crowd at Goodison Park for the Everton v Burnley match swayed and lurched.

The police went into the crowd and helped to shepherd and even carry boys from the crushing crowd over the concrete wall surrounding the pitch to the safety of the running track. Many people fainted and were treated by St John Ambulancemen.

Hundreds of Everton football fans were turned away from the ground when the gates were closed a few minutes before the kick-off.

Inside spectators were crushed against the barriers and terrace wall, and young boys – who had fainted or were in danger of being trampled upon, were passed over the heads of the crowd to St John Ambulancemen.

Spectators described the crowded conditions as the worst they had ever experienced, although there have been bigger attendances at the ground.

One spectator, who was in the 2s 6d ground part, described his ordeal as "sheer murder".

"Everything was alright until about 3pm when crowds started to surge in from the Gwladys Street end. Women, children and men were crushed against the barriers.

I was trapped against the end of a barrier and it was only by using force that I managed to free myself.

After that it was just a case of swaying and lurching with the crowd. It was impossible to do anything else," he said.

Taxi for the manager

(By Jack Rowe, Liverpool Echo, April 15, 1961)

John Moores had seen enough. Johnny Carey was invited to take a taxi.

MR John Carey is no longer manager of Everton. The club, through secretary Mr Bill Dickinson, announced the news early yesterday evening in a terse 18-word statement: "Everton announce tonight that with effect from tomorrow Mr Carey's engagement as manager with the club is terminated."

The statement came while Mr Carey and Everton's millionaire chairman Mr John Moores were in London for yesterday's Football League meeting, leading to what would become a legendary taxi ride.

Those at that meeting were last night surprised by the news that Mr Carey had finished at Everton – for he and his chairman were present for the League talk together, and less than an hour before the announcement came from Goodison Park they came out of London's Cafe Royal and walked away talking side by side.

Carey decision described as bombshell

(By Horace Yates, Liverpool Echo, April 15, 1961)

Harry Catterick was on the radar of the club board – having quit as Sheffield Wednesday boss five days previously. Carey would take over Leyton Orient that

THE YEAR OF THE CAT 151

summer. Soon after this story was published the case was left in the hands of solicitors – and settled out of court the following February. Carey would lead Orient to runners-up spot behind Liverpool to gain promotion to the top flight following a successful 1961/62.

*E*VERTON'S decision to terminate the contract of their manager Mr John Carey with effect from today can only be described as a bombshell. He knew like everyone else that he was living on the edge of a volcano with a club, which more than ever in recent months with the advent of the dynamic Mr John Moores as chairman, had only one goal – success.

There is no statement from the club regarding a likely successor but I cannot think that such a drastic step has been taken without ensuring that the man they want to take over is both ready, and available.

That man I forecast, is undoubtedly Mr Harry Catterick who this week resigned his position as team manager of Sheffield Wednesday.

Mr Catterick is an old Everton player, and if he is appointed it will mean that Everton have gone back on yet another vowed intention never to have one of their former players in charge of club affairs. This was the position after Mr Cliff Britton left Goodison Park some years ago.

Mr Carey had the bombshell broken to him from the lips of his chairman in London yesterday, where both had been to attend a Football League meeting.

Only this week, when I was investigating rumours that a move of this nature could be a possibility, he expressed to me complete surprise that such reports should be possible.

"It is news to me," he said. "If there is anything in it then somebody obviously knows much more than I do. Not by any word or deed from any member of the board have I been given the slightest clue that there is any dissatisfaction or disappointment with my work."

His charming manner produced results without the bludgeon blow. With Mr Carey it has always been a case of the velvet glove concealing the fist. He invariably got his way with men, no matter how difficult the problem. One of the players once confided to me that when one had been in for an interview with 'the boss', it was not until after he had come out that he realised he had been ticked off.

The Cat takes centre stage

(By Horace Yates, Liverpool Echo, April 17, 1961)

*W*HEN Mr Harry Catterick takes his seat at Goodison Park tonight to watch the Liverpool Senior Cup semi-final between Everton and Tranmere Rovers, it will be as manager of Everton. Yesterday club secretary Mr Bill Dickinson issued the following statement: "The Everton directors have today been in touch with Mr Harry Catterick, and it is expected he will be appointed manager. Mr Catterick is coming to Liverpool and will attend tomorrow's meeting of the directors."

Mr Catterick has already made it known that he would like to manage Everton – for whom he once played at centre-forward – so the appointment is unlikely to be delayed. He will have been unemployed for exactly one week. It was only last Monday that he resigned his position as team manager of Sheffield Wednesday.

Strangely, he will soon be retracing his steps, for on Saturday Everton play Sheffield Wednesday. To carry coincidence further, Mr Catterick's final First Division appearance for Everton was also against Wednesday.

Harry suggests a bright future

(By Horace Yates, Liverpool Echo, May 9, 1961)

Wages were on the rise at Goodison.

*N*EARLY half of Everton's professional playing strength have accepted terms for next season and re-signed.

Manager Harry Catterick said: "No one has refused terms, and we appreciate that the players like to think over these things. The majority of the first team will be earning £2,000 or more on the offers we have made to them."

Players suggest wages not high enough

(By Michael Charters, Liverpool Echo, May 9, 1961)

But was this positive spin linked to the following article that appeared elsewhere in the newspaper? It was written ahead of that night's Liverpool Senior Cup final between Everton and Liverpool at Goodison Park.

$\mathcal{O}$NLY about 50 per cent of the players are happy with their wage offer of £35 top money, plus the incentive bonus of £1extra for every thousand over 40,000 at the gate.

It was obvious, of course, that there were bound to be difficulties over re-signing. When Stanley Matthews, at 47 years of age, anticipates £100 a week from Blackpool, Everton's stars are displeased with £35 by comparison, for their club has the highest ambitions for honours next season and it is people like Young, Vernon, Collins, Parker and Co. who will be needed to win them.

The players feel they would rather have an increased flat rate rather than the pound-per-thousand bonus. On the figures of the season which has just ended, a regular first-teamer would have drawn an additional £300 bonus. The players prefer a figure in that region to be added to their salary.

Blues head across the Atlantic

(By Leslie Edwards, Liverpool Echo, May 17, 1961)

The first-team squad faced a gruelling post-season tour on the other side of the Atlantic.

$\mathcal{W}$HEN a chartered 120-seater plane touched down at Montreal from Prestwick yesterday the pilot must have felt deeply relieved.

On board was football talent including the Everton team, insured for more than £1,000,000. And that is exclusive of the insurance of multi-millionaire chairman John Moores, who was also aboard.

Everton, Shamrock Rovers, Kilmarnock and the Bangu team who appeared at Goodison Park last season all had parties on the plane. The Everton team were insured, I understand, for between £300,000 and £350,000. Alex Young, the club's Scottish international centre-forward who has been touring with the Army team and Scotland's on the Continent, is due to arrive back in Britain on Friday and will fly next day to join his team-mates in Montreal.

The question of his getting further leave to play for his club was a vexed one and Everton had to appeal indirectly to Mr John Profumo, Secretary of State for War, in order to get Young's release.

Blues threatened with suspension

(Liverpool Echo, May 22, 1961)

However, Everton were facing the prospect of a potential suspension ahead of their participation in the American International Soccer League.

$\mathcal{E}$VERTON and Kilmarnock will become liable to suspension if they take part in the American International League, Sir Stanley Rous (secretary of the FA and an executive of FIFA) said in Lisbon. The competition began last week, but Everton have still to play.

Sir Stanley said that FIFA were determined to keep a strict control on all world soccer tournaments and competitions. Their sanction was needed before these could be held.

The Americans had been asked to forward their rules and regulations for FIFA inspection. Until these had been approved the tournament was unauthorised, and UK teams taking part would become liable to suspension. Officials of the North American International Soccer League said later they were mystified by Sir Stanley's statement.

"We have heard nothing from FIFA and I am completely mystified," said Derek Liecty, an official. The league was launched last year, when Burnley represented the Football League – without objections.

Cable exchange solves power game
(Liverpool Daily Post, May 23, 1961)

Cables were apparently exchanged between Sir Stanley Rous and Football League secretary Alan Hardaker related to Everton's participation.

$\int$IR Stanley Rous is understood to have replied that Everton could take part in the competition provided the United States Football Association took full responsibility for the tournament and got the necessary sanction from FIFA to run it.

Army Game for goalscorer Young
(Liverpool Daily Post, May 24, 1961)

Everton's first game in the American International Soccer League ended in only a one-goal victory over Montreal Concordia.

CENTRE-FORWARD Young, who is on leave from the Army, scored Everton's goal after 27 minutes of the second half with a low shot that slid under Concordia goalkeeper Tony Macedo. The crowd was estimated at 8,000.

Vernon 'kicked by rival coach'
(By Leslie Edwards, Liverpool Echo, May 24, 1961)

Our man at the Echo ensured we were to learn of what really happened in Everton's first match.

$\mathcal{F}$ROM a sleepy-headed Harry Catterick awakened by my transatlantic call at 12.45pm (our time) I heard at first hand the grim facts of the battle of Montreal last night.

"Rough? They're all rough over here, but this was the toughest roughest game I ever saw. There were so many incidents going on it was impossible to keep pace with them all.

"At one stage the Concordia coach even ran on to the field and kicked Roy Vernon! There were times when skirmishes were going on everywhere on the pitch. I saw more fists fly and more blows struck last night in Montreal than I've ever seen at our stadium.

"They told us afterwards that they felt we played roughly. All I can say is that I know they did! There isn't one of our players who doesn't carry a scar or a bruise and we play Kilmarnock tomorrow – our second match within 48 hours and we've been 10 days in Canada without a match.

"The Bingham sending off happened after only 15 minutes. We had to play with a man short from that stage. No wonder the few Everton supporters who had come from the ships were delighted when we walked off as the winners.

"The referee actually gave us a free-kick after sending Bingham from the field. He had been kicked from behind and then was butted as he rose to his feet. Then he was struck and the referee caught him retaliating.

"The Concordia player sent off, Lopez, struck Jimmy Fell twice. He'd already hit Young twice with his fist. Players were being punched all over the place.

"The 6,000 fans – a good gate by their standards – didn't like to see their team losing. The Concordia eleven hardly have a Canadian. They are a mixture of South Americans, with Macedo of Fulham their goalkeeper.

"There was no doubt that the referee, who was a Canadian, lost control completely of the match, but we don't expect there to be British standards over here. They do things their own way and I'm told that other team's experiences have been similar to ours."

Collins sees off the Scots

(May 26, 1961)

*E*VERTON duly defeated Kilmarnock 2-1, two goals in seven first-half minutes from Bobby Collins ensuring victory.

Everton squad quit team hotel

(May 29, 1961)

*T*HE troubled tour raised further issues when the Everton squad surprisingly quit their hotel, used as headquarters by the International Soccer League in New York. Director Fred Micklesfield refused to discuss the matter.

Vernon sent home and offers his view

(By Roy Vernon, Liverpool Echo, June 2, 1961)

Although refusing to comment on why he was sent home from the tournament, Roy Vernon offered these views.

*E*NGLISH clubs should think very seriously before agreeing to undertake this tour.

Possibly because we are so accustomed at Everton to arrangements being made to perfection, the planning of this tour left a great deal to be desired. After our first game we faced a nine-hour journey from Montreal to New York by train and then when the time came to go training on one of the baseball pitches in Central Park we found ourselves having to travel by tube.

Subsequently we employed taxis for the job and the two-mile trip seemed much less irksome, but we had to use tracksuits for goalposts in our practice games.

The Americans have a lot to learn before they can hope to compare with English standards in organisation.

To see Billy Bingham ordered off the field against Concordia after being butted in the face twice was something I would never have thought possible.

Then in a general melee I was kicked on the leg by a coach. These trips certainly do broaden one's experience, but I cannot say memories of this tour will be among my happiest.

The Moores factor pays off handsomely

(By Michael Charters, Liverpool Echo, June 5, 1961)

Back at home, Everton were back in black.

*W*HEN Mr John Moores became an Everton director more than a year ago, and became chairman the day after the club's annual general meeting, he said he would not be satisfied unless the team reached the first 10 in the league and also made a profit on the season.

He has achieved both ambitions – the team finished fifth in the First Division and today it is revealed that a loss of £49,504 last year has been turned into a profit of £25,054 on the year ending May 6.

Chief reason for this sensational turnaround has been on transfer fees. For season 1959/60, expenditure reached £84,160; last season it was £53,300. Mr Moores, with his economy measures other than the purchase of new players, brought total expenditure down from £214,121 to £190,495 over the two years.

Players' wages took £28,195 compared with £31,358; travelling and match expenses dropped from £11,240 to £9,457; scouting expenses down from £3,751 to £2,504; ground expenses from £17,216 to £13,593.

The bill for rates and water fell from £9,515 to £4,022.

On the credit side, everything increased. Gross gate receipts from league games grew from £113,442 to £135,867, receipts from cup-ties and other games from £14,535 to £34,472, percentage from league clubs from £9,787 to £14,432, and the sale of season tickets brought £22,934, compared with £16,894.

That ill-fated venture, the electric soil-warming apparatus, comes to an end with this financial summing-up. It cost £8,200; sales of material, after the wires were removed, brought £100, and the remainder, £8,100, has been written off.

More inside information on the ill-fated tour
(By T.E. Jones, Liverpool Echo, June 5, 1961)

The Echo's Everton player contact reveals more about tour life, in New York.

I SPENT an afternoon in New York's Central Park on our last tour here five years ago, little dreaming that I should visit the park again this time for the business of training to be really fit for the games. Dressing rooms are situated in the centre of Central Park with lockers, rented at 25 cents a time with the use of hot showers thrown in. The set-up was good. We trained on the ball parks which are dotted around the area. We had a hard session and finished in a lather of sweat.

We had a tour of the United Nations buildings and the décor had to be seen to be appreciated. The high cost of living is really something. A few of us took in a cinema show and it cost 2 dollars 50, almost 18s for a cinema seat. We have been given complimentary tickets for two shows, a visit to the CBS TV studio and for a tour of Radio City where they have a large TV and radio network. We have a standing invitation to the Naval Officers' Club anytime we wish to drop in.

A second dismissal for Bingham
(June 12, 1961)

The tour rolls on – and a first defeat for the weary travellers as Billy Bingham shows more ill-discipline.

E VERTON went down 2-0 to Brazilian side Bangu at New York's Polo Grounds, their first defeat of the competition. Bangu left-back

Darcy Defaria was carried off with a suspected broken ankle at the start of the second half, before Billy Bingham was sent off by English referee Peter Rhodes for the second time on the tour 'following an incident with Bato. Ademir Da Guia and Jose Correa were the scorers in the first half, in front of a crowd of 10,721.

Reports of Bingham's sending off stated: "Bingham claimed that Bato had tugged at his jersey. After Bingham was sent off the referee called an interpreter to explain to Bato that pulling an opponent's jersey was not allowed.

Besiktas win lifts team spirits

(June 14, 1961)

*E*VERTON beat Besiktas 4-0 in the American International Soccer League in New York. Wignall, Young and Collins (2) were on target.

Everton's side: Dunlop, Parker, Thomson, Gabriel, Labone, Harris, Bingham, Young, Wignall, Collins, Lill.

7-0 as Blues clinch section championship

(Liverpool Daily Post, June 19, 1961)

Made it! Everton ended their tour with another victory – although they would have to return to play in the final in August.

*E*VERTON clinched their section championship in the North American International League at Montreal on Saturday when they beat the New York Americans 7-0.

It was Everton's sixth win in their seven-match programme and they finished with 12 points. Everton's scorers were: Mickey Lill (2), Bobby Collins (2), Billy Bingham (2) and Frank Wignall.

Everton fans can put out the flags, but there will be mixed feelings in other soccer quarters – eight Brits were in the "American" side.

New York Americans – former Welsh international Alf Sherwood is their player-manager – looked to have a chance when only 1-0 down at half-time but then came that Everton blitz, which sank the Americans.

Everton: Dunlop, Parker, Thomson, Gabriel, Labone, Harris, Lill, Bingham, Wignall, Collins, Fell. New York Americans: Harvey, Griffiths, Everitt, Chantraine, Middleton, McGuigan, Rudd, Seoane, McCole, McPherson, Tindall.

No comment, says Catterick, on tour controversies

(By Horace Yates, Liverpool Echo, June 19, 1961)

The Everton squad returned to Ringway Airport where manager Harry Catterick was coy in the face of questioning about the tour.

I ASKED Mr Catterick if he was prepared to discuss the sending home of Roy Vernon, the dismissals of Billy Bingham (twice) and Bobby Collins or the circumstances in which they sought their own hotel accommodation after that provided by the organisers of the New York America Cup competition, and to each Mr Catterick said firmly: "No comment."

When I asked about the Bangu match, the only blot on the Everton record, Mr Catterick said: "I am not making any excuses, but the temperature inside the bowl was 90 degrees, hardly the best conditions for Englishmen to play football."

The players returned bronzed and happy and their sporting headgear told anyone who did not already know where they had been.

Everton and Liverpool reject League Cup

(By Horace Yates, Liverpool Echo, July 19, 1961)

The League Cup, already deemed as an inconvenience – while the club were heading in the right direction according to the writer.

E VERTON and Liverpool will not take part in the Football League

Cup competition this season. Apparently the attempt to introduce some sort of order to replace the chaos of the first attempt last season have come too late to convince the Merseyside clubs that the competition is worthwhile, either monetarily or from the interest view-point.

Everton take the view that the American football tour, plus a return to play the final on August 3 in Montreal and on the 6th in New York, plus the strain of making an all-out effort to make this a memorable season in both league and cup, will tax the players' stamina sufficiently, without adding any extraneous matches of no great importance.

The plan to make Everton great is clearly taking shape and few would quarrel with a policy which embraced official events only.

Bobby Collins, who took over the captaincy last season after Tom Jones had lost his place, is now skipper in his own right, the sixth club captain since football was rescued after the war. The others have been: Ted Sagar, T.G. Jones, Peter Farrell, Don Donovan and T.E. Jones.

How much the players will earn this season is anybody's guess, but it would not be surprising if the top paid men began with £60 a match. This could be the way of it. From wages £35; from bonus at the rate of £1 for every thousand over 40,000 – £20 or more; from winning bonus £4. Additional satisfaction from the generous terms offered comes from an agreement to pay the same rate for the next away match as they earned at home. If Everton are not the biggest money-spinners in the country then football really has become a lucrative occupation!

It's Dukla Prague as Blues return Stateside

(By Michael Charters, Liverpool Echo, July 24, 1961)

There was a report on how Everton were about to take part in the New York International League final. They were due to meet Dukla Prague, the Czechoslovakian champions, in a two-legged final, in New York, in early August.

*M*ANAGER Harry Catterick told me that he saw Dukla play last season and regards them as one of the finest club sides he has ever seen. The only player who did not make the initial trip to America and Canada, when Everton won Section One of the competition, is goalkeeper Willie Mailey, the Scots boy. Albert Dunlop was the only goalkeeper who went originally and fortunately he was not injured and played in every match.

Outfield player Brian Harris would have deputised had the goalkeeper been Injured.

Long trip proves fruitless

(Liverpool Echo, August 3, 1961)

The Stateside journey was to prove bitterly disappointing with the Blues trounced in the first leg of the final. They would also go on to lose 2-0 in the second leg.

*T*HE victory achieved by Dukla Prague highlighted the same precision tactics used to despatch Shamrock Rovers 10-0 the previous Saturday. Everton were outclassed for most of the game, and had to settle for the financial bonus the tournament delivered.

1962-1971

Licensed premises

(Liverpool Echo, January 12, 1962)

Good news for drinkers as additional refreshments are now on offer at Goodison.

SPECTATORS attending Everton matches Goodison Park will soon be able to get an intoxicating drink inside the ground before the match. But when the whistle blows for the game to start the bars will be closed and they will not be opened again that day. This was revealed at Liverpool adjourned licensing sessions yesterday, when the magistrates granted the club permission for nine new licensed bars – three at ground level and six higher up in the stands.

Making the application on behalf of Mr William Kenneth Davies, the proposed licensee, Mr Holland Hughes said they wanted to avoid the last-minute rush which always occurred after closing time in the nearby public houses. Although this application was a novelty in the city of Liverpool, said Mr Hughes, there were 20 clubs which already had these licenses, including Tottenham. Mr Davies said that draught and bottled beer would be served in beakers.

Swoop for young England keeper

(By Leslie Edwards, Liverpool Echo, March 2, 1962)

The spending continued at Goodison as a top goalkeeper was secured.

EVERTON today signed from Blackpool England Under-23 goalkeeper Gordon West, who is not yet 20 years of age.

West knew nothing of Everton's interest in him until last evening when Everton manager Harry Catterick made a quick visit to confer with Blackpool manager Ronnie Suart. Negotiations progressed so well it was possible for West to come to Goodison Park at midday today. He had earlier trained with the Blackpool team at Bloomfield Road.

The only thing delaying his signing was the necessity – and Everton always insist on this – for a full-scale physical examination of the player by the club's orthopaedic specialist.

The coming of a new goalkeeper will surprise Everton followers. There has been talk of Everton interest in players in nearly every other position. Dunlop, who is 32 and a good club cricketer, has given Everton splendid service. He had had a benefit from the club before he finally made the first team. For some seasons he shared his position with Jimmy O'Neill, but once O'Neill went to Stoke he was rarely displaced.

Everton give no reason for his displacement from the first team. Dunlop started, some years ago, a sports outfitting business in the city, but the venture was not successful. More recently he was connected with a social club near the Everton ground. It is understood that his club did not wish him to have a commitment of this kind.

Big-spending Blues

(By Horace Yates, Liverpool Echo, March 7, 1962)

Horace Yates' 'Sport As I See It' column noted how Everton had been keeping tabs on Wrexham centre-forward Wyn Davies, and how they were also monitoring the situation of Joe Baker, who had recently been injured in a car accident. Despite scoring twice in a friendly against Brondby, Harry Catterick was said to be unconvinced.

ON Friday Gordon West was signed from Blackpool. Yesterday Dennis Stevens from Bolton and George Heslop from Newcastle joined him. According to my estimates of transfer fees, Everton have paid out £336,000 or its equivalent, in signings since 1958.

Here is the list:

O'Hara (£7,500) and Parker (£17,500), both in May 1958.

Collins (£23,500) in September 1958. Laverick (£6,000)
in February 1959.

Shackleton (£10,000) in September 1959.

Ring (£12,000), Vernon (£35,000) and Lill (£25,000),
all in February 1960.

Gabriel (£30,000) in March 1960.

Bingham (£20,000) in October 1960.

Young (£42,000) and Thomson (£16,000), both in November 1960.

Kavanagh (£4,000) in February 1961.

Fell (£18,500) in March 1961.

Veall (£12,000) in September 1961.

West (£20,000), Stevens (£25,000) and Heslop (£12,000)
in March 1962.

Mystery 'Mr X' donates £20,000

(Liverpool Daily Post, June 26, 1962)

Former manager John Carey's settlement paid by who?

$\mathcal{T}$HE cost of the court action which led to settlement of the John Carey-Everton FC dispute has been met by a supporter, club shareholders were told at their annual meeting last night.

Mr H. Holland Hughes, chairman of the Finance Committee, said: "The amount involved does not appear in this account and will not appear in next year's accounts, because I can tell you that all expenses incurred over that have been defrayed by one of our supporters."

Mr John Moores, club chairman, added: "One of the terms of the agreement was that the amount would not be disclosed."

An item in the profit and loss account was: "Donations received £20,000." Excess of income over expenditure was £12,651.

Mr Holland Hughes said: "It is only proper for me to mention that the profit and loss carry forward could not have been so satisfactory had it not been for the generosity of a benefactor of the club who had made a donation of £20,000. This benefactor desires to remain anonymous and we, of course, are bound to respect his wishes. We are none the less very grateful indeed for this most generous gift."

Mersey Millionaires close in on title

(May 8, 1963)

A convincing victory at West Brom had delirious fans dreaming of the club's first league championship triumph for 24 years...

*J*UST the two points to go... that is all Everton need to bring the First Division crown to Goodison Park for the first time since 1938/39. The Merseyside Millionaires had a big crowd of supporters in a state of near ecstasy when they routed West Bromwich Albion 4-0. And they did it to the accompaniment of the Liverpool FC supporters' battle song, "When The Saints Go Marching In," which was taken up by their fans after each goal was scored – and also at the end.

On a night of joy for everyone connected with Everton – from chairman John Moores downwards – the goals came from Alex Young (2) and skipper Roy Vernon, who kept up his remarkable season's record of never missing a penalty. And Stewart Williams, the West Bromwich left-back, joined in the scoring act by turning the ball beyond his own goalkeeper for the final goal.

A day the fans will never forget

(By Horace Yates, Liverpool Echo, May 13, 1963)

Championship glory! One for the record books; an in-depth analysis from the Echo's Horace Yates as the Blues defeated Fulham 4-1 to secure the title.

*F*OR the players it was champagne after the game; the crowd had theirs in the first 45 minutes, for after a 3-1 opening Everton became bogged down in the Fulham defence, with just two saves by Dunlop and his third goal by Vernon, seven minutes from the end, to remind the crowd that their club had assuredly punched their way to their first Football League Championship title since 1938/39. It mattered not how Spurs were faring at Maine Road, but their defeat by Manchester City merely meant that instead of completing their task one point ahead of their nearest challengers, Everton must now have at least a three points advantage. A wonderfully impressive season!

Naturally, there was a carnival spirit and atmosphere over the whole scene, with a sea of blue all round the ground and ear-splitting exhortations to finish the job, so worthily undertaken all through the season. Following their victory at West Brom on Tuesday, the Everton players had told me they hoped to finish the season in a real blaze of glory, with an exhibition of football that would leave the crowd disappointed only that this was the finale until next season. For most of the way this is exactly what happened.

The chairman, Mr John Moores, was a study in himself as the events unfolded. Seated next to another recent champion, Alderman John Braddock, whose party swept to victory in this week's polls, he showed pardonable excitement when skipper Roy Vernon took Parker's free-kick round Macedo to shoot into the empty net after five minutes.

When Vernon did it again three minutes later, again from a Parker offering, aided by a rebound between Macedo and Mullery, cautious optimism exploded into unconcealed delight.

Up in the air went Mr Moores' hat, not to be retrieved until after the match was over, and as the crowd in front of the directors' seats turned in his direction to applaud an early promise now on the high road to fulfilment, up went his clasped hands in the boxers' salute. Triumph was in the air.

He, like everybody else on the ground, decided at that moment that Everton were champions, and how they let everybody know about it!

In 10 minutes Vernon had the ball in the Fulham net once again and though it was disappointing to find the goal disallowed for offside, who cared? The tide was flowing in full flood behind an irresistible Everton.

To interrupt the celebrations was the incident in which Kay might easily have conceded a penalty as he pulled Brown back, but the decision was merciful. This proved to be only a setback delayed, for in 19 minutes Haynes squared Robson's pass and Key pulled it accurately beyond Dunlop.

Worry found no place among the happy crowd for Everton in this mood could not be denied, least of all by Fulham, bravely though they tried to occupy a share of the picture.

Composure never left the players for an instant. They fully realised they would deal with Fulham, and it was reflected in their play.

Scurvy was the trick played on the incessantly chanting supporters when they were helped to the novelty of a goal from Stevens, which would have been his first of the year – and straight away denied it.

Instead of a goal the referee awarded a free-kick to Everton, because of Keetch tugging at Young's jersey. How cruel the decision appeared! Again the denial was fleeting, for when Vernon's kick rebounded from the wall of defenders, the ball went directly to Scott, who with the aid of a deflection by an opponent, had Macedo picking the ball out of the net in 27 minutes.

Seven minutes from the end Young flicked forward Dunlop's kick with a nicely judged header and there was Vernon, darting on to the ball, controlling it in a flash and pulling beyond Macedo.

In so doing he had created a ridiculously difficult angle, but with the accuracy of the expert marksman he is when things are going well for him, he scored readily.

This long desired refresher set the crowd roaring anew and as the battery of Goodison Park crowds indicated that the end was in sight, the vast assembly took up a chant which was never stilled until 20 minutes after the players, following a hugging and caressing act, had left the field.

Only a handful defied the police and the club request to keep off the pitch, but as the players began their lap of honour, a solitary female joined a youthful half-dozen or so and succeeded in wrapping a blue and white scarf round Vernon's neck. The scene of enthusiasm is said to have been without equal in Goodison's long history, by those whose memories can go furthest back, and who can doubt it? It is difficult to know what more any crowd could have done to express their adulation.

Young, without a goal, but with the knowledge of a first-class performance behind him, came in for a large share of the lionising, and from being an almost unwelcome intruder, Tony Kay has stayed on to become a toast in himself.

Parker, too, had completely refuted the idea of some people that his best is behind him, for it would be difficult to imagine a more thoughtful and accomplished performance from any back.

Stand-in Dunlop had never given a moment's anxiety, except to Fulham, and the difficult job of controlling the lively Cook merely gave Labone an opportunity to prove his undoubted class.

Even in triumph and exultation, sight could not be lost of the splendour of Haynes, back after weeks of enforced idleness, and although England may be managing without him just now, his name will surely come up for renewed consideration next season. Haynes has the gift of making the most of every ball.

Having completed the most pleasurable lap of the ground they have ever undertaken, the team had miscalculated if they thought that was their final contact with an adoring public, for as they sipped champagne in their dressing room, the cry went up, "We want the Blues".

On and on it went and hardly anybody among the vast throng left their places. Only the seats in the directors' box were vacant, as the demand for opportunity to pay further tribute to their favourites continued.

"We want Moores" they chanted and although the minutes passed without any suggestion of reward, their enthusiasm was insatiable.

After a quarter of an hour Vernon led his players into the stand some of them carrying charged champagne glasses, with Kay smoking a cigar, and West in charge of a bottle. The crowd just roared and roared and then called for a speech from Vernon.

This is what the skipper said: "On behalf of the players and myself

I would like to thank you for your wonderful support throughout the season, and the management for the grand way in which they have backed us up. I hope this will only be the start and that we shall have many great games and highlights at Goodison Park."

So ended another wonderful day in the club history.

It is so long since there has been an opportunity for such celebrations that maybe we have all got a little rusty, but the thought did strike me that the wonderfully loyal supporters might have been spared a lot of speculation and anxiety by a simple announcement that the players would appear in the stand in a matter of minutes. They did not realise that the players were engaged in other necessary duties and were fearful only that they were not going to come back. Just a little point maybe, but we shall all know better in the light of experience. Having seen their heroes once again, everybody retired happy.

Some had danced a joyous jig on the concrete roof of the trainer's shelter. There was a cheer all to herself for Mrs Braddock and even Liverpool's point at Sheffield United was no dampener.

Casting my mind back to the opening game of the season at Turf Moor, I remember writing of Everton's victory over Burnley that "They played like champions."

Now they are champions of a competition which many rate as the most difficult of all European titles to win, and if manager Harry Catterick, so accurate in so many of his predictions, is again on target, this Everton side may only be coming into peak form next season.

To some extent this season has been a season of reconstruction and development. Next season will come the consolidation and with the average age of the side no more than 24 it would appear that by and large Everton's future is in good hands.

We may not have seen the last of the changes, but the main superstructure is there, solid and impressive. How they will fare in the European Cup competition ahead we must wait and see, but how can there be other than good grounds for hope? Tottenham have prospered in this sphere, and Everton have not done too badly in their clashes with the London club.

My view is that in the days to come Evertonians will look back on the signing of Tony Kay as one of the most important in the recent history of Goodison Park affairs. Not only is he a bundle of courage, sometimes slightly over exuberant, but curiously enough he has the quality to bring to Everton's game a control and pace adjustment, which are all the better for his coming. A future captain? Who knows what Mr Catterick may have in his mind, but as Vernon ended the season a much more accomplished leader than he began it, and has shown, especially in the vital concluding games (he has scored eight goals in the last seven matches) that the responsibility is an incentive rather than an encumbrance, what better policy could there be than to leave well alone in that respect? Well done Everton – and thank you for a season so full of happy memories.

Everton: Dunlop, Parker, Meagan, Gabriel, Labone, Kay, Scott, Stevens, Young, Vernon, Temple.
Fulham: Macedo, Cohen, Langley, Mullery, Keetch, Robson, Key, Brown, Cook, Haynes, O'Connell.
Referee: Mr. R.H. Windle (Chesterfield).
Attendance: 60,578.

Taking account of success

(By Horace Yates, Liverpool Echo, May 13, 1963)

The Mersey Millionaires tag, as the Blues were often termed due to the transfer spending undertaken courtesy of chairman John Moores, had 'bought' the championship in 1963, according to some. As a result accounts were said to reveal a loss that summer. What clubs would give for a similar loss these days.

$\mathcal{R}$ÉCORDS have fallen like ninepins in Everton's sixth League Championship season. Not only have they extended their unbeaten run at Goodison Park to 40 games, but attendance figures and receipts soar to new levels, so much so that despite the free-spending which has been necessary from time to time, the chairman, Mr John Moores, said he expected that when the accounts were balanced for the season the deficit would not exceed £20,000.

To grasp the full significance of this achievement one must remember that in bringing players like Tony Kay, Alex Scott and Johnny Morrissey to Goodison, Everton have parted with cheques amounting to well over £100,000 in addition to making the biggest payments to players of any club in the country.

When I sought some estimate of the kind of money these victorious Everton players had collected from their 25 victories and 11 drawn games, with bonuses of various kinds, I was told their income could easily exceed £4,000 a man.

Even in these days when players are more generously treated than ever before in the history of the game, that is an agreeable sort of recompense for their labours.

Mr Moores was asked about his relationship with the crowd, and in claiming them to be the best of all supporters, he said relations were excellent. There had been uncomfortable moments, he went on, mainly over the departure of Mr John Carey, but he felt that this was as much due to misunderstanding as anything else. "When you live on the hills," he said, "you must expect high winds from time to time."

Referring to the well-earned holiday the players and their wives will enjoy in Spain, Mr Moores said it had been decided that none of the directors would accompany them because it was felt that in their own company they would be better able to relax and enjoy themselves.

Perhaps it would not be fitting to close without a reference to a name less well-known than that of any of the players but who, as driver of the official coach on so many of their trips, has also played his part in the smooth running of the season – Ernie Horrigan.

There is no more enthusiastic supporter anywhere than Ernie. He counted it a privilege rather than a job when he was appointed to his duties, for he would have been at most of the matches anyway.

He told me on Saturday that after the players had lunched together at Birkdale he took them to Goodison for the Fulham game. "I was the only one in the party," he said, "who had to be given tranquillisers."

Marvellous - now for Europe

(Daily Post, May 13, 1963)

An unusual adoption of vox pops in print – 'real' people are asked for their opinion on footballing matters. Everton's triumph meant a journalist was summoned to gauge opinions on the success, and the prospect of a first venture into the European Cup. As is often the case in times of glory, there's always someone who wants a bit more.

$\mathscr{O}$N Saturday 60,578 men, women and children went to Goodison Park to watch Everton beat Fulham 4-1, win the title and enter next season's European Cup. As they left the seething stadium a reporter asked them what they thought of the triumph – and the prospects.

Two smartly dressed, attractive young women, one with hair of a coppery hue, the other a blonde, stood outside Goodison Park on Saturday evening, and chatted away gaily. There was every reason for their mood, for these two girls were Mrs Pat Gabriel, wife of Everton's right-half, and Mrs Nancy Young, wife of the side's centre-forward.

Excitedly they said: "It was great – marvellous."

What of the future, in particular Everton's European Cup prospects?

They concurred again: "They have a very good chance in the European Cup."

As she made her way out of the crush, pretty 23-year-old Jennifer Guppy, who has seen the side in each of their home matches this season, was beside herself with pleasure.

Her eyes sparkling, Jennifer of Tudor Avenue, Bebington, said: "I think it's marvellous, wonderful. It is really. I have never been so uncomfortable in my life, but it was worth every second."

Joan Atkinson, of Mendip Road, Birkenhead, and Ernest Roberts of Hatherly Street, Birkenhead, said they were pleased but they had not expected anything other than that Everton would be champions. In fact, 21-year-old Joan, who follows Everton home and away hinted that there was something unfair about the way Everton had been knocked out of the FA Cup. "We should have won the cup, too," she said.

Carol Kelly, aged 14 of Williams Avenue, Bootle, speaking for herself, her 13-year-old sister, Sally, and 14-year-old Monica Rice, also of Bootle, who was with her, commented: "We are pleased, we've been praying for them to win." She added: "My father's a great fan. He's been everywhere with them." Said her sister, Sally: "It was smashing."

Enthusiastic about the club's future were 18-year-old Glyn Jones, of Bristol Avenue, Wallasey, and 17-year-old Arthur Evans, of Liscard Road, Wallasey: "I think that next year they will get the league title and the FA Cup," said Glyn. Arthur commented: "If they play like they did today they have got a good chance of the double next year."

Not so easy to please were Mr Gerald Smallwood and his 13-year-old son, Philip, of Pilch Lane, Knotty Ash. Said Mr Smallwood: "They deserved the championship but they did not make quite the show today I was expecting. They played about too much."

Mr Fred Hopkinson, of Roxburgh Street, Bootle, one of the Goodison ground gatemen, said: "They have not been playing up to their earlier standard and they will have to improve to win the European Cup."

Mr Joe Hughes, who lives in the Southdene area of Kirkby, who has never missed seeing the side play at home this season, said of the European Cup: "They've got a good chance." A Roman Catholic priest said: "They were excellent right through." What did he think of their European Cup prospects? "They will acquit themselves quite well and represent their country well."

Echoes of a famous triumph

(Liverpool Echo, May 14, 1963)

The plaudits continued.

SIR Ivan Thompson, now a landlubber based on Anfield and Goodison Park (but once Commodore of the Cunard Line) saw Everton's triumph at Goodison. "It took me back," he says, "to 1906 when Everton first won the cup and I was a spectator at the same ground. The reserves were playing a team from Earlestown. We were anxious to know what was going on in London, but there was no public address system.

When the club got news of Sandy Young's goal they sent a boy round the pitch carrying a board on which was chalked the name 'Young'. That was enough! The crowd knew what it meant. They set up the chant, "Hey ho, Sandy scored the goal. Sandy scored the goal, Sandy scored the goal," and kept it up for the remainder of the game. I'll never forget the occasion – or the scenes against Fulham."

Congratulations from Czechoslovakia
(Liverpool Echo, May 18, 1963)

And over in the East.

$\mathcal{A}$MONG messages of congratulation was one which arrived for Alex Young from behind the Iron Curtain. The message from Josef Seplavy, Zitna 36, Praha 2, Czechoslovakia, read: "Congratulations to you and your colleagues that played it out directly, and to the other gentlemen that helped indirectly to win the Championship by working out policy of the club and tactics. Best wishes for next season."

Inter hold Everton to a Goodison draw
(By Frank McGhee, Daily Mirror, September 19, 1963)

So to 1963/64, and European Cup football at Goodison for the first time. Unlike today's European competitions, where seeding systems and UEFA co-efficients rarely throw up notable early-round clashes pitting top clubs from major footballing nations, in the early days there were open draws. The first opponents would not be a minnow, but the Italian champions Inter Milan. A goalless draw meant all hopes were lost, according to the Mirror reporter.

$\mathcal{E}$VERTON are out of the European Cup. Miracles don't happen in this class of competition. And it will take a miracle to save them in the second leg of the qualifying-round tie in the howling, screaming inferno of Milan's San Siro Stadium next Wednesday.

On last night's form they had nothing to stop Inter from brushing them aside, scoring the goals that will provide the final seal of the superiority the Italians showed at Goodison.

The muscle, effort and pace Everton poured into this match never looked enough. The Italians were better, tactically and individually.

The finest players wore the black and blue and one of the greatest was the strutting inside-left, Luis Suarez, cool, controlled and rejoicing in the space he was granted – just one of Everton's many tactical boobs.

The Italians set up a seven-man penalty area screen that Everton never looked like penetrating. But our champions can't complain.

They knew it would happen. They went out knowing the tactics to beat it.

They had the speed of Alex Scott down the right, an asset never used because on the few occasions he made himself available he didn't get the service.

Everton "tactics" seemed to consist of long balls that got lost in the forest of towering defenders planted inside Inter's area.

The Italians managed more shots at goal than Everton, 11 against 10, won more corners, eight against six.

And an even more significant statistic is that the referee, a scrupulously fair Hungarian, Gyula Gere, awarded 18 free-kicks against Everton, 12 against Inter. He also booked Everton left-half Tony Kay in the 57th minute for allegedly treading on Suarez after flattening the great man in a fair tackle.

Twelve minutes from time Everton appeared to have earned at least a slim chance of survival when inside-left Roy Vernon drove the ball home past goalkeeper Sarti.

But the roar of the 62,408 crowd was abruptly stifled when Mr Gere ruled Vernon offside.

CASH NOTE: One consolation for Everton – the £31,450 receipts was a record "gate" for an English club.

Price of a 'golden evening'

(Daily Mirror, September 24, 1963)

Ahead of the return at the San Siro, focus turned to football finances.

$\mathcal{T}$OMORROW Everton plunge anew into the maelstrom of European Cup soccer. One fears they may be overwhelmed by the might of Milan in a stadium which seats 90,000 but whatever happens the venture will have been well worthwhile. For if Everton are to reach the heights dreamed of by their ambitious chairman, Mr Moores, this is the sort of occasion to which they must become accustomed.

Last week's clash at Goodison demonstrated just what big business soccer has now become. On the one side were Everton, who have reputedly spent some £400,000 on players in the last five years; on the other Internazionale Milan, whose ace inside-forward Suarez alone cost them £210,000 and whose manager is alleged to earn about £25,000 a year. In keeping with such an occasion we had rabid supporters paying up to £2 a seat, and total receipts of more than £30,000. It was indeed a golden evening.

Yet for all the money laid out, and all the individual talent on display, not a single goal was scored. One cannot but wonder whether in the scramble for success the original object of the game is being forgotten.

Harvey thrown in at deep end

(By Frank McGhee, Daily Mirror, September 26, 1963)

Colin Harvey's debut ended in defeat – but Everton could hold their heads high as they were edged out by an Inter side who would go on to win the competition – and then retain it the following year.

$\mathcal{C}$OLIN Harvey, 18, stepped out of reserve soccer into the European Cup when he was called up by Everton for the second leg of their tie against Inter Milan. Manager Harry Catterick decided to give Harvey his first senior match at inside-right, with Dennis Stevens dropping back to replace Jimmy Gabriel, who was unfit.

In the first half every Everton player except Roy Vernon spent most of his time living dangerously on the fringe of his own penalty area. The Italians were getting a taste of their own defensive medicine, and the whistling, booing crowd hated it. There was one spell of pressure when the English champions must have been left wondering how they survived. Outside-left Corso hit one inches wide, inside-right Mazzola hit the post. Outside-right Jair from 30 yards lashed one with a vicious swinging twist that was only inches over.

Thanks to young Harvey, Jair was getting nothing like the service he got at Goodison from Luis Suarez. It was 26 minutes before the great man got a ball through to his Brazilian winger.

Italian tempers were becoming tattered and the referee was kept working overtime as a series of scuffles broke out with Brian Harris, Alex Young and Tony Kay involved in brushes with Jair, Suarez and centre-half Guarneri.

It began to look dangerous for Everton again just before half-time when Gordon West had to go down at Jair's feet.

Two minutes after the interval Jair put Inter a goal ahead. Di Giacomo took the ball upfield and passed to Jair, whose shot hit the crossbar then fizzed into the back of the net.

An ugly situation developed in another Milan attack when Jair was bowled over by Labone and Kay, who came at him from both sides. The game was stopped for three minutes when the referee tried to calm the angry players.

World Cup to come to Goodison

(By Horace Yates, Liverpool Daily Post, October 18, 1963)

Goodison Park was confirmed as an upcoming World Cup venue

$\mathcal{G}$OODISON Park, probably the finest club ground in England, will stage five games, including a quarter-final (July 23) and a semi-final (July 26) in the World Cup series of 1966. This is the sort of recognition fans have long claimed as their due, revolting as they have against the policy of taking all the leading soccer attractions to Wembley.

Many believe that the Goodison Park resources have been unwisely and unfairly neglected for representative games, but this is atonement with a vengeance! Not only are ground conditions without superior, but nowhere is there a more fanatical football population.

Rangers snub British Championship tie

(By Horace Yates, Liverpool Daily Post, December 2, 1963)

A preview of the second leg of the British Championship – and a smaller than expected Scottish invasion.

$\mathcal{R}$ANGERS' fans apparently never tire of singing, "Follow, follow, we will follow Rangers." So far as the second leg game of the British Championship match with Everton at Goodison Park tonight (kick-off 7.30) is concerned, words are not being followed by deeds.

Everton sent to Glasgow about 4,500 tickets. Yesterday, the club were informed that a large number of these will be returned in time for sale today. The only Scottish invasion tonight is by the team and judging by Saturday's 3-0 defeat by Hearts at Ibrox, the players are still somewhat caught up in the Everton whirlwind.

I understand 40,000 tickets have so far been sold. Tonight 10 shillings stand tickets will be available for the North End, South End and Lower Stand (Bullens Road). There will be cash admission at five shillings, paddock seven shillings and sixpence and boys' pen two shillings.

Thousands locked out for Leeds Cup tie

(Liverpool Echo, January 29, 1964)

An over-crowded scene at Goodison for the 2-0 FA Cup victory which saw Bobby Collins return in a Leeds shirt.

$\mathcal{T}$HOUSANDS of fans were locked out of a near-capacity attendance at Goodison Park last night, when 66,197 people, who paid £15,500 in gate money, saw Everton beat Leeds United in a fourth round FA Cup replay.

Many turnstiles were closed soon after the game began at 7.30 and ticket-holders found difficulty in getting through to take their places in the stands. Many missed the first 15 minutes play.

Some hundreds of crushed spectators, most of them boys, were taken from the crowded terracing behind the barriers at the Gwladys Street goal. Police escorted them out of the ground.

All told St John Ambulance men dealt with more than 50 casualties.

A man and a girl were taken to hospital for X-ray examination. Eighteen-year-old Margaret Orr, of Salisbury Road, Liverpool, was taken to Stanley Hospital with a suspected broken arm and Mr Joseph Davies, aged 43, of Thorncliffe Street, Everton, whose arm was badly bruised, was examined at Walton Hospital. Both were allowed home.

First-aid treatment was given to a number of others on the touchline, but a senior police spokesman said today that most of those who climbed over the barriers were uninjured.

Outside the ground there were noisy scenes for a while after the game started because a queue of 10s ticket-holders at one turnstile in Bullens Road were unable to get through in time. Some had been queuing for three-quarters of an hour.

New-look ground takes shape

(By Horace Yates, Liverpool Daily Post, February 10, 1964)

Goodison alterations were ongoing with the famous semi-circular wall being built.

$\mathcal{E}$VERTON'S barricades are down! They disappeared immediately after Saturday's derby game. That is only half the story, however, for replacing them behind each goal will be a semi-circular wall, and this is to become a permanent feature of Goodison Park.

Work on the wall will be put in hand as soon as possible. This is part of the long-term planning for the World Cup games of 1966. Inside the ground will be an oval running track. Mr John Moores, the Everton chairman, said last night: "Spectators will be kept the same distance away from the playing area, as at present, but as the track will be oval they will be at a slightly different angle."

Big money swoop for star Pickering

(By Horace Yates, Liverpool Daily Post, March 11, 1964)

More spending on players – and a new centre-forward. Hopes were high for Fred Pickering with comparisons to none other than Dixie Dean and Tommy Lawton being made. Pickering scored 56 goals in 97 appearances but never lived up to his potential. Three years later he would sign for Birmingham City.

*E*VERTON made their most spectacular plunge into the transfer market yesterday by paying £75,000 to Blackburn Rovers for England Under-23 international centre-forward Fred Pickering, to bring the total outlay made by manager Harry Catterick since he took over at Goodison Park in April 1961 to about £290,000.

At least half that amount has been recouped by the sale of players. Mr Catterick's swoop beats the signing deadline to qualify players to take part in all championship games this season by only six days.

Although there were various reports of other interested parties, Everton virtually had the field to themselves in the end.

The first question supporters will ask is: "Whose place will Pickering take?" In my view there can be only one answer – Alex Young's, despite the fine show he gave at White Hart Lane. Mr Catterick's reaction to the question was: "Everybody is trying to play up the position of Alex Young. Remember he is under contract to Everton until June 1965."

Now let me retrace the events step by step, as they occurred yesterday morning. In the morning Pickering was in Sheffield as a member of the England training squad when he received a message that his presence was required at Ewood Park.

Before Pickering arrived Mr Catterick and director Mr Holland Hughes had reached Ewood Park. They went straight into conference with chairman James Wilkinson, secretary Derek Grimshaw and manager Jack Marshall. The talks went on for about an hour before Pickering arrived and he was immediately called into conference.

Another hour elapsed with the parties still together. Then Mrs Margaret Pickering, the player's wife, appeared on the scene. She had come straight from her work as a fuse inspector at a Royal Ordnance factory in Blackburn.

About 15 minutes later she was called in. Not until after five o'clock was the news released that the transfer had been completed. A smiling and obviously happy Pickering commented: "I am very pleased to be going to a club I always wanted to join."

Mrs Pickering's comment was: "I would not have fancied a move to London or the North-East, but Everton suits us both. It is near enough to our home town, Blackburn, for us to maintain close touch."

Mr Catterick's immediate reaction was: "Pickering has been bought to fit in with our long-term policy to keep Everton right at the top. I am certain he is going to play for England and just as certain he will be in the tradition of great Everton centre-forwards of the past, men like Dixie Dean and Tommy Lawton."

Those who are inclined to express disquiet about the payment of a £75,000 fee for Pickering, have the example of Manchester United and Tottenham Hotspur to console them. Denis Law cost United over £100,000 when he came back from Italy, but the player whose three goals helped to push United into the semi-final of the FA Cup on Monday night, must have gone close to repaying that debt already.

Just imagine Spurs without Greaves! He, more than any other individual, has kept Tottenham in the top bracket. Pickering may be a rung or so lower down the ladder than these great players, but that he may play a vital part in Everton's future greatness is undeniable.

New 'impressive' tunnel for players

(By Michael Charters, Liverpool Echo, April 30, 1964)

*G*OODISON Park is to have a new players' tunnel leading to the pitch from the dressing rooms by next season. It will be moved from its present spot towards the Stanley Park end of the ground to a position nearer the centre line, and will be much larger and more impressive than the current one.

Thousands see Blues Down Under

(By Horace Yates, Liverpool Echo, June 2, 1964)

Everton travelled Down Under for the first time for a lengthy post-season tour, which was covered by the Liverpool Echo. A staggering 52,000 fans turned up to see the opening game in Sydney. The tour was a big success on and off the pitch, with the Blues winning every one of their eight games.

*E*VERTON are the greatest sporting ambassadors ever to visit Australia! That was the tribute paid by Australian soccer officials as the Everton party left for home on Saturday. When they arrived at Speke last night, in pouring rain, almost the first they had seen since leaving home, Mr Fred Micklesfield, in charge of the tourists with fellow director Mr Cyril Balmforth, revealed that a pressing invitation has been received to pay a return trip next year.

Going out to a barrage of unfavourable publicity, Everton not only lived it down very quickly, but supplanted it with a wonderful reputation of sportsmanship. "The behaviour of the boys both on and off the field was impeccable," said Mr Micklesfield. "They were a credit to Everton and English football. We can justly be proud of them."

Judging by their tans some had obviously been soaking up the sun more than others, with Brian Harris probably the best advertisement for Australian sunshine.

Chief coach Tom Eggleston regretted only one thing – that they could not have brought back the Australian climate with them. "It is supposed to be their winter," he said, "but it was glorious. Not too hot, but very pleasant, so much so that bathing was irresistible. I have travelled the world on football trips, but this was easily the best tour of my life. Of course, it makes a wonderful difference when everybody speaks the same language."

Everybody received a heroes' welcome at Speke, but their arrival at London Airport was different, for several of the players had cigarettes confiscated. They received no sympathy from non-smoking Mr Micklesfield. "They cannot blame the customs men. They were doing their job. Our boys brought back rather a lot of souvenirs," he said.

The playing side of the trip could not have been more successful. All eight games were won, 50 goals being scored against seven.

There were record attendances at every match except the last – at Newcastle. Even that attracted an outsize 16,500 with an afternoon kick-off. Just how seriously the Australians took the visit can be gauged by the fact that for the match at Newcastle, all industry stopped in the afternoon to permit everybody to see the game.

Possibly the most disappointed member of the team at Speke was Johnny Morrissey, when he learned that only a few hours before his arrival an announcement had been made that Everton were willing to consider offers for him, as well as Ray Veall and George Sharples. "No comment," said Johnny.

Skipper Roy Vernon's view was that no tour to any part of the world could have been more successful or more enjoyable. "There was only one disappointing moment," he said. "That was the accommodation provided for us at Perth. It was British Week there, however, and there was just nothing anybody could do about it.

"Elsewhere the arrangements were wonderful. We cannot thank those likeable Aussies enough. What a grand bunch! The telephones at our hotels hardly stopped ringing, former Merseyside people going out of their way to invite the boys out to their homes for meals. Hospitality was simply fantastic. No other word could be adequate.

"This was a trip all of us will talk about long after our playing days are over. The only snag about it all is that wherever we may go in the future we shall always find ourselves comparing that country with Australia, and it will have to be sensational to warrant a rating.

"Never before have I seen such sadness on the part of the people as we left the country. Some of the officials at Sydney Airport were unashamedly wiping back the tears – and, come to think of it, what was that lump doing in my throat?

"And so farewell Australia, and thanks for a memory that will never die."

Fred's luggage goes West!
(Liverpool Echo, June 2, 1964)

*A*VERY relieved Mr Fred Micklesfield rang me up last night to tell me that three overnight bags belonging to him, which disappeared after Everton's arrival at Speke Airport, had not been lost after all.

George Heslop, lending a hand with the disposal of luggage, had put them in Gordon West's car – and so all was well.

"They were full of souvenirs," said Mr Micklesfield. "I was delighted to tell the police to call off the hunt."

E-V-E-R-T-O-N
(Liverpool Echo, October 3, 1964)

Inevitably, with The Beatles making waves and the Merseybeat scene thriving, the club branched out into music.

*E*VERTON footballers are chasing a new double for this season: top of the league and top of the pops. Fans at the ground for today's match will not only see the team – they will hear them, too, when the loudspeakers relay a record the boys have just made.

The songs are aimed to set the fans singing. The titles: "E-V-E-R-T-O-N" and "Everton For Me" explain what they are all about. They are sung by Canadian John Dunbar, but the appeal lies as they say, in the backing: by 12 of Everton's leading players.

The idea springs from Scotland. Glasgow Rangers have already made two records for their fans – and sold 50,000 copies of them. Two months ago Celtic entered the soccer league and have already sold 8,000 discs. Why Everton? "It is not because of the number of Scots on their books!" said 29-year-old Mr Tony Wright, who is handling the distribution on behalf of the makers on Merseyside. "They are having a good run – and that's the time to put it on the market."

At the Everton Supporters' Club yesterday afternoon, the players gathered to give the record a send-off – the first 500 copies are in Liverpool shops today.

The disc is a standard 45 and will sell for 6s 8d in the shops like any pop record. The lads hope that soon they will be adding record royalties to their bulging pay-packets.

Match Of The Day's FA Cup first

(January 9, 1965)

*E*VERTON made their Match of the Day FA Cup bow, a home tie with Sheffield Wednesday being the first FA Cup match televised on the show.

It was unusual for Everton to be featured at Goodison, as boss Harry Catterick did not welcome the cameras. This was highlighted by the fact that the next time a Goodison league game was screened was not until August 1967, a 3-1 win over Manchester United.

The tie saw Everton lead at the break thanks to an Andy Burgin own goal, although a thigh muscle injury to Sandy Brown saw the defender revert to the right wing, with Johnny Morrissey coming back into defence. The change lifted the visitors and lax defending at corners saw Wednesday turn around the deficit to lead 2-1 in the second half.

The Blues pressed, with Alex Scott swapping wings with Brown but their direct approach was failing to yield success. But with visiting fans chanting "easy, easy", Fred Pickering popped up to earn a replay – in which they eased to a 3-0 victory, with all the goals being scored by half-time.

Goodison passes World Cup test

(By Horace Yates, Liverpool Echo, July 16, 1965)

Goodison was given the green light as a stadium for the following year's World Cup.

$\mathcal{G}$OODISON Park has passed its World Cup examination with honours! Anyone who has seen the ground, trim and immaculate, will hardly be surprised at the excellent impression Everton's home has created on Dr. Helmut Kaser, secretary-general of FIFA, who made a tour of inspection yesterday. To conform with World Cup requirements the pitch has been extended. Although the dressing room accommodation is superb by any standards, Everton intend to install more shower baths.

"The work done at Goodison has been admirable and we are delighted by it," said Dr. Kaser. "We are completely satisfied with everything we have seen and grateful for the co-operation we have received from Mr Moores and his colleagues.

After seeing the dressing rooms, medical room and stands, the deputation inspected the Press centre which is to be established in the Supporters' Club premises in City Road.

They were informed that arrangements are being made for the installation on the ground of a scoreboard, on which will be recorded details of all other World Cup matches being played simultaneously with those at Goodison Park, so that the crowds will be given a complete picture.

'Don't drink, don't smoke...'

(By Horace Yates, Liverpool Echo, July 23, 1965)

Positive words as the players are welcomed back ahead of the 1965/66 campaign.

$\mathcal{O}$NLY Sandy Brown, Everton's Scottish full-back, was missing when the club's professional staff reported for their first day's training at

Goodison Park yesterday, where they were welcomed by the chairman, Mr John Moores. Brown has been given special leave because of the death of his father-in-law on Wednesday, to travel to Scotland.

Mr Moores' address of welcome is always an outstanding feature of this first day.

The players look forward to it because they realise that not only is Mr Moores laying down club policy, but that he does it clearly encouragingly and entirely without ambiguity.

"I think we have very good prospects," he said.

"Don't forget, our success is your success. If we do well we can give you more and more incentive bonuses. We have got to play good football in league and cup.

"Ask me which I would rather win and I would say that either will do – and we have a team that can do it."

There were congratulations too for the other club sides, with a special word for the youth team. "We can feel very satisfied for the future with such youngsters coming up," Mr Moores said.

The chairman concluded with a fatherly word of advice for the players. "Stanley Matthews," he said, "did not last as a player until he was 50 by drinking and smoking. You have to dedicate yourselves to your game.

"You have to be completely fit. I would advise you – don't drink, don't smoke. Don't stay out all night at night clubs and expect to be chosen by England. I hope

"I have not been too much of a 'square'. It is a magnificent life and I want you to enjoy it."

Mr Harry Catterick, Everton manager, also announced the signing of four 15-year-old boys – Alan Whittle, a Liverpool and England inside-forward; Frank Thornton, a Scottish international schoolboy inside-forward; Robert Humphreys, a Cheshire schoolboy goalkeeper; and Billy Brindle, a Liverpool and Lancashire schoolboy wing half-back.

Moores stands down as chairman

(Liverpool Daily Post, July 30, 1965)

Moores decision rocks the club.

*I*N a shock announcement, Mr John Moores last night announced his resignation as chairman of Everton Football Club.

Revealing his intention at the club's annual meeting, Mr Moores said he had come to this decision for compelling private and business reasons. Fellow directors were told of Mr Moores' decision shortly before the annual meeting began at Liverpool's Exchange Hotel.

Mr Moores, who is chairman of Littlewoods Mail Order Stores Limited, became chairman of Everton in June 1960. He told the surprised meeting: "Now I have reached the decision that this year I must withdraw my name. There are certain compelling private reasons and, in addition, there are business reasons for my decision to resign. My company have quite a lot of business on the Continent and we are investigating trade there on a much wider scale," said Mr Moores.

"This means I will be travelling a great deal to the Continent in the future, and will be absent from Goodison. I do not think it wise to have an absent chairman in a year when there will be a number of World Cup matches at Goodison Park. This being so, it would be unwise for me to be chairman – apart from any difficulty I might have myself."

Goodison work continues

(By Leslie Edwards, Liverpool Echo, August 17, 1965)

Goodison improvements continued, with an eye on the following summer's World Cup. Next up was the Park End area of the ground.

*F*AMILIES from a dozen houses adjoining the Everton football ground, in Goodison Avenue, whose homes are to be demolished as part of the club's plan to give World Cup spectators next year a wider and better approach to Goodison Park, are to be rehoused at the personal expense of Mr John Moores, the club's president.

The cost of rehousing is estimated at £30,000. Disclosing this today at the Everton club offices, Mr E Holland Hughes, who succeeded Mr Moores recently as chairman, said that demolition would probably start towards the end of the month.

The benefits of a more spacious approach to the ground at the Stanley Park end are many. One of the walls of the houses scheduled for demolition eats into seating accommodation of the Stanley Park goal stand. This stand is to be modernised, though there will be little structural alteration, at a cost estimated at £110,000.

£15 down the drain

(Liverpool Daily Post, August 23, 1965)

Can I mind your car, Mister – no really, I'm skint.

*P*RIVATE enterprise took a heavy knock at Goodison Park on Saturday when the Corporation opened their two new car parks for match traffic. There was gloom among young street car minders as they watched 325 motorists pay 2s 6d each to use the Corporation enclosure at Stanley Park.

Fourteen-year-old Stanley Evans, who has been minding cars in the area on match days for the last five years, said: "They would have been worth a shilling each to us – that's about £15 gone down the drain."

'The dirtiest team I have ever seen'

(By Michael Charters, Liverpool Echo, August 29, 1965)

An Inter-Cities Fairs Cup clash with Nuremberg in West Germany was not for the faint-hearted. Even the trainer got his marching orders from the referee.

*T*HE most fantastic incident of all took place 15 minutes from the end when Everton trainer Tom Eggleston was ordered off the ground by the referee for refusing to take the injured Morrissey off the field.

Morrissey, who was injured in a tackle by Wenauer which manager Harry Catterick described as the worst he had ever seen in football, was writhing in agony some 15 yards from the German goalmouth when trainer Eggleston went on to attend to him.

The next thing that happened was that two men carrying a stretcher ran on to the pitch and the German goalkeeper Wabra joined in the argument. There was some jostling in a crush of people and the referee then ordered Eggleston out of the ground. The German goalkeeper picked up Eggleston's medical equipment and hurled it off the pitch.

I understand that the referee literally ordered Eggleston to leave the stadium, but a Nuremburg official permitted him to sit on a bench by the side of the pitch.

Subsequently the Everton reserve goalkeeper Rankin went on to the pitch to attend to Wright when he was injured near the end.

Mr Catterick commented angrily: "I'm no softie, but this German team is the dirtiest I have ever seen."

Beware the Hungarian 'beach balls'

(By Michael Charters, Liverpool Echo, November 3, 1965)

Next up in the competition was a trip to Hungary, and a test for the usual English stereotype of fair play and sportsmanship. The hosts ended up victorious.

*E*VERTON trainer Tom Eggleston, who is in charge of the team in the absence of manager Harry Catterick, spent several hours today trying to ensure that the Hungarians do not try to pull a "fast one" before the Inter-Cities Fairs Cup tie with Ujpesti Dozsa here tonight.

After training at the Nep Stadium yesterday morning, he was so disturbed that the footballs provided for their work-out were so much smaller than those in use in England, that he described them as "beach balls".

He told me: "They are smaller than the regulation size laid down by international law. If the match ball tonight is the same, it will be a handicap to our boys and a help to the Hungarians."

'Catterick out, Young in!'
(January 22, 1966)

*W*ITH his Everton side showing patchy league form, manager Harry Catterick had decided to drop crowd favourite Alex Young the week before and brought in a 16-year-old centre-forward named Joe Royle for his debut at Blackpool.

The change backfired badly on "The Cat" and resulted in a 2-0 defeat and angry fans confronted Catterick outside the ground after the game.

As a result of that disappointment, a fan wielded a placard before the FA Cup third-round tie with Sunderland in 1966 bearing the misspelt legend: "Cattrick [sic] out, Young in".

Although the fan failed to get his wish about Catterick, he at least saw the return of "Golden Vision". Young was brought back in for Royle and impressed in the 3-0 victory (claiming the third goal). With Gordon West, Jimmy Gabriel and Ray Wilson also returning to the side, the XI would be the same all the way through their FA Cup run that year apart from centre-forward Mike Trebilcock.

New-look Bellefield
(By Michael Charters, Liverpool Echo, February 11, 1966)

The final touches were being made to the club's new state-of-the-art training ground.

*W*ORK will be completed soon on Everton Football Club's training ground at Bellefield, West Derby, which will make facilities there the best in Britain.

When it is complete, the club will have achieved the ultimate in training arrangements, with the players only reporting to Goodison Park on match days.

At present, the playing staff arrive at Goodison each morning and are taken by coach to Bellefield for training, returning to headquarters for baths and a midday meal. But within the next few weeks, Bellefield will become a self-contained unit. The players will report direct there each morning, train, bath and have a meal in a pavilion which sets a new standard in dressing room accommodation.

The most notable feature of the work, however, is a superb indoor playing area, which resembles an aeroplane hangar in size and scope. It is 200 feet by 100 feet, with the roof towering more than 60 feet above an all-weather playing surface.

The walls have been left bare so that the ball can rebound truly off the surface. Every conceivable type of training exercise can be conducted there without interference from the weather. Upstairs [in the pavilion] there is a dining room, superbly-fitted kitchen, a lounge for the players and also a room for the manager, Mr Harry Catterick, who will work from there instead of his present office at Goodison Park.

This office has been designed in a corner of the building, with two windows overlooking the two outdoor training pitches, so that the manager will be able to get an overall view of activities outside.

Mr Catterick told me: "I will be able to supervise the training schedule with the coaches as well as attend to routine office work."

The present wooden pavilion, built more than 30 years ago when the ground was used by a shipping company as a sports field, is to be pulled down. A car park will be constructed on the space.

The cost of this work is in the region of £100,000. For that, Everton will not only possess the finest training ground in the country, but also a centre which should bring the club untold benefit in the future.

Everton first used Bellefield for training 20 years ago, when the leased the ground. Before they decided to spend £100,000 on these improvements, they negotiated to buy Bellefield three years ago at a cost of £30,000. It is money well spent.

View to a thrill
(March 21 1966)

Fans were pictured sitting watching the Merseyside derby from St Luke's Church roof. Anything to get a decent spec.

*L*OCKED out of the Everton-Liverpool game at Goodison Park (there were 62,000 chanting fans inside), about 40 youths risked broken necks or worse to gain a church roof view of the game. One kept a precarious hold on the church's cross. In vain, police and fire brigade officers on a snorkel tried to persuade the supporters to come down.

Meanwhile a wedding service went on more or less undisturbed in the Goodison Road church. Explained the Rev Robert Campbell: "The roar of the crowd pretty well drowned out the roof noises."

There were no arrests when the youths climbed down after the match.

Labby's pre-match nerves
(By Jack Rowe, Liverpool Echo, March 23, 1966)

The thoughts of skipper Brian Labone ahead of the FA Cup quarter-final at Second Division Manchester City.

*M*ATCH days are usually the worst," admits Brian Labone. "Everybody gets churned up inside but that is something you have to conquer. I find I can't eat much before a game, and on Saturday I shall not have breakfast. For lunch I'l just have a steak on its own."

Even an experienced pro like Labone feels extra excitement before a cup tie. It's impossible to treat it as just another match. Thousands of fans will meet the team when the coach reaches the ground.

"That can get you a bit as well," comments Labone. "You become conscious that you must not let them down, but we all know that once we get out on the pitch and have a job to do you have not time to think about anything else."

Catterick under fire for 'squad rotation'

(Liverpool Echo, April 18, 1966)

After seeing off City in the quarter-final, Everton were set to meet Manchester United in the last four. A week before the FA Cup semi-final, mid-table Everton fielded a much-changed side (known as "squad rotation" in modern parlance) at Leeds. The side, with an average age of 20 years and 11 months, went down 4-1.

JOE Richards (president of the Football League) said that Everton are likely to be asked why they fielded a side made up almost entirely of reserves against Leeds at Elland Road. "My guess is that the League management committee may decide to ask Everton for an explanation, although I know nothing of the facts apart from what I have read in the newspapers and heard on television," commented Mr Richards.

Everton manager, Harry Catterick, explained that eleven of the squad were on the injured list and that he saw no reason to expect an inquiry into the strength of his side. "We had so many players under medical care and treatment that I thought it was a good opportunity to give some young players the vital experience against first-class opposition, which has been denied them because of our run in recent weeks. In that time we went 14 games without defeat," said Mr Catterick yesterday.

League rules state that clubs must play full strength teams in all league matches unless they have a satisfactory reason for not doing so. Five years ago Burnley were fined £1,000 when the League management committee did not consider their explanation satisfactory.

Harvey the hero as Blues march on

(By Horace Yates, Liverpool Daily Post, April 25, 1966)

Despite injuries to Fred Pickering and Tommy Wright, Colin Harvey would be Everton's FA Cup semi-final hero.

FROM the depths of despair in January to ecstatic heights of triumph in April! That was the story book recovery by Everton, as they soared to their first Wembley cup final for 33 years, by defeating Manchester United in the semi-final at Burnden Park, Bolton, on Saturday. That they were value for their victory I have no doubt and I am equally certain that they have the will, the skill and experience to keep the trophy, won by Liverpool last season, on Merseyside for another year.

Nobody will pretend that Everton overthrew the tarnished might of Manchester United by play that delighted the heart of the purist. They won because they were superbly fit, magnificently drilled tactically and had the confidence to make and take their opportunity when it appeared. If I had an award to make for the finest sportsman of the hour, I would unhesitatingly confer it on Matt Busby, the United manager. In victory, it is easy to be magnanimous. It is heart-rending defeat that offers the challenge.

At a time when his heart must have been in his boots, Matt's reaction to the catastrophe, far more made him an even greater giant among men than he already was. "Everton deserved to win. They were the better team today. I could not see us pulling this game off," he said. Could any man be fairer than that?

There were delirious champagne scenes in the Everton dressing room. I am sure the players hardly knew whether to laugh or cry. All the tension had gone and a dream come true left them with a more rewarding sense of achievement than they have ever known.

Outside the fans, intoxicated with happiness, sang their songs, their chants and gave vent to their feelings, and as the players began to appear the victory throng broke out into "Auld Lang Syne."

A great day indeed!

Skipper Brian Labone, just as much in command of this situation as of the most trying moment on the field, commented simply: "I thought we were the better side. We were stronger than they were and we had more in hand at the finish. United played as we wanted them to do and the rest was up to us."

Manager Harry Catterick, proud and delighted, gave full credit to his boys. "They were magnificent to a man. I was delighted with the way they played the game. It went exactly the way we planned it. We realised they were a strong attacking side and it was our plan to get them coming at us into forward positions and then to strike back from defence. Harvey took his goal brilliantly and Trebilcock could not have fared better in his first cup tie for the club." The senior member of the team, Brian Harris, found difficulty in making words express his feelings.

"The greatest day of my life," he said. "I knew my chances of going to Wembley were running out, but now we want that cup."

Colin Harvey, wearing a grin that would not come off, had not only earned a place at Wembley, but had scored the goal that had made it possible. What more could a 21-year-old ask of life?

"When I hit the ball I knew it was going in, and yet I hardly dared look. I have only scored two cup goals in my life, but this is the one that counts. It's great, just great."

The limited impact of Charlton's prowess was the measure of Gabriel's triumph. He disciplined himself perfectly, laid off wisely and so heaped hard labour on the accomplished Charlton.

Labone and Harris shared the duties of curbing Law and Herd superbly. Their understanding was one of the most remarkable features of the game. I doubt if the two have ever dove-tailed their responsibilities more ably. Assuredly I have never seen either more dominant or more ruthlessly efficient.

Probably the name most frequently mentioned in terms of admiration was that of Mike Trebilcock. At Leeds last week I suspected that Everton here have a prize whose worth has not yet been fully appreciated. The events at Bolton underlined his qualities.

Everton have struck football gold in Trebilcock. I hope I am not allowing excitement to colour my judgement when I say that he was the most dangerous individual attacker on the field!

True, the role of forward striker was allotted to him, so that when Everton attacked, Trebilcock was almost invariably in it. I saw him tangle with Bremner last week and Stiles on Saturday in a way which satisfied me the lad is not lacking courage.

Unless I am very much mistaken Trebilcock is a name likely to be included very frequently in future hymns of Everton praise. His powers of marksmanship are exciting and even at this late stage he must come very seriously into the reckoning to complete the job at Wembley which he started so successfully at Burnden. As thrilled as anybody was Fred Pickering, the man ruled out of consideration by the very necessary yielding to a policy of caution.

He told me: "Last Wednesday I had a tremendous try-out and came through in great style. I was sure I was fit and when the boss told me I was out, that he could not afford to take the chance of a break down, I could have cried.

"In calmer moments I realised Mr Catterick was right. To have saddled the lads with the risk of taking on United with 10 men was unthinkable. Now we are through!

"I must use the remaining three games to prove that my knee is perfectly sound again. I must prove beyond all doubt that I am fully fit again. Wembley is tugging at me very hard."

Everton: West, Brown, Wilson, Gabriel, Labone, Harris, Scott, Trebilcock, Young, Harvey, Temple.
Manchester United: Gregg, Brennan, Dunne, Crerand, Foulkes, Stiles, Anderson, Law, Charlton, Herd, Connelly.
Referee: Mr. E.T. Jennings (Stourbridge).
Attendance: 60,000 (receipts £29,386).

Blue is the colour

(By Leslie Edwards, Liverpool Echo, April 26, 1966)

The boys would be in blue.

*E*VERTON have won, by the toss of a coin, the right to play in their traditional blue in the FA Cup final at Wembley on May 14.

Sheffield Wednesday, their opponents, play in blue and white, and there was a colour clash.

This was resolved at Goodison Park last night, where Everton manager, Mr Harry Catterick, won the toss against Wednesday manager, Mr Alan Brown.

Two more coins must yet be spun – to decide which dressing rooms the teams will use, and the choice of ends. Everton fans will be saved thousands of pounds in changing the colours of their favours.

The final will be re-lived in sight and sound by fans through the co-operation of the BBC with a firm manufacturing 8mm film.

Wembley premonition
(By Leslie Edwards, Liverpool Echo, May 12, 1966)

A MAN, who has never attended a football match, wonders why the figures '33 33 31' appeared to him in a dream in blue and black. Only when he read next day of Everton's Cup win in 1933 and their appearance in a final 33 years later did he come to the conclusion that the final set of figures (31) represented a score of 3-1 to Everton on Saturday. Happily my correspondent from Wirral says he doesn't believe in dreams. But he hopes this one will prove him wrong.

Catterick's selection surprise
(By Leslie Edwards, Liverpool Echo, May 13, 1966)

Harry Catterick would announce his side a day before the final, at the club's 'secret' headquarters at Selsdon Park, Surrey.

C ATTERICK said: "Wright is preferred to Brown at full-back after considering ground and tactical conditions for this match. Whilst Pickering appears to have fully recovered physically from injury, he has had insufficient time to recover his confidence and form for me to risk him in such a vital game as this.

"These decisions were the most difficult I have had to make in my fifteen years of football management. Both Pickering and Brown are excellent club men and I have had a particularly difficult duty to inform them of these decisions. Trebilcock, Brown, Wright and Pickering were called in to our private lounge at the hotel after training this morning and informed of these decisions."

Pickering and Brown heartbreak
(By Michael Charters, Liverpool Echo, May 14, 1966)

*T*HERE are strong reports in London today that Pickering is going to reveal his exclusive thoughts on the subject in a newspaper tomorrow. He said last night: "I don't want to do anything hasty which might upset the boys in the team, but I feel I have been unfairly treated.

"I have told Mr Catterick that I haven't been given a chance to show whether I was in form or not after my knee injury. With the cup final coming up the lads didn't bother too much about creating opportunities in league games. What happens after the final will affect my future."

The other man omitted from the FA Cup final team, full-back Sandy Brown, has remained true to character in that he is prepared to accept his bitter disappointment as part of the game and has not rushed to his manager with transfer demands.

'That's it, it's Wednesday's Cup'
(May 14, 1966)

One of the most memorable FA Cup finals, Everton had gone into the match with Sheffield Wednesday having secured only one win from their last eight First Division games – although they had not conceded a goal in the competition. The following extracts are taken from the match reports and the subsequent coverage given the final in the wake of the success.

*A*FLYING start from the Owls saw the Blues a goal down inside five minutes – the first they had conceded in the competition that year, Jim McCalliog's shot deflecting in off Ray Wilson. Wednesday were on top despite Alex Young first having a goal ruled out for offside, before being brought down by keeper Ron Springett in the area – only for the referee to wave play on. McCalliog had an effort blocked soon after they opened the scoring but they were comfortably ahead at the break.

Young's effort early in the second half was brilliantly saved by Springett while McCalliog again went close before Everton found themselves 2-0 down after 57 minutes, David Ford following up after Gordon West had parried a fierce Fantham effort. Ford's strike encouraged commentator Kenneth Wolstenholme to declare: "That's it, it's Wednesday's Cup."

But suddenly the Blues hauled themselves back from the brink with two goals from young Cornishman Trebilcock. The first came on 59 minutes after Derek Temple's header had been blocked, Trebilcock firing home the loose ball from 12 yards before the equaliser stunned Wednesday further five minutes later. Alex Scott's free-kick into the area was half cleared by Sam Ellis, and Trebilcock crashed home as the ball dropped from the edge of the box. That goal prompted Eddie Kavanagh, a former Everton youth player, to run from the crowd and make a mazy run across the pitch, finally being brought down courtesy of a policeman's rugby tackle just outside West's penalty area.

With 17 minutes left a mistake by Gerry Ford, who failed to control a Colin Harvey long ball, let in Derek Temple, who raced from just inside the Wednesday half one-on-one with Ron Springett. Temple made no mistake and fired home to complete a remarkable triumph. "I knew the instant I hit it that it was going in. But I wouldn't like to be in that position again at Wembley, unless there was the same outcome." Trebilcock was denied a hat-trick by Springett soon after while Fantham missed a late chance for Wednesday, but that was it, leaving skipper Brian Labone to collect the trophy from Princess Margaret.

(Liverpool Echo)

The Everton fans grouped behind the West goal in great voice and certainly louder than the Wednesday contingent at the other end of the ground. As last year when Liverpool were at Wembley, the Everton fans drowned the community singing with their own chants and applause. They wanted to sing their own songs.

When the M.C. called for the singing of 'When The Saints Come Marching In', the Everton supporters drowned it with a chorus of boos and whistles.

Among the many telegrams of good wishes the Everton team received was one from the players of the last Everton Cup winning side of 1933, at the match as guests of the club.

The attendance was given as the usual 100,000 of course, but the receipts of £109,600 was a record for any match at Wembley.

Everton: West, Wright, Wilson, Gabriel, Labone, Harris, Scott, Trebilcock, Young, Harvey, Temple.

Sheffield Wednesday: Springett, Smith, Megson, Eustace, Ellis, Young, Pugh, Fantham, McCalliog, Ford, Quinn.

A royal blue homecoming

(Liverpool Echo, May 16, 1966)

About 250,000 turned out on the Sunday to welcome home the team. Behind the players' coach in another vehicle rode the club directors and behind that a car containing the club's mascot, Bernard Gamble and Mother Noblett, Miss Shiela Radcliffe. Having left Allerton Station soon after five o'clock, they arrived at St George's Hall two hours later where a crowd of around 20,000 were waiting.

*W*HEN the players came out on to the steps of St George's Hall a few minutes later to hold up the Cup again, Lime Street re-echoed to ear-splitting cheers. The Lord Mayor (Alderman David Cowley) tried to make a speech – but the roar defeated him. The team finally disappeared inside the Hall after spending about 15 minutes on the steps, and the satisfied crowd dispersed very quickly with the same good humour there had been throughout.

Afterwards, Mr Herbert Balmer, Deputy Chief Constable, said: "We had every available policeman on duty in the city centre today. All leave was cancelled. The crowd have behaved extremely well especially as so many Liverpool supporters have turned up owing to a rumour that the

Liverpool team was coming as well. There have been no clashes and I am very pleased at the way everyone has behaved."

Casualties and injuries were well down on last year – 395 with just over 30 sent to hospital. Last year 600 were hurt, 300 sent to hospital.

At the celebration banquet on Saturday evening, the club presented Mr Catterick with a silver tea service and each player and trainer Eggleston with a gold wristlet watch.

Among the principal guests were Mr Denis Howell, the Minister for Sport, the Lord Mayor of Liverpool, Alderman David Cowley, Mr Joe Mears, president of the FA, and Mrs Bessie Braddock. In addition, most of the Liverpool directors were there, headed by president Tom Williams and chairman Sidney Reakes

Mr John Moores replied to the toast of the Everton club, proposed by the Lord Mayor and asked the Everton Cup-winning team of 1933 to stand up and take their applause from the guests.

He also gently gibed at the Lord Mayor, who despite protestations to the contrary, is a fervent Anfield fan. "I'm sure my Lord Mayor would have preferred to see red ribbons on the Cup tonight!"

Charity begins at home

(By Jack Rowe, Liverpool Echo, May 24, 1966)

Local talk turned to the FA Charity Shield – Liverpool were league champions so would be meeting the Blues in August.

*R*ÉPRESENTATIVES of Everton and Liverpool will meet to toss a coin, and on it will depend where the Charity Shield match between the FA Cup winners and the league champions will be played.

Both clubs have been notified by the Football Association that the match has to be played on Saturday, August 13, and according to the FA ruling they must toss for choice of ground. I hope for the sake of 10,000 soccer fanatics in this city that Everton call correctly.

We are lucky to have two fine grounds in this city, but as everyone knows it is Goodison Park which can take the bigger number of spectators with a capacity in the region of 65,000.

Tempers fray in Istanbul
(Liverpool Echo, June 7, 1966)

It's just as well there weren't many successes on the close-season tour.

*F*A Cup winners Everton beat Turkish Cup semi-finalists Fenerbahce 1-0 after scoring from a penalty in the 13th minute. Tempers frayed in the second half of a rowdy game and the referee sent off Everton centre-forward Fred Pickering and Turkish full-back Oazer after a midfield brawl. Hundreds of angry spectators hurled bottles at Pickering as he left the field. Everton manager Harry Catterick said: "The referee was bad, the spectators were worse."

A profitable season
(By Michael Charters, Liverpool Echo, July 21, 1966)

There was more money rolling around the Goodison coffers.

*E*VERTON report a profit of £22,773, compared with £13,331 the previous year. As the financial year ended the week before the club won the FA Cup, the income from that game is not included in accounts. Wages, bonuses and benefits totalled £71,895 (£76,687), while there was no expenditure on incoming players, as against £33,925 in 1965.

World Cup hero Ball signs
(Liverpool Echo, August 16, 1966)

A World Cup winner was on his way to Goodison for a record fee.

*E*VERTON last night signed World Cup hero Alan Ball from

Blackpool for a record £110,000 – but only because they got their bid in first. Everton manager Mr Harry Catterick revealed last night: "Leeds United were vying with us by telephone and, indeed, had equalled our offer, but as ours had been first Blackpool accepted it.

"The important thing is, however, that although Stoke were also in the hunt at the finish, Ball wanted to come to Everton. He will report for training tomorrow and will be in our side on Saturday. I think he will fit in well in our set-up."

Ball said: "I can still scarcely believe it has happened. I was having a cup of coffee in Blackpool when the club sent me a message asking me to return to Bloomfield Road. There were lengthy negotiations and I decided to go to Everton because of the crowd at Goodison Park."

Ball told Mr Catterick that he was delighted to be joining such a great club and was thrilled at the prospect of playing for them, besides having his future settled.

Negotiations for the transfer lasted about two-and-a-half hours. The fee paid by Everton is a record between English clubs. Only Manchester United, who spent £115,000 to bring Denis Law back from Turin, have paid out more for one player.

Ball arrival fuels great expectations
(September 2, 1966)

Ball's signature was a factor in record season-ticket sales.

*S*UCCESS – the winning of the Football Association Cup – and enterprise – the spectacular £110,000 signing of Alan Ball – have combined to give Everton a record financial start to the season. Banked already from the sale of season tickets is the staggering sum of £97,500, easily the highest figures in the club's history.

This means that about 14,000 season tickets have been bought. It is unlikely to go very much higher than that, for the flood of applications has now slowed down to a more manageable trickle. The demand has been not only for seats, but for paddock and ground tickets too.

Secretary Bill Dickinson told me last night: "It is true that because applications were on an unprecedented scale we ran out of both paddock and ground tickets and had to order a reprint.

"We are still waiting for some of these books to be delivered and in the meantime are having to issue tickets for individual matches to members who have paid but still await their tickets.

"The rush has been going on for quite a long time now, ever since we won the cup and then when Alan Ball joined us there was another flood of applications."

Bad news for club mascot

(Liverpool Echo, October 13, 1966)

It was all over though for one Goodison youngster.

*B*ERNARD Gamble, 11-years-old unofficial mascot of Everton Football Club, has received a letter from the club forbidding him to go on the pitch any more.

The reason given to the boy's father is that his presence tends to detract from the effect of the Supporters' Club official mascot, the Toffee Lady, who, decked out in traditional Mother Noblett outfit, distributes toffees to terrace spectators before matches start.

Everton FC secretary, Mr Bill Dickinson, said when asked to confirm that Everton have asked the boy not to appear again: "This arises from a request from the Supporters' Club that the Toffee Lady should be the only mascot.

"It is nothing personal – the boy is a nice lad and could not be better behaved. It is a matter of principle. The board gave the request full consideration before they made their decision."

Bernard's father, Mr Jimmy Gamble, who lives at 27 Strawberry Lane, Norris Green, emphasised that he had no quarrel with Everton.

He said: "My son could not have had kinder treatment from the club or players. They got him tickets for the cup final and could not have done more to help him. The trouble, I think, is jealousy. There have been boy mascots for six years at Everton now and it has taken the Supporters' Club a long time to discover that their presence detracts from the effect of the Toffee Lady.

"My son is very disappointed indeed. Fortunately he was giving the job up at the end of this season, because he's getting too tall to be a mascot. We always kitted him out in Everton colours at our own expense and he always paid to go into the ground.

"I don't suppose anyone has supported the team, home and away, as regularly as Bernard has these past three seasons. He's so upset today I haven't had the heart to send him to school."

Chairman of Everton Supporters' Club, Mr George Bailey, told the Liverpool Echo: "We are the only supporters' club in the country with a girl mascot who is officially recognised. Naturally we guard this distinction carefully.

"It is not a personal vendetta against the boy. After Everton won the cup there was doubt in many people's minds as to who was the official mascot. This has rather brought the matter to a head.

"Our Toffee Lady for the past few seasons, Miss Sheila Radcliffe, has resigned because she now has a boyfriend. The new one is Miss Catherine Dunne."

Spanish frustrate spirited Blues

(By Ian Hargraves, Liverpool Echo, November 24, 1966)

Credit to the referee as Everton bow out of Europe.

*T*HE cast-iron control of a giant German referee, Herr J. Weyland, prevented the second leg of Everton's European Cup-Winners' Cup tie with Real Zaragoza at Goodison last night developing into a shambles like the first leg in Spain.

Fighting back against a two-goal deficit, Everton generated such spirit that it was all the Spaniards could do to hold out for a 2-1 victory on aggregate. Their time-wasting tactics aroused the fury of the 56,077 spectators who paid £22,000 to watch, as well as the home players.

Fortunately Herr Weyland was quick to dampen the numerous potential flash points before they could explode into trouble.

The crowd also behaved reasonably well. One solitary firework was thrown into the Spaniards' goalmouth and the visitors were booed continually, but that was the extent of the trouble.

The Zaragoza trainer, Senor Fernando Daucik, said he was quite satisfied with his side's performance. "We came to eliminate Everton rather than to play brilliant football," he pointed out.

Undersoil heating experiment ends

(By Horace Yates, Liverpool Daily Post, December 22, 1966)

Under-soil heating problems would require a re-think.

EVERTON are to remove their soil-warming apparatus at the end of the season. This statement was made last night by Mr Jack Sharp, chairman of the ground committee, and follows sharply on the postponing of the league game with Sunderland on December 10 and the very heavy state of the ground for the Fulham match last Saturday.

Whether or not this is the end of the experiment, of which Everton were pioneers, is not stated. Mr Sharp told me: "The future of it will be decided later. The experiment has proved a success in every way since we began it four years ago, but we wondered if the few occasions when it was called into service made it more important than combating excessive rainfall. The main body of argument seems to be in favour of guarding against water and chancing our luck with the frost. There have always been difficulties in adequately forking ground in which wires are buried so close to the surface. It is felt a well-drained ground will be of greater advantage to the team."

Derby cup tie hits the big screen

(March 1967)

After overcoming Burnley, fans looked forward to an FA Cup fifth-round derby, with the added attraction that the Goodison game would be televised on a big screen erected across the Park. The screen at Anfield needed to be reinforced due to 40mph winds although, with over 40,000 in attendance, the experiment proved a success.

*H*UGE interest surrounded the FA Cup fifth-round tie between Everton and Liverpool. The first cup derby for 12 years (when the Blues had been humiliated 4-0 at Goodison in 1955) caught the public's imagination. The match was set to be screened on closed-circuit cameras at Anfield.

Plans were made for 30 minutes of pre-match entertainment from Goodison for the benefit of the viewers at Anfield, which would include general pictures of crowd scenes from Goodison and interviews with Harry Catterick and Bill Shankly from their respective dressing rooms. Any first-half goals would then be shown at half-time, while along with two commentators, Tommy Lawton was summarising.

Such was the clamour for tickets that a sell-out was announced at Goodison with another 40,500 capacity attendance for the "TV show" at Anfield.

Any spares?

(Liverpool Echo, March 6, 1967)

The other dominant subject related to the Everton v Liverpool tie of 1967 was the massive demand for tickets. Stories circulated regarding forged tickets for the Lower Bullens Stand. At an early stage it was clear that the remaining tickets for Goodison available for general sale would be nowhere near sufficient to meet demand.

*I*T'S the day of the big queues. The day when thousands have been streaming to Goodison, Anfield and Liverpool Stadium to queue for the 75,000 tickets available for Saturday's Cup-tie and the TV showing at Anfield. Throughout the morning the crowds grew solidly outside Goodison and by mid-afternoon, it was estimated that there were about 20,000.

The queue, four deep, stretched from the entrance gates along Walton Lane, and right onto Church Road, almost a mile away.

At times, some sections of the crowd grew a little restless, and began to surge forward, but police swooped quickly to restore order. "What this will be like by tonight? I hate to imagine," said a police officer.

Because he did not have a ticket, one man, 20-year-old Paul Gray decided to put an advertisement in the Echo offering to exchange his 1957 Ford Consul car for a ticket.

A few hours later, Paul had his ticket and a young Bootle man had the car. Paul, of Coronation Avenue, Formby, who is a car salesman, said: "I don't care what sort of ticket it is as long as it gets me into the ground." The man who exchanged the 5s 6d ticket for the car is 23-year-old Mr. Trevor Roberts of Litherland Road, Bootle, a Liverpool supporter.

Record crowds see Ball nick it

(By Michael Charters, Liverpool Echo, March 13, 1967)

Over 250 police would be on duty for the match and to add further spice to the occasion, Everton had signed Howard Kendall from under the noses of Liverpool on the eve of the tie. Everton held on for the 1-0 win, with the final whistle seeing 'scores of young fans run on to the pitch'. With nearly 65,000 inside Goodison and 40,500 at Anfield, a combined total of 105,000 saw the tie – an FA Cup record. It was Liverpool's first FA Cup defeat away from home since 1959. Match report extracts from Monday's Echo:

*T*HE ground was full half-an-hour before kick-off and there was crushing in the Stanley Park End, where the majority of the Liverpool fans were. Ambulance men had to deal with half-a-dozen casualties, people being pulled out of the densely packed crowd. The inevitable fan ran on to the pitch while the players were taking position before the kick-off and shook hands with Alex Young.

Ball went headlong, but play went on until Young was flattened by Stevenson. West ran 30 yards out of goal to run in among a group of players and push St John.

Milne tried to find Lawrence with a back pass, but Husband was on it like lightning as the ball went past Yeats, and as Lawrence came out Husband and the Liverpool goalkeeper collided, the ball bounced free and Ball, following up quickly, turned it into the net from the narrowest of angles.

No reputations had been made in this match whatsoever, but I suppose you could call it typical, hard cup-tie football with the wind being so troublesome that it must have been very difficult for the players to control the ball well. The crowd deserved much better than this unsatisfactory, untidy game.

The 64,000 dollar question

(By Michael Charters, Liverpool Echo, May 2, 1967)

In a rare interview with the media, Harry Catterick gave his thoughts on the 1966/67 season, the future of the side and his views on one or two players. His thoughts on up-and-coming striker Joe Royle were also revealed.

QUESTION: Everton supporters have been brought up on a long line of great centre-forwards. The 64,000 dollar question: Do you think that Joe Royle can develop into another famous Everton leader now that Fred Pickering's slow recovery from injury has affected his chance of regaining a first-team place?

Answer: I think Joe can, but he has a lot to learn to my mind. The boy wants to learn and he has many attributes, but only time and more experience can tell before anyone can say whether he will ever take over the mantle of the two really great Everton centre-forwards of the past – Dean and Lawton.

Confidence in Catterick

(By Chris James, Liverpool Echo, July 28, 1967)

Was it the "dreaded" vote of confidence for the Everton manager?

ALTHOUGH he has come under fire from a section of the fans for selling wing-half Jimmy Gabriel, Everton manager Harry Catterick was given a hearty vote of confidence by the club's shareholders at last night's annual meeting.

The vote proposed by Mr George Bailey, came after Mr Catterick had given the shareholders prospects for the future.

"Since Mr Catterick took over as manager we have always been in a respectable position," said Mr Bailey.

Mr Catterick had told about 50 shareholders present: "I am quite confident that the policy we have adopted of recruiting schoolboy players and turning them into first class players is the right thing. I personally feel that the side may be a little too young for very big things. It is only the run of the ball that makes the difference between success and failure so small."

There were, he thought, eight teams in the First Division in with a chance of major honours this season, but Everton was one of them. But "lack of experience of the young players may have a detrimental effect at first. But to play them in the first team is the only way to give them that experience."

One shareholder attacked Mr Catterick for not signing a good reserve goalkeeper as a stand-in for West. But Mr John Moores leapt to the manager's defence. "If Mr Catterick had wanted to sign another goalkeeper we would have thought he was mad. We had the best staff of goalkeepers in the whole country."

After Mr Moores and chairman Mr Jack Sharp had been re-elected to the board unopposed, Mr Moores said: "We can only promise you we will do our best. We can't promise you we will win both the cup and the league but we will have a damn good try."

The club's new director, Mr G.A. Watts, appointed upon the death of the chairman, Mr E. Holland Hughes, was introduced to the shareholders. He promised: "Apart from playing centre-forward, I will do all I can to further the interests of Everton." Before the meeting began, a short silence was observed for Mr Holland Hughes.

In his report, Mr Sharp said the loss on the year of £45,000 was "entirely due to the expenditure of £178,250 on the acquisition of new players during the year, and, in the opinion of the board, should prove to be a sound investment for the future of the team."

Travelling fans go Dutch

(By Ian Hargraves, Liverpool Echo, August 1, 1967)

A new innovation – supporters travelling to continental Europe for pre-season.

*F*IFTY Everton supporters are flying to Holland next Wednesday to see their team's friendly match against Ajax.

The Liverpool firm P. and M. Travel have chartered a B.A.C. 1-11 jet, which will take the party to Amsterdam on Wednesday morning and bring them back the following afternoon.

"Interest has been remarkable, considering so many people are away on holiday," Mr H Langley, one of P. and M.'s directors, told me. "Perhaps the fact that Ajax beat Liverpool so convincingly in the European Cup last year has had something to do with it."

Seven more years for the boss

(By Michael Charters, Liverpool Echo, October 10, 1967)

The Everton manager committed his long-term future to the club, being made one of the highest paid managers in the country in the process.

*E*VERTON manager, Harry Catterick, has been offered, and has accepted, a new seven-year contract by the club which makes him one of the three highest-paid managers in the country.

This is the first time the Everton club have ever offered a contract of such length to any manager and indicates, as chairman Mr Jack Sharp told me today, their complete confidence in Mr Catterick's handling of playing affairs. Mr Sharp said: "I have great pleasure in announcing that the Board of Directors have offered a seven-year contract on more advantageous terms than the existing one to Mr Catterick and he has accepted.

"This is a practical expression of the Board's complete confidence in Mr Catterick, based on the facts that, since he took over as manager, the club has won the First Division championship in 1963 and the FA Cup in 1966, and this year he has produced a team which is largely composed of young players of whom we expect to gain honours in the near future."

In the past few months, Mr Catterick has been the target of some criticism based on his hectic transfer activity. He has transferred Fred Pickering, Jimmy Gabriel, Derek Temple and Alex Scott in that time as part of his team-building plans, while paying about £120,000 for the incoming Howard Kendall from Preston and Ernie Hunt from Wolves.

The battle of St James's Park

(Football Echo, October 30, 1967)

A 1-0 defeat at St James's Park saw two men sent off including Gordon West – with Sandy Brown having to take over between the sticks. The game would also have an impact on several other members of the Everton squad's international plans.

TOMMY Wright, one of nine Everton players injured during Saturday's soccer brawl at Newcastle, will miss an international cap as a result.

Everton manager Harry Catterick said yesterday that Wright, who received a bad ankle knock, will be unfit to play for England's Under-23 team against Wales at Swansea on Wednesday.

Wing-half Colin Harvey, who was on reserve for England, will be unable to travel, and Howard Kendall and John Hurst – also in the England squad – will have to receive treatment. The manager added that other casualties were Morrissey, who left the field after 40 minutes; Wilson, Ball, Hunt and Young.

But Mr Catterick refused to comment on the sending off of goalkeeper Gordon West, as did Everton chairman Jack Sharp.

Newcastle full-back Burton was also sent off in a rough game which Everton lost by a twice-taken penalty in the closing minutes.

Ball, Harvey and Kendall by the seaside
(January 27, 1968)

The attraction of Everton's three midfield stars had fans queuing up at Southport.

*T*HE rise to prominence of the "Holy Trinity" coincided with an FA Cup fourth-round tie at local rivals Southport (managed by former Blues favourite and future manager Billy Bingham).

A crowd of 18,795 packed into Haig Avenue, yielding gate receipts of £6,175 – a Southport record, although Liverpool Echo reporter Michael Charters would later question the decision of their directors not to switch the game to Goodison. Their share would be less than £2,000 – while they could have earned four times that amount at Everton. It was left to Joe Royle to head a glorious winner against the Third Division side 11 minutes from time.

Computer says 9-0
(March 9, 1968)

*A*BIZARRE prediction prior to Everton's fifth-round tie against another local side in Tranmere Rovers claimed that Tranmere would win 9-0. The computer, programmed by Rovers chairman Chris

Hodgson, had taken into account results from Tranmere v Coventry (2-0), West Brom v Coventry (0-1), West Brom v Southampton (3-2), Southampton v Everton (3-2) and Coventry v Everton (1-3). Other results were 4-0 and 3-0 wins for Tranmere, while just programming the results of either side's wins over Coventry yielded a narrow Rovers win.

Nearly 62,000 crammed into Goodison, although it proved a disappointing one-sided affair with only Tranmere goalkeeper (and Lancashire pace bowler) Jim Cumbes preventing a rout, being cheered for his efforts at the break and at full time by the home support.

Royle maintained his goal-a-game record in the cup while Johnny Morrissey also netted in the first half as Third Division Tranmere failed to test Gordon West throughout.

Incidentally, it turned out that an Everton fan came nearest to predicting a correct result – 3-0 was his forecast, having dreamt the scoreline.

The Golden Vision

(By Ken Irwin, Daily Mirror, April, 1968)

A BBC play, The Golden Vision, was due to be screened for the first time that evening at the mysterious hour of "9.5" – or 9.05 in modern parlance.

NEWSCASTER Gordon Honeycombe will be in a hurry to finish his shift at the ITN studios tonight. He will read the news at 5.55 – and three hours later he will be at home tuning in to the rival channel.

For Gordon is having his first TV play produced by the BBC.

He is co-author, with actor/writer Neville Smith, of the Wednesday Play "The Golden Vision" (BBC1 9.5). It is not so much a play, more a documentary.

And it promises to be a most unusual piece, for it centres around the lives of Everton Football Club players and a handful of the team's fans.

The play, produced by Tony Garnett and directed by Kenneth Loach, was filmed entirely on location.

Loach let his cameras run and left it to the footballers and fans to provide a lot of the action. The play shows the fantastic gulf which exists between the fans and the players they idolise.

Says Gordon Honeycombe: "We wanted to show how the fanatical worship of sports heroes really exists. The fans live in a dream world. They never even get to within touching distance of the heroes they adore."

And in the play the fans admit to being crazy about Everton.

There is John Coyne and his two sons, Vincent and Johnny.

There is Joe Harrigan, and a 70-year-old known as Mr Hagan, who has stood on the same spot on the terraces for 50 years.

Everton stars, including captain Brian Labone, goalkeeper Gordon West and forwards Alan Ball and Alex Young were filmed at training, relaxing at home and in action.

The BBC must be extremely pleased that it singled out Everton for they are still in the running to win the FA Cup.

Wembley again as Leeds dumped out

(By Michael Charters, Liverpool Echo, April 29, 1968)

After a quarter-final success over Leicester City, Leeds United stood in the Blues' way of a return to Wembley. It was Everton who edged through, Johnny Morrissey's 42nd-minute penalty proving enough. Liverpool Echo reporter Michael Charters noted that "there wasn't a weakness in the Everton side, but outstanding performances had come from Labone, Harvey and Kendall." Incidentally, it was Leeds' 61st game of the season (including League and Cups), while the £51,000 gate receipts were a record for any game in England outside Wembley.

*E*VERTON'S victory will have caused considerable pleasure throughout professional football. Whether they know it or not, Leeds have few admirers among the people who control and play the game and Everton had the support of many more than their own fervent fans. Their win, to face Albion in what should be a classic Wembley final, was what most professionals were hoping to see and many of them told Everton officials they wanted it before and after the game.

Harry Catterick said: "I am delighted that we have got through. I thought that Leeds looked a tired side, but I feel that we did very well when one considers the tremendous blow of being robbed of Alan Ball, Sandy Brown and John Hurst. I regard Hurst as the king pin of our defence. The greatest win in my years of management."

Plans for a giant new stand

(By Horace Yates, Liverpool Echo, May 9, 1968)

Big thinking at the club would see Goodison Park transformed.

*E*VERTON plan to erect a gigantic new cantilever stand to replace the existing building on the Goodison Road side of the ground, and the plan envisaged may follow the lines of the stand Manchester United have built at Old Trafford, an enterprise which would cost around £500,000.

It was while discussing the inability of the club to accept any new applications for stand season tickets next season that Mr G.A. Watts, a club director, told me of the enterprise that could convert Goodison Park into the finest ground in the country.

"We don't know at this moment when we may be able to go ahead with the scheme," he said. "The new stand would provide additional seats and there would be complete cover of that side of the ground. We also aim to cover all the other standing areas eventually."

The Goodison Road stand has 3,189 seats, but only about 3,000 of these can be allocated to season- ticket holders, because of provision that has to be made to visiting clubs in cup ties.

In all 18,000 spectators can be seated at Goodison Park at present.

Mr Watts added: "The main purposes are to increase the seating capacity and to make the ground more comfortable for spectators. More and more they are demanding to see the matches in comfort, and quite rightly so."

Admission prices on the up

(By Michael Charters, Liverpool Echo, May 10, 1968)

There was no escaping price increases for supporters.

$\mathcal{E}$VERTON FC are to increase prices all round for next season, in line with the general trend in the Football League.

Admission to the ground will cost 5s (4s this season), the paddock 6s 6d (5s), stand cash prices 8s (6s 6d) and the boys pen goes up from 1s to 2s. All season tickets will cost more. For the ground, the price will be £5 5s from £4 5s, and the paddock £6 16s 6d from £5 5s. Increases in stand tickets will be: £8 goes up to £9 10s, £8 10s to £10, £9 to £11, £10 to £12.

Fortune forsakes Everton

(By Chris James, Liverpool Echo, May, 1968)

A second FA Cup wasn't to be in this decade. FA Cup final woe was hard to take, as lady luck decreed West Brom to prevail 1-0 – only a couple of months after Everton had beaten the Baggies 6-2 at The Hawthorns.

$\mathcal{E}$VERTON'S gold shirts lay in a crumpled heap in their Wembley dressing room on Saturday, sadly tarnished by a cruel trick of fate as can ever have struck a team in a cup final.

Everton, although never being allowed to reach top form by a rugged West Bromwich Albion side, had done enough to be worthy winners. But luck, that abstract thing upon which so much often depends, forsook them in their hour of need.

As a showpiece to demonstrate through television to people across the Atlantic, in Europe and the millions in Britain all that was best with English football, it failed miserably.

It was billed as a football feast between two teams who on form can be the most scintillating in the country. Even before half-time, the

100,000 packed into the bowl were being forced to chant, "We want football" – the thing they came for, but were denied for long spells.

It was Albion's tactics at the outset that prevented the play reaching the pinnacles of brilliance. Albion decided to put Everton out of their stride with ruthless, and sometimes crude tackling that in the final count saw them conceding 32 of the 49 fouls that littered the game.

Towards the middle of the second half, Everton surging forward, with the flame-coloured hair of Alan Ball at the burning heart of every move, looked certain to take the cup back to Goodison Park for the second time in three years.

But in the space of 21 minutes, Jimmy Husband, and how sorry I felt for him, missed three chances that often he would have gobbled to complete a hat-trick.

It was Ball who earned the Everton honours and most people felt his disappointment and frustration with him as he walked dejectedly round the stadium afterwards. Here was Ball, with most of the game's honours showered on him already, missing a winners' medal which he utterly deserved.

My feelings, too, went out to Howard Kendall as, at 21, he collected his second runners-up medal. He played his heart out. Colin Harvey too showed many of the touches that rank him as a player with the football world at his feet.

Fairs Cup door bangs shut

(By Michael Charters, Liverpool Echo, July 6, 1968)

A one club, one city rule had been restricting Everton's opportunity for European experience in the Inter-Cities Fairs Cup

*E*VERTON'S hopes of joining Liverpool in the Inter-Cities Fairs Cup next season have ended with a shock decision by the Cup committee which is doubly disappointing after they had been named as first reserve club if any of the original entries dropped out.

At the annual meeting of the Fairs Cup clubs in Copenhagen recently, the committee chairman, Sir Stanley Rous, gave Everton an assurance in an open meeting that they would be first reserve.

It was expected that the Swedish club Malmo would withdraw because they have also qualified for the European Cup. Yesterday Malmo informed the Fairs Cup secretary Petre Joris, in Basle, that they were concentrating on the European Cup, thus apparently leaving the way open for Everton to be nominated for the Fairs Cup.

However, Mr Joris said last night: "The Brussels team, Daring FC, go in as a straight swop for Malmo. Everton will be considered if there are further withdrawals, but that is now most unlikely."

Everton chairman Jack Sharp, who had represented his club at the Fairs Cup meeting in Copenhagen, spent several hours contacting Sir Stanley Rous and Mr Joris for clarification of the position and a possible explanation of the change of mind by the Fairs Cup committee.

Mr Sharp told me today: "I am very disappointed that Daring have been named as substitute for Malmo, who have withdrawn, as we anticipated being the team who would take their place. I have spoken to Sir Stanley Rous and we have no alternative but to accept the committee's decision."

Mr Sharp did not wish to make further comment but it is clear that he has been puzzled by the decision in the same way as other club representatives who were at the Copenhagen meeting.

Had Everton been accepted, it would have been the first time that two teams from the same city had taken part in the competition.

It is this rule which came under criticism at the annual meeting of the Fairs Cup because it bars a team like Everton and yet opens the competition door for Newcastle United, who finished 10th in the First Division, compared to Everton's fifth place.

It seems obvious to me that the assurance by Sir Stanley Rous that Everton would be first reserve caused some resentment among other members of the Cup committee.

England already have four representatives – Liverpool, Leeds United, Chelsea and Newcastle. If Everton had become the fifth, representatives of other European countries would have been annoyed at the high proportion of English clubs while they had been limited to one entry in some cases.

But it would have been preferable if this reasoning had been made known at the Copenhagen meeting rather than bar Everton at the last minute, so to speak, when they had been given every justification for believing that they would be playing in the competition again.

It is likely that the rule preventing two clubs from one city competing will be amended next year when the Fairs Cup organisation will come under the jurisdiction of the European Union of Football Associations.

But that is 12 months too late for Everton as they now find the Fairs Cup door banged firmly in their face.

Moores: I'll walk away

(By Ian Hargraves, Liverpool Echo, August 9, 1968)

A stormy club AGM made news ahead of the 1968/69 season.

*T*HERE were pre-season fireworks at Everton's annual general meeting last night, when former chairman Mr John Moores offered to resign from the board after complaints by a minority group of shareholders that the club was in danger of becoming a closed shop.

The controversy stemmed from the resignation of two directors, Mr Fred Micklesfield and Mr Jack Taylor, and the nomination by the board of two new figures, Mr John Hacking and Mr Will Scott, to succeed them.

Mr Jack White, a former Bootle Cricket Club captain and long-time Everton supporter, complained that the first shareholders knew of the directors' resignations was when they read about them in the annual report. It was then too late for nominations to the board to be accepted.

"I am worried that this club is getting mixed up too closely with Littlewoods," he said. "After all it is a sports organisation. Who are these two nominees – I've never heard of them. I ask you, Mr Chairman, can you assure us that they are not also connected with Littlewoods?"

Mr Jack Sharp, the chairman, replied: "They have no connection with Littlewoods at all so far as I am concerned."

The two candidates identified themselves and received a sympathetic reception. Mr Hacking, who said he felt deeply embarrassed, is managing director of Sun Valley Nut Products of Birkenhead, and a keen sportsman who has driven racing cars and flies his own aeroplane.

Mr Scott, chairman and managing director of Scott's Bakeries, has followed Everton since before the war and has actually trained at Goodison while a member of the Liverpool Ramblers' amateur football club.

Mr Moores said that the board had not known about the resignations until comparatively late in the day and he pointed out that in any case the shareholders' association had the opportunity to make nominations if they wished to do so.

"Mr [G. A.) Watts [another director] and I will resign here and now if that is the will of the shareholders."

Last year Everton made a profit of £25,541 compared with a loss of £44,952, mainly due to a gain on transfer fees of £78,250.

The business of football
(By Michael Charters, Liverpool Echo, February 3, 1969)

The club decided to expand their off-field operations.

*E*VERTON today announced the expected appointment of a promotions manager – the first time the club has had one in its history.

He will be purely concerned with the commercial side of the club's affairs and one of his principal jobs will be to design and edit a new style match programme. He is 31-year-old David Exall, now commercial manager at Birmingham City. He will take up his job at Goodison Park on April 1.

New coach signs in

(By Harold Wolfe, Liverpool Echo, July 28, 1969)

A new coaching appointment brought an FA Cup winner to the club. Stuart Imlach's son, sports presenter Gary, would later document his father's career on and off the field in the award-winning My Father And Other Working Class Football Heroes.

*S*TUART Imlach, former Scottish international winger and Notts County coach, was today appointed to Everton's coaching staff and will take charge of the youth team.

A native of Lossiemouth, Imlach began his career in English football with Bury, and subsequently had a spell with Derby County before signing for Nottingham Forest in the 1955 close season.

While with Forest he won a place in Scotland's team in the finals of the 1958 World Cup in Sweden, and also gained a Cup-winner's medal the following year.

Transferred to Luton in 1960, he had only a short spell at Kenilworth Road before joining Coventry City, and later Crystal Palace, with whom he ended his career as a player.

Too many games on TV

(By Michael Charters, Liverpool Echo, February 4, 1970)

What price a club, in the 21st century, trying to ban TV cameras from Goodison?

*B*ECAUSE they feel that too many of their games have been televised this season, Everton have banned the scheduled televising of their next home game, against Arsenal, on February 14.

Everton chairman Mr Jack Sharp told me today: "A report that we have banned the TV cameras indefinitely from Goodison Park is not true.

"We were in the Football League programme for the Arsenal match to be recorded. The board considered it, but as we feel we have been over-exposed to television this season, we turned it down and wrote to the League to tell them.

"We feel we have had too much of it and think other clubs should get a chance. Our decision has nothing to do with tactical moves being exposed on the screens. This is no crusade against TV. We are not against TV recordings of matches.

"If we were asked later in the season by the League for one of our home matches to be televised, it would be considered by the directors. Of course, we have no control over our away fixtures being televised."

In the agreement which the League has made with the television companies, the home club has the final word. The League arrange a programme of matches to be screened a month in advance.

Everton games have appeared on TV screens in 15 out of 25 weekends so far this season, on either the BBC or ITV channels.

A spokesman at League headquarters said today: "We will do our best to meet Everton's request. We view it with sympathy."

Defending the new stand experience

(Liverpool Echo, February 14, 1970)

A letter to the paper. Subject: the new stand experience fails to please.

*A*FTER spending the coldest two hours of my life in the new stand at Everton when they played Wolves, I was astounded to read in the Liverpool Echo that night that "external work on the first section of the new stand is now completed".

If this is the case, we season-ticket holders are in for a miserable time, no matter how well or badly the team performs. The lack of a side panel acting as a wind-break at the church end of the new stand meant that a force 10 gale swept the seats. Is there ever going to be a side panel, or must we all buy fur coats?

Those of us, incidentally, who tried to get a cup of tea during the interval, found after queueing for 15 minutes that the supply of cups was exhausted and the only drink available appeared to be orangeade (iced). The hot meat pies also ran out and all there was to eat was a packet of crisps. So much for the modern catering facilities!

Other faults in the new stand seemed to be:

a) Only two turnstiles – and they must be the narrowest in the country – meant excessive queueing to get in.

b) Inadequate toilet facilities meant a long, long wait at half-time.

c) The much-vaunted "perfect view for everyone" just does not obtain – the thick pillars see to that.

The club took the issues on board. And here is their answer:

*W*HEN the stand is completed next season, the church end will be weather-proofed. The directors are considering now three schemes about how far they can build over Goodison Place.

Catering arrangements are temporary. They will be greatly improved.

The weather at that game was the coldest for six years. Thirty per cent more tea was sold than ever before in the catering manager's experience. At only two of the 20 catering points did the supply of tea, meat pies, etc, run out.

There are four turnstiles – two at each of two entrances. They are the same size as other stiles on the ground or any other ground.

Toilet facilities already conform to local authority requirements. When the stand is finished, they will far exceed bye-law demands.

When the stand is completed, there will be four pillars. Two at each end will not interfere with the view of the pitch. The other two will be equally spaced along the front and are essential because the stand is double-tiered. The present pillar has extra bracing but this will be taken off eventually.

If Everton had had the space to move the stand back, with one deep tier, there would have been no need for pillars – as at Hillsborough. But pillars are essential to support the top level and roof. When the stand is finished, it will compare with any in the country.

VIP treatment

(By Horace Yates, Liverpool Echo, February 27, 1970)

A new opportunity for fans, the 300 and 500 clubs set to open for business.

*E*VERTON shareholders and £12 season-ticket holders are being advised of a club plan to provide them with first-class seats and deluxe social amenities in the new Goodison stand.

The idea is to introduce exclusive "300" and "500" clubs, whose main activities will be on match days. As their names imply the clubs will be limited to that number of members, and of the two the "300" members will enjoy the more luxurious accommodation.

For that they will pay an entrance fee of £20 (payable once only). Seats, with amenities, will cost £40 a season, but will be available for all home games, including cup ties and European matches.

Tea will be provided at half-time without extra charge, and a complimentary programme will be available. Colour television will be installed and a service of half-time and full-time scores laid on.

On the crest of a wave

(By Michael Charters, Liverpool Echo, March 21, 1970)

All well on and off the park.

*E*VERTON must be just about the wealthiest club in England which was, he [Everton Shareholders' Association chairman Donald McPhail) said, "The result of planning and hard work by the directors."

I reckon Everton's financial resources are in the healthiest state in the history of the club. Only Glasgow Rangers, who, I understand, have about £1,000,000 invested – have more cash behind them, among British clubs. Apart from the money which pours in through the turnstiles, with average gates nearing 50,000, I estimate Everton make a profit of more than £100,000 a year from fundraising schemes.

Naturally, the club will not disclose figures, but Mr David Exall, the promotions manager, tells me: "I have been astounded at the response of supporters to our ticket schemes. We have not had to hard-sell. The supporters have responded as agents and ticket buyers."

The masters kick off new decade in style

(By Horace Yates, Liverpool Daily Post, April 2, 1970)

The most convincing of Everton's seven titles up to this point, secured with victory over West Brom at a packed Goodison. The success, at the start of the new decade, appeared to put the team in pole position to dominate for years to come.

*E*VERTON are champions – and have the League trophy on their sideboard to prove it. Secret arrangements had been made for Mr L Edwards, of Manchester United and a member of the Management Committee to present the trophy in the event of West Brom being beaten at Goodison Park last night.

Nothing could have been better stage managed for here was the last home game of the season with a capacity crowd exulting over their team's success.

Throughout the last few minutes the crowd chanted their favourite songs and slogans, but at first obeyed the club appeal to keep off the pitch at the end while the players made a victory lap of honour.

Rarely, if ever, have such wild scenes of enthusiasm been witnessed anywhere. This was the moment all the supporters had waited for and who could blame them for celebrating in the grand manner.

Once again the hero of the night was Everton's youngest player, 18-year-old Alan Whittle, for he it was who scored the vital first goal in 19 minutes that sent Everton coasting to victory.

Colin Harvey made certain with a spectacular second in 65 minutes. The game finished to a chorus of song, "We shall not be moved" and the players jumped in the air with arms raised above their heads, congratulating and back-slapping each other.

Manager Harry Catterick was first on the pitch to hug his players and the crowd roared their approval as the manager lifted Whittle and Ball into the air.

This normally undemonstrative manager was clearly elated at this high water mark to his career and it was fitting that last night it should be announced that he had been voted Manager of the Month.

Whittle's goal began with Kendall dropping a high ball into the middle. Harvey tried a first-time shot which cannoned across to Whittle. The youngster brought it down, killed it with consummate skill and with great deliberation hit the ball towards the goal.

It struck a defender in flight, but finished where all the home fans wanted to see it — in the back of the net.

What a fantastic impact this slightly-built blond teenager has made on the Everton side. He was scoring for the sixth successive game and it was his 11th goal in 14 games.

Before his goal he had looked ordinary in the routine role of winger but whenever he moved into the middle he became a stick of dynamite.

The roar that greeted the goal threatened to tear Goodison Park apart for everyone felt then that this was the final nail to clinch the championship. With two games still to play Everton are out on their own. They are nine points ahead of Leeds, who have only four league games to play.

As Brian Labone, the club captain, joined the players for the lap of honour a terrific ovation was directed to him.

As the players made their way round the pitch all the good intentions disappeared and some of the crowd invaded the field.

How well Everton have lived down the taunt of "Merseyside Millionaires" that used to be hurled at them in the days when they were buying to build, but last night's team cost a mere £275,000 with £110,000 of that for Alan Ball.

This was a night for Everton celebration. Everybody let themselves go in an extravaganza of cheering, waving and singing. It was a night few of them will forget.

West Brom forced Everton to take the title the hard way, for they conceded not an inch willingly, tackled as though they themselves were defending honours and could not have yielded ground more grudgingly.

Only rarely did Albion threaten danger, for the attack was monopolised by Everton.

Although it always looked as if one goal would be enough, it was still just a shade precarious so that when Harvey thrashed home a superb solo goal in 65 minutes, it set up a succession of exultant chants that persisted for the rest of the match.

What a goal it was by Harvey. First he moved towards goal, changed his mind and veered out as though to bring Morrissey into play.

Seeing Morrissey was covered he doubled back to the edge of the penalty area and while on the run sent a crashing drive soaring into the net with Osborne leaping spectacularly, but vainly across goal.

Prior to this Whittle had almost scored with an overhead shot and then Royle hit a post. Hurst almost made it three when he headed Ball's cross against a post. Everton put on a fine show that will carry their fans through hopefully to next season. I think they realise what a lucky lot they are for no crowd in the country has been treated to more skilful or exciting play.

In a great side I thought Kendall looked a supreme artist but for that matter so did Harvey and Ball. With the three in this mood Everton could hardly fail to serve up model football. Morrissey's wing raiding was as powerful as ever and although Royle had to struggle for his achievements against Robertson, Albion could never afford to take any chances with him. Hurst was the defensive kingpin with an adventurous eye for opportunity.

Kenyon indeed will be difficult to move from this side. He improves with every match and is already a model of composure with a bite in every tackle. Wright and Brown were rarely in trouble so it was not at all surprising that West had another trouble-free night.

West Brom were up against the masters – and the difference showed as Everton stroked and caressed the ball to their bidding.

Everton: West, Wright, Brown, Kendall, Kenyon, Harvey, Whittle, Ball, Royle, Hurst, Morrissey
Sub: Darcy.
West Brom: Osborne, Hughes, Wilson, Fraser, Robertson, Merrick, Cantello, Suggett, Astle,
Brown, Hope. Sub: Hartford.
Referee: Mr. L. Callaghan (Merthyr Tydfil).
Attendance: 58,523.

And there's more to come, says Harry

(Liverpool Daily Post, April 2, 1970)

"*T*HEY have a long way to go before they reach their peak."
This was the statement made by a delighted Everton manager Harry
Catterick as he toasted his team's League Championship triumph.

"I have been too long in football to make predictions about results,
but if you have good players playing good football the results will come.

"I am just coming up to the end of nine years as manager of Everton,
and in that time we have won two Championships and the FA Cup.
There must be room for a lot of satisfaction in that.

"It is a mistake to think of the European Cup as the ultimate. Sides
have won the European Cup that could not have won the English First
Division – and I don't mean British sides. To have to play 42 matches
in a season in all kinds of weather must make terrific demands.

"Remember, Everton have not been out of the top six for seven years.
Many of these boys in tonight's team I took straight from school, lads
like Wright, Hurst, Whittle, Kenyon, Royle, Harvey and Husband.

"Whittle has had a phenomenal run. I said three years ago that he
would be the toast of Goodison. We wanted to win this Championship
on merit and I feel we have done that. We were not interested in
anything Leeds did.

"We have achieved our results with a freer expression of the game as
opposed to method football. We don't play any assassin stuff. We don't
have players nobbling key players."

Club chairman Jack Sharp said: "I am tremendously happy and
proud at our achievement. I feel that as directors we are very much
back-room boys. All the honour and glory go to the manager and his

players. At the same time we feel we fulfil a necessary function and we are happy to play our part.

"Injuries to players were the only reason we slipped. Once we got the lads together again we won seven matches off the reel."

Skipper Brian Labone, still not match-fit, said: "It has been a thrilling struggle. We first won the Championship, lost it and won it again. We have had to withstand a lot of criticism, but it has all worked out well.

"Now people are saying Leeds have presented the Championship to us. That is wrong. We have won 28 games. They simply had the good sense to realise they could not cope with the League Cup and European Cup."

This was also the theme developed by Alan Ball, the acting skipper. "We were three points clear of Leeds before they started sticking their reserves in," he said.

"I believe that as well as being champions we are the finest team in the country. I can see five great seasons ahead. This team is certain to go better. We have lots of skill and every player works hard for each other. With that behind us how can we fail?"

Trainer Wilf Dixon's view was: "There are still one or two things to sort out. I feel they are going to be a great side."

Gordon West said: "This match was worse than a cup final. The pressure has been pretty hectic over the last few games, but tonight was unbearable. It was worse than any cup final because we realised we had to win because the Championship rested on it, and because we knew all our supporters were convinced we could do it. We simply couldn't let them down.

"It seems hard to realise it, but at last we can relax. I missed the last few games of the 1963 Championship season with a dislocated shoulder, and it was disappointing to miss the final game. Perhaps that's why I felt so sorry for Labby tonight."

Last night's attendance of 58,523 was the biggest of the season and hoisted the aggregate to 1,045,565.

Incredible scenes as the trophy is lifted

(By Peter O'Sullivan, Daily Mirror, April 2, 1970)

*E*VERTON are the Football League champions of 1970.

They clinched the title last night with a 2-0 victory over West Bromwich Albion – and sent the 58,523 Goodison Park crowd – biggest of the season – wild with delight.

There were incredible scenes as the league trophy – brought from Leeds in anticipation of an Everton win – was presented.

Thousands of fans flooded the pitch, ignoring loudspeaker appeals to keep off, and roared their approval as acting skipper Alan Ball received the trophy from Mr Louis Edwards, chairman of Manchester United FC and a member of the league management committee. Then, as the team went to the dressing room, the exultant fans began a dance of triumph along the length of the pitch.

The congratulations flooded in for Mr Catterick and his team and among them was a telegram from Don Revie, the Leeds United manager who last night saw another trophy slipping from his team's grasp. "Heartiest congratulations. You are true champions" said the telegram.

Mr Revie took time off to offer his congratulations to Everton immediately after his own side had been beaten 1-0 by Celtic in the European Cup semi-final, first leg, at Elland Road.

He added: "Everton came at just the right time. They have had some fine wins recently and these have enabled them to clinch the title. I say, 'Well done, Everton'."

Sporting Evertonians praised

(By Michael Charters, Liverpool Echo, May 29, 1970)

*E*VERTON fans have been highly commended for their sporting behaviour last season, as part of the John White awards scheme, run in conjunction with the Football League.

Back to Europe

(By Jack Rowe, Liverpool Echo, July 7, 1970)

The dawn of the new season meant Everton would also learn who their European Cup opponents would be. Would they be given more luck than being drawn against the Italian champions first up this time?

*E*VERTON'S first venture into European football for nearly four years takes further shape when the draw for the first round of the European Cup is made in Geneva. They go into the hat, as champions of England, with 31 other clubs from the European Continent ranging from Keflavik of Reykjavik in Iceland to Floriana in Malta.

Manager Harry Catterick is not travelling for the draw and he said: "We shall know soon enough and then we shall get down to the job of learning all we can about the club we have to meet first. European football is a tough baby – all clubs have got to be good to get through."

The European Football Union are also expected to announce rule changes that will substitute a penalty shot contest for the old method of tossing a coin to settle drawn matches. Under the current system, which usually works for the vast majority of the two-leg ties, away goals count double during the normal 90-minute period.

Ice-breaker

(By Stan Liversedge, Liverpool Echo, July 8, 1970)

A tie against the champions of Iceland would surely provide an easier test – they were already "virtually through", according to the Echo reporter.

*B*ARRING accidents, Everton are virtually through to the second round of the European Cup. They drew unknown and unfancied Keflavik of Iceland, whom they play at Goodison on September 16 and away on September 30. At the end of 90 minutes at Goodison, Everton should have piled up a big-enough lead against the no-hopers from Iceland to make the second leg a formality.

Everton were one of only four teams seeded. The others were Italian champions Cagliari, Spartak Moscow and West Germany's Borussia Munchen Gladbach (sic).

Appeal for stars' missing boots

(Liverpool Echo, July 25, 1970)

Blame it on the boot boys?

*F*OUR pairs of boots have gone missing from Goodison – and Everton want to get them back – quickly. Police are investigating the disappearance, but it's not so much the cash value that concerns Everton, as the fact that the boots are worn in matches by players.

Gone from the dressing room are the boots worn in Mexico by right-back Tommy Wright. And the other three pairs belong to skipper Brian Labone, Gary Jones and Alec Clarke.

Everton secretary Bill Dickinson said: "These boots have all been broken in by the players – and it could cause trouble for the lads if they have to start breaking in new boots, with the season so close at hand."

Return of The Greatest

(Liverpool Echo, August 1, 1970)

Dixie's thoughts on the class of 1970.

*W*HILE the players chatted and laughed at a special reception before dinner, and talked about the coming season, for one man the occasion meant only memories. And that man was perhaps the greatest idol Goodison Park will ever know, Bill "Dixie" Dean.

At the reception, apart from a few words with his modern-day counterpart Joe Royle, "Dixie" stood in a corner away from today's team – and chatted with an old friend. He said: "The game isn't what it used to be – it's all big business now. I think this present team is good. They will be among the honours again because they are better than they were last season."

Another piece of silverware

(By Michael Charters, Liverpool Echo, August 10, 1970)

*T*HE message was loud and clear – Everton are better than ever. As new captain Alan Ball walked off the Stamford Bridge pitch on Saturday to receive the FA Charity Shield, I thought: "He'll have to get used to this; it won't be the only trophy he'll be collecting this season."

Everton's all-round display beating Chelsea 2-1 to win the Shield for the fourth time in the club's history was highly impressive.

It stemmed from two factors. They showed the defensive stability to contain a top-class team like Chelsea, the resilience to absorb persistent attacks, and then the talent to switch into attacking gear themselves with an attractive flair of a very high order indeed.

Manager Harry Catterick was delighted. His pre-match comments that it was just part of his training programme, that the result did not really matter, were genuine. He was putting this annual fixture into perspective. But his pleasure at winning the trophy was equally sincere. It put him in great heart for the real business which starts on Saturday.

As he ordered champagne for his boys on the rail trip home, he told me: "What pleased me most was the way we won, the attractive football we showed.

"Whether we win anything or not this season, this team is going to please fans everywhere with the quality of their play."

The turning point came with a glorious goal from Whittle seven minutes before the interval. Taking a pass from Ball, he cut inside the bearded Webb and unleashed a right-foot shot from 18 yards for a goal which will be difficult to better all season.

Whittle has established his growing scoring reputation by his sharpness in snapping up half-chances. This one he made all himself and finished with a power of a shot which rivalled a Charlton special.

From then on, it was Everton who stamped their class and talent on this lovely pitch. Ball, Kendall and Harvey, the trio who master-mind the whole set-up, took over midfield and cut Chelsea to ribbons in the second half. Kendall nodded a beauty from a centre of inch-perfect placing by Royle, and although Hutchinson scored a late Chelsea goal – the only time West could be faulted – the glory and the Shield belonged to Everton.

Skipper Ball, an inspiring personality, said it all with: "The boys were great."

Mystery of the struggling champions

(By Horace Yates, Liverpool Daily Post, September 4, 1970)

Despite the early season plaudits for the team, the title defence faltered – and it was only the first week in September. A World Cup hangover for Everton's England contingent perhaps?

*E*VERTON, third from bottom of the First Division without a win, are the biggest soccer conundrum of all time. It is the sort of mystery story from which even an Edgar Wallace would recoil from writing, because it is a tale without a solution.

Manager Harry Catterick honestly confesses himself nonplussed at the blight that has descended over his team and so, because it is the outsider who sometimes sees most of the game, I turned to Manchester and Joe Mercer last night for his views.

Even the City manager, who knows most of the answers, scratched his head in puzzlement. "I thought they played very well against Leeds United," he said. "In the first half against Manchester United they were great. Against us, in the second half they did a bit.

"This is just one of those things. You can never tell from match to match. I wouldn't bury them by any means. The only thing is if the run goes on much longer the Championship is going to be up the wall, but surely they can't be as bad as their results suggest.

"Ask anybody what is wrong with Everton and he just wouldn't know, any more than I or anybody else. Look what they did last season with the same players. It was fantastic. Anybody who says he can put his finger on the trouble is just kidding you.

"All of a sudden they will start winning again and the mystery will be over without anybody knowing why. Even their worst enemy would not call them a bad side.

"If I could offer a constructive criticism in an effort to be helpful I would say they are getting a bit anxious and perhaps a bit panicky at times when they make a slip. They have a big young fellow up front in Joe Royle and keeping putting the ball up to middle to him as teams have done to Tony Hateley. This, I believe, is not the way they normally play. Perhaps they are overdoing it.

"After watching Everton we decided that if we could make it difficult for Joe to get the ball Everton would not give us a lot of trouble. That is just what we did."

Time to say a prayer

(Daily Mirror, September 5, 1970)

A picture accompanying this article shows the teenager lighting a candle.

*L*IKE many other Everton fans, Chris Anderson is worried about his team not winning a game since the season started.

So yesterday Chris, aged 13, of Ditton in Kent, went to a local Roman Catholic priory, lit a candle and prayed for the Blues.

Yesterday was the 10th time Chris has lit a candle for the team.

Says Chris, who wants to play for Everton: "I decided at the end of last season to light a candle for Everton. They won, so I kept on lighting them." Father Richard Hearne, the priory superior, said: "We have no objection to Chris coming here. Many people say prayers for other than spiritual things. Provided he respects the priory and is sincere, as he obviously is, then he is welcome."

Skipper Ball under pressure

(By Ron Wills, Daily Mirror, September 16, 1970)

Alan Ball's captaincy of under-performing Everton was coming under scrutiny.

*A*FTER five weeks of controversial captaincy at Everton, Alan Ball emerged as the most likely to lead England in future World Cups.

The 23-year-old forward will skipper the Football League side against the Irish League in the season's first representative match at Norwich next Wednesday. And that is a vote of confidence from England team boss Alf Ramsey for the footballer who, in the past five seasons, has been dogged with a "firebrand" image.

Ball was appointed captain of the champions in the summer, and soon ran into trouble. On August 22, as Everton slumped to a 3-2 defeat at Leeds, Ball reprimanded embarrassed team-mate Keith Newton in front of 46,000 fans. Afterwards Ball confessed: "I realise now there are better ways of doing my job."

Everton manager Harry Catterick later warned his new skipper "tone it down", but Ball was still criticised as Everton went in search of their first victory – and that didn't arrive until September 5.

Ball captained the Football League against the Scottish League at Hampden Park in March 1969 – because no other World Cup footballer was playing. The nomination as captain is indication that Sir Alf is looking to the day when England are without Bobby Moore.

The nationwide search for talent

(By Harry Catterick, Liverpool Echo, October 8, 1970)

The Everton manager noted how he and his scouts had already checked on 86 of the 92 Football League clubs that season in a bid to consider new signings.

I WAS interested in the Preston midfield player Archie Gemmill. He would have suited us, but I put a price on him which I thought to be right and I would not go above that when Derby signed him.

Fees must be regarded in the light of the needs of the clubs – at the time of the transfer. With Ball, Harvey and Kendall, our need for another midfield performer was not as urgent as, say, Derby County's.

Derby paid around £65,000 for Gemmill – but that does not mean Derby paid too much. They needed him, so the price was right for them. If I had wanted another midfielder, I would have gone higher. But it was not necessary, and that is why I dropped out of the transfer.

The end for the Holy Trinity?

(By Dave Horridge, Daily Mirror, October 14, 1970)

Money was thrown at the problem as Everton's league form continued to frustrate

*H*ARRY Catterick made big transfers fashionable again when he bought Henry Newton from Nottingham Forest. The Everton chief used his Irish wing-half Tommy Jackson as a £25,000 makeweight in the £150,000 move – the third highest in British soccer history.

The signing poses an intriguing question for fans – who steps down from the Kendall-Ball-Harvey midfield trio, rated the best in the First Division, to make room. Catterick could play all four by moving Alan Ball up and dropping a forward, but I visualise Kendall stepping down.

British soldiers cheer on Euro Blues

(By Michael Charters, Liverpool Echo, October 19, 1970)

A large away contingent was likely to cheer on the Blues in the European Cup second-round clash in West Germany. Everton would progress to the quarter-final – a 1-1 first leg draw away and a 1-1 draw after extra time at Goodison meant penalties – with Everton edging through, the first winners by this method in the competition's history.

*F*IVE thousands British soldiers will be cheering Everton, when they play Moenchengladbach in Germany in the second round of the European Cup. This clash between the English and German champions has roused tremendous enthusiasm in the garrison town, and a capacity crowd of more than 30,000 is certain.

The home side admit to being apprehensive about tackling the English champions. Skipper Gunter Netzer says: "Our players are a little afraid of Everton. They are a fine team and a hard side."

Coach Hennes Weisweiler said: "We are wary of Everton, and I believe we need TWO goals and THEN we can get through on aggregate." Weisweiler has a victory plan and he was briefing his players on it this afternoon. One of the things he will impress upon his men: "Stop Alan Ball." Weisweiler, who with skipper Netzer saw Everton lose 4-0 at Highbury last Saturday, says: "Ball was impressive and he is a danger man to us."

Bosses go head to head

(By Michael Charters, Liverpool Echo, March 8, 1971)

Harry Catterick faced an unwitting head-to-head with his opposite number, Dick Graham after Colchester United were defeated in an FA Cup sixth round tie.

COLCHESTER manager Dick Graham launched his blast last night. Here it is, point for point, with the replies of Harry Catterick.

GRAHAM: "Everton's players clapped us off at the end. That was wonderful and my boys deserved it, but I did not like other things that happened. We were not given the usual courtesy of having half a dozen practice balls for a warm-up in the dressing rooms. I think it was pettiness, as well as gamesmanship."

CATTERICK: "This is the practice in most clubs. You can't have balls in the dressing room because you could cause damage if you start kicking them around. Both teams receive their balls 10 minutes before the kick-off for use on the pitch, which is routine at Goodison."

GRAHAM: "There was another incident before the match. Our

club mascot was not allowed into our dressing room to change."

CATTERICK: "I don't know anything about that. If he was in the official party, anybody could go into the dressing room and change. I can assure Mr Graham that mascots are not allowed into Everton dressing rooms. The ticket which all visiting clubs have for entrance to the ground is for players and officials – not mascots."

GRAHAM: "Harry Catterick did not come to see me before or after the match. I read in Friday's paper that he was calling us a hard and rough side – this was stirring it up. When we beat Leeds, they showed dignity. I didn't think Everton showed much – except the players."

CATTERICK: "I said earlier in the week that they were a hard and rough side. Does Dick think they are not a rough side? I never go into the visitors' dressing room before the game – that is the wrong time. After the match, I had to go to the far side of the ground for a TV interview. When I came back Dick was not in the board room and I understood he had left for the station. He did not come to the directors' room with other Colchester officials."

Supplies packed for trip to Greece

(By Horace Yates, Liverpool Daily Post, March 13, 1971)

'You don't want to be eating any of that foreign muck' – Everton in Athens ahead of the European Cup quarter-final second leg, with the tie poised at 1-1.

*E*VERTON are going to unprecedented lengths to make their players feel at home in Greece, when they travel to Athens for the second leg of the European Cup quarter-final.

They are taking with them their own caterer, Mr Ken Davies, the catering controller of Messrs Littlewoods, and acting manager for Everton's exclusive "300" club at Goodison Park.

Stored away in their chartered plane will be ample supplies of steak, bacon, eggs, potatoes, bread, cheese, fruit and all the liquids, including orange juice and water, they are likely to need.

Nothing is being left to chance. This is no reflection in any way on Greek hotels or catering, but merely an attempt to play safe with the food, so that the players will go into the match in peak condition.

The Greeks have already received permission to postpone a league game on the Sunday before the Everton match, so that there will be no interruption of their special training and no risk of last-minute injury.

Whether it is a form of conceit over English clubs' team strength or merely indifference to Europe, there is no such co-operation from the Football League for continental adventurers. In Greece national prestige is at stake and the whole country is ranged solidly behind Panathinaikos. Dangling in front of the players' noses is a golden carrot in the shape of a £1,200 bonus offer if they win the tie. This is a staggering inducement that will make Everton, once dubbed the "Millionaires of English football", feel like poor relations.

Panathinaikos win bonus

(By Erlend Clouston, Liverpool Echo, March 23, 1971)

The Greeks ended up quids-in – a 1-0 victory putting Everton out and progressing to the last four. They would eventually reach the final, before being well beaten by Ajax at Wembley.

$\mathscr{P}$ANATHINAIKOS have been put on 10,000 drachmas (£150) a man to win, and there is talk of Government medals being struck for the players in the event of victory.

The match is being hailed in Greece as one of the most important club matches ever played there. Fifty-pence tickets (the cheapest) are being sold on the black market for £28. It is said to be impossible to buy one of the 20,000 stand tickets.

Ferenc Puskas, Panathinaikos' manager, is confident of success: "We should win here," he says. "At the worst, we will force a play-off."

A report from the Government meteorologist has cheered up the locals. The temperature for the 2.30 kick-off is set to be in the high 70s.

Club turned off by TV plans

(By Chris James, Liverpool Echo, April 8, 1971)

Everton try to ban Match of the Day.

$\mathcal{E}$VERTON'S hostilities with the television cameras could develop into open warfare at the Football League's annual meeting. I understand Everton have put forward a suggestion to the League which would ban the BBC's "Match of the Day" programme on Saturday nights.

At League headquarters at Lytham St Anne's today, a spokesman confirmed that Everton had written to the League expressing their views on television coverage of football. He added that Everton were the only club so far to express in writing their disagreements.

Twice in the last year, Everton have complained about their over-exposure and now they are believed to have put forward the view that matches televised on Saturday should be shown no earlier than Sunday.

Everton would prefer these recordings to be held over and shown during the next week. Other views expressed by Everton include a rationing system for teams to prevent over-exposure and a doubling of the £250,000 that both channels pay for football coverage.

Texaco Cup snub

(June 21, 1971)

A new competition? No thanks.

$\mathcal{E}$VERTON have turned down the Football League's invitation to take part in next season's British Isles Cup – better known as the Texaco Cup – because of other fixture commitments.

The competition is open to 16 clubs from England, Scotland, Northern Ireland and Eire, and although Everton were not one of the original qualifiers, they were offered a place because Manchester United withdrew.

Fears over Ball's future

(By Michael Charters, Liverpool Echo, August 6, 1971)

There were worrying developments concerning the future of Alan Ball. Were the club considering his departure?

*H*AVE Manchester United tried to buy Alan Ball from Everton? It is a question which has been intriguing Merseyside football followers for some time. I put it to Harry Catterick months ago and he treated it as though he was handling a time-bomb. He replied with a counter-question: "Would United sell us George Best?" To my knowledge there has never been a straight "yes" or "no" reply to this huge talking point.

Ball was also the principle figure in the other main feature of an otherwise routine meeting. Shareholders George Beattie and Jack White asked about the captaincy without mentioning Ball by name.

Mr Beattie said: "I should like to see an improvement in the captaincy. We don't want to see any more tantrums and fist-shaking on the field."

Mr White said: "The captain is a great player but if we could control the tantrums side of him, it would be wonderful."

Mr Catterick replied: "I can think of two other great captains, Dave Mackay and Billy Bremner, who do a lot of fist-shaking. If you have an extrovert as a captain, half the work for the manager and coach is done. Ball was a little rash at times, but you have to remember that he is a new skipper and has a lot to learn. A quiet player, quietly spoken, cannot always get the desired performance from the players."

The Blue Streak dolly girls

(Liverpool Echo, August 11, 1971)

A picture showed six ladies posing in front of a train, complete with blue sash with the legend 'Everton' in white. They were the 'blue streak dolly girls'.

*M*EET the "dolly girl" information service for Everton's "Blue

Streak" special trains to away games. Kitted out in blue and white, the girls will be on board to see the fans have a smooth trip.

The girls will have detailed dossiers on the Blues, ready to answer any questions. All fans will have to sign a good behaviour pledge.

Technology arrives

(By Michael Charters, Liverpool Echo, August 12, 1971)

The electronic era is ushered in at Everton...

$\mathscr{G}$OODISON Park will have two new features by the time the first home game of the season comes around against promoted Sheffield United a week on Saturday.

Those fans at the game against the Israeli champions on Monday night will have seen the permanent advertisements around the ground.

The other innovation will be in place next week – a £13,000 electric scoreboard which will supplement the loudspeaker address system.

Eventually the club plan to install another scoreboard at the Gwladys Street end, operating simultaneously, so that people in all parts of the ground will be able to see one of them without difficulty.

Chairman George Watts told me: "We have tried in recent years to improve facilities for spectators. I think the new scoreboard will extend those facilities. The advertisements will bring us a lot of additional revenue, which will play its part in the general financial structure of the club. We will, of course, spend it on the team and spectator facilities."

Shock as Ball heads to Arsenal

(By Alan Ball, Daily Mirror, December 23, 1971)

Unwelcome pre-Christmas news as Alan Ball is sold for a British record £220,000.

$\mathscr{A}$LAN Ball, ex-Everton and now Arsenal! I couldn't believe it when it started to happen and I still can't believe it.

Alan Ball, Everton skipper and Number One Fan, sacked, sold and more than satisfied – all in 24 of the craziest hours of my life.

Alan Ball, the lad they called England's energy-pack after the 1966 World Cup, whacked out, physically and mentally shattered by the whirlwind way London wooed him and won him in less than a day.

In the morning I am going to wake and ask myself: 'Has it REALLY happened?' On Tuesday I was down – as low as you can get. Shaken by the shock news that my beloved Everton were ready to sell before Arsenal came in. All right, I'd had a stinker at Derby last Saturday.

I'm not making excuses but there was an understandable reason. Last Friday my wife, Lesley, gave birth to our second daughter and that night I didn't sleep. I'd hoped the boss might understand. He didn't and that was that. I was angry but I wasn't going to rush into the first offer that came along. Otherwise I would have signed right away when Bertie Mee, Arsenal's manager, came up to interview me.

But I had made up my mind that I would never kick another ball for Everton. It wasn't just my pride that had been hurt. My faith in the club to whom I had given everything for five years had been shattered. How could I be worth over £200,000 to Arsenal and not worth a first-team place to Everton? The only conclusion I could come to was that Harry Catterick must have thought I was going over the hill. Burned out at the ripe old age of 26? Well, everyone's entitled to an opinion.

It's hard to imagine that I'm about to leave Merseyside. It's hard, too, to think of those wonderful Everton fans as mere memories. There will be a big welcome to Highbury for them from Alan Ball if they come down for my home debut on January 5 against...wait for it... Everton.

1972-1981

'Enry's happy

(Liverpool Echo, February 29, 1972)

One man pleased with Alan Ball's sale was a famous Arsenal fan.

*H*ENRY Cooper, former British, Commonwealth and European heavyweight boxing champion, was guest of honour at the Everton sportsmen's dinner last night. Looking around the well-appointed 300 Club, Cooper, a self-confessed Arsenal fan, quipped: "I would just like to thank you on Arsenal's behalf for Alan Ball – and I am delighted to see you have spent the money so wisely."

Thomas on his way

(By Michael Charters, Liverpool Echo, March 7, 1972)

Dave Thomas was among the new names linked with a switch to Goodison.

*W*ITH the transfer deadline only 48 hours off, Everton fans will be expecting their club to make a dramatic move in the transfer market. Everton are reported to be interested in Burnley's Dave Thomas. I know they have been interested in Thomas for many months. They have not always been totally impressed by their scouts' reports on this 21-year-old Under-23 star, but he has such exciting potential that he looks the best bet. Henry Newton has also been mentioned, with Alan Whittle, in a reported part-exchange move to bring Asa Hartford, of West Bromwich, to Goodison.

The computer age

(By Michael Charters, Liverpool Echo, May 2, 1972)

Progress was being made in the ticketing department.

*E*VERTON tickets next season will be sold through a new and revolutionary computer system which the club believes will be of major help to supporters. They are creating a new ticket office in Bullens Road, where the computer will be installed. It will provide many advantages over present methods, not least of all in service to the public, security and immediate accountancy, at the touch of a button.

Embracing sports science

(By Chris James, Liverpool Echo, May 17, 1972)

Injury to several key men was another factor cited for Everton's relative struggles since their championship success. Sport suddenly became a "science"…

*I*NJURY prone or unlucky? That was the question raised most at Everton last season as the 1970 champions slumped into the bottom half of the First Division.

Almost every player in the team had spells out through injury. In fact, only goalkeeper Gordon West played in every match. As a result, Everton were rarely able to field a settled team, results and performances were poor and the Blues and their fans were not satisfied.

Everton have now called in Dr. Vaughan Thomas, a sports scientist from Liverpool Polytechnic, to try to cure their ills.

Sports science in this country is scarcely known, but it is widely practised in Russia and the Under States and, says Dr. Thomas, is one of the reasons for the success of these nations in the world of sporting events. "Everton are not happy with anything less than the best, and even though I don't think they knew that people like me existed, they thought sports science might be able to help them."

Plastic fantastic

(By Horace Yates, Liverpool Daily Post, June 7, 1972)

Artificial surfaces – plastic pitches – were beginning to enter footballing parlance as a potential option for clubs.

$\mathcal{I}$S there a future for pitches of artificial turf in Football League games? It is far too early to say, but experiments have reached an advanced stage and already one pitch has been laid at Islington.

Everton have taken the lead in drawing attention to this revolutionary project. Their chairman, Mr George Watts, emphasises that Everton at this stage have no intention of pushing ahead in a pioneering role.

Mr Watts aired the topic at the League's annual meeting and last night told me: "We are not interested in putting down such a pitch, but we are interested in exploring possibilities. If such a pitch was a success it would mean constant turf throughout the season and goodbye to annual re-seeding. It could also mean that the ground might be used for other events during the summer, something that is out of the question at the moment."

How far?

(By Michael Charters, Liverpool Echo, July 29, 1972)

The early days of foreign pre-season tours would often raise some unforeseen logistical issues.

$\mathcal{E}$VERTON complete their Swedish tour with a friendly game on the East Coast which involved a 400-mile journey they would never contemplate for a match in England.

By deciding to return tomorrow, instead of Monday, the team had to make a 10-hour journey by coach today, to and from Oskarshamn. Apparently, when Everton first checked how far Oskarshamn was from Hindas, they were told 20 miles. What they didn't know was that a Swedish mile is the same as 10 English miles.

The players are clearly bored. As Joe Royle said to me after finishing training yesterday: "I am now going to play my 800th game of cards since we came here." Cards are the main means of relieving the boredom of being confined to this isolated camp in poor weather. The players are also able to play table tennis but there is a limit to this.

E.F.C

(By Michael Charters, Liverpool Echo, August 8, 1972)

Two consecutive poor seasons was beginning to tell on the supporters.

*E*VERTON'S stand season-ticket sales are down by about 15 per cent – the supporters' reaction to the disappointments of last season. Last season, Everton sold around 13,000 stand season tickets, bringing in £210,000 revenue. Sales at present are under 11,000.

[Harry Catterick] has also ordered a slight change in the playing strip for next season, first choice and change strip.

The royal blue jerseys will now have white collars and white inset at the neck, and have the motif E.F.C. embroidered in white on the jersey. These will be worn with white shorts and stockings.

The change strip is amber with blue collars and blue inset at the neck. Blue shorts and amber stockings complete the outfit – and very smart they look, too.

For-Ever Everton

(Liverpool Echo, October 26, 1972)

The Everton squad were pictured in casual wear 'singing' with song sheets in hand.

*E*VERTON yesterday became the latest soccer team to try their hand at pop singing. Eleven members of their first-team squad went to a Stockport recording studio to cut a song called "For-Ever Everton."

A poor reception

(Liverpool Daily Post, January 17, 1973)

Had this problem been considered when developing the new Main Stand? Locals were unhappy that their televisual viewing was being compromised.

$\mathcal{A}$NGRY residents living in the shadow of Goodison Park, have complained to their MP that the new stand is ruining their TV reception. Tenants in Oxton Street, which runs roughly east-west from the ground to County Road, approached Mr Eric Heffer, Labour MP for Walton, and told him that people in the street who have recently bought new colour or 625-line sets, have not been able to get a proper reception since the new stand was completed. Mr Heffer said: "The least Everton could do would be to provide a communal aerial system."

Jam in the loaf

(By Horace Yates, Liverpool Daily Post, February 7, 1973)

A shock FA Cup defeat at home to Millwall, and a league position in the lower reaches of mid-table meant patience at boardroom level was wearing thin.

$\mathcal{E}$VERTON chairman Mr John Moores made it clear yesterday that his patience is not inexhaustible. Everyone at Goodison is now on trial – and if the situation is not brighter by the end of the season, in three months, the axe could fall.

Thoroughly disappointed by the Millwall defeat, Mr Moores pulled no punches in an exclusive interview. "I am not happy with anybody at the moment. I am not even happy with myself," he said. "But the manager has to be given a little more time to improve the situation. No matter what may have happened, Harry Catterick has got together a fairly good side. It now remains to be seen whether he can go through with it and make it into a very good side. He is good. He buys the right men, but badly wants a bit of a break. We need somebody to set the attack moving and somebody to set up the goal flow. Once he gets the forwards moving, he is through the barrier.

"Three seasons of disappointment is a long time and we want to end the sequence at the earliest possible moment. Mr Catterick has been away sick for some of the time. We have to make allowances for that, but I feel we must have a good team again by the end of the season.

"All Harry now needs is a little bit of jam for the Goodison loaf and we are on our way."

Bernie the bolt

(By Michael Charters, Liverpool Echo, February 15, 1973)

Bernie Wright's short Goodison stay and subsequent departure was noted – perhaps a further example of the club's increasingly scattergun transfer policy?

*T*HE background to the Everton suspension and subsequent transfer of striker Bernie Wright, who has now rejoined his old club Walsall, is revealed today by the Football League.

Wright appealed to the League against Everton's decision to give him 14 days notice to end his agreement, for what has been described as "serious misconduct".

The official language of the League report on the hearing reveals the outline of what must have been a rare scene at Bellefield, the club's training ground.

Everton's reason for their action was: "On December 22, when Wright reported for training, he was under the influence of alcohol and created a disturbance. Subsequently, he absented himself from training and match duty without permission from December 22 to December 27 inclusive."

The commission which heard Wright's appeal, at League HQ, consisted of League president Len Shipman and vice-president Sam Bolton. Everton were represented by secretary Bill Dickinson, assistant-manager Tom Eggleston and chief scout Harry Cooke.

The commission found that Wright was guilty of being under the influence and causing a disturbance. Because of conflicting evidence about him being absent for five days, the commission were not able to resolve this.

They found that Wright was guilty of a serious breach of his agreement and dismissed his appeal.

Wright joined Everton in February last year from Walsall, at a fee of more than £30,000. After being sacked, five weeks ago, he was transferred to Walsall for £10,000.

Ball's ghost

(By Horace Yates, Liverpool Daily Post, March 6, 1973)

Six winless games in league and cup, and dipping levels of performance – where could Everton turn to? If only they still had Alan Ball.

*O*NE midfield man and one striker could be the answer to Everton's dream, but many leading clubs share the problem.

I wonder, if in retrospect, [Harry Catterick] now believes he did the right thing in releasing first Alan Ball and then David Johnson. Playing as they are now for their present clubs, Ball and Johnson could have assisted a Goodison rescue act.

I admit that when Ball went to Arsenal I thought Mr Catterick had made a fine deal, for Alan was not only looking stale, but seemed to have left his best football behind him.

Arsenal have revitalised him. Whether Everton could have done as much I don't know. But just now Ball's ghost struts around Goodison.

Johnson, I am told, is twice the player now than he was at Everton. Even so, Johnson, I thought, was always the most talented youngster produced by the Bellefield machine.

I was sorry to see him go and I fear the passage of time will only make Everton more deeply conscious of their loss.

The end of the Cat

(Liverpool Echo, April 11, 1973)

A 2-0 Saturday home victory over Coventry City would prove to be Harry Catterick's final game in charge. By the following Tuesday he had gone, with coach Tommy Eggleston taking caretaker charge for the final six games of the 1972/73 season. The club's then most successful manager, Catterick left the Blues 15th in the First Division having won two league titles, one FA Cup and two FA Charity Shields during his 12-year tenure – as well as becoming regular competitors in Europe.

*H*ARRY Catterick's 12-year reign as Everton team manager ended this afternoon. The announcement came as Mr Catterick and the team were leaving for the game at West Brom tonight. The statement from the board was as follows:

"Everton are pleased to announce they have reached an arrangement with Mr Catterick under which he will continue to serve the club for the term of his present contract but will act in a senior executive capacity, not responsible for team selection and management.

"This will free the position of manager and the board invite applications to fill this appointment. The manager will have complete charge of team and playing affairs. The directors wish to place on record their appreciation to Mr Catterick for his services during which the team achieved many successes. They are happy that Mr Catterick can continue to make a contribution to the success of Everton."

Who next?

(By Bob Whiting, Liverpool Daily Post, April 12, 1973)

The circus had now begun – who would land one of the most coveted jobs in English football? An early favourite was Brian Clough.

*D*ERBY County manager Brian Clough must be the favourite to take over the now-vacant managerial chair at Everton.

Money is no object – and the winning applicant's jackpot could be soccer's top salary, perhaps even as high as £20,000 a year.

Until recently the most tipped man to take over at Goodison has been Wolverhampton Wanderers manager Bill McGarry. But who can rule out Clough? He can't be ruled out of any job from No. 10 downwards.

Favourite among the younger managers is Bobby Robson, the man who has brought the best out of Ipswich Town, but he signed a new contract just before Christmas.

Another First Division manager who cannot be overlooked is Birmingham City boss Freddie Goodwin, who brought the St Andrew's club back into the First Division last season.

An ex-Evertonian who must be considered is Norwich boss Ron Saunders. From the Second Division comes the name of Queens Park Rangers' Gordon Jago.

Burnley's Jimmy Adamson and Bournemouth's John Bond could be considered – and from the ranks of the unemployed there springs the names of Frank O'Farrell, the charming chap whose Old Trafford career ended so distastefully.

If you wanted to look further afield, there's the name of Argentinian-born Helenio Herrera, rated one of the world's top coaches. He's available – because Roma fired him on Monday.

Revie says no

(Liverpool Echo, May 25, 1973)

Leeds United's Don Revie was the man the club approached – but failed to land. The approach, and the figures being bandied around prompted mention in Parliament…

$\mathscr{D}$ON Revie has turned down the invitation to become £25,000-a-year manager of Everton FC. This blow to the hopes of the Goodison Park club came today in a statement from Leeds United, later confirmed by Everton FC.

The Leeds statement said: "Don Revie, whose future as manager of

Leeds United has been the source of recent speculation, is to remain with the club. He notified his decision today from his holiday hotel in Greece in a telephone conversation with secretary/general manager, Keith Archer. He said: "I'm very happy to announce that I will be staying as manager of Leeds United."

Everton FC, seeking a successor to Mr Harry Catterick, have also been rejected by Bobby Robson, manager of Ipswich Town, and Jimmy Armfield, manager of Bolton Wanderers.

Everton's reported £25,000 pay offer was referred to in the House of Commons this week and yesterday a Government Pay Board spokesman said both clubs had been reminded of their obligation under the Government Pay Code.

Bingham told: Get Everton back on top

(Liverpool Daily Post, June 4, 1973)

Eventually it was a former Everton player who was lured, handed the task of restoring the club's reputation as regular challengers for silverware.

*F*LIGHT BE 457 winged across Europe today carrying Everton's passport to the future. On board B.E.A.'s morning flight from Athens was Billy Bingham, the man the Blues have chosen to put them back among soccer's elite.

Bingham, a former Everton player and now the man they hope will be their £10,000-a-year revivalist, was arriving at Heathrow early this afternoon and connecting with a flight to Manchester.

After two years coaching the Greek national side, Bingham has turned down offers of highly-paid coaching jobs in Greece to become the Goodison trouble-shooter. His mandate is clear: Get Everton back on top. Tomorrow he will set about the task and, during the rest of this week, he will take stock of his staff and have talks with the man he replaces, Harry Catterick.

One era ends as another begins

(By Horace Yates, Liverpool Daily Post, July 16, 1973)

John Moores also took the decision to again stand down from the boardroom as Billy Bingham embarked on the club's pre-season preparations – at Ainsdale beach.

 *E*VERTON'S father figure, Mr John Moores will step down from the chair next month. When Everton players reported for the new season at Bellefield on Saturday, Mr Moores said: "It is my intention to hand over to Allan Waterworth, but I'll be there to help and guide him, a sort of shadow chairman, while he needs me."

"Harry Catterick," he told me, "was the best manager Everton have ever had. He had a lot of very good qualities." But clearly he is hoping that Billy Bingham will prove even better and that he will find the remedy for the mystery blight that has fallen over Everton.

Mr Bingham told his new charges: "Don't look on me as a new man. I am an old man steeped in the traditions of the club. We all know the sort of playing pressures you will have to face, but together we must learn to ride them. Bad times will come and go. Together we can move them on that much quicker."

His planned, scientific approach to training begins on Ainsdale's sandhills today, a scene they will familiarise themselves with for a week. The plan is dovetailed to suit individuals.

There will be a log recording the case history of every man. "It is a programme I have tried and proved I am confident it will work for Everton," he said.

Irksome irritations have already been removed. There will be no clocking in each day. Players will no longer have to look over their shoulder when talking to a Pressman.

Already players are convinced they will have a happier dressing room, but his demands for good behaviour have left the impression that behind that ready smile is a demanding streak.

A fine start

(By Erlend Clouston, Liverpool Echo, August 17, 1973)

Bingham makes his mark early – as lateness is punished.

*E*VERTON manager Billy Bingham last night fined three players a week's wages for breaking club curfew in Sweden. Roger Kenyon, Joe Harper and Mike Bernard will each lose about £100 – more than £2 a minute for the 45 minutes they were late reporting back to the hotel.

Bingham said: "The players were given Wednesday evening off, but were told to be back in the hotel by 11pm. The three concerned were spotted returning at 11.45pm by trainer Stewart Imlach. Action had to be taken. The club secretary, Chris Hassell, will hand them letters informing officially of my decision. It will all be done coldly and clinically. They must know who is in charge." One of Mr Bingham's first acts as manager was to do away with the business of the players signing in for training. They had found it petty. "It will put the players on trust," he said at the time. "But serious breaches of discipline will obviously be severely dealt with." He proved his point last night.

Big Bob signs in

(By Dave Horridge, Daily Mirror, February 14, 1974)

Goals had continued to be a problem – and a solution was sought in the form of a new centre-forward, with Howard Kendall departing as part of the deal.

*E*VERTON will hoist the British record transfer fee to a staggering £350,000 when they buy Birmingham striker Bob Latchford.

In return for the player manager Freddie Goodwin last year said money couldn't buy, Birmingham will get Everton midfield man Howard Kendall and left-back Archie Styles, plus £80,000 cash.

With Kendall valued at £180,000 and Styles at £90,000, the deal smashes the previous record by £100,000. The 22-year-old Latchford will collect £17,500 as his share of the fee. The deal was set up days ago, and the parties met near Manchester yesterday afternoon.

I understand the three players involved have agreed terms and the deal will go through today. Birmingham supporters will be shocked at the departure of a player they regard as vital to their hopes of avoiding relegation from the First Division.

Latchford, who has scored 60 goals in the last three seasons, is again their top-scorer with 18. He won his first Under-23 cap recently. In November, Latchford hit two hat-tricks in four days. Shortly afterwards Goodwin claimed he would rather be sacked than sell him.

Under the spotlight

(By Kevin Moseley, Daily Mirror, February 16, 1974)

Would the record fee prove a problem? Meanwhile, the manager would have to wait for his opportunity to assess his new charge in first-team action.

*B*OB Latchford, Everton's £350,000 buy from Birmingham, spoke last night about the pressures of being Britain's most expensive footballer on the eve of his debut at West Ham today.

"Every move, pass and shot that I make will be closely watched," he said. "I'm constantly reminded that I'm the first £350,000 player. I've hardly had the ideal preparation. I only caught a glimpse of my new team-mates at Euston before being whisked away for a TV interview."

Billy Bingham, the Everton manager, will miss Bob Latchford's debut at West Ham today. He was treated in hospital after a pan of hot fat had spilled over his feet at his Southport home.

A narrow escape

(By Ken Lawrence, Liverpool Daily Post, January 6, 1975)

The Blues almost came a cropper against non-League opposition in the FA Cup. Beforehand Northern Premier League side Altrincham fancied their chances of an upset. The confidence was highlighted by the following Liverpool Echo piece:

'Lifelong Everton supporter Phil Smith was aiming to knock the Blues out of the Cup as an Altrincham player. The 25-year-old, a teacher at Quarry Bank School in Allerton, said: "I've been an Evertonian all my life. It really is like a dream come true. I happened to see the Carlisle game, but that was the first time I had seen Everton since the time of Kendall, Ball and Harvey. I don't think they're in the same class as then. They work harder, but they don't seem to have the same skill."

*T*HE man who makes the wisecracks over the Goodison loudspeakers, who expressed the hope that Altrincham might tire themselves out in their pre-match warm-up, must, for a long time on Saturday, have felt that providence had kicked him in the teeth.

This match was anything but a laughing matter. In the space of nine minutes, the no-hopers took the lead; tragedy struck when John Connolly was carried off with a leg fractured in two places; and midfielder Gary Jones, who had earlier shown the right kind of aggression, showed the wrong kind, with a short, sharp right hook which felled Altrincham's Morris and left the referee with no choice but to send him off.

Forward the 10,000

(Liverpool Echo, January 21, 1975)

A trip to Third Division Plymouth in January is hardly the visit most would relish, but for Everton supporters, buoyed by the side's resurgence – they were top of the table – that would be the journey of choice. Over 7,000 were set to flock to the south west for the FA Cup fourth-round tie (with 3,000 Liverpool fans going to Ipswich for their cup clash, thus the above headline). On a heavily sanded surface, Everton went through 3-1, with Jim Pearson and Mick Lyons on target. Unfortunately, the Blues would be shocked in the following round, by eventual cup runners-up Fulham

*A*BRITISH Rail spokesman said: "Normally we only get this number travelling for the semi-finals and the final." Blues secretary Chris Hassell said: "We are going to have a colossal following and it will be tremendous for the team to have all those fans behind them."

A shattering end

(By Ken Lawrence, Liverpool Daily Post, April 21, 1975)

A run of two wins from the final 10 games shattered the club's championship charge – although in the final reckoning, it was believed defeats home and away to relegated Carlisle United were the biggest factors in a failure to secure the title. The final home game of the season, against Sheffield United, was the final nail in the coffin.

*T*HE seat cushions and crumpled programmes which rained from the Goodison stands, on Saturday, provided a crude monument to Everton's league title aspirations. The dream for this season was over. But what a way to end it all. Whether Everton would have won the championship, even if they had beaten Sheffield, remains to be seen. The chances are they would not. But if they had to submit in the end, did it have to be in this shattering fashion?

To be two goals up at half-time, then to lose three in the second half is, for a championship-chasing side, not the kind of thing one expects. It was certainly the most unexpected occurrence for the frustrated Everton supporters.

For while their supporters might have remembered this season as one in which Everton tried, but failed valiantly, they may now only remember it as the season that Everton failed – again.

Europe confirmed

(By Alex Goodman, Liverpool Echo, May/June 1975)

Everton had finally benefited from the abolition of the one city, one club rule in European competition – with the club's fourth-place finish allowing entrance into the UEFA Cup. Other clubs weren't so happy.

*E*VERTON are back in Europe for the first time in five years. But immediately their nomination was confirmed, Stoke City manager

Tony Waddington claimed: "We have been stabbed in the back."

The angry outburst from Mr Waddington came after yesterday's annual meeting of the Football League in London when top League officials said that Stoke, their original choice for the UEFA Cup, would have to step down.

Mr Waddington added: "Everton should be charged with bringing the game into disrepute. They should have stepped down. But it seems that although they are rich enough they are not big enough."

At the end of the season Stoke finished below Everton in fifth but because of the League ruling that only one club per city could compete in Europe, Stoke were put forward for the UEFA Cup as Liverpool had already qualified. But UEFA officials pointed out that they did not recognise this rule and told the League that they would not accept Stoke's entry. England's UEFA representative, Dick Wragg of Sheffield United, went to Paris to plead Stoke's case but he was rejected.

League secretary Alan Hardaker said: "There is no other choice for us. Even if we withdrew Everton, UEFA would put in a reserve team and I do not think this would be Stoke. It would simply mean that we would have three teams in the competition and not four."

Everton, led by chairman Alan Waterworth, maintained all along that they have not been trying to get into Europe by the back door. Secretary Chris Hassell said: "All we ask is that the rules are observed."

Praise from Trap

(By Brian Glanville, Daily Mirror, September 12, 1975)

Ahead of the club's UEFA Cup first round tie with AC Milan, one Italian footballing legend ran the rule over the Blues.

$\mathcal{G}$IOVANNI Trapattoni, the former international left-half who watched Everton beat Derby County, was impressed by them, and had some pleasant words to say about Martin Dobson.

"A team," said Trap, "with all the most salient English characteristics;

speed, good exploitation of the wings, crosses to Latchford who is a centre-forward a little bit like Chivers.

"Everton are a classically collective team. For example, in defence they use the offside game and the centre-backs often switch. These English are well organised and have their strength in dynamism and in team work. They'll be a hard job, like every English team."

The wrong type of cushion

(By Horace Yates, Liverpool Daily Post, September 18, 1975)

Milan opposition at Goodison in a European tie, and another goalless draw – although this time there was a final cushion call.

$\mathcal{E}$VERTON'S first entry into European competition since 1970/71 ended in sensation in the last minute of their UEFA Cup first round, first-leg tie with AC Milan, when Mick Bernard was sent off. It was for an offence on Benetti, and early in the game he had had his number noted but had not been booked.

The decision produced a hail of boos and cushions rained down from the stand. This was repeated as the players left the field and there was a demonstration for several minutes. The surprising feature was that Everton had scarcely been in any disciplinary trouble, while four Milan players had been booked.

A bitter defeat in the San Siro

(By Alex Goodman, Liverpool Echo, October 2, 1975)

Unfortunately, there was another second leg repeat at the San Siro. As they had done 12 years previously, Everton bowed out of Europe by the odd goal. Mick Lyons and Billy Bingham were left to rue what might have been.

$\mathcal{M}$ICK Lyons flew into Liverpool early today with an ugly two-inch gash over his left eye as the sole reward for his efforts in attempting to take Everton through to the next round of the UEFA Cup.

Lyons had to have six stitches inserted in the wound before he flew out from Italy last night following the 1-0 defeat by AC Milan in the San Siro Stadium.

And it was a handling offence by Lyons that brought the penalty that produced the only goal in the two legs of the tie.

It came after 67 minutes of the game and Lyons said: "I controlled the ball with my feet and then it bounced up and flicked my hand."

And he summed up the disgust of the Everton party over the handling of the game by East German referee Rudi Glockner when he said: "If he had not given a penalty then he would have invented some other offence by us."

Manager Billy Bingham was equally scathing with his after-the-match comments.

He said: "I am terribly disappointed because we thought he was a quality referee. But it was obvious that we would have to get a clear-cut goal for it to count."

Everton had two penalty claims rejected in the game. In the first half Gary Jones was fouled 10 yards inside the penalty area only for a free-kick to be given just outside the box and after the break Jim Pearson was knocked down – again inside the area. But play was waved on.

A post-war low

(By Alex Goodman, Liverpool Echo, April 8, 1976)

Crowds dropped to worrying levels as the 1975/76 season petered out.

*T*HE Goodison Park attendance for last night's game with Stoke City was a meagre 16,974, the club's lowest First Division gate since the war.

Mr Jim Greenwood, the Everton secretary, said today: "It was very disappointing but a sign of the times. People are finding that money is short but it is success they want. I am expecting a better gate for Saturday's home match with Arsenal."

Blues in the red

(By Horace Yates, Liverpool Daily Post, July 13, 1976)

Predictably falling gates was a factor in the club recording a loss. Public note was also made of player earnings.

*I*N view of Everton's disappointing playing record last season, nobody will be surprised at the revelation in the club's annual report that a loss of £43,721 had been incurred. This would have been substantially reduced had it not included a late £35,000 outlay to Luton Town for the signing of Andy King, for in fact there was still a profit of £5,949 apart from signing fees. The club had one employee in the £15,000 to £17,500 bracket, two received between £12,500 and £15,000 and three were paid more than £10,000.

Brucie bonus

(By Horace Yates, Liverpool Daily Post, December 9, 1976)

Having considered his options, a new midfielder had agreed to come in alongside a player who would become a fans' favourite.

*E*VERTON last night pulled off their second signing in successive days when Derby County's Bruce Rioch changed his mind and agreed to move to Goodison Park for a £180,000 fee.

He will join newcomer Duncan McKenzie in a debut game at Coventry on Saturday.

The signing took place in the Prince of Wales Hotel, Southport, about 9.30pm yesterday and ended a day of speculation.

Rioch, who is 29, had a lot of things going for him in the Midlands. He is the proprietor of a 'Do-it-yourself' shop in Kingstanding, and has recently bought an exclusive £40,000 house overlooking Moor Hall Golf Club.

Dixie smiles on

(By Frank Corless, Daily Mirror, December 29, 1976)

Dixie Dean made news, having been forced to have a leg amputed.

THE legendary courage of soccer hero Dixie Dean kept him smiling yesterday. He was even able to joke about the amputation of his right leg.

"I'll have an artificial leg, and with a spring fitted I might even do a bit for Everton," he laughed. "And goodness knows they need someone!"

Dixie, who will be 70 next month, reckons that the leg which had to come off scored half his total of almost 400 goals.

Since his operation, hundreds of cards, letters and telegrams have arrived from all over the world at his daughter's home in Upton, Merseyside, where Dixie lives. The leg had to be amputated when complications occurred after an operation in November.

Dixie, a widower, said: "People have been marvellous and it's helped me to keep my chin up. It was no use being a coward. The leg had to come off."

Just before Christmas Everton sent Dixie a basket of fruit and a huge spray of dyed blue flowers.

Bingham goes

(By Horace Yates, Liverpool Daily Post, January 11, 1977)

A little over a month after being permitted to bring in two new players, days after making FA Cup progress and with a two-legged League Cup semi-final to come, the manager was axed.

EVERTON last night sacked manager Billy Bingham – with 18 months of his contract still to run.

Team coach Steve Burtenshaw, former manager of Sheffield Wednesday, takes over while Everton look for a successor.

The news came in a dramatic 9pm statement, issued by club secretary Jim Greenwood. The official statement said: "Given the very considerable resources, a club of Everton's standing can put at its manager's disposal, the ultimate responsibility for the performances on the field must rest with the manager."

Mick Lyons, the Everton captain: "It has really surprised and shocked me. I was quite happy with the way things were going with Mr Bingham."

Duncan McKenzie, signed from Anderlecht only five weeks ago, was astonished to hear the news. "Blimey!" he blurted out. "This has come as a tremendous shock and a surprise. It's incredible. I'm not quite sure what my thoughts are at the moment."

Terry Darracott: "This is amazing news, I'm absolutely stunned. I found Mr Bingham a good manager. He was certainly fair and square with me."

Lee takes the hot seat
(January 31, 1977)

A variety of names were lined with the vacant Everton job, including Aston Villa's Ron Saunders, Bobby Robson, Don Revie and apparent "people's choice" Brian Clough. But it was a man whom, only days before, had reportedly committed his future to his club, that decided to take on the challenge.

$\mathcal{G}$ORDON Lee yesterday became Everton's £20,000 a year manager for the next five years after resigning from a similar post with Newcastle United. He travels to Merseyside today when he is expected to announce the acceptance of Steve Burtenshaw as his chief coach.

"Everton are a big club with wonderful facilities," he said. "There can be none better, but I definitely shed a few tears at leaving the players at Newcastle, where we had a marvellous relationship.

"I am leaving a team challenging for the title and going to one struggling. It is my job to improve that position. I am optimistic it can be done."

Back at Wembley

(By Ian Callister, Liverpool Echo, March 14, 1977)

Having edged past Second Division Bolton – who fielded a young Peter Reid in their line-up – the Blues faced Aston Villa in their first-ever League Cup final. Unfortunately, the final turned into something of a damp squib with a replay required. The fans made the most of the occasion though.

*T*HE support had been arriving in London from early on Friday morning. Euston Station early on Saturday morning looked like a gigantic doss-house with an Evertonian's head on every available resting place. Then came the main invasion and countless reunions with Welsh, Irish, Lancashire and Cockney fans among the hordes sporting the Royal Blue.

The London Bobby was much in evidence, but there was little trouble and in fact the boys in dark blue appeared to be enjoying the party as much as anyone. Said one young Scots constable: "One mob came up to me and looked most disappointed when we told them that there would be no ticket touts about. I can't think why."

With every pub on the way to Wembley packed with the blue and white of Everton, the scouse voice round every corner asked the eternal question, "Any spares?"

Judging by the number of Evertonians inside the national stadium – estimates range from 40,000 to 50,000 – many of the ticket hunters must have struck lucky. Said West Ham fan Jim Oxford: "I've been to more finals than I can remember, but I have never seen so many fans from one club here."

Welcome home, boys

(By Steve Oldfield, Liverpool Echo, March 14, 1977)

*F*IFTEEN thousand fans welcomed Everton yesterday on their return from Wembley. There was no trophy to display, yet well-wishers put on an emotional and enthusiastic greeting which will boost the side's confidence for Wednesday's replay against Aston Villa.

Blue and white lined the route – if at times sparsely – from Allerton Station all the way to the city centre where a right Royal (Blue) reception waited for the team at Picton Library.

There, something like 5,000 fans stood swaying in the street and roared, sang and chanted as their heroes moved on to the building's balcony for the traditional salute.

There was just one minor problem when the team bus struggled to make a sharp uphill turn less than 100 yards from the library – "I had been in second gear all the way and I think the engine overheated as I tried for first" said driver Harry Dobson, – and the bottom deck of officials and directors had to disembark before it could re-start.

Manager Gordon Lee, clearly delighted, promised the fans "one cup and possibly two."

He told them: "I think we put up a good show. I think our supporters had the better of Villa's – and that's a good sign."

He introduced the side individually from captain Mick Lyons – "one of the great guys I have met; a man with blue blood in his veins" he said – through to substitute George Telfer and other players, who made the trip.

British Rail also expressed delight over the behaviour of the fans.

Latch keeps us alive

(By Alex Goodman, Liverpool Echo, March 17, 1977)

The final was set to go to a third game after Bob Latchford's late intervention.

$\mathcal{B}$OB Latchford has scored many goals in his career, but none so vital as last night's equaliser in the League Cup final replay against Aston Villa at Hillsborough.

There was less than a minute of normal time left and the cup was halfway to the Midlands when Everton pushed themselves forward for one last effort, and Latchford did the job he knows and likes best –

scoring goals. Now after 210 minutes of football, the teams must meet a third time. And after two tremendous performances, the odds may now be tilting slightly in Everton's favour.

Yet it looked as though a tragic own goal from Roger Kenyon would be enough to shatter all Everton's hopes after they had done so well in Saturday's goalless draw at Wembley.

Then, with referee Gordon Kew already checking his watch closely, Everton won a throw out on the right. Duncan McKenzie, Mike Bernard, Ronny Goodlass and Jim Pearson were all involved with Pearson getting the final flick on for Latchford to ram the ball past John Burridge from close range.

A kind of magic

(By Charles Lambert, Liverpool Daily Post, March 17, 1977)

Momentum appeared to be with the club on and off the pitch.

*S*O many times in the past, Goodison Park has worn an air of detachment, the spectators looking on politely like ancients watching the youngsters at play. Goodison would hardly have recognised the scenes at Hillsborough last night, just as it would not have recognised those at Wembley on Saturday.

There is a new spirit on the terraces – and the stands too, for last night the chant of "Everton are magic," a chant which looks like becoming their new theme song, came from the stands as much as from the other parts of the ground.

It is a spirit which is not easily related to the days, not so very long ago, when Goodison echoed not to hymns of adulation, but to the thuds of cushions landing on the turf.

Everton have still not won anything. The fans are not waiting for success before making themselves heard; they are weighing in with their contribution in a bid to achieve that success.

Last night proved it. They outshouted the Villa clans from before the start, but did they pack up when they went a goal down? Did they sidle away when the last seconds were running out? Did they hell! They kept up the chorus of "Everton are magic," and Bob Latchford proved they were right.

It was a united effort we saw last night, fans and players rooting for one another from the word go. When the team came out, Mick Lyons raised clenched fists above his head in acknowledgement of the crowd's roar as if he was saluting victory. When at last it was all over, the whole team ran to their supporters in spontaneous salute; only when Villa saw what they were doing did they follow suit.

So the communion was celebrated. It could mark the start of a new era in the relationship between Everton and their fans. Win or lose, this League Cup series will be remembered for more than just the football that was played.

A man called Clive
(April 23, 1977)

Unfortunately, despite taking an early lead through Bob Latchford, the League Cup would be lost, Brian Little's 118th-minute extra-time winner securing a 3-2 triumph at Old Trafford. Ten days later, there was an opportunity to bounce back and reach a first FA Cup final in nine years. Standing in their way? Champions-elect and European Cup finalists Liverpool, who Everton had failed to defeat in over five years.

$\mathcal{E}$VERTON, minus the injured 24-goal Bob Latchford and Andy King, went behind early on to their great rivals when Terry McDermott sent a superb chip over David Lawson.

A torrential downpour less than half-an-hour before the kick-off had left the pitch in an awful state and it played a part as Everton hit back just after the half-hour mark. Emlyn Hughes slipped trying to clear to let in Jim Pearson. The forward, who had replaced Latchford, found McKenzie with his cross and he made no mistake.

With the wind at their backs for the second half, the Blues seized control. Michael Charters' Football Echo report indicated the performance of McKenzie. He said: 'McKenzie beat Smith brilliantly and took the ball on a 30-yard run before passing to Pearson, whose half-hit shot was easily saved. McKenzie nearly got through again but Hughes took the ball away with a brilliant interception which McKenzie applauded, a nice touch.'

Despite this it was Liverpool who went back in front with less than 20 minutes left – Jimmy Case heading over the stranded David Lawson.

After 81 minutes Everton brought on Bryan Hamilton in place of Martin Dobson and almost instantly it was all square. Again McKenzie had a say, setting up Bruce Rioch for his first goal for the club.

In the dying minutes Ronny Goodlass cut in from the left and centred for McKenzie. His flick-on fell for Hamilton who deflected the ball past Ray Clemence and as Everton celebrated, Liverpool's players looked beaten. However, one of the great moments of derby controversy now unfolded.

Charters' Football Echo report noted: 'Hamilton chested the ball past Clemence, but the "goal" was disallowed, presumably for offside.'

Referee Clive Thomas had stepped in, disallowing the effort and awarding a free-kick to Liverpool, who got on with the game. Thomas later felt that from the angle of Hamilton's contact, there was no way he could have scored without handling the ball. An astonished Hamilton commented:

"I could tell that Emlyn Hughes, Ray Clemence, Joey Jones thought it was a goal and it was finished. It hit me on the hip, because it came at a difficult height. It was in between head and foot, and I just turned my side on it and it hit my hip-bone and went in the far corner. Unfortunately it wasn't the winner, but for me it was a goal, and it will always be the one that would have taken Everton to Wembley."

Everton, again without Latchford and this time Hamilton, away on international duty (Andy King returned on the bench), went down in the replay 3-0 four days later. Skipper Mick Lyons summed up everyone's thoughts: "We are sick."

Something blue

(By Gordon Hughes, Daily Mirror, June 18, 1977)

One fanatical Evertonian made the news when his love for the club collided with his marriage...

 YNNE Boswell's marriage blues started when her husband stripped for bed on their wedding night.

For his underpants were in the royal blue colours of his favourite soccer team.

And that was only the start of a tortured marriage that auburn-haired Lynne, 21, had to share with Everton Football Club. Husband Harold, 21, was such a fanatical Blues supported he:

PAINTED the front of their terrace home blue and white.

BEDECKED it with Everton banners and slogans.

NAMED it Goodison Park in letters a foot high.

AND even painted the street lamp outside blue and white.

That wasn't all. He registered their blue-eyed baby son Jason in the surnames of the entire Everton playing and coaching staff. He put pendants over the windows of their home in Olive Mount, Birkenhead, Merseyside. He decorated the fridge, cooker, washing machine and bedroom walls with Everton slogans and pictures of his favourite players. And when he went to sleep it was under a blue and white bedspread.

But now Lynne's marriage to soccer-crazy Harold is on the touchlines She is suing for divorce on the grounds of mental cruelty – and blaming Everton FC as the cause of the break-up.

After their registry office wedding four years ago, the pair celebrated at a small reception. But Harold made an excuse that he was slipping out for a pint and sloped off to cheer on his Goodison heroes.

Yesterday Lynne was back with mum in Kings Mount, Birkenhead. She said: "I always knew that Harold was an Everton fan but I didn't realise how much until our wedding day. I nearly died when I saw those underpants. He wasn't so bad to begin with, then he became more and more fanatical. If his team lost he wouldn't say a word."

Harold said: "Lynne said she even saw blue when she was watching TV. That was because I painted the frame of our set blue.

"She wasn't very pleased when I showed up at the wedding in a £75 blue and white suit. And it was like the beginning of the end when she saw my blue and white underpants on our wedding night.

"I've known her since I was 12. She must have known I was like that."

Last word from Lynne: "I've watched Everton only twice, and that was before our marriage – just to see George Best play at Goodison."

Shirt sponsorship on the way?

(By Charles Lambert, Liverpool Daily Post, June 27, 1977)

Having been influential figures in the effect of televised football, shirt sponsorship began to dominate the agenda as clubs looked to boost income.

*E*VERTON are to lead a bid by a number of clubs to persuade the Football League to give them the go-ahead to introduce advertising on players' shirts in time for the new season.

This follows the latest moves by the Football Association on the advertising issue, which has been a prominent topic for discussion since last season ended.

Some weeks ago the FA gave their consent to clubs displaying advertisements on their shirts, but on Saturday they decided that this would not apply to the FA Cup competition. But this still leaves the way open to clubs to conclude deals with commercial organisations with regard to matches played in the League and the League Cup.

All it now needs is for the League to give their consent, and the way is clear for English clubs to follow the trend already established on the Continent.

Everton, one of the leading exponents of the advertising theory, contacted the League today to check on their attitude to the situation.

It would appear that the League is reserving its position at present and Everton secretary Jim Greenwood said there was a chance that Everton would get together with Derby and Bolton, two other clubs who have shown particular interest in the idea with a view to pressing the League for a decision.

Said Mr Greenwood: "The League haven't yet decided what their attitude will be which makes life a little difficult if you are trying to negotiate with people."

Everton and the other clubs will want a quick answer to the question because there are many likely side-effects. Time is becoming increasingly short before the season begins, and once a deal has been signed there is the question of television coverage. Clubs – and sponsors – will want to know what the television companies' attitude is to shirts bearing advertisements.

The BBC has a strict code governing the televising of sport where advertisements play a big part, and there may be problems in keeping both them and the advertisers happy.

Moores leaves the board

(By Michael Charters, Liverpool Echo, July 8, 1977)

Despite stepping down from various boardroom roles in previous years, this was now apparently going to be the end for John Moores.

MR John Moores, who has been "Mr Everton" in the eyes of the football world since he became an Everton director 17 years ago, today resigned from the club board.

The move is not unexpected. Mr Moores, head of the giant Littlewoods empire and a life-long Evertonian, pumped cash, enthusiasm and his tremendous expertise into Everton when he came onto the board.

But now, at 79 years of age, he feels he has done enough, although I am sure he will remain a potent force in the background whenever the club needs him.

Mr Moores has assured the club if his continued backing and interest. "I will always be a 100 per cent Evertonian," he added.

He joined the board in March 1960. He was chairman from July 1960 until July 1965 and again in 1972/73. He then became vice-chairman and held that role until now.

The pen is no more

(By Charles Lambert, Liverpool Daily Post, August 26, 1977)

New safety regulations were in force ahead of the 1977/78 season which saw the Goodison Park capacity reduced to 35,000. Capacity the previous season was 56,000. It meant that changes to the ground were necessary with the end for the famous boys' pen.

*E*VERTON have been given the green light to add almost an extra 10,000 to their gate. This takes the club's spectator capacity well over the 40,000 mark once again, the most significant change spectators will notice is that the boys' pen at the Gwladys Street End has been removed. By doing this, the club has made available to the general terraces two extra staircases which previously led only to the pen.

Call Chris

(By Charles Lambert, Liverpool Daily Post, June 5, 1978)

Check out our secretary's number! The club installs a 24-hour phone service.

*F*ELLAS, this is what you've been waiting for – the chance to note lovely Chris Welch's phone number, and ring her 24 hours a day!

Chris is Everton's girl with all the answers, and supporters can cash in by dialling 051 523 6642. That's the number of the new Everton information service, an automatic telephone-answering device which relays recorded messages about forthcoming fixtures and ticket arrangements. Until now, any success by Everton on the field has meant extra work for Chris who, as the receptionist at Goodison, has had to answer countless inquiries from fans. Now she simply records the information on tape and lets the machine do the work.

Fenced in

(Liverpool Echo, June 21, 1978)

Ground improvements – and bad news for wannabe pitch invaders.

$\mathcal{G}$OODISON is getting the fenced-in look. Work is now well underway on Everton's £65,000 project which will cut out the risk of pitch invasions. The decision to erect fences around the ground was taken over a year ago, but a start was delayed until the end of last season. Everton's qualification for Europe has been an added spur, as the UEFA authorities have shown they will clamp down hard on any club whose crowd control precautions are inadequate.

A side-effect of the fences is the removal of the semi-circles behind each goal. These were originally installed to reduce the risk of missiles being thrown at goalkeepers, but now the terracing is being replaced and the capacity at the Park and Gwladys Street ends will therefore be increased. Putting up fences is the latest phase in a series of ground improvements at Goodison over the last 12 months. In all the club has spent over £300,000 on the various operations.

Chairman Carter

(Liverpool Echo, August 4, 1978)

A familiar name takes over the club chairmanship.

$\mathcal{E}$VERTON have a new chairman – Mr Philip Carter, who takes over from Mr Bill Scott, chairman for the last two years.

Mr Carter, managing director of the Littlewoods organisation, formally stepped up at the club's annual meeting last night.

Though Glasgow-born, he has been an Everton supporter since the age of five, and has been a director for the last three years. He said: "It's a very great honour to be chairman of a club of this stature. We've had a tremendous record in the past, and I hope we have a glorious future."

Andy does us all a favour

(By Frank McGhee, Daily Mirror, October 30 1978)

The day a seven-year wait came to an end, while the goal hero and BBC interviewer Richard Duckenfield were shoved off the pitch by a burly copper.

LIVERPOOL fans won't like me for saying so but Everton did the whole of football a favour at Goodison Park on Saturday.

And it wasn't just because they beat the league leaders 1-0 to close to an attainable two points the gap at the top of the table – a gap which, with a different result, might have become a frightening six points. Everton provided them with a rude awakening. And that is the most important service they provided to football last Saturday – Liverpool CAN be beaten in the league.

Liverpool will have to live with the fact that all of the many arguments which inevitably raged long afterwards in pubs and clubs and around TV sets, about who was the best player on the park, had one common factor. The only names mentioned were those of Everton players.

There was, for an obvious start, Andy King, the midfield man whose spectacular volley in the 58th minute deservedly won a game Everton dominated. Dave Thomas figured largely in the "man-of-the-match" arguments because of the way his bare, bandy legs carried him at speed so many times past Case and Neal to fire good crosses.

But for me the most eye-catching performance was that of Everton's 20-year-old central defender Billy Wright.

He did superbly against both David Johnson and Kenny Dalglish and is already obviously one to watch for the future.

Yet for me the real heroes of the day were not on the pitch, they were all around it – 53,131 of 'em – two passionately opposing, singing, shouting, banner-waving sets of fans.

All I want for Christmas is

(By Horace Yates, Liverpool Daily Post, November 2, 1978)

Dave Thomas held his hands up as Everton's European adventure was cut short – this time in Czechoslovakia.

$\mathcal{E}$VERTON are out of Europe because of the rule that away goals count double in the event of equality. After the 2-1 win in the first leg at Goodison, a goal 10 minutes from the end in Prague yesterday was sufficient to take Dukla into the third round of the UEFA Cup.

"I was to blame," said Dave Thomas, Everton's international winger, discussing the goal 10 minutes from the end.

"I hold my hands up," he said. "I thought Gajdusek was closer to me when I tried to flick the ball over his head, but that's life. There's nothing you can do about it now. It's over and done with. You are up one minute with victory over Liverpool and you are down the next. Now we have to get on with it and concentrate on Nottingham Forest."

Bolton blizzard

(By Ian Hargraves, Liverpool Daily Post, January 2, 1979)

A league game at Bolton Wanderers – who wore red to distinguish themselves in the blizzard-like conditions – was abandoned after the wintry conditions turned the spectacle into a farce. It was to prove a painful experience for a future Evertonian.

$\mathcal{A}$T 3pm yesterday the A58 which runs through Bolton was probably a better surface for football than the Burnden Park pitch. Certainly, it could have been no harder than the frozen rock that passed for soil and grass – and the Highway Department salt at least melted the snow that drove down throughout a bleak afternoon.

Those of us from Liverpool who crept and skidded down the side roads to Burnden Park were both grateful and amazed that the game should have started at all.

But there they were – Bolton in red shirts instead of their normal white so that we could see them in the blizzard, and Everton looking blue in more ways than one.

It was chance in the 12th minute that directed a back pass from Neil Robinson into a patch of soft snow and allowed Frank Worthington lurking like a snow Apache in his red shirt and headband to slither in and prod it past Wood left footed into the net.

It was Ross who ran up unmarked when King took a ball from Thomas, cut through the centre and took what seemed to be ages before he turned it to his right to allow the Everton strong man to waste no time in shooting past McDonagh from 18 yards.

There was drama at the other end when Wood, diving bravely forward to cut out a through ball, crouched with it in his arms and was stationary when Peter Reid, the Bolton midfield player, skidded into him. While everyone expected Wood to be the one injured it was Reid who lay brushed with snow until he was carried off.

Barnsley referee Trelford Mills was at the centre of the controversy over his decision to start the match which was abandoned at half-time. Both managers said after the match they were against it ever starting.

Everton manager Gordon Lee said: "As I understand it people have paid the money to see football played in football boots on grass and there was no way this was anything like that."

Bolton manager Ian Greaves said that his midfield player Peter Reid may have suffered ligament trouble in a collision caused by the state of the ground.

"There is no way this game should ever have started," said Mr Greaves. Referee Mills blamed the intensity of the snow storm for making a mockery of his decision to start the game.

A million reasons to say no

(By Charles Lambert, Liverpool Daily Post, February 17, 1979)

Everton were unwilling to go to seven figures to secure Trevor Francis, who would soon become the country's first £1m player.

$\mathcal{E}$VERTON opted out of the chase for Trevor Francis because they felt that signing him at a fee of £1,000,000 was not in the overall interests of the club.

That is chairman Philip Carter's answer to supporters who are puzzled at Everton's decision to watch from the sidelines while Nottingham Forest, one of their biggest rivals for honours, snapped up the best player to become available since Kenny Dalglish and Kevin Keegan were transferred. Mr Carter said the asking price was unrealistic.

"Everyone at Everton was of the opinion that Francis was a first-class player but that a million pounds was a ridiculous price," he said.

"If paying ridiculous figures means we unsettle the stability of the club, and therefore could have long-term consequences, then the board and myself would not condone that sort of irresponsible behaviour."

Everton have often been said to have an impersonal relationship with the public, and I took the opportunity of mentioning this to Mr Carter. He said: "I would disagree violently. Everybody does a damn good job in projecting the general image of the club. I don't think you can isolate the club's image from the fans, and the fans we have both at home and away are a credit to us, and are part of our total image."

UEFA qualification secured

(Liverpool Echo, May 8, 1979)

European football was secured for a second successive season courtesy of a fourth-place finish.

$\mathcal{E}$VERTON completed their league programme, and their 1-1 draw at White Hart Lane on Saturday has ensured their participation in the UEFA Cup next season.

Brian Kidd's goal enabled them to get the point needed and, although one or two other clubs have still to settle their differences, Everton have at least gained something, from a generally disappointing season.

Welcome to Hafnia

(By Charles Lambert, Liverpool Daily Post, August 3, 1979)

With commercial opportunities continuing to be sought off the pitch, Everton now appeared to have changed their stance on televising the club. However, they were unhappy about restrictions on shirt sponsorship.

*E*VERTON chairman Philip Carter has launched a bitter attack on the television companies for keeping shirt advertising off the screens.

And he is demanding that the recent 10 million pound TV contract with the BBC and ITV be renegotiated to allow clubs a bigger share of sponsorship revenue.

Mr Carter's comments were made at Everton's annual meeting last night, after he had revealed that the players' shirts will be sponsored by the Jaka Foods company, New Brighton, this season.

The shirts will carry the name Hafnia, one of Jaka's brand names, in all non-televised league and League Cup matches.

Everton officials would not reveal the amount of money Everton will receive from this form of sponsorship. But it will be only a fraction of the cash that would flow in if the TV companies lifted their ban on shirt adverts. "Sponsors of nearly every other sport receive coverage on television which is denied to football," said Mr Carter. "To me this doesn't make sense.

"It is not unreasonable for us to ask the Football League to renegotiate the situation with the television companies, to see if we can get the added advantage of television revenue from sponsorship."

New blood required

(By Charles Lambert, Liverpool Daily Post, May 11, 1979)

Andy Gray was linked with a move to Goodison – with Bob Latchford heading the list of possible departures as Gordon Lee sought bring in new blood.

$\mathcal{B}$OB Latchford in a swap for Andy Gray – that could be Everton manager Gordon Lee's answer to the club's goals shortage.

With Aston Villa striker Gray demanding a move, I believe Mr Lee will be among the first managers to make inquiries. And he could offer Latchford, the current England number nine, in an exchange package.

And whether that deal comes off or not, the Goodison careers of Latchford and team-mates Mike Pejic and Dave Thomas are likely to end in the near future.

All three players are believed to want away from Everton, although Mr Lee denied reports that they have submitted transfer requests.

Meanwhile, Everton have withdrawn from the hunt for Chelsea's Ray Wilkins. Mr Lee had talks with Wilkins yesterday, and was unable to persuade the England midfielder to move to Goodison.

"He is grateful that we were interested in him, but he wants to stay with Chelsea for the time being," said Mr Lee. "It is another setback and I am very disappointed."

Something blue, part two

(By Peter Cain, Liverpool Daily Post, May 20, 1979)

It's that man Harry again – although he wasn't going to miss out on his big day... at Goodison...

$\mathcal{H}$ARRY Boswell kicked off his second marriage with the wedding day blues. For he "deserted" his bride hours after the ceremony to watch Everton lose 4-2 in their opening fixture of the season to Norwich. This was a 'replay' of his first marriage, which ended in divorce.

Harry, an Everton fanatic, turned up for his wedding at Birkenhead Registry Office sporting a new suit in the club's colours. He even had on blue underwear and wore a club scarf under his jacket.

Even his "Match of the Day" fixture was arranged for the day of the big kick-off to bring Everton luck. But the wedding's lucky horseshoe did not work on the Goodison boys.

After Saturday's ceremony Harry, 31, and his new bride Tina Sinnett, 21, went to their council home in Quigley Street, Birkenhead, where they cut into a blue and white wedding cake in the shape of a football pitch. Then the reception for nearly 40 guests was interrupted while Harry took his bride to Goodison Park for a specially arranged handshake with Everton boss Gordon Lee.

After the game he said: "Naturally I was disappointed at the result but feel sure the team will improve. Anyway I have a new season ahead of me with my new bride."

His fanaticism for Everton was one of the reasons his previous marriage was kicked into touch.

Harry's first wife objected to him painting their Olive Mount, Birkenhead, home blue and white and naming their son Jason after the entire Everton team which won the league championship in 1970. The couple divorced in January.

Czech-mate

(By Charles Lambert, Liverpool Daily Post, October 3, 1979)

Ahead of the UEFA Cup first-round, second-leg tie at Goodison with Feyenoord – one-up from the first leg - the opposition were hopeful of defeat.

_M_EANWHILE Vaclav Jezek, the Feyenoord coach, arrived in Liverpool last night with a surprising view of tonight's game.

"I hope Everton win," said the Czechoslovakian-born coach, adding with a smile: "But only by 2-1."

Such a scoreline would be enough to put Feyenoord into round two on the away goals rule. But behind Jezek's comment was affection for Everton which goes back six years to the time when, as coach of the Czech national team, he visited Everton to study their training methods. "I have been an Everton supporter ever since," he said.

Feyenoord dash European dream

(By Charles Lambert, Liverpool Daily Post, October 4, 1979)

Another European campaign ended prematurely as the Dutch side ran out 1-0 winners on the night, 2-0 on aggregate.

$\mathcal{G}$EOFF Nulty was one of Everton's stars on the field last night – but they had nearly 30,000 stars who didn't kick a ball. And Nulty led the tributes to the supporters, who did their best to inspire the team throughout last night's match against Feyenoord.

Said Nulty: "The crowd were great. They lifted us tremendously. Feyenoord never gave us a problem until they scored – and even then the crowd kept cheering us on. Feyenoord are a team who have been unbeaten for 12 months, and I don't think many people expected us to do as well as we did against them."

Nulty also spoke about the effect on the other players of Bob Latchford's return, as a 67th-minute substitute. "It was good to see Bob back. He is a quality player, and when you see an England international coming off the bench it makes everyone feel six inches taller."

Derby mayhem

(Liverpool Echo, October 22, 1979)

A 2-2 derby draw at Anfield contained many memorable moments – a calamitous Mick Lyons own goal and a streaker being just two of them.

$\mathcal{W}$HAT they said about the derby. Liverpool manager Bob Paisley: "Everton must be the luckiest team to take a point here this season. They did not put two passes together all afternoon."

Everton manager Gordon Lee: "We showed tremendous character. A lot of sides who had given away a goal like the one Mick Lyons did would have been beaten. Probably an own goal like that could only happen in a local derby. But Mike did not let his head drop, he came battling back. This will do us a lot of good."

John Gidman, who spent his first Saturday as an Everton player watching from the dugout: "I have never been so excited. I was so excited I did not even notice the streaker."

Staying afloat

(By Alan Gordon, Daily Mirror, November 7, 1979)

Two Merseyside lads used football as a tool in simply staying alive, having been left ship-wrecked...

*T*EAM spirit – that's what kept shipmates Don Crane and Mark Fook alive when their ship sank under them. And the teams were those great Merseyside rivals, Liverpool and Everton. Don, 21, is an Everton fan. His close friend Mark, 18, supports Liverpool.

With their fellow crewmen dead, they clung desperately to floating wreckage in the icy, storm-lashed English Channel. The lads knew their only chance of survival was to keep up their spirits. So they sang their teams' songs and chanted their rival slogans at each other.

Four-and-a-half hours later, when a rescue helicopter clattered overhead, they were still croaking out "Ee aye addio."

Don, of Wallasey, Merseyside, and Mark, of Hough Green, Widnes, Cheshire, were the only survivors of 15 people aboard the coaster Pool Fisher, which capsized and sank off the Isle of Wight.

From his hospital bed last night, Mark said: "We knew we would be saved if only we could hang on. To keep up our spirits I thought of my girlfriend Jean and we chanted Liverpool and Everton songs until we were hoarse."

Patience wearing thin

(By Nick Hilton, Liverpool Daily Post, February 11, 1980)

The pressure was on Gordon Lee after a drubbing at home to high-flying Ipswich Town left the club languishing in 17th – and with another bill to replace some cushions.

$\mathcal{E}$VERTON chairman Philip Carter last night denied rumours that manager Gordon Lee's future at the club rested on their staying in the FA Cup.

And he underlined his backing for Lee after Saturday's 4-0 defeat by Ipswich which had a posse of fans demonstrating outside Goodison chanting: "We'll support you if Lee goes."

Carter said talk about Lee losing his job was "idle gossip." He went on: "He is the manager and we are backing him. He's going through a bad patch and so is the team. But he's the same manager now as he was in the last two good seasons when we finished third and fourth in the league. The team has changed and he is having problems getting it settled down."

A section of the 31,000 crowd on Saturday chanted for his dismissal immediately after the final whistle, and 300 gathered in the street outside the main entrance afterwards until dispersed by police.

A cushion was thrown onto the pitch soon after Ipswich's second goal, and a shower of them poured down after the final whistle which was greeted with a chorus of jeers and boos.

Mr Lee, who has been Everton's manager for three years, said after the game that his team's performance had been "a shambles" and that he was "ashamed of them".

But he faced the fans' criticism squarely last night when he said: "After a display like that it was only natural that the fans were frustrated. They are entitled to something better and I have got to take the stick just as you take the praise when you are doing well.

"It was my team selection and I could make a million excuses. But that's not me. If I was a fan I would be very disappointed and I can't blame them.

"They pay their money and what they saw was disastrous. It was so bad it was untrue. It was a nightmare. Defensively we were diabolical and Ipswich looked like scoring every time they went up."

Tributes to the greatest centre-forward ever

(Liverpool Echo, March 3, 1980)

The great William Ralph "Dixie" Dean passed away towards the end of an Everton v Liverpool derby clash, fittingly at his beloved Goodison Park.

*T*RIBUTES have been pouring in for the legendary Dixie Dean, who died on Saturday at Goodison Park, the scene of many of his greatest goal-scoring glories.

Dixie, who was 73, complained of feeling unwell towards the end of the derby. He was taken to the players' gymnasium where he was examined by a doctor but died before an ambulance could reach him.

The tragic news – broken to officials and players from both clubs shortly after the Everton-Liverpool game ended – cast a shadow over the derby occasion.

Dixie, the son of a Birkenhead railwayman, spent the last years of his life confined to a wheelchair following a leg amputation in 1976. Despite the handicap, he remained a regular at Everton home matches.

Everton chairman Philip Carter said: "Dixie Dean was synonymous with the name of Everton. Wherever he travelled he was Everton through and through."

Former Everton chairman John Moores said: "I was present when Everton beat Arsenal and Dixie established the new goalscoring record. He was always good for the game and always gave young players a lot of encouragement."

Former Liverpool manager Bill Shankly described Dixie as "one of the all-time greats". He added: "The hardest thing to do in football is score and he was a past master. To stop him from scoring you would have to hold his legs. When he headed the ball it frightened the life out of people."

Everton manager Gordon Lee said he felt Dixie had helped the Goodison club to greatness.

"He helped Everton to become the great club it is both as a player and a person. Each generation throws up a player – a Stanley Matthews, a Tom Finney – a person who embodies public belief in what the footballer should be. Dixie Dean was one of the select band."

Highs and lows for Kidd

(By Charles Burgess, Liverpool Daily Post, April 14, 1980)

With Liverpool facing Arsenal in the other semi-final, there was the opportunity to set-up the first-ever all-Merseyside FA Cup final. Second Division West Ham were no pushovers though. They held Everton to a 1-1 draw for whom Brian Kidd was sent off, having earlier opened the scoring at Villa Park. The controversy regarding the referee's showing was considered in the wake of the tie. The Blues, backed by 30,000 Evertonians at Elland Road, would go on to lose the replay 2-1 four days later. Frank Lampard Snr's header deep into extra time won it. Skipper Mick Lyons reportedly told Kevin Ratcliffe, playing only his second senior game: "You've got plenty of time to get to another final. The rest won't get another chance." Gordon Lee exclaimed: "The only reason Lampard was there to score was because he was too knackered to get back to his defensive position."

*T*HE saddest man in British football yesterday was Carlisle referee Colin Seel. He took last week off work from a local print works to prepare himself for Saturday's semi-final at Villa Park, refereed as best as he thought he possibly could and woke up yesterday morning to find himself being slated for his performance. His fee was £35, taxed at source.

Criticism has been levelled at him for giving Everton a penalty, for not sending off Trevor Ross, already booked, after a bad looking tackle and for sending penalty scorer Brian Kidd off on the advice of a linesman after Kidd and Ray Stewart were involved in a fracas.

Said Seel yesterday: "I was happy after the match that I could not have done any better." On Wednesday night Seel will be the man in the middle again at the replay at Elland Road, a match he is looking forward to. He will do his best again. Receipts will be well over £100,000. Colin Seel will get £35, the same as he received for officiating at Tranmere a few weeks back. I wish him luck.

Lee in for Reid

(By Ian Hargraves & Charles Lambert, Liverpool Echo, July 11, 1980)

With Lee seeking to improve on a disappointing 19th-place finish, he looked to reinforce the midfield.

*E*VERTON manager Gordon Lee was locked in secret talks with Bolton's midfield star, Peter Reid, today, in a last-minute bid to bring the former England Under-21 skipper to Goodison Park for a fee expected to be about £750,000.

Reid, whose contract with Bolton expired at the end of last season, has been made a "fabulous" offer of £800 a week to stay at Burnden, but has made it clear he is not prepared to play in the Second Division. He has already had talks with Wolves, who are prepared to meet Bolton's asking price and is due to meet their manager John Barnwell again to discuss personal terms this weekend.

Mr Lee has made no secret of his admiration for Reid, who was out of the game for more than a year following a serious knee injury suffered in a collision in a match against Everton on New Year's Day, 1979.

He made an impressive return to the Bolton side last spring, and proved his complete recovery during a run of 20 matches when he was easily Bolton's outstanding player.

Sources close to Reid say that the Liverpool-born player would prefer to come to Goodison. He is thought to have a deep-rooted admiration for Everton's potential and tradition.

Also in Everton's favour is that Wolves operate a rigid pay structure and are known to be reluctant to pay a new "star" more than the rest of their players. If Mr Lee is ready to match Bolton's pay offer, or at least get close to it, he may be able to lure Reid to Goodison.

The asking price of £750,000, if paid in full, would be an Everton record for a player – but the Goodison club have always been among the pace-setters in the past, and they badly need a new personality to spark off a revival.

Who holds the shares

(By Ian Hargraves, Liverpool Echo, July 16, 1980)

A share issue – local readers were given the opportunity to see who had interests in both Everton and Liverpool. There's one or two interesting names who feature, with the Moores family – and Littlewoods – still retaining a big interest.

*K*EEPING an accurate picture of who actually holds all the shares of either club is a complicated business, as they spread over a vast area, with hundreds of people owning a mere handful each. Many shares are held in other people's names, and some still stand in the names of people who have been dead for several years.

A classic example of this is supplied by the case of the late Frank Sugg, who was still listed as a shareholder of both Liverpool and Everton as recently as 12 months ago. Sugg, who played football for Everton, Sheffield Wednesday, Derby County and Burnley (and who also played cricket for Lancashire and England) was born in 1862 and died in 1933!

With Sir John Moores now in partial retirement, and none of his family showing any obvious interest in following in his footsteps, many are wondering what will eventually happen to this powerful interest in one of Britain's premier clubs. Sir John Moores is, of course, also a major shareholder at Liverpool, as is his son John junior, but he has always been content to hold a watching brief at Anfield.

GUIDE TO WHO OWNS OUR TWO BIG CLUBS

Everton (Shares issued: 2,500)

Directors' shareholdings (as of August 16, 1979)

Philip Carter	23
Bill Scott	3
George Watts	3
Alan Waterworth	6
John Search	3
Keith Tamlin	20
David Newton	3

Other leading shareholdings (as of August 16, 1979)

Sir John Moores	751
John Lindop	92
Alfred Fisher	40
John Borthwick	34
Grenville Hinton	33
John Moores Jnr	32
Ada Butter	32
Frank Linaker Legge	28
Bertram Hackney	26
Evelyn Baxter	21
Enid Stevenson	19
Alastair Turnbull	17
David Moores	15
Teresa Hamilton-Sugden	15
Fred Micklesfield	11

Other local shareholdings of interest

John Behrend	3
William Borthwick	5
Arthur Colenso	1
Peter Dutton	3

Robert Hepburn	3
Alan Isaac	1
Solly Isenwater	4
Ingram Legge	3
Joseph Mercer	3
David Mars-Jones	3
Howard Neve	3
Barton Mills	1
Peter Parry	1
Sidney Reakes	3
Michael Reece	3
John Searle	3
Bill Shankly	1
Anthony Shone	1
*Frank Sugg	1
John Tushingham	3
John Lyall White	2

Now deceased

What price?

(Liverpool Echo, July 18, 1980)

What odds the Blues these days!

 *B*LUES' fan Robert Legge saw red when he discovered Everton were quoted as 50-1 shots for next season's league title in his local betting shop.

He smashed the screen on the counter after an argument with the manager and at Wirral Magistrates Court, it cost him a £20 fine and £43.15 compensation when he admitted causing damage.

Legge (36) said in a statement it was a disgrace Everton should be quoted at such a price.

A long time coming

(January 24, 1981)

There was little reason to suspect that Arsenal's impressive FA Cup record in the previous three seasons – three finals, one win – would end against the Toffees, who found themselves on the slide in the First Division. There was the first real blooming of progress in the club's youth policy, with defenders Kevin Ratcliffe (20) and Billy Wright (22) beginning to make their mark. The Blues deservedly claimed the spoils, making the breakthrough six minutes from time when Joe McBride's hard cross into the box glanced off Kenny Sansom and past Pat Jennings. With time ticking away, substitute Mick Lyons made it 2-0 in the last minute. A bigger challenge lay ahead with a tie against the European champions from across the Park.

*I*N front of nearly 53,000 (providing Everton-record gate receipts), Everton created the better chances in the tie even after goals from Peter Eastoe and Imre Varadi. The latter received a meat pie to the face having netted at the Park End where Liverpool fans were congregated. Martin Hodge was given a dramatic call-up, having not played in the first team since the previous April after Jim McDonagh was ruled out with an ankle injury. Avi Cohen came in for the injured Alan Kennedy on the Liverpool side and referee Clive Thomas was given a torrid reception by the home faithful.

Substitute Jimmy Case, on for the injured Kenny Dalglish pulled a goal back with 14 minutes left, although Bob Paisley admitted afterwards that his team had been outplayed.

It was the first and only time Mick Lyons had played for the victorious side in 20 derbies and hundreds poured onto the pitch at the end. Lyons declared afterwards: "At the end I didn't want to be on the pitch. I wanted to be on the terraces with the fans."

Reds' boss Bob Paisley admitted: "In all my years at Liverpool I have never known an Everton team that has been stronger than us, but in the first half they were stronger. I hope now that Everton go on and win the Cup."

The final word goes to former chairman and major shareholder

Sir John Moores (who had turned 85 on the Sunday): "After years of having our noses rubbed in it, it is at least some solace to have beaten them at last."

Blue heaven

(By Graham Bell, Liverpool Daily Post, January 26, 1981)

It's safe to say the fans enjoyed a famous victory.

 *T*HERE was a special air of ecstasy about every pub in Goodison Road on Saturday night.

A bobbing, weaving tubful of blue-and-white splashed out of the Winslow in a sea of Whitbread bitter. They were banked atop tables and chairs as tightly as on the Gwladys Street terraces, their faces lit like beacons and their voices shrieking like sirens.

Mick Lyons and his crew were caught in the wash and swept in with the tide. The more reserved shook the victors by the hand and patted them on the back, the less inhibited grabbed them in a bearhug and planted kisses.

What has so often been Everton's chapel of mourning after derby defeats became a temple to worship heroes. Former favourites like Duncan McKenzie, in trench-coat and Austrian homburg, were just as welcome at this banquet of beer.

For big-hearted loyalists like Lyons it must have been an emotional reception. This is the first time he has been on a derby-winning side in 20 games.

"I can't thank the fans enough," he said. "They gave us such a tremendous lift. At the end I didn't want to be on the pitch, I wanted to be on the terraces with them. There are so many scousers in our side and I think that gave us greater commitment than ever before.

"Every tackle was like a battle. When we went two-up I kept looking at Steve McMahon and pointing to my heart. 'It's up here now,' I told him – and that's where we won it."

Big screen, small crowd

(Liverpool Daily Post, January 26, 1981)

Fans also watched in Liverpool Stadium and at local cinemas – but it was an experiment that was unlikely to be repeated, particularly with prices at £5.50 for a cinema ticket. Top prices for a stand ticket at Goodison was £3.20. The following piece summed up the viewing experience

$\mathcal{G}$ET your spot-the-crowd tickets," chanted the lugubrious gent decked out in Liverpool red. "First prize a Goodison season ticket. Second prize two Goodison season tickets." The joke was lost on the harassed Viewsport official, whose own spot-the-crowd calculations were no laughing matter.

Twenty minutes to go before the "match of the season" and disaster was already written large on his glazed countenance. "Lucky if you get 300," pined a cheery steward, peering into the murky depths of Liverpool Stadium.

Here and there a sprinkling of spectators – looking for all the world like refugees from the world's end – stared grimly at the closed-circuit TV gadgetry as if daring something to happen.

Erected in the boxing ring, the screens resembled nothing more than a hastily-erected bathing tent. Without the bathers.

"Saw more excitement at me auntie's funeral," quipped a weighty Evertonian. "No cheering, please," chided his mate, making a great play of finding a vacant seat in the echoing emptiness.

"Free tea at the interval," announced the man at the door. "And you'll only need one teapot," came the lightning-fast rejoinder. By now the screens' checkerboard pattern had been replaced by the Everton centenary emblem, which caused a minor stir.

Suddenly, it happened, as they say in all the best melodramas. One minute we're gazing blankly at a 12ft by 9ft chessboard, the next transported to what appears to be a ploughed field. Relief all round when it appears to be Viewsport's monochrome version of Goodison

Park, and then a focus close up of the pitch ushering us in.

So this was what soccer looked like in black and white. All it needed was Stanley Matthews in knee length shorts and it would have been a ringer for All Our Yesterdays. That sort of nostalgia we could've lived with, what followed we most definitely could not.

"Oh no, it's him," shrieked a voice from the gloom. "It's him!" And it was indeed "him." Not the dreaded Clive Thomas, lapping up the boos centre stage, but the cobwebbed Kenneth Wolstenholme dredged up from the soccer commentators' valhalla for another taste of the big time.

"It's up to you to make your own enjoyment," he told us. "Create your own atmosphere. Cheer as loud as you like."

Well we didn't. And if we did it couldn't be heard above the Goodison roar. I tell a lie. The Evertonians did raise three cheers – it may possibly have been four – and at least 10 heads were seen to gyrate when Varadi put the tie beyond doubt.

The Liverpudlians lay crumpled in their seats, trying hard not to believe it. They managed a spasm or two when Jimmy Case scored, but for the rest it was really Mr Wolstenholme's day.

"You'll be glad to know that Bristol City have equalised against Carlisle." We weren't. Not ever.

"Don't worry about the bandage on Phil Neal's leg. It's just to keep his stocking up, not to staunch the blood." Thanks, Ken.

His moment of glory came just after half-time when it took him what seemed like half an hour to discover that Dalglish was no longer on the field. We all helped him, but he didn't hear.

And so to the end, when all the smiles wore blue scarves, and at least two Liverpudlians, headed bowed as if in prayer, had to be prised away to face cold, stark reality.

Outside, a solitary policeman chortled when I asked about crowd trouble. "What crowd?" he asked. He was still laughing like a drain when I left him.

An unlikely hero

(February 17, 1981)

Southampton were seen as one of the toughest possible draws when the Blues were handed a trip to The Dell in round five. But with Jim McDonagh inspired in the Everton goal, the Blues earned a 0-0 draw on the south coast backed by 6,000 visiting fans in The Dell's 24,000-capacity ground.

*I*NTEREST was high in the replay, with fans queuing outside Goodison Park for tickets the day before the game, which was not all-ticket. There was little to choose between the sides at a packed Goodison Park (nearly 50,000 crammed in, virtually twice the average First Division attendance). But the extra time period saw the Blues edge into the last eight thanks to a player who was playing non-League football for Mossley only months earlier – Eamonn O'Keefe.

O'Keefe, a man who two years before was delivering newspapers for a living, wrote his name into the headlines. The match-winner revealed: "Seeing the ball fly into the net was the greatest moment of my life.

"When it went in we knew we had won. Having beaten Arsenal, Liverpool and Southampton, I reckon they should give us a bye straight into the semi-final."

Lee days numbered

(By Nick Hilton, Liverpool Daily Post, April 13, 1981)

A defeat to 20th-placed Norwich City in front of less than 17,000 at Goodison appeared to signal that the end was nigh for Gordon Lee. Meanwhile, a familiar name had been proving his managerial credentials in Lancashire.

*H*OWARD Kendall will be the next manager of Everton.

I understand the club's concern over their rapidly declining support will lead to the appointment of Kendall, the public's favourite, as successor to Gordon Lee. Chairman Philip Carter's statement following the 2-0 home defeat to Norwich on Saturday, which revealed that the position of manager and his coaching staff were under review, has, I believe, spelled the end of Lee's four-and-a-half years at Goodison.

Kendall, currently manager of promotion-chasing Blackburn in the Second Division, would jump at the chance of returning to the club he skippered in the 1970s and helped to their last championship success 11 years ago. As odd-on favourite for the job, his appointment will probably be at the end of the campaign, as Everton are unlikely to break the League club's gentleman's agreement over not taking a manager from another club during the season.

Lee's future is in doubt because Everton are hovering dangerously close to the relegation zone following a run of eight league matches that have yielded one point.

A big task for the new boss

(By Ian Hargraves, Liverpool Echo, May 7, 1981)

*E*VEN those Merseysiders who did not think Gordon Lee was the ideal manager for Everton must have felt considerable sympathy for him over the last few weeks as he soldiered bravely on in the face of adversity. His honesty, his courage and his immense enthusiasm have all earned him great respect, and it must be hoped that he will have further opportunities to demonstrate them with another club.

Like one or two others who have just been sacked, he has come out of his own personal ordeal with more credit than many of those firing the bullets. The question now is who will be offered – and accept – the tremendous task of revitalising Everton, a great club who have come increasingly under the shadow of their distinguished neighbours.

Few will doubt the potential there, but over the last decade there has always been a lingering feeling that something vital was missing, perhaps a spark of genuine inspiration or one hundred per cent determination to live up to the club's historic demand for Nothing But The Best. What the critics, and the board, must remember is that for all their great history neither Everton nor any other famous club have a divine right to be successful. Like Liverpool, Manchester United, Arsenal or indeed Tranmere Rovers, they will get exactly what they deserve in terms of dedication, planning and sheer hard work.

Everyone will hope that Everton eventually find an outstanding manager with the qualities to restore former glories. But let nobody be under any misapprehension about the magnitude of the task facing him. He will need all the help and understanding he can get.

Kendall is the choice

(By Ian Hargraves, Liverpool Echo, May 12, 1981)

With Howard Kendall appointed, he wasted no time in making changes.

*H*OWARD Kendall made his first decisive moves as Everton's new manager today when he sacked "with great reluctance" his predecessor's assistant Geoff Nulty and chief coach Eric Harrison.

"It's not a pleasant task to have to do something like this," he told me.

"But I believe you have to make your mind up and then act as soon as possible. It isn't fair to the people concerned to keep them hanging about."

Kendall's famous midfield playing partner of the glory era, Colin Harvey, has agreed to continue in his present position as reserve-team coach, and the new manager is hoping to persuade his chief coach at Blackburn, Mike Heaton, to join him at Goodison.

Reinforcing Everton on tour [to Japan] will be the 22-year-old striker from Queens Park, Alan Irvine, whose signing should have been completed late yesterday afternoon. "At the last minute we discovered there was a technical snag and that he couldn't sign for us before May 15," Kendall explained. "I haven't seen him myself, so I can't claim any credit but I respect the judgement of the people who have seen him, and they rate the lad an outstanding prospect."

All change

(Liverpool Echo, August 26, 1981)

"New" was the recurring theme ahead of the 1981/82 season.

$\mathcal{A}$ NEW era is dawning at Goodison Park where yesterday Everton unveiled its 11 new executive boxes and reception rooms under the Main Stand. Each box, on lease at £5,000 a season – and they have all been snapped up – has an uninterrupted view of the pitch, its own television, bar and sink unit and comfortably seats 10.

Other changes at Goodison include a new pitch and new seating in the Bullens Road stand.

And there's a new look on the field too. New manager Howard Kendall has brought in Neville Southall, Mick Ferguson, Mike Walsh, Mike Thomas, Jim Arnold, Alan Ainscow and Alan Biley.

Thomas shipped out

(By Ian Hargraves, Liverpool Echo, November 5, 1981)

The new manager didn't take long to get tough, off-loading one of his seven summer signings before the year was out.

$\mathcal{E}$ VERTON were today hoping to complete the sale of Welsh international midfielder Mickey Thomas to Brighton for £400,000 – because he refused to play in the reserve match at Newcastle last Saturday. "Thomas had recovered from the injury that kept him out of a couple of games, and wanted to come straight back into the first team against Manchester City," Kendall told me today.

"There was no way I was going to change the team that had played so well against Coventry, especially as Thomas' replacement Paul Lodge had an outstanding game. So I told Thomas he would be playing for the reserves. He refused to play, and that was that. There is no way any player on our staff tells the manager who he puts in this team."

1982-1991

Building for the future

(By Ian Hargraves, Liverpool Echo, March 23, 1982)

Everton were heading in the right direction, with youth apparently the key to the club's future success.

*E*VERTON chairman Philip Carter has told his fellow shareholders that he is confident the club are now on the right lines.

"We said last year that we were resolved to build for the future on the basis of youth, and that is exactly what we have done," he emphasised. "One thing we thought important was that we must not look for instant success. We must be patient.

"We cannot expect success immediately. We now have the basis of a squad for the future, but they are still young and need time to fit into the First Division cauldron."

Manager Howard Kendall also told the shareholders at last night's meeting that he was confident about the future, though he warned: "We still need two or three more players. I believe that we are on the right lines and that we have something to offer. In the near future we will have something to excite you, and we will soon be ready to win a trophy or two."

However, Kendall warned that it was no longer possible to go out and buy the players the club required. "The key will be player exchanges," he said.

"Business will be done where we have two good players for one position and we find another club in a similar position. Then we can talk."

Ten available for transfer

(By Nick Hilton, Liverpool Daily Post, April 10, 1982)

Howard Kendall was hoping to bring in some much-needed funds by offloading several players.

$\mathcal{H}$OWARD Kendall paved the way for a wholesale clear-out at Everton yesterday by making 10 players available for transfer.

The League clubs will be circulated with details next week of one of the biggest sales of talent by an unendangered club in the history of football. The players could be valued at around £1 million even in a collapsing market.

Among the listed 10 are three of manager Kendall's signings this season, although only one, Trevor Ross, currently commands a first-team place.

Five of the players, Peter Eastoe, John Bailey, Ross, Joe McBride and Martin Hodge refused to sign extensions to their current contracts last December and will become free agents in July.

Kendall said his three listed purchases, Mick Ferguson, Alan Biley and Mike Walsh felt particularly frustrated at being left out of the side. "They have to realise that if this club is the best place for them they have to get on with it and fight for their places."

Paul Lodge, a midfield player with experience over three seasons, and reserve midfield player Dean Kelly make up the 10.

Mind games

(By Ian Hargraves, Liverpool Echo, November 25, 1982)

A seven-match winless run in league and cup saw the club offered help from an unexpected source.

$\mathcal{E}$VERTON'S fading fortunes have touched the heart of a leading Liverpool clairvoyant, who has offered to help the players.

"I am sure lack of confidence is their biggest problem at the moment and I would like to help them if I can," the lady in question, Dorothy Wright, told me today.

"I have approached their chief coach, Mr Heaton, and he has promised to discuss the matter with the manager, Howard Kendall, and come back to me on Monday.

"What I have in mind is the use of mental telepathy, by which I communicate with the players sub-consciously. I can apply it in any case, even if they do not wish to co-operate, but it will undoubtedly be much more effective if I can meet the players concerned and get to know something about them."

Cynics will doubtless burst into rude laughter at Dorothy Wright's suggestions – until they learn that she has already applied her techniques with considerable success on the other side of Stanley Park.

"I've been a Liverpool supporter all my life," she explained. "Recently I became concerned because Ian Rush, who scored 30 goals for them last season, seemed to have lost his touch, so I concentrated on him, thinking about him every day and willing him to become more sure of himself.

"The Saturday after, he came out and scored four goals against Everton. He told everyone that even before the start, he'd never felt so confident.

"I have also helped Sammy Lee with some success. As you know, he's often a bag of nerves before a big match, so when he was picked for England last week, I spent a long time communicating with him and willing him into greater confidence.

"You saw the result – he ran out and played the game of his life. I know people tend to be sceptical at first, but ever since I was young, I knew I had unusual powers and could influence people's actions by thinking about them."

Dorothy's sudden concern for Everton comes from her loyalty to Merseyside as a whole and her disappointment at the decline in the rivalry between the two big clubs.

"I've always been a Liverpudlian first and foremost, but recently I've started to feel rather sorry for Everton because nothing has been going right for them recently. We need two successful sides in the city and I shall be delighted if I can help them to begin a revival," she said.

"Though I've only seen them on television and read about them in the Echo, it seems that their main trouble is a loss of confidence. There is no doubt they have some very talented players, who are not doing themselves justice.

"I intend to start with one at a time and I thought I would begin with their centre-forward Graeme Sharp. He is a very talented young man who seems to have lost his touch.

"After that, I would like to go on to some of the others like Steve McMahon and Billy Wright – preferably with their help."

Dorothy Wright describes herself as a professional clairvoyant, but she has nothing to do with fortune telling or communicating with the so-called other world.

A former manageress of a city pen shop until incapacitated by successive ear illnesses, she is well known for her ability to find out things about people simply by holding objects belonging to them.

She has sometimes applied her undoubted gift medically, by pinpointing ailments that had previously remained undetected and has developed her powers of telepathy to a marked extent.

Meanwhile Sammy Lee said today that he had not noticed any difference before the start of the England game. "I'm always nervous before the kick-off," he admitted, "but it usually goes as soon as I touch the ball. I don't know Dorothy Wright, but good luck to her if she can help the Everton lads in any way."

Holders vanquished as Blues march on
(February 19, 1983)

*F*A Cup winners in 1981 and 1982, Tottenham arrived at Goodison for an FA Cup fifth-round tie with visiting boss Keith Burkinshaw expecting a difficult afternoon.

He said: "It's always a tough game up there. It's not like a League match, it's a muck and nettles affair."

How right he was. Spurs were backed by around 8,000 fans, but Howard Kendall's young side, with Steve McMahon dominant in midfield, proved more than a match, claiming an impressive victory.

Andy King broke the deadlock early in the second half and Graeme Sharp tapped in Kevin Sheedy's free-kick for No 2, after Ray Clemence had collided with King.

King revealed: "We said at half-time if we kept playing the way we had done, something would break for us. It's pleasing to be in the next round and it's also great to give our fans something to shout about."

Late, late heartbreak

(March 12, 1983)

*T*HE young Blues were rated as clear underdogs when they travelled to Manchester United for the FA Cup quarter-final clash. However, roared on by 15,000 Evertonians in a 58,000 plus crowd – the biggest attendance anywhere in England so far that season – the Blues more than held their own.

Spectators included Andy King who was recovering from his recent knee ligament operation. He declared: "It will take more than a pair of crutches to keep me away."

There were chances at both ends, but the game was still goalless when United sub Lou Macari headed a Ray Wilkins pass into the path of Frank Stapleton, who shot into the roof of the net two minutes into injury time.

Howard Kendall said: "It was disappointing to lose after playing so well, but I was proud of the team.

"We are trying to build something big at Goodison, and in the process we want to win friends and win matches.

"We are certainly winning friends with our football – even the United fans applauded our coach away from Old Trafford – and now we have to start winning matches."

Looking to the future

(Liverpool Daily Post, May 18, 1983)

Having secured eighth and now a seventh-placed finish in his two seasons at the helm, questions were now asked as to what the future may hold for the club and their manager.

*W*ITH Kendall now halfway through his four-year contract, the Daily Post approached him for his views on his future.

Everton now seem reluctant or unable to provide the sort of top player the fans have come to expect. Are Everton still a "big club"?

"Yes, this is still a big club. We just aren't in a position to go for highly valued players. We aren't prepared to go overboard and spend money we haven't got. Those clubs which do, take a gamble which could backfire."

A few months ago you were being linked with the then Ipswich striker Alan Brazil. What was the situation?

"I couldn't go after him although I would have liked him in my side. He was too expensive."

And Celtic's Charlie Nicholas?

"I haven't seen much of him, All I know is that he is a proven goalscorer."

Did you ask your board for more money to buy players during the season?

"I am very limited. I am fully aware of the financial situation at the club. Times are still hard. The fact that I have put so many good players on free transfers should be a pointer. I was told to cut the wages bill. I have released more than I needed to because I hope to bring in new players before next season."

Do you think that some of your buys were influenced by your time in the Second Division with Blackburn Rovers? Were they simply Second Division players who were always going to struggle to make the grade in the First Division?

"Not all of them. If you can't bring the best to your clubs then your risks are obviously greater. Take Alan Biley for example. He was a proven goalscorer who had played in the First Division. We decided to take a chance which sadly didn't work out. It's a difficult situation. Biley went to Portsmouth and he scored 26 goals for them this season. If a First Division manager was looking around today for a lower division player to take a chance on it would probably be him."

Did you at any time during the season feel your job was on the line?

"No. I still feel I have the backing of the board. The board and the fans have, I feel, stood by me. With regard to the fans, the sensible ones know the problems I face and know how difficult this job is."

If Everton fail to win anything again next season, do you feel your job will be at all threatened?

"I was offered a four-year contract. I want to stay here much longer than that. I think if we finish next season in the same position as we have finished this one the board would look at the situation and see if anyone else could do a better job.

"I don't think anyone could do a better job. This is the hardest job in football. I wouldn't have it any other way. I want our fans to have success and I want to be here when that happens. I remember the scenes when we won the League Championship in 1970. When we win something I will stay up celebrating all night with the supporters."

What are your targets for the 1983/84 season?

"I want to win something, naturally. If I had a choice it would be the League Championship because that is always won by the most consistent side in the league.

"I was so optimistic at the start of this season. Our pre-season preparation went very well. You are kidded to a certain extent by some individuals. They aren't capable of consistency. It is no good having a team which contains four or five players you are concerned about before they step on to the pitch. Some players have let themselves down this season. The demands here are great. It is a situation which can't be tolerated for very long."

Can Everton win something next season?

"We must always believe we can. That is very important. We will be in a better position next year. I was probably more confident in them this time than they were in themselves."

Will Everton eventually reverse roles with Liverpool and become Merseyside's top club once again?

"It is taking time to catch up with them. The Liverpool system will carry on even though Bob Paisley has stepped down."

How do you rate your supporters?

"They are in a different class. They gave the side a great reception after the game against Ipswich on Saturday and we hadn't even played well. They have had a long wait for success but I am responsible for the last two years not the last 12."

Do you still enjoy the job?

"I love it. It is my dream job. There is nothing I would rather do. I love the club and everything concerned with it."

Blues in profit

(By Ken Rogers, Liverpool Echo, August 3, 1983)

Continued cost cutting meant the Blues were in far better shape than many of their Football League rivals.

*I*N a year when many leading Football League clubs faced up to financial disaster, Everton battled their way back into the black with a profit of £45,547. This overturned a loss for 1982 of close on £100,000 and reflects a determined cost-cutting exercise at Goodison Park almost right across the board.

Wages were down by nearly £23,000 as the club reduced its staffing levels to sail a tighter ship. Only one Everton employee earned more than £40,000 last year and there was nobody in the £35,000 to £40,000 wage bracket. Only two people received salaries in the region of £30,000 to £35,000. By comparison there were 14 men at Anfield who earned in excess of £40,000 with two men topping £80,000.

Carter backs Kendall

(By Ian Hargraves, Liverpool Echo, October 19, 1983)

The Blues were languishing in 15th after a 1-0 home defeat to Luton Town, with home crowds regularly falling below 20,000. However, the board were continuing to back their man.

*E*VERTON manager Howard Kendall has the full confidence of the club's directors, despite his side's disappointing start to the season.

Mr Philip Carter, who has been Everton's chairman for the last five years, said last night: "We are not complacent about our present problems. We are most concerned. But let me state unequivocally that our manager Howard Kendall has the fullest and the absolute support of the board.

"He is a little more than halfway through a four-year contract and the board have not, and are not exerting any pressure on him. We look forward to seeing an upturn in attendances coupled with improved Goodison results. We have every confidence that the team will achieve that under Howard Kendall.

"That is not just a club chairman trotting out a hackneyed phrase – I am stating that categorically.'"

Mr Carter's assurances will doubtless give Mr Kendall's confidence a major boost. It is rare for a chairman to commit himself so completely to an employee's performance.

Clearly board and manager stand to triumph or fail together, as Everton face up to the mounting problems caused by disappointing results and falling attendances. Mr Carter explained that the board is most concerned about gates at Goodison which have dropped alarmingly from an average of 39,500 only five seasons ago.

"Our average this season is now slightly below 18,000 and our financial break-even figure is 20,000, taking into account our fund-raising activities," he said.

"Compared with the attendances for the first five games last season we are 25 per cent down – yet we are more than 15 per cent up on last season's fixtures with the same clubs."

Mr Carter denied suggestions the club have put a ban on signings.

"In just a few months since the end of last season, we have spent £500,000 on signing Trevor Steven from Burnley, Alan Harper from Liverpool and Terry Curran from Sheffield United," he pointed out.

"Before that we paid £700,000 for Adrian Heath from Stoke. It is true we did not attempt to sign Charlie Nicholas but then most other clubs decided that the price was out of reach.

"Howard Kendall is constantly searching for new talent but he has to be satisfied it would be right for Everton. If he does find a player he considers is the right type, he knows he can put the matter to the board and we will consider it."

Leaflets call for Kendall and Carter to go

(By Ian Ross, Liverpool Daily Post, October 27, 1983)

Unconvincing Milk Cup progress was not enough to stop the discontent in the stands. Howard Kendall duly hit back at his critics.

*E*VERTON manager Howard Kendall brushed aside calls for his resignation after he and club chairman Philip Carter were made the targets of an orchestrated demonstration by a small group of supporters, following the draw with Fourth Division Chesterfield.

At the end of the latest in a series of poor home performances, an angry section of fans distributed leaflets expressing their disgust at the way they claim the club is being run.

As the players made their way off to wholesale booing, photostat copies of the hand-written message were thrown into the air. The leaflet read: "30,000 stay at home fans can't be wrong. Bring back attractive winning football to Goodison Park, Kendall and Carter out."

Kendall admitted he was upset by the demonstration but re-emphasised his determination to stick with the job.

"I do not intend to go; I have no intention whatsoever of resigning and I am sure that Mr Carter feels the same way. It hurts when something like this happens. I obviously do not like it. I am here to do a job and I intend to stick with it."

The first sign of disenchantment with Kendall's reign came on the night the club played host to its lowest recorded gate for a senior game.

Only 8,067 people passed through the Goodison turnstiles despite a 25 per cent reduction in admission prices. A series of poor home results has seen Goodison attendances plummet since the opening day of the season. Kendall acknowledges that the Everton faithful have had little to shout about so far this season.

"The fans were rightly disappointed with tonight's performance but how do they think I feel? It concerns them that we threw away a game and it concerns me. We conceded sloppy goals, there was reaction from the fans and there was reaction from me. Things have been sticky at home and that has resulted in increased pressure.

"I have a job to do here and I am going to do it. The fans are not bothered about clean sheets, they want pure football and goals. The gate was poor as expected. I am concerned with the team not the attendances; gates are down all over the country at the moment."

Howard: I will bring success back to Goodison

(By Ken Rogers, Liverpool Echo, October 27, 1983)

*E*VERTON manager Howard Kendall is more determined than ever to see out his contract and bring glory to the success-starved Goodison faithful. He said: "I've got more ambition and determination than when I arrived two years ago. I'm proud to be manager of such a great club. This is probably the biggest challenge in the game. Every club in the country is trying to match Liverpool and their achievements. We are on the doorstep and so the challenge is that much bigger.

"The fans have got a right to expect a certain standard of football, but I will say this: No-one else could do a better job under the circumstances that exist. The fans must accept this and let us get on with it."

"The distribution of those leaflets got more publicity than the good things that happened in the game. I thought Trevor Steven's goal was the best strike seen at the ground since Graeme Sharp's memorable televised effort against Spurs.

"Trevor has been excellent in certain games away from home. He scores his first goal at Goodison and it's a cracker. This morning no-one is talking about it."

Kendall reflected on the attendance of 8,067 and said: "There were only 9,000 people at Anfield for the Brentford game. People don't argue that their fans stayed away because of the standard of the football."

From mediocre to magnificent

(By Ian Ross, Liverpool Daily Post, November 10, 1983)

Under pressure Kendall was grateful for two late goals which secured passage into the fourth round of the Milk Cup.

*E*VERTON temporarily silenced their critics with a stunning late, late show at Goodison Park last night. Trailing 1-0 with only minutes remaining Howard Kendall's brave youngsters stormed their way into the Milk Cup fourth round with a dramatic injury-time winner.

After Adrian Heath had levelled things 12 minutes from time, limping Graeme Sharp, who had been little more than a passenger during the closing stages, dragged himself off the ground to head home at the far post 90 seconds into stoppage time.

To say they left it late would be the understatement of the year; no sooner had Coventry's disbelieving forwards restarted the game than referee Arnold Challinor blew for time to set Goodison Park alight for the first time in many weeks.

The saddest thing was that only 9,080 people, the lowest crowd on record for an all-First Division match on Merseyside, bothered to turn up for a game which suddenly switched from mediocre to magnificent.

While it may not have totally pacified those who scent hierarchy blood at the club, it did at least temporarily silence them and take some of the pressure off Kendall.

The Goodison boss has been awaiting what he has diplomatically labelled a "turning point" for the best part of a month; he may now have found it.

Kendall threw on substitute Peter Reid in place of young Trevor Steven. The decision was rather unpopular at the time but proved rewarding in the end.'

Sharp, Everton's limping last-minute hero, said: "I felt tremendous when I headed it in. Luckily I did not have to jump for it because I was limping on the left leg and that's the one I spring off. I did not think we were going to do it. But the crowd lifted us. They were marvellous."

When Skies are Gray

(By Ian Hargraves, Liverpool Echo, November 29, 1983)

The signing of Andy Gray appeared to signal the end for another Everton forward.

$\mathcal{D}$AVID Johnson will never play for Everton again.

That was the reaction of manager Howard Kendall to the transfer-listed striker's refusal to stand by for duty at West Ham. Kendall needed Johnson because of doubts over Graeme Sharp's fitness.

A furious Kendall said: "Johnson told me he did not want to be considered because he was on the transfer list, and did not think he was in the right frame of mind. To say I am disappointed is putting it mildly. So far as I'm concerned the sooner he leaves this club the better.

"Although he has been out of the picture, and knows we have signed Andy Gray, this was an opportunity to bounce back. It is an attitude I don't like. It means that if we have to manage without Graeme we shall have to take the field with a weaker team than we should – but there is no way I am going to select someone not willing to battle and scratch with the rest of them. Effectively I have reduced my squad by one professional – only unfortunately I still have to pay him."

Fans inspire cup victory

(January 7, 1984)

*E*VERTON began their FA Cup campaign against Stoke City at the Victoria Ground. Howard Kendall opened the dressing room window before the game to let the players hear the backing of the fans in a bid to inspire them. Such was the noise generated by more than 10,000 fans, he told his players: "That's how much they want you to win. If you can't do it for them today you'll never do it for anybody."

On a wet and windy day it seemed to work as the Blues, with only 14 senior players available, came through 2-0. Andy Gray's superb diving header from a free-kick broke the deadlock, with Alan Irvine's fierce left-footer doing the trick.

Back at Wembley

(By Ken Rogers, Liverpool Echo, February 23, 1984)

The Blues progressed to the semi-finals of the Milk Cup, and led 2-0 from the home leg against Aston Villa. Future Evertonian Paul Rideout pulled one back for Villa, but Kendall's men held on to claim an aggregate success and a first all-Merseyside Wembley cup final. Everton lost the final replay but proved they were more than a match for Liverpool. This was the start of the great Everton revival.

*H*OWIE'S Army took Villa Park by storm to inspire the Blues towards an epic Wembley showdown against arch-rivals Liverpool.

I joined the 13,000-strong Merseyside invasion of the Midlands on a night when the fans did Everton proud. They out-sang, out-joked and out-chanted the home supporters from start to finish.

The North Stand was a sea of blue and white as the teams kicked-off with the Blues defending a 2-0 first-leg lead. There were a few around me who thought they were auditioning for the GPO's Talking Clock.

As referee Keith Hackett signalled the start someone shouted: "How long to go?" The Wembley countdown was on in earnest and the players responded magnificently.

The Villa fans were a nonentity until that shock second-half opener suddenly brought them to life. "I thought it was a cardboard cut-out up the other end," said a fan next to me.

There were incredible scenes on the final whistle. Alan Irvine was carried all round the pitch when he failed to escape to the dressing room. Ten minutes later, with thousands refusing to go home, the players returned to join in the celebrations.

I walked into a village pub in Cannock later to find it overflowing with Evertonians. The bar staff ran out of glasses, they ran out of lager, they ran out of brown. The manager had seen nothing like it.

There was no trouble, no problems, just relief and delight that Merseyside's great Wembley dream was finally on.

Marching on
(March 10, 1984)

*E*VERTON remained on course for Wembley in two competitions as they saw off Notts County 2-1 in the FA Cup quarter-final, to the delight of 10,000 travelling Evertonians. Kevin Richardson and Andy Gray, with a remarkable diving header from literally inches off the ground, secured a semi-final spot. Howard Kendall later joked: "Andy rotivated the ground with his nose as he slid in to meet the ball!"

Heath's header sends Everton into ecstasy
(April 14, 1984)

*T*HE FA Cup semi-final against Southampton at Highbury could have gone either way, with both goalkeepers Neville Southall and Peter Shilton in top form. Danny Wallace was a constant threat for Everton, but it was left to Adrian Heath to head home the only goal to the delight of the 22,000 Evertonians with three minutes left of extra time, after Peter Reid's free-kick had been touched on by Derek Mountfield.

Blues' boss Howard Kendall later explained the winning goal: "Frank Worthington was playing for Southampton, and it was a case of 'Try and hit his area' because Frank wouldn't want to go back and defend. It happened in extra time. Derek Mountfield did get the touch on and Adrian Heath finished it off, in Frank's area. It's down to a little bit of planning or a little bit of luck on the day. Who knows?"

Lawrie McMenemy, the Southampton manager, said: "No disrespect to Everton, but I feel we contributed much to our failure to reach Wembley again. I felt we had the ability to beat Everton, and were performing well enough, but on the day some of our players just froze."

New contract for Kendall

(Liverpool Echo, May 17, 1984)

FA Cup final week and the local press was littered with stories related to the struggle for tickets. Those who did go were rewarded with the right result.

$\mathcal{E}$VERTON have rewarded manager Howard Kendall and coaches Mick Heaton and Colin Harvey, by giving them new contracts.

Kendall has signed on for a further four years. Said Kendall: "I'm delighted, and I hope it's not the last contract I get at Everton because I would never want to leave. I don't see my future as being anywhere else. Even when we had problems earlier in the season I believed I was doing the right thing, and the chairman and the board have been tremendous, because they supported me during that period."

Blue heaven

(By Ken Rogers, Liverpool Echo, May 21, 1984)

$\mathcal{W}$HAT a day, what a season. Merseyside's Big Two stand supreme, the untouchables of English soccer. The League Championship, the Milk Cup, the FA Youth Cup and now the FA Cup itself all reside within the city. Liverpool can still add European glory to this stunning array of silverware, but for the moment their famous rivals Everton are basking proudly in the spotlight, winners again after 14 long years.

Saturday's 2-0 victory over Watford saw Howard Kendall's blue and white army take Wembley by storm. It was an occasion to cherish; the friendly final when rival fans shared a laugh and a joke before the game, posed with each other for photographs and revelled in the atmosphere and excitement of a marvellous occasion. But cup finals are all about winners and Everton's unshakable determination to claim that elusive piece of silverware was to prove decisive.

Watford boss Graham Taylor had talked about enjoying the match and being part of a great day. His rival Howard Kendall, a two-time Wembley loser, could only talk about winning. Goals from Graeme Sharp and Andy Gray were to give the Blues' boss possibly his proudest ever moment, surpassing even his achievement in helping win the League Championship for Everton in 1970. The Ball-Harvey-Kendall midfield trio was to become legendary at Goodison. Now the Kendall and Colin Harvey backroom link has proved just as potent. They both choked back the tears as Kevin Ratcliffe held aloft the FA Cup. A season of swinging fortunes had ended on an unforgettable high note.

Even before a ball was kicked Everton knew that the biggest threat to their chances would come from the talented John Barnes. The young winger was to live up to his exciting reputation, shaking the Blues early in the game with his pace, strength and superb skill. It's a pleasure to watch Barnes in full flight, a player who can light up any match with his natural ability. The task of containing him fell to another impressive young player, Blues' right back Gary Stevens. He was to rise to the challenge magnificently and as Everton imposed themselves on their opponents, the fans were to salute the adventure of another bright talent – Trevor Steven. What a game he was to have, finally laying on the cross from the right that saw Gray kill off Watford with typical spring and strength after 51 minutes. From that point there could only be one result with Everton firmly in the driving seat and their opponents struggling to pick themselves up off the floor.

It was an outstanding first half, Adrian Heath setting off on a twisting chase for goal before attempting a chipped shot that was deflected for a corner. Watford bounced back, the Barnes magic flickering as his body swerve took him away from both Gary Stevens and Derek

Mountfield. He got in his shot on the edge of the box with Southall spreading himself, but it was Mountfield who recovered to block the effort. The pressure wasn't over for the Blues with Les Taylor arriving to hammer inches wide of the left hand post. Both sides had created good opportunities and Peter Reid, Everton's Player of the Year with 11 man-of-the-match nominations in the Echo during the season, showed his strength to shake off Kenny Jackett before curling a tremendous effort wide of the upright.

The momentum and the vast number of scoring chances at both ends made this an intriguing and entertaining final. Everton began slowly, then stepped up a gear to live up to their billing as favourites. The decisive blow came after 38 minutes. Wembley erupted in a sea of blue and white as Sharp suddenly found himself with the space just inside the box to strike a brilliant opener. Gary Stevens had won a challenge with Barnes, the ball breaking forward for Sharp to control and lash his shot into the corner of the net with goalkeeper Steve Sherwood completely helpless. The fans roared their delight.

Watford were forced to dig deep into their reserves of character and spirit, but six minutes into the second half it was effectively all over. Trevor Steven's skill took him past full-back Neil Price. The midfield man sent over a teasing cross that looked ripe for the keeper to hold but Gray rose with power and suddenly the ball was in the back of the net. Watford, pushed by Bob Wilson later on Match of the Day, complained that Sharp's effort was offside and that Gray had fouled Sherwood for the second. But to suggest that this victory was anything but fully deserved is an insult to a memorable match. The headlines in the Echo's Wembley souvenir edition, sported in many cars on the motorway, had already said it all for the Evertonians: WE'RE BACK.

Everton (4-4-2): Southall, Stevens, Bailey, Ratcliffe, Mountfield, Reid, Steven, Heath, Richardson, Sharp, Gray, Sub: Harper.

Watford (4-2-4): Sherwood, Bardsley, Price (Atkinson 58), Taylor, Perry, Sinnott, Callaghan, Johnston, Reilly, Jackett, Barnes.

Referee: Mr. J. Hunting (Leicestershire)

Attendance: 100,000

"Unbelievable" crowd welcomes cup-winners home
(Liverpool Echo, May 21, 1984)

*M*ORE than 200,000 people turned out to give a magnificent Mersey welcome to Everton when they came home with the FA Cup yesterday.

A Merseyside police spokesman said that the day had passed off without a single problem, despite the "unbelievable" crowd which he estimated at up to 250,000.

"It was an excellent turnout and everyone was so well behaved. God bless them all," he said.

The special trains carrying the Everton party arrived at Broadgreen Station at 3.45pm on the Sunday – more than 30 minutes late. 5,000 sang and cheered as the team boarded their open deck bus.

Banners on the journey included:

'Everton give Elton the blues';

'Howie's got more hair than Elton'.

The siren-blasting motorcade included 16 police motorcycles, and was led by an official car carrying city council chairman Hugh Dalton.

The coach was almost brought to a halt outside Goodison Park and nearby Spellow Lane where at least 20,000 more supporters were waiting. Then came a faster section down Scotland Road – chased for more than a mile by a black and white mongrel – before the team arrived in the city centre.

In Lime Street, where it all began for so many Evertonians on Saturday morning, at least 50,000 supporters waved and cheered and even tried to kneel down in front of the players' bus.

The crowd there had been among the most patient all afternoon, and were given some free entertainment when a group of Scottish pipers turned up and performed a lively jig.

Outside the bigger houses along Catharine Street and Princes Avenue and the players spent some time dodging the low lying branches before their bus arrived in Wavertree.

University examination awaits

(By Peter Went & Ian Hargraves, Liverpool Echo, July 11, 1984)

Back in Europe, it was predicted there would be an easy passage in the first round of the Cup-Winners' Cup.

$\mathcal{E}$VERTON could hand out a European Cup-Winners' Cup caning to the soccer intellectuals from University College Dublin.

The clubs formed an unlikely first-round pairing in yesterday's draw and UCD manager Theo Dunne came out with a comment to match the occasion. "Bless us and save us," said Dunne, a card-carrying member of the Everton supporters' club (Dublin branch).

"It's a great draw; so good, I almost don't believe it."

Dunne once acted as Everton's scout in Dublin – but this time he will try to ensure that UCD are well prepared for their European debut.

Everton chairman Philip Carter was also delighted with the draw, though he added: "There is no way we will underestimate the Dubliners. Lots of Irish people travel across regularly to watch Everton so it will be quite a family occasion."

Everton scrape past part-timers

(Liverpool Daily Post, October 3, 1984)

Irish part-timers UCD proved tougher opponents than had been predicted.

$\mathcal{T}$HE most astonishing thing was that even after Graeme Sharp stole in to collect his fourth goal in as many games, to effectively stamp Everton's passport into the next round, the back-pedalling Irishmen refused to alter their killjoy tactics. A blanket defensive operation which was about as palatable as a dose of sustained toothache was still rigorously employed. Had Everton managed to sneak on their five substitutes they would still have struggled to find a way through a wall which made the Aswan Dam seem positively tiny in comparison.

Bolt from the Blue!

(By Ian Hargreaves, October 22, 1984)

A first victory at Anfield for over 14 years — coincidentally in a season when the Blues had last landed the league title — was achieved courtesy of 'that' Graeme Sharp goal.

*W*HAT a difference 12 short months can make in football. This time last year Liverpool were heading for a unique treble in League, Milk Cup and Europe, while Everton were fighting the threat of relegation with their manager Howard Kendall being quoted as favourite for the Great Sack Race.

On Saturday it was Liverpool's turn to struggle against opponents who seem to have banished the kingsize inferiority complex that has bedevilled their efforts over the last decade.

Inspired by their performance in the two-legged Milk Cup final, and again in the Charity Shield when they discovered their neighbours could be beaten, they played to the form that has taken them near the top of the table and looked a really good side. Now, as the champions concentrate on rebuilding another great team, it is Everton who must surely carry Merseyside's best hopes in the League and who, for the moment at least, are the standard bearers for tomorrow.

In a blustery, hard-fought struggle, full of entertainment and outstandingly refereed by Salford's Neil Midgeley, Everton always had the edge. They were much quicker, both in thought and execution, and their lively central trio of Adrian Heath, Peter Reid and Paul Bracewell were always a step ahead of their opposite numbers, whose lack of pace has proved such a problem this season. Reid was outstanding.

Although he did not have a spectacular game, he was always there beating John Wark and Jan Molby to the ball, feeding Heath or Sharp with swift, accurate passes and generally tidying up in midfield. Behind him Kevin Ratcliffe and Mountfield kept a firm grip, not only on the welcome if match-rusty figure of Ian Rush, but on the much livelier

Kenny Dalglish, who could have swung the match given better support.

Gary Stevens confirmed his steady development at right-back and he hit a shot from a free-kick that Bruce Grobbelaar did well to push round the post. Yet in the end it was one superb strike, by that exciting centre-forward Graeme Sharp, that decided the game.

Other chances came and went at both ends, but the one that counted was a sharply dipping 30-yard volley from Sharp, who pounced on a long, upfield pass by Stevens, shooting before Mark Lawrenson could get in his usual stifling challenge.

Grobbelaar, who had what is best described as an exciting game, had no chance with this effort. It is a long time since I have seen so many blue jerseys at Anfield, especially in the Kop.

Like most who have watched both clubs this season, they could sense that Everton's moment had finally arrived, and that they were about to claim their first league victory on the ground for 14 years, and only their third anywhere against Liverpool in 34 League and Cup games.

For the moment the glory is Everton's and it is they who have cause for celebration. Long may they enjoy it; they have waited long enough.

Liverpool (4-4-2): Grobbelaar, Neal, Lawrenson, Hansen, A. Kennedy, Wark, Molby, Whelan, Dalglish, Rush, Robinson. Sub: Lee.
Everton (4-4-2): Southall, Stevens, Mountfield, Ratcliffe, Van Den Hauwe, Harper, Reid, Bracewell, Steven, Heath, Sharp. Sub: Gray.
Referee: Mr. N. Midgeley (Salford).
Attendance: 45,545.

Blues' title rivals in a spin

(By Ian Hargraves, Liverpool Echo, October 29, 1984)

A week later Championship favourites Manchester United were outclassed 5-0.

*T*HAT magnificent old Evertonian Joe Mercer put the victory over Manchester United in its true context when he said afterwards: "It was the best performance by any Everton side I remember." Even allowing for the natural enthusiasm of the moment, he wasn't far wrong.

You have to go back to the playing days of Kendall and Harvey, whose coaching skills were behind this latest triumph, to recall anything comparable, and it overshadowed the whole of the last decade. Manchester United arrived at Goodison as championship favourites, stuffed with internationals, and having lost only one match previously.

They were outclassed by opponents whose speed and inventiveness made a mockery of United's title pretensions. Now manager Ron Atkinson faces the task of rebuilding their shattered confidence in time to avoid a repeat when the adversaries meet again on Tuesday night.

Only two things give him much cause for hope. In the first place Everton may be without Kevin Sheedy, whose two-goal comeback after injury triggered off the rout; secondly United centre-back Kevin Moran will have recovered from concussion or will have been replaced.

Moran collided with Sheedy as the latter headed Everton's first goal after only four minutes, and thereafter played in a complete daze until replaced by Stapleton 22 minutes later. He had every excuse for not knowing what was going on round him, but there were plenty of occasions when his colleagues looked even more bewildered.

United could not match the Blues' astonishing speed to the ball, let alone the precision of their passing. The scene was set in the opening seconds when United kicked-off but immediately lost possession as Sharp and Reid homed in like guided missiles.

Mountfield could have scored before Sheedy did. The Irishman got his second after 23 minutes and Heath made it three soon after.

The only miracle was that United somehow survived further setbacks until the last 10 minutes, when Stevens and Sharp gave the scoreline a more accurate appearance. Everton hit the heights, as their rapturous reception confirmed.

Everton (4-4-2): Southall, Stevens, Mountfield, Ratcliffe, Van Den Hauwe, Steven, Reid, Bracewell, Sheedy (Gray), Heath, Sharp.
Manchester United (4-4-2): Bailey, Moran (Stapleton), McQueen, Hogg, Albiston, Moses, Strachan, Robson, Olsen, Hughes, Brazil.
Referee: Mr. G. Tyson (Sunderland).
Attendance: 40,769.

Fortuna favours the Braveheart

(Liverpool Echo, March 7, 1985)

An inspirational frontman found some vintage form to help guide the Blues towards the semi-finals of a European competition for the first time, courtesy of a treble against Fortuna Sittard in the first leg of the ECWC quarter-final.

*I*T was vintage Andy Gray – a performance combining brains and bravery. Gray, who took the match ball home with him, said: "It was very sweet and just the right time for my first hat-trick in seven years. But my finishing was A.OK in the second half."

Harry Catterick dies

(By Ken Rogers & Ian Hargraves, Liverpool Echo, March 9, 1985)

*A*S Evertonians mourned the loss of former manager Harry Catterick today, one of the first tributes to come in was a moving salute to the legendary royal blue figure from across the park at Anfield.

Liverpool boss Joe Fagan said: "I shall be forever grateful to Harry for all he taught me about the coaching side of the game. I learned more about that from him than any other person and he gave me an invaluable insight into what is a very tricky business. He gave me my first job as a coach with Rochdale and later on he recommended me to Liverpool. For me he was a really good manager."

Catterick (65), the man who inspired Everton to two Championship successes and an F.A. Cup, died on Saturday – minutes after watching his old club snatch a thrilling F.A. Cup draw against Ipswich. He collapsed in the Directors' Box from a heart attack and desperate efforts to revive him failed.

Two of his greatest players, former Championship captains Roy Vernon (1963) and Brian Labone (1970) reflected today on his qualities.

Vernon said: "Everton came before everything else with him. At times he seemed to do things the players – and some of the supporters

– didn't like. But in his heart it was always for the best of the club."

Labone said: "I don't think he was as ruthless as he was painted. He was a strict disciplinarian, but it wouldn't do some of today's players any harm. He was a character and his epitaph is the tremendous ground and training facilities we see today."

Euro Blues into last four

(Liverpool Echo, March 21, 1985)

*B*RING on the big guns. That was the bold message from Peter Reid as the Everton players looked ahead with supreme confidence to tomorrow's European Cup-Winners' Cup draw in Geneva.

The Goodison midfield general was an outstanding performer in Holland last night where the Blues secured a 5-0 aggregate victory over Fortuna Sittard to reach their first-ever Euro semi-final.

He said: "We are in there now with three class sides in Bayern Munich, Dinamo Moscow and Rapid Vienna, but it is enough to say that we fear no one. That's not being over-confident.

"If we continue to play to our strengths there is no reason why we can't go all the way in this competition. We haven't conceded a goal in six European ties this season and that is the real secret at this level."

Bayern await

(Liverpool Echo, March 22, 1985)

Next up in Europe were the favourites, Bayern Munich.

*E*VERTON manager Howard Kendall said: "It's going to be a big game for us. It has got a ring to it.

"Bayern are the favourites to win the competition but we have not conceded a goal so far and there's no reason why we shouldn't go through. We are delighted to be away from home first."

Bayern trainer Udo Lattek said: "Bayern against Everton – that's really the final. Whoever wins this semi-final will also win the cup."

Captain Klaus Augenthaler said: "My God, that's a hard draw. For me, Everton are the hardest semi-final opponents, because German teams find it very difficult to deal with English teams."

Theft halts Howie's homework

(By Ken Rogers, Liverpool Echo, April 2, 1985)

Video nasty (surprise) for Kendall?

*H*OWARD Kendall has had his hopes dashed of doing some early homework on European Cup-Winners' Cup rivals Bayern Munich.

The Everton boss had his car broken into at Goodison Park last night while attending the shareholders' annual dinner. He said: "A video tape was taken of the Roma v Bayern Munich quarter-final. I had taken it home to have a good look at the strengths of the West Germans. The tape was removed from a bag and I just hope that whoever has got it will quietly return it to the club as quickly as possible."

Scoreless draw in Munich sets up return

(Liverpool Daily Post, April 11, 1985)

A solid showing in Munich's Olympic Stadium secured a valuable goalless draw, and showed that the team could compete against one of the continent's best sides.

*E*VERTON produced another magnificent continental black-out in Munich last night to move within striking distance of a first-ever European final.

Howard Kendall's battlers, a side which has scored an astonishing 100 goals this season, stunned a partisan crowd in the Olympic Stadium with as fine a display of the defensive art as you are ever likely to see.

The Goodison boss punched the air in delight at the final whistle before rushing forward to congratulate his 11 blue-shirted heroes.

Bayern Munich: Pfaff, Dremmler, Willmer, Eder, Augenthaler, Lerby, Pfluger, Matthaus, Hoeness, Rummenigge, Kogl.
Everton: Southall, Stevens, Van Den Hauwe, Ratcliffe, Mountfield, Reid, Steven, Harper, Sharp, Bracewell, Richardson.
Referee: Paulo Bergamo (Italy).
Attendance: 67,000.

Reid delighted by excellent job

(By Ken Rogers, Liverpool Echo, April 11, 1985)

*I*NFLUENTIAL midfield man Peter Reid summed up the feeling of the players when he said: "The lads showed what a good side we are. It was never going to be easy, but we stopped them, frustrated them and could have won in the end. We might have looked a bit pensive early on, but it was a case of having a good look at them and we were never really in trouble. Once we got the pattern right the team settled in and did a tremendous job against one of the top sides in Europe.

"We know we did an excellent job on the night. Who would have thought on Merseyside 18 months ago that we would not only be top of the league, but contesting a European semi-final in such fine style."

Howard Kendall said: "This result will make people sit up and take note. We've played seven games in Europe and have yet to concede a goal. I am very proud of that record."

Sheedy keeps treble dream alive

(April 13, 1985)

Days later, Luton Town were the opponents in an FA Cup semi-final at Villa Park.

*U*NFANCIED Luton Town, with the wind at their backs, deservedly went into the interval a goal to the good thanks to Ricky Hill's strike. There were chances at both ends but the Blues' grip on the trophy seemed to be slipping, as well as the end of their 20-match unbeaten run.

But with five minutes remaining there was a lifeline. A free-kick was awarded for a foul on Derek Mountfield 20 yards out. Kevin Sheedy stepped up and somehow the ball bobbled into the corner.

The Hatters looked a beaten side and Derek Mountfield, so prolific from set pieces, headed the winner seven minutes from the end of extra time from a Sheedy set piece. Cue pitch invasion.

Post-match, Mountfield said: "The boss sent me forward and the move paid off. I was fouled, and Kevin Sheedy scored from the free-kick. Then we got another free-kick near the end of extra time and I threw myself at it."

Massive crowd expected for semi showdown

(By Ken Rogers, Liverpool Echo, April 24, 1985)

With the Blues heading towards an eighth league title and having reached a second successive FA Cup final, the treble dream was close to a reality. Excitement was building ahead of the European Cup-Winners' Cup semi-final, second leg against Bayern Munich.

$\mathcal{G}$OODISON Park promises to be a cauldron of excitement as Everton bid for a place in the final of the European Cup-Winners' Cup with a victory over Bayern Munich. A massive crowd of over 48,000 is expected, beating this season's previous best of 47,402 for the FA Cup tie against Telford.

Manager Howard Kendall said: "It's going to be a tremendous occasion, absolutely electric. I recall the 1970 Goodison clash against another German team, Borussia Moenchengladbach.

"There was an unbelievable atmosphere that night and the fans will remember the excitement as we eventually won 4-3 on penalties. I don't want it to get that tight and hopefully we can finish it."

Everton had only 1,500 seats left when the Box Office opened and it is expected that they will have been sold before kick-off. Admission to all terraces, including the Park End, is by cash at the turnstiles.

The game of games

(By Ken Rogers, reflecting in his 'Goodison Glory' book)

T will go down in history as the greatest Goodison Park clash of modern times.

Everton 3 Bayern Munich 1 . . . let the scoreline roll off the tongue and feel the passion of that never-to-be-forgotten night of April 24, 1985, when the Blues blitzed the pride of Germany to power into their first ever European final, having already disposed of University College Dublin, Slovan Bratislava, and Fortuna Sittard.

Everton gave one of the greatest club sides in Europe a one goal start in this finely balanced second leg and then battered them into submission with a breathtaking display of power.

Goodison exploded as goals from Graeme Sharp, Andy Gray and Trevor Steven broke the hearts of Bayern Munich. The West German league leaders thought they had the tie in the bag when Dieter Hoeness squeezed them in front after 37 minutes. But Everton, inspired by 11 heroes on the pitch and 49,000 never-say-die supporters on the terraces, hit back with a vengeance.

The courage, determination and commitment that inspired the triumph and earned a final clash with Rapid Vienna was epitomised in the displays of the goalscorers. Sharp and Gray gave the Germans a pounding with as bold a display of front running as you will see. It was the very best of British in terms of aggressive centre-forward play.

They were rewarded with a goal apiece in the second half when Bayern were on the rack and on the run with the Evertonians roaring their men forward. If that wasn't enough, Steven brought the house down four minutes from time like some latter day Bobby Charlton, racing clear and unleashing and unstoppable shot from the edge of the box that flew past Belgian international 'keeper Jean-Marie Pfaff.

On the final whistle, Gray was last off the pitch. He thrust his fists high into the air and the cheer must have rattled the Bayern dressing room door as they sat disconsolate, reflecting on a remarkable game.

German coach Uli Hoeness, who waited in the tunnel, spat out a frustrating aside to Gray: "That was not football. You are crazy men."

What he really meant was: "We've just been played off the park by a team of giants."

Hoeness later told the gathered press: "Everton are the best team in Europe, but Gray should be playing rugby, not football."

Gray's response was totally defiant: "The lads were determined to show that they were the best in Europe, and that's just what they did."

An elated Howard Kendall declared: "We had decided to bomb them and put them under immediate pressure rather than getting involved in a patient, slow build-up routine. I felt that if we moved forward slowly from the back, it would be playing right into their hands. It was a cash of cashing in on our strengths and it paid off."

It certainly did. The game will live forever in the minds of Evertonians, and I was one of those whose was supremely proud to declare: "I was there."

Everton: Southall, Stevens, Van Den Hauwe, Ratcliffe, Mountfield, Reid, Steven, Sharp, Gray, Bracewell, Sheedy. Subs not used: Arnold, Wakenshaw, Richardson, Atkins, Harper.
Bayern Munich: Pfaff, Dremmler, Willmer, Eder, Augenthaler, Lerby, Pflugler, Matthaus, Hoeness, Nachtweih, Kogl. Subs not used: Durnberger, Beierlorzer, Wohlfarch, Rummenigge, Mathey.
Referee: E. Frederiksson (Sweden).
Attendance: 49,476.

The fans sucked it in

(By John Osborne, Liverpool Echo, April 25, 1985)

*B*AYERN boss Udo Lattek admitted: "On this showing Everton are the best team in Europe. They put us under pressure and in the final analysis they were simply just too strong for us."

Andy Gray said afterwards: "The fans out there were absolutely tremendous. It was their victory as much as ours in the way that they got behind us. In fact, my goal should be credited to them for I didn't hit it that hard, the fans sucked it in!

"The boss was happy with us at half-time even though we were one down. We always knew that we could do it, then we got the break and by God we showed the Germans that we can play."

Everton boss Howard Kendall said: "I have not known many nights like this. I feel pleasure for everyone concerned at the club. Getting into a European final is a new experience and we mean to enjoy it."

New sponsors set for £1m deal

(By Keith Ely, Liverpool Daily Post, May 4, 1985)

Everton's impressive season had not gone unnoticed by blue-chip sponsors.

*A*BIG switch in the sponsorship of Everton FC looks possible, with Japanese computer giants NEC stepping into the arena.

It is believed that the present sponsorship deal with Wirral-based food importer Jaka – which uses its Hafnia label to back Everton – may not be renewed.

The value of the existing sponsorship contract, which has been running for three years, has never been disclosed but it is unlikely to approach the sort of payments being made elsewhere in the sport – about £500,000 for two years.

The outstanding success of Everton this season has made the club a very attractive proposition to would-be sponsors.

Word in the marketing industry is that Everton's deal could be worth up to £1m over three years.

Champions, champions

(By Roy Hayes, Liverpool Daily Post, May 7, 1985)

An eighth league title, the first for 15 years, was confirmed with victory over QPR.

*E*CSTATIC Everton are the new kings of English soccer.

The Blues ended 15 years in the shadows of neighbours Liverpool when they wrested the league title from the Reds with a 2-0 win over Queens Park Rangers before a packed 50,000 house at Goodison Park.

The players ran a lap of honour to a thunderous ovation and the celebrating continued well into the night with jubilant fans proclaiming Howard Kendall's heroes the new pride of Merseyside.

"It's an unbelievable feeling," said Kendall. "Winning a trophy means so much to this club and the fans. We got the win we wanted and we got it at Goodison Park, which is great. And to win the title with five games remaining is unbelievable."

The goals came from Derek Mountfield and Graeme Sharp and stretched Everton's unbeaten run to 27. The target now is a fabulous treble of league, FA Cup and European Cup-Winners' Cup – and certainly the fans were in no doubt as they chanted "We're going to win the lot" long after the final whistle sounded yesterday.

Everton will be presented with the league trophy, which they last won in 1970, before tomorrow night's home clash with Division One strugglers West Ham. A memorable day was crowned by the Player of the Year award to keeper Neville Southall and the Bell's Manager of the Month award to Howard Kendall.

A team to be proud of

(Liverpool Daily Post, May 7, 1985)

A period of dominance was predicted.

*I*F everything goes according to plan Everton's success story could run longer than "The Mousetrap."

It came as little surprise to yours truly that practically everyone connected with English football's premier club was at great pains, shortly after 5pm yesterday to point out that this was just the beginning – the dawning of a new golden age at Goodison.

For the time being at least people like Howard Kendall, Kevin Ratcliffe, Andy Gray and Joe Public on the terraces will be content.

The force-fed diet of broken promises is thankfully at an end and the legions who have suffered in silence as the Red enemy from across the park swept all before them, at last have something to crow about.

Actually, the word "something" is both inappropriate and insufficient. Everton supporters young and old, far and distant, now have a team they can be proud of. The side Howard built is a cracker.

There was a time, five or six weeks ago, when I honestly thought the thoroughbreds who inhabit White Hart Lane were preparing to sneak the title in a dramatic end-of-season smash and grab raid. Rather stupidly I had forgotten one simple and undeniable fact – Everton don't lose any more. Where we mere mortals have blood oozing through our veins, Kendall's young lionhearts seemingly have neat adrenalin.

They have the courage of a gladiator, the determination of a wounded prize-fighter and the skill of a circus acrobat.

With the age-old adage "when the going gets tough, the tough get going" pushed to the sharp end of their collective mind, the new aristocrats of our much maligned national game set about deftly reinforcing the bubble we had all been reliably informed would eventually burst. Well the Blues bubble hasn't burst – it's gone up.

Yesterday's game was never going to be an easy one. QPR may have unwittingly gatecrashed the year's biggest private party, but they most certainly weren't going to lie down and surrender, as the script decreed.

For in a bone-crunching encounter at Loftus Road back in December, tempers and composure were occasionally lost as boots, fists and knees sought refuge in the fleshy parts of opposition bodies.

Aware that their boss had already made it perfectly clear that there would be no final whistle celebrations unless victory was attained, Everton were uncharacteristically nervous for the most part.

The breath-taking football, which has helped turn boys into men, was rarely in evidence as they tentatively rolled forward in search of the goal which would inevitably release much of the pressure.

After numerous near-misses it duly arrived midway through the half as a direct result of one of 10 pre-interval corners. Kevin Sheedy's kick was helped into the path of Gray by a Rangers defender; the spring-heeled Scotsman directed it towards Pat Van Den Hauwe and there was Derek Mountfield to latch on to his defensive colleague's header to thrash the ball home via the crossbar and Peter Hucker's legs.

Gary Bannister so very nearly spoiled the afternoon with just 17 minutes left when he headed firmly against the foot of a post, then with the seconds ticking away Graeme Sharp neatly tucked away his 30th goal of the campaign to officially launch the jamboree.

Everton: Southall, Stevens, Van Den Hauwe, Ratcliffe, Mountfield, Reid, Steven, Sharp, Gray, Bracewell, Sheedy. Sub not used: Richardson.
QPR: Hucker, Chivers, Dawes, Waddock, Wicks, Fenwick, Robinson, Fillery, Bannister, James, Gregory. Sub not used: McDonald.
Referee: J. Hough (Macclesfield).
Attendance: 50,514.

An unforgettable afternoon as the title comes back

(By Ann Cummings, Liverpool Echo, May 7, 1985)

Emotional scenes as dreams are realised.

*T*HERE was hardly a dry eye in the place, as Everton brought the league championship back to Goodison Park after 15 years.

Emotion spread from Gwladys Street to the directors' box, where Mrs Rita Carter, wife of Everton chairman Philip, wept openly.

And Sir John Moores, millionaire chairman when they last won the title in 1970, could hardly contain his joy, as he said: "I never thought that I'd live to see another league championship come to Goodison. It's great to feel free of the domination of Liverpool."

The sight of a delirious fan tying a scarf round Sir John's neck summed up the heady atmosphere, shared by everyone present.

So did the scenes on the pitch, when referee John Hough blew for time at 4.40pm to signal that the Blues were the kings of English soccer.

Manager Howard Kendall could not resist dancing a little victory jig on the pitch, and the players ran to hug him with joy. The jubilant fans sang: "There's only one Howard Kendall," and the chants of "Champions" rang from all corners of the packed stadium, when the players started the traditional lap of honour.

The supporters, who had thronged the streets in blue and white mass hours before the kick-off to swell the gate to more than 50,000, realised the elusive "treble" was a possibility, with the FA Cup and European Cup-Winners' Cup finals to come. So they started singing: "We're going to win the lot."

Celebrations went on until the early hours of this morning, and there were a few hangovers, as people reported back to work today after the Bank Holiday. A new page was written in the history of Merseyside soccer folklore, which was crowned by the news before the game that goalkeeper Neville Southall had been named Player of the Year.

Manager Kendall was presented with the Bell's Manager of the Month award, the rain stopped, and the sun came out just before the kick-off. It was a day when nothing could go wrong for the Blues.

The champions' coronation

(By John Osborne, Liverpool Daily Post, May 9, 1985)

The championship trophy was presented two days later, ahead of the home game with West Ham.

*T*HE long wait is over. After 15 years in the First Division wilderness, the League Championship returned officially to Goodison Park amid scenes that would have been unbelievable 18 months ago.

When Football League president Jack Dunnett handed over the Canon League Trophy to Everton skipper Kevin Ratcliffe before the 3-0 win over West Ham, Goodison erupted. And the man behind the Blues' dramatic rise, Howard Kendall, has extra reason to celebrate.

As Ratcliffe raised the trophy to the ecstatic Gwladys Street end, Kendall stood quietly on the sidelines, perhaps reflecting that it was exactly four years to the day since he took over at Everton.

For him it was as much a personal triumph as a team victory for only a year last Christmas he and his backroom staff were hot favourites for the axe as the club tumbled almost hopelessly towards the foot of the

First Division table.

The Blues extended their unbeaten run to 28 matches with a goal from Andy Gray and two from centre-back Derek Mountfield, who took his tally this season to 14. Kendall, as ever low key, described the evening as "magical".

"It was a smashing night out for the fans who have been tremendous throughout the season and a great moment for all the players and everyone else connected with the club."

Attempting to conquer Europe

(By Ian Ross, Liverpool Daily Post, May 15, 1985)

The club were on the verge of their biggest moment, a first European final and a chance to secure the second of three trophies in the space of 12 days. Everton were also many neutrals' favourites ahead of the Rotterdam clash – including Celtic fans.

*E*VERTON carry the standard of English football into a showpiece European final for the first time in their 107-year history.

A season of quite monumental proportions moves to the continental stage as Howard Kendall's young champions boldly bid to land the second part of a staggering treble by carrying off the Cup-Winners' Cup at the expense of controversial Austrian hard-men Rapid Vienna.

Already hailed at home as the game's new aristocrats, the all-conquering Goodison side now stand on the threshold of a triumph which would serve to underline their growing stature and signal the dawning of a glittering new era.

But although the confidence which swept Everton to a first title success in 15 years is still high, Feyenoord's magnificent stadium will be no place for faint hearts.

Rapid, still furious at the public outcry which followed UEFA's decision to order a replay of the infamous second-round tie against Celtic, are convinced they can shatter the dreams of a side labelled the finest in Europe by semi-final victims Bayern Munich.

Ironically, it was that much-publicised incident at Parkhead – in which a Rapid player claimed he was felled by a missile – which may well come back to haunt the Austrians.

Everton carry a tidal wave of Scottish support into the game and are anxious to prove it is players and not bureaucrats who still have the final say in modern football.

"We have received many letters from north of the border wishing us all the best and urging us to beat Rapid to put the record straight," said midfielder Peter Reid.

"I have always been interested in the fortunes of Celtic because my grandfather was a big fan of theirs. I felt they were very hard done by when the tie was ordered to be replayed.

"It just did not seem fair. It would be nice to bring the cup back home and it now looks as though we will have Britain on our side.

"We have adapted to European football very quickly, which I think has surprised many people. The continental game suits our style; we don't give the opposition time or space."

As expected, Kendall, who was in Vienna last Friday to watch Rapid go down 1-0 to fierce rivals FK Austria, has named his strongest side, Kevin Sheedy having fully recovered from a slight ankle knock picked up during the defeat at Nottingham Forest on Saturday.

"We are looking forward to the challenge; I am delighted that all my players are fit and that we go into the game injury-free.

"Now we want to complete the job. I was disappointed not to be able to name my strongest side at the weekend," said Kendall.

"I am proud to be here. We want to bring the club's first European trophy back home to Merseyside. I think Rapid will possibly give us more space than Bayern did. I am amazed we have adapted so well, we look as though we have been playing in Europe for many seasons."

The First Division's most celebrated double act arrived in Rotterdam in buoyant mood. Everton's twin strikeforce of Andy Gray and Graeme Sharp were yesterday called up to the Scotland squad for the clash with England at Hampden Park on May 25 and the World Cup qualifier against Iceland the following Tuesday.

"This simply serves to underline how well the side has played all season. I am absolutely delighted for the pair of them. This means that only Derek Mountfield has not been called up but I am hopeful his turn will come," said Kendall.

Gray said: "This is a tremendous boost for me. Everything has gone right since I moved to Everton. I never really thought about getting back into the Scotland set-up; I just kept trying my hardest for the club." Said Sharp: "This is magic. A lot of the credit must go to Andy, he has helped me a great deal this season, in fact, he was one of the main reasons why I signed a new contract. It is now up to me to take my chance if I am included in the starting line-up."

Rapid overwhelmed by super Blues

(By Ian Hargraves, Liverpool Echo, May 16, 1985)

The 3-1 victory rounded off a proud night for players, staff and fans, 25,000 of whom made it to Holland. Praise was generous.

*M*AGNIFICENT! That is the only word to describe Everton's performance in over-running Rapid Vienna in Rotterdam last night to claim their first European trophy.

Rapid's former Golden Boot winner Hans Krankl summed it all up when he said: "Everton were just too good for us. It is a very long time since we have played against anyone of their class.

"In all other games in Europe we have been given the chance to win at some time, but Everton gave us no chance at all.'"

Few teams since the war have given such a complete demonstration of all-out, controlled football. Wolves, Spurs, the pre-Munich Busby Babes and more recently, one or two of Liverpool's very best teams, may have matched it from time to time; none have surpassed it.

If Kevin Sheedy and Trevor Steven were not swinging over centres for the ever-dangerous Andy Gray and Graeme Sharp, Peter Reid and Paul Bracewell were threading passes through the middle.

And right behind them was young Derek Mountfield, powering through from the back at every opportunity, and adding to the general unease surrounding goalkeeper Michael Konsel.

For a side at the end of a testing season it was a remarkable achievement.'

Everton's dominance on the pitch was matched by their supporters off it. The 25,000 fans who turned Rotterdam into a cauldron of noise in the morning and who entertained the locals with their humour and their footballing expertise during a series of impromptu matches in the city centre, also set the stadium rocking with their vocal support during and after the match.

Rapid's green-clad supporters were hopelessly out-shouted and would have disappeared totally but for the fireworks they fired onto the pitch and the fire they stupidly started by igniting a banner.

Given such a reception it was unthinkable the Blues should lose, and the only surprise was that they did not wrap it all up well before the interval.

In the opening 20 minutes Rapid barely crossed the halfway line as Everton came at them from all angles. Konsel beat out a fierce right-footer from Sheedy while Bracewell fired a shot only inches wide.

Kranjcar did manage to engineer a couple of promising breakaways for the beleaguered Austrians but Everton were soon back in control.

Gray actually netted in 39 minutes, after Mountfield had headed a Sheedy free-kick back inside, and though the whistle went for offside, it must have been desperately close.

Rapid caused a few flutters of unease on the resumption when Van Den Hauwe was forced to head a Kranjcar shot against his own cross bar and Ratcliffe intervened at the last moment to foil Krankl, but once Gray had put Everton in front in the 57th minute the match was as good as over.

Sharp's speed of anticipation enabled him to beat Konsel to a poor back pass and his squared pass was volleyed into the empty net by a delighted Gray.

Steven almost increased the lead when he turned his man superbly at the end of an intricate move involving half a dozen players, only to see his shot saved by Konsel, but made amends by adding the second goal after 72 minutes.

Rapid's defence were all at sea as Sheedy curled in a typical corner, and the ball flew straight through to Steven who could hardly miss.

Understandably, Everton then relaxed, and although they suffered a minor shock when Krankl snatched a goal back after rounding Southall, they re-emphasised their dominance by scoring again immediately.

Straight from the kick-off they swept downfield with almost contemptuous ease, and Sharp's diagonal pass set Sheedy free to hammer the ball home.

That goal put the finishing touch to a memorable performance. Not only had Everton shown their ability to beat a top Continental side, but they had done so with the kind of style now associated with the modern Goodison. You can't ask for more than that!

Everton (4-4-2): Southall; Stevens, Mountfield, Ratcliffe, Van Den Hauwe; Steven, Reid, Bracewell, Sheedy; Sharp, Gray. Subs not used: Arnold, Bailey, Harper, Richardson, Atkins.
Rapid Vienna (4-4-2): Konsel; Lainer, Brauneder, Weber, Garger; Kranjcar, Kienast, Hrstic, Pacuit (Gross, 60); Krankl, Weinhofer (Panenka, 66). Subs not used: Pregesbauer, Stadler, Feurer.
Goals: Gray 57, Steven 72, Krankl 85, Sheedy 86.
Corners: Everton 10, Rapid 2.
Bookings: Stevens, Weber – both for fouls.
Referee: Paolo Casarin (Italy).
Attendance: 45,000 (estimated).

Party time for the pride of Europe

(By Andrew Edwards, Liverpool Echo, May 16, 1985)

*E*VERTON and their royal blue army were the pride of Europe today after last night's magnificent and historic European Cup-Winners' Cup victory in Rotterdam.

The 25,000 Evertonians who descended on the city won a huge tribute from the Dutch authorities. And Everton impressively proved themselves as a major new force in European football.

It was a day when Merseyside showed the world all that was great about British soccer. The blue and white army of fans drank the city dry before the match, but still upheld the name of the club they adore.

During the match they turned the beautiful Feyenoord Stadium into a cauldron of noise and colour, outnumbering the Austrian supporters three-to-one. Andy Gray's opening goal for Everton in the second half sparked the start of some amazing scenes of celebration.

"It was a pleasure having the Everton supporters here in Rotterdam. They were a credit to their country," said Rotterdam chief inspector Johan Smits.

Everton chairman Philip Carter said: "Our supporters have been absolutely marvellous. What a great night for Everton. Our fans have upheld the reputation of Everton FC and given a tremendous boost to the British image abroad. I am very proud of our team and I am proud of our supporters. All day they mixed with the Dutch people, the police and the Austrian supporters. They've swapped hats and scarves and even had a game of football with police – and that's what the spirit of European football is all about."

Everton manager Howard Kendall said: "The fans have been great ambassadors for this club. We are proud of them."

Team skipper Kevin Ratcliffe said: "Our supporters have proved to everyone what we already know – they are brilliant. Wherever we have played this season, at home or abroad, they have done us proud.'"

Liverpool Airport was today scaling down their operations after their largest single movement of people. They transported an estimated 4,000 Blues out of Liverpool and back in just 24 hours – as well as coping with their usual customers.

Two out of three is Scouse poetry
(May 18, 1985)

*J*UST three days later, Manchester United stood in the Blues' way of a treble. Things looked up when Kevin Moran was sent off by referee Peter Willis for a foul on Peter Reid in the second half – the first such instance in 105 years of FA Cup finals. But on a humid day with energy sapped, Norman Whiteside curled home a goal worthy to win any final in extra time. This gave United a first win in four attempts that season against the Blues. It was also the first instance of a match in Britain generating gate receipts exceeding £1 million.

Despite the disappointment, an estimated 250,000 people welcomed the team home on their open-top bus tour of the city. One banner proclaimed: "Two out of three is Scouse poetry." On the bus tour, Derek Mountfield said: "Our name just wasn't on the FA Cup yesterday afternoon. But it has been a tremendous season for everybody connected with Everton. This welcome home is wonderful."

Derby double for record-breakers
(Liverpool Daily Post, May 24, 1985)

Completion of the Merseyside double.

*E*VERTON'S unsung heroes emerged from the shadows to claim their own piece of history. Howard Kendall's champions, lacking the services of five of Saturday's FA Cup final side, completed their first derby double in 20 years to prove conclusively that the future of English football's new premier club is in safe hands.

New-boy Paul Wilkinson capped his senior home debut with the game's solitary goal midway through the second half. This victory takes the title holders on to 90 points – a new First Division record.

Damages sought for Euro ban
(By Ian Hargraves, Liverpool Echo, June 27, 1985)

English clubs including Everton were already looking into the implications of the European ban.

*E*VERTON will tomorrow claim cash damages as they stage a court bid to wipe out the European soccer ban on English clubs.

It emerged that the Blues are asking for compensation after losing their European Cup place following the Brussels disaster. They are being joined in their High Court action by Manchester United and Southampton. However, Tottenham have decided not to back the action and Norwich City look set to pull out too.

Everton claim the decisions of the FA, UEFA and FIFA are void because they breach the rules of natural justice.

The clubs are also claiming a declaration that the decisions represent an unlawful restraint of trade against the clubs and their players.

Against the FA, the clubs are alleging breach of contract.

Tomorrow's hearing will be before Mr Justice Walton, who will be asked to order the FA to submit the four club's names to UEFA immediately. The deadline for qualifying clubs' entries is next Monday.

FA secretary Ted Croker said yesterday he believed the clubs were "chasing a lost cause".

Lineker: 'Everton team of the moment'

(By Ken Rogers, Liverpool Echo, July 18, 1985)

A new striker was raring to go.

$\mathcal{G}$ARY Lineker completed his first Bellefield training session with the kind of enthusiasm that you might expect from a man with his sights firmly on the top with Everton and England – and then spoke with confidence and conviction about his Goodison Park dream.

The pacy centre-forward said: "I moved from Leicester because I intend to try and win trophies with a top club and it goes without saying that Everton are one of the biggest. I've only been here a day, but I've been impressed by everything at Everton, the manager, the players and the club itself. It's clear everyone in this city lives for football."

Both Manchester United and Liverpool were keen to sign him, but he was more than happy to move to Goodison, reflecting: "Everton are the team of the moment."

Blues in whites

(Liverpool Echo, July 18, 1985)

Lineker impressed on his Everton bow – in Wallasey – although it was the manager who guided the side home.

$\mathcal{E}$VERTON'S new signing Gary Lineker made his debut for the Blues yesterday in the unlikely surroundings of Wallasey Oval. Players and staff were taking on Parkfield Cricket Club in their annual friendly to help raise money for Parkfield's pavilion appeal. And Lineker proved he's just as deadly near the wickets as he is in front of goal.

He took a spectacular catch to see the host team finish at 113-3. Man of the match John Williams was 54 not out and Alan Harper took 2-27. In reply Everton were 116-8, Howard Kendall playing a real manager's innings, making 48.

Huge demand for season tickets

(Liverpool Echo, July 26, 1985)

Unsurprisingly supporters' enthusiasm was high.

$\mathcal{E}$VERTON are set to smash their season-ticket sales record following the most successful campaign in the club's history. Sales are already up by a staggering 70 per cent on last term and the Goodison staff are expecting another surge just before the big kick-off in August.

Gray: "The happiest years of my life"

(By Ken Rogers & Ann Cummings, Liverpool Echo, July 25, 1985)

There was a fond farewell from a striking great, who made such a big impact during his short spell at Goodison.

$\mathcal{A}$NDY Gray was overwhelmed by the mail he received when he left for Villa. He sent a personal letter to the Echo, saying: "It would be impossible to thank everyone individually. I have never felt so moved or humble as I did when the cards started to arrive. I thought the supporters and I were close, but never realised how close.

"I have so much to thank the fans for. I am proud to have been part of Everton's revival. Goodison will always be special. Everton gave me the two happiest years of my life.

"So thanks for the memories – to you, the fans, to Howard, Colin, Mick Heaton, Terry Darracott, and 'Clinks' (John Clinkard) for putting up with me and to the best bunch of lads I have worked with.

"God bless you all, and long may your amazing success continue."

Europe hopes ended in High Court

(Liverpool Daily Post, July 29, 1985)

There was to be no joy for English clubs in their appeal over the European ban.

A HIGH Court judge ended Everton's slim hopes of playing in Europe next season. Mr Justice Vinelott threw out an appeal following the Brussels disaster ban "in the interests of the game and its future".

The ruling also ended the Euro dreams of Manchester United, Southampton and Norwich. Along with the Professional Footballers' Association the clubs had sought to declare the ban on them illegal. Everton must now sit out the prestigious European Cup competition. They had qualified for it for the first time in 15 years and will now lose thousands of pounds. The clubs had claimed the bans were an unlawful restraint of trade, in breach of natural justice, against European Community law and an interference in contractual obligations.

Mr Justice Vinelott said the clubs had no automatic right of entry in Europe via the FA's nominations. One reason was that UEFA and FIFA would have ignored such orders as being made by a court which had no power over them. But more important, said the judge, was the tragic background to the bans.

Champagne celebration

(Liverpool Echo, August 16, 1985)

There were joyous scenes at the club AGM.

*E*VERTON gave their shareholders a champagne AGM at Goodison Park last night, with added sparkle from the massive show of trophies won in a memorable season.

With the forecast running in his ears that the Kendall Kids would become as famous as the Busby Babes, manager Howard Kendall paid tribute to his backroom staff as well as players and supporters with a special mention for the now departed Andy Gray.

Said Kendall: "Andy was like a two-year-old in training and a tremendous example. I understand the reasons he moved on and want to wish him all the best at Villa this season – apart from the two games."

Team of the year

(By Ken Rogers, Liverpool Echo, November 19, 1985)

Europe – and now the world!

*E*VERTON were named in Paris today as "European Team of the Year" – a fitting reward for the most successful season in their history.

Their achievement was immediately acknowledged from an unexpected source, Manchester United boss Ron Atkinson admitting that there was only one team in it.

The man who is desperately hoping to relieve the Blues of their championship crown this season, said: "There were no other worthier contenders for this award than Howard Kendall's men. Everton thoroughly deserved to win the title last season and they performed superbly in Europe. I'm sure they are going to be around again this season when the prizes are handed out."

Iraq trip cancelled

(Liverpool Echo, January 10, 1986)

A planned trip abroad was cancelled.

$\mathcal{A}$T a special meeting of the Everton board today, the Goodison Park club decided to call off their trip to Baghdad next week.

They were due to play two games against the Iraq national side, but the escalating problems in a trouble-torn war zone led to the decision to cancel the journey.

Told you so

(Liverpool Echo, April 7, 1986)

The Blues were chasing a possible Double for the second successive season, and had already beaten FA Cup semi-final opponents Sheffield Wednesday twice during the campaign. A 2-1 Everton victory at Villa Park ensured the first-ever all-Merseyside FA Cup final – although for one person the fixture was never in doubt.

$\mathcal{L}$IVERPOOL psychic and medium, Mrs Ivylea Turner predicted that Liverpool would meet Everton in the FA Cup final. The 66-year-old grandmother says she has a number of predictions for this year which will remain under wraps for the time being.

League out of Everton's hands

(Liverpool Daily Post, May 1, 1986)

A cruel late defeat meant the defence of the league title was out of Everton hands…

$\mathcal{E}$VERTON manager Howard Kendall remained defiant last night after his side's crushing defeat at Oxford.

A goal two minutes from time by United midfielder Les Phillips cruelly robbed the Blues of a vital point in the title chase. They must now pray for a Liverpool defeat at Stamford Bridge to stand any chance of retaining their league crown.

But Kendall insisted: "The league isn't over yet. We'll all be in there fighting on Saturday. I have suddenly become a Chelsea fan! We wanted to win our last three games. The title was in our hands, now it's not and that's the most disappointing thing."

Title slips away

(Liverpool Daily Post, May 5, 1986)

A 6-1 victory on the final Saturday of the First Division season proved academic – but there was still all to play for

*H*OWARD Kendall yesterday pushed aside the bitter disappointment of seeing Everton's league crown snatched away to gaze optimistically at next weekend's FA Cup final.

Everton surrendered their title despite hammering Southampton 6-1 and must now defeat West Ham United at Goodison tonight to clinch the runners-up spot behind Wembley opponents Liverpool.

But Kendall is convinced his leg-weary stars can dig deep for one last effort as they go in search of a silver lining to another superb season. "I don't think I have felt so low after a 6-1 victory. We have had another great season and the lads made a tremendous attempt at retaining the title. It is to their immense credit that they went so close," he said.

Kendall admitted that for a time he was lulled into a false sense of renewed hope, believing Liverpool had fallen behind to Chelsea. "I wasn't in touch with that game but you pick things up from the supporters. I did get a bit excited when I heard the roars from the crowd," he said. "I heard one huge scream and then another and thought Chelsea were two-up but we were told at half-time that it was Liverpool who were in front. We kept waiting for some sign towards the end that Chelsea had equalised because it would have given hope."

Lineker matches Latchford

(Liverpool Daily Post, May 6, 1986)

Victory in the final league game at least ensured second, and a confidence boost ahead of the FA Cup final.

$\mathcal{G}$ARY Lineker claimed a place in football's Hall of Fame last night as Everton maintained Merseyside's vice-like grip on the English game.

The man who will head our assault on the World Cup in a few weeks time became only the second First Division player since Bob Latchford eight years ago to hit 30 league goals in a season. It brought his personal tally since his £800,000 move from Leicester City to a remarkable 39.

Lineker's double blast was the high spot of a breath-taking display by Howard Kendall's side which lifts them above West Ham and clinches the runners-up spot behind FA Cup final opponents Liverpool.

Ditching the bib

(Liverpool Daily Post, May 6, 1986)

There was to be a return to an ALL blue home shirt for 1986/87.

$\mathcal{H}$OWARD Kendall's Goodison heroes will have a completely new look next season. Everton have kicked their much-criticised team strip into touch, favouring a dominant royal blue shirt – long regarded as traditional dress by the club's die-hard supporters.

So Everton's "white-bibbed" style shirts disappear after just one season. They were initially given the thumbs down but, ironically, became best-sellers in the sports shops. Manufactured by Le Coq Sportif, the strips will make their last appearance in the FA Cup final.

Umbro will take over the contract and insiders say the look will be traditional, the royal blue shirts being complimented by white shorts. There have been rumours Everton might opt for blue shorts, but the Chelsea look wouldn't go down well with the Gwladys Street faithful.

Merseyside heads south

(Liverpool Echo, May 10, 1986)

There was a mass exodus south for the FA Cup final. An estimated 30,000 fans were set to travel without a ticket. Despite leading at half-time through Gary Lineker's 40th goal of the season, Liverpool hit back early in the second half with Ian Rush and Craig Johnston turning the game on its head. Graeme Sharp had an effort brilliantly saved and having sacrificed Gary Stevens for Adrian Heath, Rush took advantage in space to fire home the third.

$\mathcal{B}$Y breakfast time, fans were pouring from trains, cars, coaches and their overnight pavement spots to the Wembley dry zone carrying Scouse briefcases – plastic bags loaded with beer cans.

One fan said as he set out on a six-mile march to the stadium with his mates after last night's merry-making: "We've had a good time already and win or lose, we'll have another one tonight."

Reid misses bus tour

(By Harry Harris, Daily Mirror, May 12, 1986)

Prior to the game both sides had agreed to do an open-top bus tour of the city on their return. The one man who missed it? Peter Reid, who had also been linked with a move to West German side Cologne.

$\mathcal{P}$ETER Reid last night angrily denied that he snubbed the Merseyside fans by not turning up for yesterday's FA Cup parade.

After missing the joint tour of the city by Liverpool and Everton, the Goodison midfield star said: "I didn't go because of personal reasons. I didn't go missing for secret transfer talks with Cologne or anyone else and the fans will know I wouldn't snub them."

But despite Reid's assurances, manager Howard Kendall was seething last night: "We deserved an explanation," he said.'

Reid revealed to me last night: "I want to carry on playing for Everton. If everything is right I'd be happy to sign a new contract. I've not spoken to any other clubs. To suggest I have flown out to Cologne is sheer nonsense." Reid's solicitor Zac Harazi said: "Peter didn't meet any club, it was just that he was very upset. He comes from Liverpool, he's a winner and the result probably got to him more than it got to the others. That was the explanation."

Barcelona bound?

(By Harry Harris, Daily Mirror, May 12, 1986)

Everton's star striker was dismissing speculation linking him with Barcelona.

$\mathscr{B}$ARCELONA, willing to pay £2.2m for Gary Lineker, will be shocked to hear the striker say: "I don't want to go."

Lineker, depressed after Everton's Cup final defeat, talked to me at Wembley about his future. And he said: "I've another three years to go on my contract and I'm perfectly happy at Everton.

"It's flattering that a club like Barcelona are linked with me, but honestly I'm not bothered. No-one has spoken to me about it and as far as I'm concerned it is speculation."

Lineker took a realistic view when he said: "If Barcelona do make an offer, obviously I'll listen. But I won't be looking for a move. I'm sure we'll win something next year."

Facelift for Goodison

(By Ken Rogers, Liverpool Echo, July 16, 1986)

Ground improvements were in the pipeline – as well as a transfer move.

$\mathscr{E}$VERTON are planning a fan-tastic season, both on and off the pitch. A £600,000 plan will unfold over the next 12 months, elevating Goodison Park to super stadium status. And the Blues plan to have a team to match with Leeds United's outstanding England Under-21 midfielder Ian Snodin firmly in their sights. Elland Road boss Billy

Bremner describes Snodin as the hottest young property in the game.

In the meantime, they have unveiled details about a number of exciting new projects at Goodison – including the roofing of the Gwladys Street terraces in time for the 1987/88 season.

Sharing the burden

(By Chris James, Daily Mirror, August 16, 1986)

Gary Lineker had now departed after finishing as top scorer during the World Cup.

*G*RAEME Sharp, Everton's Scottish World Cup striker, last night warned the soccer world: "We won't miss Gary Lineker."

Everton go into today's Charity Shield game at Wembley knowing that they will have to be firing on all cylinders to topple arch rivals Liverpool. And they have to do it without 40-goal Lineker, who has moved to Barcelona in a near-£3m deal.

But Sharp reckons his partnership with Adrian Heath can achieve all his pairing with Lineker did last season. He even believes the loss of Lineker might benefit the team by providing extra goal power.

Sharp explained: "Gary's 40 goals last season was a fantastic achievement, but we suffered in other departments with goals not being spread round the team.

"Now, hopefully, everyone will start contributing to the scoring. While it would be nice for me to equal the 24 I scored last season and possibly do better, hitting goals doesn't count much if you don't win anything."

Back on top

(Liverpool Daily Post, May 5, 1987)

*E*VERTON were yesterday crowned the new Kings of English soccer. A Pat Van Den Hauwe goal after just 45 seconds sealed a 1-0 win against Norwich City at Carrow Road and took the league title back to Goodison Park for the ninth time.

Everton supporters invaded the pitch at the final whistle and cheered captain Kevin Ratcliffe on a lap of honour. After a champagne celebration manager Howard Kendall said: "It is a magnificent day for us." Ratcliffe added: "You could sense the lads wanted to do it today. We were determined not to let it slip once we had got our chance. Everybody is delighted and again I would like to thank our fans."

It is expected that the old League Championship trophy will be presented at Saturday's home game against Luton. And those other boys in blue, the Police, were also rejoicing for there was very little trouble after Everton's triumph.

The most successful Everton manager of all time

(By Ken Rogers, Liverpool Echo, May 5, 1987)

*H*OWARD Kendall arrived at Bellefield today, surveyed the magnificent training ground that was once the domain of his mentor, the late Harry Catterick, and glowed with pride at a title triumph that has made him the most successful Everton manager of all time.

Victory at Norwich secured Howard Kendall his second managerial Championship crown, matching Catterick's 1963 and 1970 successes.

Like his former boss, he has won one FA Cup, but has taken his side to three finals against Catterick's two. Unlike Kendall, Catterick never won a European crown – putting the present Goodison boss at the head of the pack in the royal blue managerial hall of fame.

He said: "I'm a very proud man today, although I never set out to surpass Harry. The most important thing was to match our great rivals from across the park. When I arrived, they were the team and the club which had monopolised the English scene – and Europe – for years.

"My aim was to try and strive to be the best, not just for one season, but over a long period. It's a building process and we have laid the foundations. You can never talk about dominating for years to come. People said that the 1970 Championship side would be the team of the decade. You just take it season by season. What we have got is a very strong squad and to have secured the title again is very special."

Kendall reflected in more depth on his achievement. He said: "When you sit back and see what has happened to us, it makes it an even greater achievement than our title two years ago. What has been our secret this season? Good players, a tremendous team spirit and a collective effort from everyone concerned."

Everton wasted no time at Carrow Road to rock their opponents. A blockbuster of a shot straight out of the Kevin Sheedy shooting manual exploded from the right boot of a man who is more renowned for his ferocious tackling than his lethal finishing.

It wasn't so much Van den Hauwe as Van den Howitzer as the ball flew into the net like an Exocet missile. It triggered off an ecstatic response from the 7,000 Evertonians who had made the long trek to East Anglia. Their triumphant deafening roar must have carried on the wind all the way to Merseyside.

You could sense from the word go that it was going to be a royal blue day. It was as if the Gwladys Street had been transported lock, stock and barrel to the Carrow Road terraces.

On the pitch, the key ingredient was balance. Howard Kendall had produced a vintage champagne blend and his reward must surely be the Manager of the Year award. Anything less would be an insult.

Norwich City: Gunn, Brown, Spearing, Bruce, Phelan, Butterworth, Williams, Drinkall, Rosario, Biggins (Fox, 59), Gordon.
Everton: Southall, Stevens, Van Den Hauwe, Ratcliffe, Watson, Reid, Steven, Heath, Sharp, Snodin, Power. Sub not used: Harper.
Ref: Jeff Bray (Hinckley).
Att: 23,489.

A team effort

(Liverpool Daily Post, May 5, 1987)

*H*OWARD Kendall spread his praise wide and admitted it felt even better than two years ago because of their injury-hit season.

"It means a tremendous amount because we missed out last season. We've had our upsets and it's a compliment to those who've come in.

"When you sit back and see what has happened to us in terms of injuries this is a great achievement. We owe a lot to a tremendous lot of players. We have used 23 this season and everyone of them has contributed. Last season our fans were so disappointed when Liverpool pipped us. Today I think they have got over it."

"I sensed a determination to do it today. I told the players we were going to be champions beforehand. There was never any doubt we would achieve it and it's good that we have done it today. That kills the ifs and buts. It's done and we can look forward to an occasion to savour on Saturday at Goodison. It's nice to have turned the tables on Liverpool but it doesn't matter who you take the title from."

Captain Kevin Ratcliffe said: "It could not have been more pleasing after the year we have had. We struggled with injuries and the title is credit to all the squad."

Ian Snodin said: "I have proved my point. I came to Goodison to win medals and I have got one in my very first season."

"I can't believe that I've got my hands on a championship medal at this time in my career. It is a wonderful feeling and has to be the greatest day of my footballing life," said another new Blue Paul Power.

For ex-Norwich star Dave Watson it was a unique experience: "I'm delighted that we managed to come and do it here. A year ago I got a Second Division championship trophy at Norwich so our timing couldn't have been better. I came to Everton for success and have got it in my first season."

Euphoria as Goodison basks in a golden glow

(By Ric George, Liverpool Echo, May 11, 1987)

The trophy presentation was made back at Goodison following the penultimate game of the season, against a determined Luton Town side.

LUTON Town, the club that bans away supporters from their ground, must have wished their team was barred from Goodison Park as Everton celebrated their Championship triumph in style.

The Hatters left Merseyside madder than ever and should have known better than to expect success on the day the Blues received their title trophies.

Even with the league already clinched, the script had been written for another Everton victory, and try as they might The visitors were not going to spoil the Goodison party. After a dream start they were forced into a catalogue of complaints and disasters as this explosive match slipped totally from their grasp in a 15-minute spell.

Flags, banners, ticker-tape reception for the team, and even sunshine – the setting was perfect for the new champions to produce another winning display before skipper Kevin Ratcliffe was presented with the championship and Today league prizes, to wild applause.

However, the carnival atmosphere lasted only four minutes as Luton, aiming to finish the season in their highest-ever position, took a shock lead through a fierce Mark Stein shot.

Inspired by the combative Reid, Everton swept forward, virtually camping inside the visitors' half. The midfielder saw Sealey turn his close-range effort for a corner and when Ratcliffe drove a free-kick towards goal the Luton keeper again produced a flying save.

But then it all went wrong for the Hatters. Just before the break, Sealey took a kick in the face from Sharp, requiring lengthy attention for concussion. There were fears he had swallowed his tongue and that he had received the kiss of life. Fortunately, we learned he had not.

But the blow on the head turned Sealey into an angry man. This was evident in the 52nd minute when Everton got their expected equaliser. Reid showed magnificent skill, beating two men on the edge of the box and as his chip came back off the bar, Johnson handled in a melee.

The Luton keeper particularly objected to the penalty decision, hurling the ball towards the referee. Trevor Steven remained cool, though, and slotted home the spot-kick before the disgusted Sealey was booked for booting the ball away. Three minutes later Steven repeated the act after he had been fouled by North. This time Les kept his mouth shut and his protests to a minimum.

Sharp turned in Stevens' drive on the hour to illustrate Everton's superiority and after the match, trophy-laden Ratcliffe led his team on a lap of honour to the euphoric chant of "Champions, Champions." It was an act of mutual respect.

Everton: Southall, Stevens, Watson, Ratcliffe, Van Den Hauwe, Steven, Snodin, Reid, Harper, Heath, Sharp. Sub not used: Adams.
Luton Town: Sealey, Johnson, North, Donaghy, McDonough, Nicholas, Hill, Preece, B. Stein, M. Stein (Wilson 73), Newell.
Referee: George Tyson (Sunderland).
Attendance: 44,092.

Howard for Bilbao – and Colin is the people's choice

(Liverpool Echo front page exclusive by Ken Rogers, June 18, 1987)

Howard Kendall's decision to step down after six years, to take on the challenge of managing Athletic Bilbao, saw his number two Colin Harvey take over at Goodison.

*E*VERTON manager Howard Kendall is considering a sensational offer from Spain to become the new boss of Athletic Bilbao.

The shock news surfaced today amid reports that Kendall has been offered a 45 million peseta (£220,000) signing-on fee, plus wages and fringe benefits. The Blues' boss returned from a club tour to New Zealand, Australia and Hawaii on Monday to find the Spanish offer on the table.

Bilbao have been tracking him for some considerable time on the recommendation of Terry Venables, who now looks certain to remain at Barcelona for a further year.

Evertonians, still elated at last season's Championship triumph, were expecting their manager to sign a new deal this week. An announcement was expected on that within 24 hours, but now it seems that the man who has transformed the club's fortunes could be on his way.

The Spanish swoop, involving a king's ransom, has forced Kendall to consider the future very carefully indeed. If developments progress, Everton will be encouraged by the fact that they have a ready-made

364 THE OFFICIAL EVERTON AUTOBIOGRAPHY

replacement waiting in the wings. I believe that coach Colin Harvey will be thrust into the Goodison limelight if Kendall takes the plunge and moves to Spain.

Harvey commands the respect of players and fans alike, is an Evertonian through and through, and he would be the people's choice ahead of any rival candidates – including Brian Clough.

Up to now, Harvey has been happy to remain in the background. He is a modest individual, never seeking headlines, but his impact has been immense. He has worked with Kendall to bring Championship, FA Cup and European Cup-Winners' Cup honours to Goodison.

Everton will almost certainly ask Harvey to take the reins should they lose a man whose success has captured the attention of clubs all over the Continent. Kendall's name has constantly been linked with foreign outfits, notably Barcelona who missed out on the Spanish championship race on Sunday to arch-rivals Real Madrid. At the other end of the table, Bilbao have been in desperate trouble, figuring in the relegation play-offs. They survived, but now want a new man to replace boss Jose Angel Iribar.

As manager of Bilbao, it would be unlikely that Kendall would be in a position to sign any Everton players. Traditionally, the Spaniards have refused to play anyone born outside the Basque region. They are fiercely proud of their local identity, looking on themselves as a country within a country.

Real lesson for wounded Blues

(By Philip McNulty, Liverpool Daily Post, August 27, 1987)

Everton faced Spanish champions Real Madrid in front of 76,000 at the Bernabeu Stadium, competing for the prestigious Santiago Bernabeu Trophy. A weakened side were demolished 6-1.

$\mathcal{R}$EAL Madrid left the pride of English soccer battered and bruised – the deadly striking duo of Hugo Sanchez and Emilio

Butragueno left champions Everton in total disarray.

They both struck winning doubles – as only Bobby Mimms and a helping of good fortune prevented the score reaching double figures.

Everton's illness and injury-ravaged squad – missing eight stars – were ripped apart as they appeared overawed by the wave of attacks which rained down on them.'

Skipper Kevin Ratcliffe reflected: "We have a good squad, but we were never able to get going. At half-time it was a case of trying to get some discipline in our play, but then they scored from a free-kick that went through our wall and once again we were under pressure."

Manager Colin Harvey said: "The Spaniards were the better team by a long way. It was a prestige game and they came out on top. They are a very special side and some of their football was magnificent. We have 11 disappointed players who have not performed as well as they should have done. We refuse to hide behind injuries.

"We didn't perform as well as an Everton side should have done. It was all over by the end of the first half. We were dead, simple as that."

Real Madrid: Buyo, Chendo, Solana, Tendillo, Sanchis, Gordillo (Llorente, 60), Butragueno, Michel, Sanchez, Gallego, Vazquez. Subs not used: Ochotorena, Mino, Santillana, Pardeza.
Goals: Butragueno (15, 30), Harper (17, og), Sanchez (29, 63), Michel (65).
Everton: Mimms, Harper, Pointon, Ratcliffe, Watson, Sheedy, Adams, Clarke (Ebbrell, 46), Marshall, Snodin, Power. Subs not used: Chamberlain, Van Den Hauwe, Reid.
Goal: Power (62).

Absentees pile up

(By Ian Hargraves, Liverpool Echo, October 1, 1987)

Colin Harvey believed a return for key players would be a welcome boost – with only three men now out with long-term problems. Gary Stevens, Peter Reid and Ian Wilson were close to a return.

*T*HE injury situation has caused us a lot of heartache over the last 18 months or so," he admitted. "And it has worried the fans, because we have been inundated with letters offering all kinds of suggestions.

"We have spent hours analysing every injury in detail, and we are satisfied that almost all of them have been unavoidable, because they have resulted from incidents in the heat of a match.

"We have made some changes in our training routine, to cut down the amount of running and the amount of physical contact, and I can assure you nobody here has dropped out because of strains received in that way, except for the odd freak incident."

Bayern back for celebration

(Liverpool Daily Post, November 24, 1987)

A return to European competition was forecast ahead of a clash with West German champions Bayern Munich, which Everton went on to win 3-1 at Goodison Park.

EVERTON chairman and Football League president Philip Carter forecast that English club sides will be back in Europe next season. He believes Everton's Centenary Challenge against West German champions Bayern Munich can help end the UEFA exile.

"It's a very good opportunity for us to show that European clubs coming here can be accommodated without any difficulty," said Mr Carter. "It's an important element in the argument that I have to produce for UEFA next February."

It is the third season that clubs have been denied European soccer since the Heysel Stadium disaster claimed 39 lives in May 1985 – and there are those who believe the time is still not right for a return.

But Mr Carter said: I'm quite convinced they will bring us back next year. How they will bring us back is debatable. Whether they'll say, 'We'll bring you back into the UEFA Cup and not all the competitions', I don't know. But I'm quite sure that they are as anxious to get us back as we are to get back."

Bayern Munich arrive on Merseyside today to finalise preparations for tomorrow's friendly. Coach Jupp Heynckes will be fielding his strongest available side, with on-loan Mark Hughes leading the attack.

Penalty defeat in the desert

(By Philip McNulty, Liverpool Daily Post, December 9, 1987)

Everton's 'Battle of Britain' with Rangers ended frustratingly, beaten 8-7 on penalties – Ian Snodin's spot-kick being saved by Chris Woods – after a 2-2 draw in Dubai. Man-of-the-match Kevin Sheedy, who picked up a golden boot from match sponsors, and Dave Watson were the Everton scorers in Al Nasr's Al Maktoum Stadium. Robert Fleck and Ally McCoist hit back in the final 10 minutes before the shoot-out. The club would pick up £25,000 for their troubles.

$\mathcal{E}$VERTON skipper Kevin Ratcliffe and player-coach Peter Reid summed up the team's mood of bitter disappointment after the penalties defeat against Glasgow Rangers in the Dubai Super Cup here last night.

"I have played for Everton for nearly 10 years and we have never won a penalty shoot-out as far as I can remember," said Ratcliffe. "We lost two daft goals. We dominated the first half but then they got the first goal and they seemed to build on that and made it hard for us."

Reid was angry at Everton's failure to hold on to the two-goal lead they had secured in such style.

He said: "To be two-up and then to lose two goals in the last 10 minutes is not good. You have to be disappointed with that. We created the best chances and we played some nice football, so it is disappointing to lose it on penalties."

Rangers suffered as an astonishing six 'goals' were ruled out for a variety of offences. Their player-manager Graeme Souness joked: "It's a bit much when you've got to get two goals out of eight to get a draw."

At the fourth time of asking

(January, 1988)

$\mathcal{I}$T took four games to separate Sheffield Wednesday and Everton in the FA Cup third round. Three 1-1 draws – the first at Hillsborough and two at Goodison – were followed by a fourth meeting, back in

South Yorkshire. Going into the fourth game, which had already yielded £200,000 for each club, boss Colin Harvey remained confident, telling the Liverpool Echo:

"Wednesday may be thinking that the advantage is now with them, but I don't see it that way. In two recent games at Hillsborough we looked the better side. We must remain as confident as ever."

Everton took advantage of a pre-match injury to Owls defender Lawrie Madden, who had been a rock for Wednesday in the previous games and which forced the Owls to revert to a four-man defence for the first time in the tie.

A hat-trick from Graeme Sharp – which many visiting fans missed having been caught in heavy traffic – helped the Blues to a 5-0 romp, with Adrian Heath and Ian Snodin also on target before the break.

The visitors cruised through the second half with Paul Bracewell coming on in the second half, his first senior appearance since the 1986 FA Cup final due to injury.

Between January 1 and January 27, Everton played Wednesday five times and discounting the tie against Bolton in 1887/88, it is the longest FA Cup marathon in Everton history.

Cottee arrives in record deal

(By Ken Gaunt, Liverpool Daily Post, July 27, 1988)

Injuries and inconsistency saw the defence of the championship end in a fourth-place finish. With money in the bank, the Blues sought reinforcements. Club record fee. Tony Cottee was the pick of the four newcomers.

*C*OLIN Harvey last night promised to carry on spending – even though he has splashed out close on £5m already this summer.

The Everton manager completed the signing of £2m West Ham striker Tony Cottee in a press conference at Goodison Park.

Then Harvey declared: "If any other quality players become available we will be interested. That has always been the club's policy. You have got to go after players even if their market value is high. I know the fans would rather have a quality player than £2m in the bank."

The Blues won the race with Arsenal to secure the services of the 23-year-old England player, who was born and brought up in London. But Cottee, who starts training today, was quick to stress that he is moving North for football and not financial reasons.

"I believe that by moving to Everton I will have a better chance of winning titles and trophies as well as improving my chances of international selection," he said.

Cottee said his decision was in the balance right up to the moment he put pen to paper for manager Colin Harvey at a London hotel on Monday night.

"They are two great clubs and it was such a big decision for me. I wanted to take as much time as I possibly could and I am definitely certain that I have made the right decision," he said.

"There were two main factors. I was very impressed with Colin Harvey and his thoughts on football and the role I would play in the team. I was also a bit disorientated by London and needed a new start. I don't think I will have any problems settling into life in the North.

"I don't feel under any pressure because of the fee. I am just glad the talking has finished and that I can get on with the job I do best – playing football."

Cottee's decision to join Everton was a bit of a blow to his agent Jon Smith – for he is an Arsenal fan. "I am absolutely gutted," he joked.

TV's big day at Goodison

(By Peter Went, Liverpool Daily Post, October 29, 1988)

The match attracted more print coverage than normal.

SOCCER'S £44m jazzed-up TV coverage kicks off tomorrow at Goodison Park. And the first innovation that will hit viewers is the unfamiliar starting time for Everton v Manchester United of 3.09!

It is all to do with commercial breaks – and nothing to do with fans being allowed to settle into their armchairs following the extension of Sunday licensing hours.

For the same reason half-time will be 16 minutes instead of the traditional 10, ITV also requiring extra-time in order to re-run all of Saturday's First Division goals.

It is a feature the commercial channel hope will make "The Match" the most exciting soccer coverage to hit the screens.

Executive producer Jeff Foulser admitted: "It really is all about the match; we are just bringing it into people's homes. We just hope it's a ruddy good game of football."

Without that ingredient, ITV could fall flat on their faces after the months of bitter wrangling that saw the clubs finally accept their cash package for exclusive four-year coverage.

There were casualties along the way, with League president Philip Carter and Management Committee colleague David Dein both being voted out of office in the wake of the summer affair.

It is somewhat ironic that Carter's Everton are the first to benefit from the new deal. They will collect a £150,000 fee and also gain from spin-offs such as perimeter advertising.

Everton have in turn assisted ITV's coverage by agreeing to two new camera positions, and Foulser said: "We will have more cameras (10) than ever before and the use of graphics will give it a different feel."

Cottee rescues point on an intrusive day

(By Philip McNulty, Liverpool Daily Post, October 31, 1988)

*E*VERTON and Manchester United ultimately failed to provide the five-star soccer spectacular television's excessive demands required at Goodison Park.

The opening episode of the latest expensive small screen soap opera provided a hectic but uninspired storyline following the hype accompanying the new £44m television deal.

Heroes did emerge from a collision between two sides with envious eyes on Liverpool's title crown. The two most expensive members of the all-star cast – strikers Mark Hughes and Tony Cottee – demonstrated their goalscoring prowess and Neville Southall again showed why he is the best in the business.

The obvious intrusion of TV cameras failed to impress an undersized Goodison audience, who were kept waiting for over a minute at the start of the second half as advertisers were accommodated and television punters gave their verdict.

But what threatened to be the proverbial damp squib was lifted by an eventful second period which saw both sides come close to victory.

Ratcliffe record

(By Ric George, Liverpool Echo, March 1, 1989)

Another much-derided competition, the Simod Cup, at least provided the club – and record-breaking skipper Kevin Ratcliffe – another Wembley visit.

*E*VERTON star Kevin Ratcliffe is set to lead out his team at Wembley for a remarkable 10th time following last night's Simod Cup win over Queens Park Rangers.

The Welsh defender has already skippered the Blues in four Charity Shield matches, three FA Cup finals, one Milk Cup final plus last season's Centenary Tournament dating from 1984, and is relishing the prospect of returning to the Twin Towers to face Nottingham Forest on Sunday, April 30.

Goodison manager Colin Harvey paid tribute to his centre-back, saying: "It's unbelievable, a record any player would be proud of."

Ratcliffe commented: "I'd not realised I've been there so many times. I'm lucky because so many great players haven't even been there at all. I suppose, counting things like schoolboy matches, I'll have played at Wembley 14 or 15 times. Not bad for someone who's not English!

"The thought of getting to Wembley was incentive enough. You can say what you like about the competition, but it's nice to be going back."

Everton stand to make a profit from the tournament as they battle for the £60,000 first prize, with half that sum for the runners-up.

Winger Pat Nevin revealed the secret behind last night's winning goal – extra training on headers. The tiny Scot, the smallest man on the field, nodded home the only goal from Ian Snodin's cross, and said: "We play lots of head tennis at the club and I've not been doing very well, so I've been staying behind after training to practise my heading."

Dons downed

(March 19, 1989)

*H*AVING drawn 1-1 with Wimbledon in a stormy league encounter a month earlier (which had seen Vinnie Jones sent off for clashing with Kevin Ratcliffe), a lively FA Cup quarter-final tie was expected. Colin Harvey said: "It's just good to be at home. Our previous meeting won't come into it. As far as we are concerned, it's all in the past."

Kevin Ratcliffe said: "We are certainly not afraid of them, and I hope Vinnie Jones plays. We must battle with them and prove we can match them in that sense. Then it's vital that we get our passing game together and use our skill to try and win the game. The cup generates a very special atmosphere, particularly amongst Evertonians. I know our fans will be right behind us."

Everton recovered from an eighth-minute penalty miss from Graeme Sharp to edge through, Stuart McCall sliding home the only goal from close range. McCall said: "It was about time I scored one. I couldn't really miss because Kevin Sheedy's trusty left boot put it on a plate."

United in sorrow

(By Ken Rogers, Liverpool Echo, April 17, 1989)

Everton faced a tough task against Norwich City in their bid to reach their fourth FA Cup final in six years in what was their 22nd semi-final. Backed by 25,000 fans at Villa Park, Everton sneaked through thanks to Pat Nevin's scrambled effort after 26 minutes. Referee George Courtney blew the final whistle at around 4.42pm, signalling a pitch invasion. Harvey punched the air before moving along the touchline, stopping only to wave to family and friends in the crowd. Pat Nevin also took an age to reach the dressing room, having been carried shoulder high from one side of the pitch to the other. But within 20 minutes of the final whistle, Everton's celebrations had ended because of the realisation of what had happened at Hillsborough in the match between Liverpool and Nottingham Forest in the other semi-final. Radio and television reports revealed a shocking tragedy had unfolded in Sheffield.

*E*VERTON secured their fourth F.A. Cup final appearance in six years with a battling victory over Norwich City on Saturday.

But the Villa Park celebrations lasted only as long as it took for the news to filter through from Hillsborough that a disaster of frightening proportions had unfolded in the other semi-final.

Within minutes of the final whistle, the Cup was no longer about red or blue, or about winning or losing. It was all about Liverpool people in the Midlands showing nothing but concern for their friends – and in many cases relatives – in Sheffield.

At that stage, the scale of the tragedy was still unknown. But we knew there had been fatalities and we knew that all of the mayhem had unfolded at the Merseyside end of the ground.

Everton had just achieved a feat that in normal circumstances would have turned the M6 into a sea of blue and white. But on the journey home, there was no chanting or singing, no banter between supporters who had just seen their side achieve a glorious victory over Norwich.

There was only a feeling of helplessness and uncertainty. All we could do was tune into our car radios and wince as the death toll rose with every mile we covered between Birmingham and Liverpool.

Merseyside fans have always been able to stand shoulder to shoulder. In that way we are unique. Evertonians recognised that it could have been them at Hillsborough. The demand for tickets would have been just as great. The recipe for disaster would have been just the same.

In the end, a Pat Nevin goal gave Everton victory. It was Colin Harvey's greatest day as a manager, but he used his press conference

374 THE OFFICIAL EVERTON AUTOBIOGRAPHY

to send a message of sympathy to the families of those who had lost their lives. Suddenly victory had a very hollow ring about it. A giant cloud hung over Villa Park. There were tears too. And try as it might, the sunshine just couldn't break through.

Everton: Southall, McDonald, Van Den Hauwe, Ratcliffe, Watson, Bracewell, Nevin, Steven, Sharp, Cottee, Sheedy. Subs not used: Clarke, McCall.
Norwich City: Gunn, Culverhouse, Bowen, Butterworth, Linighan, Townsend, Gordon, Allen (Fox, 72), Rosario, Crook, Putney. Sub not used: Goss.
Referee: George Courtney.
Attendance: 46,553.

An eerie afternoon

(By Nick Hilton, Liverpool Daily Post, April 24, 1989)

The following week's fixtures – minus Liverpool – went ahead, with pause to remember those who died.

*I*T was eerie at first. There were no more than a hundred people scattered across the corner terrace of White Hart Lane reserved for Everton supporters. A gateman said they'd sold only 20 advance tickets for this section of the ground.

The public address system played cold jazz guitar music, then Roy Orbison as a few more drifted in, so slowly that it appeared only the most fanatical of Evertonians could find the stomach for football one week after Hillsborough.

The gathering was solemn. People spoke little, so it was hard to tell those who had come alone from groups of fans sharing their silence together. A man wearing two scarves, one blue, one red, took his young son, dressed in full Everton kit, to the front of the terrace where earlier in the week Tottenham had torn down the perimeter fences. It stayed quiet, a calm, patient quietness, as the Everton support swelled with people who marked their arrival with nothing more than a murmured "excuse me" as they sought a spec.

Almost imperceptibly the terrace became so full that by kick-off time some fans were ushered into a small wing stand above to avoid any chance of crushing. The filling of the terrace brought with it a change in mood: the warming that comes from being with people of your own kind during times of adversity.

I don't recall a cheer on the Everton terrace all afternoon, but there was generous applause for the public address announcer who said there would be no birthday record requests played at this match; for the elderly steward and the young ball boy who brought floral tributes to the front; and at the end of the minute's silence for those who lost their lives at Hillsborough.

During that minute a middle-aged man in front of me raised a red Liverpool scarf above his head, high and proud, and his friend stretched to touch it. There was one moment of anger when a posse of photographers gathered in front of the Everton terrace, cameras clicking; Scouse fans out of the cages and into the goldfish bowl.

Cries of protest and indignation brought a senior police officer who sent the photographers back up the touchline to more applause. The photographers carried on taking pictures of us with zoom lenses.

Later, they were welcomed back to take pictures of the floral tributes donated by the Tottenham club and its fans.

It wasn't a bad game. People encouraged and cursed, as they always do, but they were private rituals. There was no chanting on the Everton terrace, no common roar. On the Spurs terrace they sang about how much they hated Arsenal.

Paul Walsh scored a goal that showed how beautiful a game of football can be, wriggling from a knot of tackles on the edge of the box to chip a shot of great precision over Everton goalkeeper Neville Southall's dive and into the top corner.

Neil McDonald equalised, then Walsh scored a minute from time to give Tottenham victory. Everton did not deserve to lose but no-one complained because it did not matter. What mattered was being there.

More people than anyone had expected gathered on the Everton terrace at White Hart Lane to pay respect to the Hillsborough dead in the best way they knew; to leave a memento on the main gates of a distant ground and to reaffirm their commitment to football as an important part of their lives.

Police blocked the exit from the Everton terrace to the street at the finish, then thought better of it, allowing us to mingle freely with the Spurs' fans filing home. Most people left as they had arrived, in silence.'

Simod defeat after final thriller

(By Philip McNulty, Liverpool Daily Post, May 1, 1989)

There was Wembley woe in the Simod Cup in an eventful final.

$\mathcal{B}$RIAN Clough turned Wembley scene-stealer again last night as Nottingham Forest claimed the Simod Cup.

The unpredictable Forest manager grabbed the Wembley limelight when Forest won the Littlewoods Cup against Luton Town.

And he was once more the centre of attention, bounding up the Wembley steps to grasp the much-maligned trophy after a magnificent victory over brave Everton.

Clough broke with Wembley tradition to move ahead of Forest skipper Stuart Pearce and pick up the cup.

Everton led twice in a topsy-turvy encounter, but striker Lee Chapman became Forest's hero, scoring twice in extra time to clinch a highly entertaining game.

Tony Cottee was on target twice for Everton, along with Graeme Sharp, but two goals from midfield man Garry Parker added to Chapman's double gave Forest their triumph.'

Edged out again by Liverpool

(May 20, 1989)

$\mathcal{T}$HE spectre of the Hillsborough disaster loomed large as Merseyside united at Wembley for the FA Cup final. Kenny Dalglish commented beforehand: "You can't pick and choose your opponents, but if we could have chosen it would have to be Everton. They have made their own contribution to the city of Liverpool and they have helped a lot of people. Everton have brought a lot of joy here during the 1980s and they are there on merit. They have our total respect as a club and as a team."

Unlike previous finals, each side was allocated more tickets than normal – in this case 37,000 each. Liverpool were strong favourites, having won 19 of 22 games in an unbeaten run which had taken them to within reach of a second double.

Colin Harvey said: "Our cup campaigns this season have been very good and while we haven't been able to turn it on in the league, we have been able to divorce one from the other and we just hope we keep it that way on Saturday."

Liverpool dominated much of the game, but led only through John Aldridge's fourth-minute strike as the final entered injury time. Then a break from Pat Nevin set up Dave Watson whose shot was parried into the path of sub Stuart McCall to take the tie into extra time.

Fellow sub Ian Rush put the Reds ahead again early in the extra period, but it was McCall again who hit back, volleying home from 20 yards. However, Rush struck again just before the end of the first half of extra time. This time it was the winner.

Colin Harvey said: "The game was competitive. What both teams wanted was a game played in the right spirit, and the crowd to watch it in the right spirit, which they did. The barriers were down, and people came on the pitch but I don't think that meant a thing on the day."

Stuart McCall said: "It was beyond my wildest dreams to get two goals at Wembley. When it has sunk in, I will be delighted personally in a little way for my family who were watching. But it was a real sickener for the supporters who have backed us through our cup campaign."

Tony Cottee added: "I didn't do myself justice and felt very tired after the first 15 minutes. When I put my foot on the accelerator there was nothing there. The whole day was a very tiring experience."

New men in, sales up

(Liverpool Daily Post, July 18, 1989)

There was good news all round as the squad – featuring new faces – reconvened ahead of the 1989/90 campaign.

$\mathcal{E}$VERTON got a £1m boost as the players reported back to Bellefield for pre-season training. Season-ticket sales have already soared past that magic figure, and chief executive Jim Greenwood is confident that last year's 15 per cent rise will easily be surpassed.

Said Greenwood: "The figures are very encouraging, particularly as the bulk of ground season-ticket holders are still sending in their application. With five weeks to go before the start of the new season, the figures are very promising indeed."

Also smiling was Colin Harvey as his players arrived for pre-season training. Said Harvey: "It's a relief to have everyone reporting fit and well, unlike the past when we've had to wait for players to get themselves fully fit. It's also good to have real competition for places, with Stefan Rehn, Mike Newell and Martin Keown putting pressure on the men in possession. That has to be a benefit for us."

Everton's pre-season plans have not been finalised, but they will fly out on July 30 for a series of games in Japan and will then travel to Thailand for a match against the country's national side. The club are still involved in negotiations to play another match in Malaysia.

Big Norm's immediate impact

(By Ken Gaunt, Liverpool Daily Post, August 2, 1989)

One of the new-boys made an immediate impact – against his former club.

$\mathcal{N}$ORMAN Whiteside brought down the old pals axe on his former Manchester United colleagues today as Everton got off to a splendid start on their four-match Far East tour.

Colin Harvey's £750,000 midfield buy scored a spectacular goal in only his second game for the Blues as they chalked up an impressive 3-1 win in the Japanese port of Kobe.

Everton swept into a 3-0 lead at half-time in today's showpiece friendly with goals coming from Kevin Sheedy, Neil Pointon and Whiteside. United made a brief comeback with Neil Webb pulling a goal back, although Everton were never really troubled.

Harvey said: "It was a competitive game, just as we had expected and an excellent work-out. We played well, especially in the first half and all the goals were good strikes."

Greenwood reflects on what might have been

(By Brian Reade, Liverpool Daily Post, October 26, 1989)

There was the fear that English clubs – including Everton – were being left behind by the rest of Europe.

*N*OWHERE in English football has the pain of the UEFA ban been felt so cruelly than at Goodison Park. To be an Evertonian in May 1985 was to be in ecstasy after a glorious march to the league title was followed by one of the most breathtaking European triumphs for years as the Blues tore Rapid Vienna to pieces in Rotterdam. There seemed to be no limits to what Howard Kendall's young lions could achieve. Then came Heysel.

"It was galling," recalls chief executive Jim Greenwood. "At that stage we had a team that was just developing into a truly great side. It hadn't had a great deal of European experience but it achieved that marvellous victory.

"The UEFA ban meant that side missed out on two attempts at the European Cup, and with all respect to the UEFA Cup and the Cup-Winners' Cup, the European Cup is the one everyone wants to win.

"It was a great tragedy that that side missed out on having a crack at those two European Cups.

"There is no doubt that we also missed out on the huge amounts of cash that have been at stake in Europe over the past four years," admits Greenwood. "It's all down to television and the fact that when you play in Europe you negotiate your own agreement with the TV companies.

"You're not stuck with this 92-club structure we have in England which is so frustrating for big clubs like ourselves.

"Every time you try to progress with television everything gets bogged down with how the money's going to be distributed.

"But it's the big clubs who attract the television audiences. They're the ones the fans want to see and the ones the TV companies want to show. So logically they're the ones who should be rewarded.

"You can't go on defying economic forces forever. The league have been doing so for a long time but the economics will work their way through. If we're going to compete with large clubs across Europe then the large English clubs must be given the chance to earn the money that will enable them to compete."

Greenwood is a great believer in the Football League. He holds no truck with ideas of a European Super League organised by a television magnate. "That sort of thing is just not on in the foreseeable future. The football authorities would never allow TV to hijack football.

"We want to stay in the Football League, but we want to see changes in the structure. Changes will come in football through the great expansion of television and the league has got to accept it. It's in their own interests if they want their overall structure to stay intact. The big clubs can't go on playing 42 games a season plus a few cup games.

"The world's changing, people are becoming better informed, matches will be beamed all over the world, our big clubs are going to be invited to play all over the world and will want to go."

Greenwood feels a major obstacle to the big clubs achieving their ambitions has been themselves.

"Our public relations has been dreadful. Certain sections of the media have hijacked the situation and claimed the big clubs just want to take all the money that's at stake. That's just not true. All we're asking for is what happens all over the world. We need to be able to make our own agreements to compete with the rest of the world. If we're not allowed to then we won't attract the best players, in fact we'll lose our best players and England will decline as a footballing nation."

Greenwood the businessman can see the vast opportunities television will bring in the next decade. His frustration over the inability to take advantage of opportunities presented in the last half of this decade make him more determined that Everton will not be left behind once the UEFA ban is lifted.

"With pay-as-you-see television around the corner the sky's the limit for successful clubs but we have to be in a position where we can make our own decisions. At the moment we can't. It will have to change."

Horror show as Everton hit for six

(By Philip McNulty, Liverpool Daily Post, November 6, 1989)

An unexpected TV nasty at Villa Park, with the Blues lying fourth before kick-off, suggested a title challenge was an unrealistic expectation.

*E*VERTON'S first venture of the season on to the nation's television screens should have carried a triple X-certificate after a shameful shambles at Villa Park.

Aston Villa inflicted a clinical execution on an Everton side that had the backbone of a jellyfish. Colin Harvey's side treated the viewing millions to a display which would have been greeted with derision in a lower-class Sunday league. It was an horrific combination of shuddering surrender and sheer ineptitude, and Graham Taylor's in-form Villa took full advantage.

Everton's attempts to move to the top of the table were undermined by a display which must rank as the most abysmal by the Merseysiders for many years. David Platt and Ian Olney struck twice, with Gordon Cowans and Kent Nielsen completing a shocking 90 minutes. Not even a late Tony Cottee strike and an own goal from Paul McGrath could paper over the alarming cracks in the Everton line-up.

Fury after Southall out of step

(By Philip McNulty, Liverpool Daily Post, November 23, 1989)

Neville Southall became embroiled in controversy during a Littlewoods Cup clash against Nottingham Forest. It led to a brief trend for loud and deliberate counting of how long opposition goalkeepers held the ball.

*T*HE agony went on for Neville Southall as Everton tumbled out of the Littlewoods Cup in controversial style last night.

Southall – the centre of transfer speculation earlier this week – was penalised for time-wasting in his own penalty area in the incident which led to Nottingham Forest's last winner. As Everton coasted towards a draw with just six minutes left, referee George Tyson blew for an infringement and booked Southall as he stood with the ball at his feet in the penalty area.

In an atmosphere of anger and confusion, Lee Chapman touched home Nigel Clough's free-kick to end Everton's Wembley dream. There were furious scenes at the final whistle, with Everton players surrounding Tyson and manager Colin Harvey restraining his players before exchanging words with the Sunderland official. The referee was led away by police, with Everton players continuing their protests as they disappeared down the tunnel.

Rebuilding required after Oldham defeat

(By Ken Rogers, Liverpool Echo, March 12, 1990)

The pressure was building after the realisation of a third season without a trophy.

*C*OLIN Harvey will not be found wanting in the battle to resurrect Everton's shattered season.

The Goodison boss, devastated by Saturday's FA Cup exit at Second Division Oldham Athletic, has made it patently clear that he will not be backing away from a mighty Goodison Park challenge.

He said: "I was deeply upset for the supporters on Saturday, not least those who have watched us in all of the cup ties. We must get something out of the remainder of the season for them.

"It's up to every one of us to be totally positive. At the start of the season you think you have a good enough squad to go on and challenge for honours. Looking back, we have to accept that our away form has once again been a bugbear.

"Now I must think about a form of rebuilding. It would be wrong just to dive in. If it means waiting a little longer to get the right quality, then I will do it. Equally, if I could get one this week then I would do that as well. We've always had high standards at this club. I want to set them even higher. If it means bringing in new players, younger players or changing things around, then I'm going to do it."

Shared stadium kicked into touch

(By Ian Hargraves, Liverpool Echo, July 30, 1990)

The new stadium idea was shelved with finances key to the decision.

MERSEYSIDE has lost the chance to house Britain's first super soccer stadium, a £120m development capable of seating 67,000.

Both Liverpool and Everton have decided that the development involves too great a financial risk, and informed developers Mersey Stadium that they do not wish to become involved.

Everton turned down a move some time ago, but kept their decision quiet so as not to influence Liverpool. They argue that Goodison Park is big enough for their requirements and that it would become a white elephant if they moved, as no alternative use seems possible.

"We were informed by Everton that they did not wish to move from their present ground, and so the economies resulting from dual use were not available," said Liverpool chief executive Peter Robinson.

"The cold fact is that it would have taken about £31m a year just to cover interest charges and repayment, while the combined income of our two clubs at present is about half that figure.

"With both clubs coming in, and increased revenue from greatly improved facilities, the plan might just have worked, but with only one club it makes no sense at all."

Everton have always had considerable reservations about the scheme, ever since it was put forward. Chairman Philip Carter told me that if it was adopted his shareholders would be left with virtually no assets, as players cannot be shown on a balance sheet and Goodison Park would have little value save as a football ground.

These days Everton's average gate is well below Goodison's capacity, with only the occasional derby match and cup-tie posing any kind of a problem, and nobody had come up with any realistic plan for it to be used profitably in a different way.

Both Liverpool City Council, who welcome the scheme enthusiastically, when it was put to them, spending time and money on finding a suitable site, and a good many football fans will be greatly disappointed at the collapse of the development.

Neither Anfield or Goodison is ideally situated, and neither ground offers much in the way of car parking, while local residents have often complained about noise and other nuisances on matchdays.

Moreover, I can disclose that the overall scheme would have included provision of a fine indoor arena next door, giving Merseyside a major facility it has always lacked.

Members of Kirkby Golf Club, who would have faced a move to an alternative site on the other side of the M57 had the development gone through, will doubtless be relieved, but overall, the feeling can only be one of great disappointment.

Most upset of all are Mersey Stadiums, who have already spent a considerable amount of time and money on the project.

Managing director Bill Young says they were prepared to go ahead with the support of just one club, in the hope that Everton would eventually change their mind.

Southall and Sheedy ask to go

(By Ken Rogers, Liverpool Echo, August 14, 1990)

Two unsettled stars were causing concern for Colin Harvey.

*E*VERTON manager Colin Harvey jetted out with his team to Turkey today, aware that two of his players had once again slapped in transfer requests. Both goalkeeper Neville Southall and midfielder Kevin Sheedy seem intent on leaving Goodison Park.

Southall's request is his third in three months and how Harvey deals with the situation remains to be seen. The keeper has signed a long-term contract. The club say that he is their highest-paid player and they are extremely reluctant to sell.

But just how long the manager can continue to play a cat and mouse game with Southall is open to debate. It's a highly frustrating state of affairs for the fans and like Harvey they are beginning to lose patience.

Southall, it seems, will not relent until his transfer demands are met and Harvey was assessing the situation, as well as weighing up the Sheedy situation. It seems likely the Republic of Ireland star will be told he can go – for the right fee. Unlike Southall, Sheedy goes into the new campaign unsure of his place. He wants a new challenge following a fairly successful World Cup and could attract interest from abroad.

Southall sit-in overshadows Leeds loss

(Liverpool Daily Post, August 27, 1990)

Neville Southall's half-time sit-in made the headlines as the Blues began the season with a 3-2 defeat – a stirring fightback from three-down ultimately proving fruitless.

*C*OLIN Harvey will hold showdown talks with Neville Southall after his disgruntled star's bizarre solo sit-in at Goodison Park. The Everton boss is anxious to discover why transfer-seeking Southall left his team-mates in the dressing room at half-time and trudged on to the pitch to the bewilderment of the 34,412 crowd.

They stared in amazement as the 31-year-old Welsh international made his way to the Park End and propped himself against a goalpost for several minutes before the rest of the players returned to the pitch.

Knowing that Southall has had three transfer requests rejected in his desperate desire to move – despite being on a long-term contract – some Everton fans jeered the man they used to idolise.

They believed he had stormed out after a dressing room bust-up, but Harvey insisted last night: "You can be sure of one thing – there was no bust-up at half-time between Neville Southall and myself."

After the match, Harvey denied any knowledge of his goalkeeper's apparent sit-down protest.

"Incident. What incident?" he asked.

"I knew he had left the dressing room early, but I didn't know he was out on the pitch."

Southall refused to explain his behaviour – although it is understood heated words were exchanged between the keeper and the manager.

Said Harvey: "I'll be talking to Neville on Monday morning, but I'm not saying anything about it until then."

What's good for the goose

(By Ken Rogers, Liverpool Echo, October 4, 1990)

Another fixture change – but not for the cameras.

*E*VERTON'S immediate priority is Sunday's game at Nottingham Forest. The game was switched, not for the benefit of the live TV cameras, but because of the city's historic Goose Fair which began today and finishes on Saturday.

It proves that the Sheriff of Nottingham is still bigger than Brian Clough, who doesn't like Sunday football. The Goose Fair, held north of the city centre at a place called The Forest, has been going for 696 years and is the biggest show of its kind in Europe.

A Royle appointment?

(By Ian Hargraves, Liverpool Echo, November 1, 1990)

The decision to dismiss Colin Harvey was taken in the wake of a League Cup defeat at Sheffield United, after a run of only one win in 10 league games that had left the Blues in the bottom three. Speculation immediately linked the club to former centre-forward Joe Royle, who had led Second Division promotion-challengers Oldham Athletic to the League Cup final the previous season.

$\mathcal{A}$S Everton began their search for a replacement for Colin Harvey, they could face problems in landing a new manager in mid-season. Joe Royle has emerged as the fans' favourite, but League regulations rule out an approach to a person already under contract.

Royle is tied to Second Division leaders Oldham and so could not apply for the vacancy, which is to be advertised. However, if the board wanted Royle there could be a way forward. When Manchester City were searching for a manager last year, they asked Oldham chairman Ian Stott for permission to approach Royle, and were given it.

In the end Royle declined to move, the job going to Howard Kendall, but that precedent suggests a similar application by Everton chairman Philip Carter might be granted. Royle has refused to make any comment, but I believe he would relish the challenge.

There is no certainty that for all his popularity with the supporters, Royle is the Everton board's first choice. He seems to have the right qualifications, having transformed little Oldham in the space of eight years and masterminded their FA Cup victory over Everton last season.

The problems of approaching a manager already contracted to a club also apply to candidates like Steve Coppell and Ron Atkinson, whose names have already been mentioned, which probably explains why Everton have decided to invite applications for the vacancy.

Two people who might soon be available are John Toshack, under pressure at Real Madrid, and former England boss Bobby Robson, facing similar problems with PSV Eindhoven.

Guessing game continues

(By Philip McNulty, Liverpool Daily Post, November 6, 1990)

Uncertainty surrounded the potential new appointment.

*E*VERTON expect to name the new Goodison Park boss within the next 48 hours – and last night the guessing game about the identity of the man in question reached fever pitch.

Joe Royle remains favourite, but the silent treatment being employed by Everton has heightened speculation that a mystery contender could be in the frame.

Royle heads the pack waiting to land the Everton vacancy, but Sheffield Wednesday boss Ron Atkinson is still an outside contender... speculation in Manchester yesterday even linked former Everton favourite Peter Reid with the job.

But Manchester City chairman Peter Swales denied Howard Kendall's influential midfielder was about to make a shock return.

Joy as Kendall renews his 'marriage' vows

(By Ken Rogers, Liverpool Echo, November 7, 1990)

The secret was out – Howard Kendall was returning home.

*F*OOTBALL seems to take a daily battering in the media and yet it seems there is still room for a real-life fairytale to unfold. Goodison could easily have been named the 'Field of Dreams' when a stunned soccer world learned that two of Everton's greatest soccer sons were teaming up again to try and put the Blues back on top.

When a press conference is called and hard-bitten soccer hacks are seen punching the air in triumph, thrilled like little boys by the events about to unfold, you know something special is happening. I stood alongside Everton's chief executive Jim Greenwood and director Bill Kenwright as Howard Kendall and Colin Harvey trooped into one of the plush executive suites to explain this genuine soccer miracle. It wasn't just a welcome back. It was a welcome home.

Colin Harvey qualifies for an immediate place in the Guinness Book of Records. Sacked on Wednesday, born again the following Tuesday. He was clearly delighted to be back in business. I revealed last week how he had spent his final night as Everton manager sleeping at Bellefield, pondering what seemed to be a dismal future. He revealed that he would not have returned as right-hand man to anyone but Kendall.

The pair run a mutual admiration society. Kendall summed up his own feelings after his spells with Bilbao and Manchester City: "When you talk about a love affair with Manchester City, you are talking about a marriage with Everton." It was perfect.

Bill's delight at second coming

(By Ian Herbert, Liverpool Daily Post, November 7, 1990)

Others offered their reaction.

*I*T was actor and producer Bill Kenwright, now an Everton director, who led the salute to the prodigal son.

"This is the Second Coming," he declared. "If I had put it in a movie no-one would have believed it. It was a magnificent ending tonight, seeing Colin and Howard together again. It's a dream to me."

Concerts ruled out

(By Andrew Edwards, Liverpool Echo, February 6, 1991)

Goodison was to remain a non-football free zone.

*E*VERTON Football Club today ruled out the possibility of staging pop concerts and boxing events at their Goodison Park ground.

Chief executive Jim Greenwood said: "We have had a number of approaches but have always made it quite clear that any event where there was any encroachment on to the playing area was just not on.

"Having seen the condition of the Manchester City pitch following the Rolling Stones' concert in August 1990 we are even more determined that we should not follow a similar path, even though the revenue generated would be welcome in assisting us to implement the Taylor recommendations."

4-4

(February 20, 1991)

*F*OLLOWING a goalless draw at Liverpool in the FA Cup fifth round, the replay was played three days later at Goodison.

Four times Everton were behind, yet four times they hit back to earn a second replay. Graeme Sharp struck twice after Peter Beardsley's double had twice given Liverpool the lead and Ian Rush's header looked to have won it for the Reds.

But up popped sub Tony Cottee to take it to extra time. John Barnes curled a shot past Neville Southall, but late on Cottee again took advantage of poor defending to make it 4-4. The result signalled the end of Kenny Dalglish's first spell in charge at Anfield.

Howard Kendall said: "It was a magnificent game, one of the greatest cup ties of all time – and one of the greatest derbies. It was pure theatre, and I am proud to have been involved. I simply couldn't have asked any more from my players in terms of effort and commitment."

Sharp said: "It was different class, the greatest game I have ever played in. I don't think you will ever see a game like that again."

Cottee's delight at his rescue act

(By Richard Tanner, Daily Mirror, February 22, 1991)

*T*ONY Cottee, the saviour of Everton's FA Cup dreams, declared a double ambition. The £2.2m striker, whose season has had more highs and lows than a weather chart, said: "I want to win back a regular place – and score more league goals."

Late super-sub Cottee took his season's tally to 13 on Wednesday with his stunning double in the epic fifth-round replay at Goodison Park – described as the best Merseyside derby of all time.

Remarkably, 11 of his haul have come in cup competitions, and he last found the net in the First Division way back on September 29.

Despite being Everton's leading scorer, the former West Ham star has been unable to command a regular place under Howard Kendall. And while his exhausted team-mates enjoyed a lie-in after their extra-time exertions against Liverpool, hero Cottee was ordered in for a training stint. But the 25-year-old had no complaints, and said: "I didn't mind. I've got to build up my fitness to help me find consistency."

Watson wins it

(February 27, 1991)

*T*HE second replay at Goodison (Everton having won the toss of a coin to stage the game) failed to live up to expectation.

A match of few chances was won when Dave Watson scrambled the ball home after Martin Keown's effort was parried by Bruce Grobbelaar on 12 minutes to send managerless Liverpool to their first derby defeat since March 1988.

Hero Watson said: "We defended very well. Liverpool threw everything they had at us but our back line held. We hung on in there."

All-seater Goodison on the way

(By Ken Rogers, Liverpool Echo, April 5, 1991)

The intention to transform Goodison into an all-seater stadium, including a two-tiered Park End, was mooted.

*E*VERTON have confirmed their intention to turn Goodison Park into an all-seater stadium in line with Government requirements. The present capacity is 41,266 of which 29,396 are seats. When the work is finished, the new all-seated capacity will be 40,013.

Phase one, due to be completed for the opening of the 1991/92 season, is the seating of the Gwladys Street terrace area which provide extra seating for 6,982.

Phase two, to be completed in 1992/93 subject to financial constraints, involves the demolition and replacement of the existing Park Stand. It will be replaced by a completely new 6,000 seater double-decker cantilever stand, designed so that the roof line is a continuation of the Gwladys Street and Bullens Road stands.

The end of an era at the Street End

(By Ken Rogers, Liverpool Echo, May 6, 1991)

It was the end for the Gwladys Street terrace after an end-of-season date with Luton.

I JOINED the faithful to say goodbye to an old friend. The Gwladys Street terrace, as we know it, is now just a part of Goodison folklore. Everton's answer to the Anfield Kop will be all-seater for the start of next season and so the game marked the end of an era.

Saturday's odyssey was very special. It was the first time I had stood at the Street End for 28 years. It was fascinating to climb onto the shelf, that slightly elevated section of terracing halfway up the Gwladys Street, reclaim my old "spec" behind the goal and listen to the banter and views of the only sponsors who really matter in football – the grassroots fans who are the lifeblood of every club.

I took along my two young boys, Colin and Peter, and regaled them with memories of great Gwladys Street days.

But for 20 minutes on Saturday there was hardly a murmur from the faithful, but in their defence the first half was abysmal to say the least with hardly a chance at either end worth shouting about. Thankfully, things warmed up in the second half.

They say there's a very narrow line between love and hate. Nowhere is this more apparent than on a football terrace where fans blow hot and cold, saluting individuals one minute and calling them fit to burn the next. Cynicism is part and parcel of every supporters' make-up and you learn to take it with a pinch of salt.

So when an exasperated voice screamed "Go on, pass it back Ratcliffe," everyone knew that what he was really saying was: "Skipper, can we have a positive forward ball!" Many such quips were delivered as the afternoon progressed, parcelled and tied up with barbed wire.

The sun came out and things were looking up, especially when Luton's Richard Harvey blasted a shot a mile wide. "Going down, going down!" I'd hate to have this lot on the jury if I was in the dock. No leniency whatsoever. But that's the name of the game and the sooner Luton are down the better.

At 35 minutes someone remembered the significance of the day. A tuneful ditty spewed forth, the lyrics suggesting that the seats planned for this section should be stuck up a certain part of the anatomy.

It was time to whip things up and get behind the lads. Everton, now attacking the Street End, began to find their feet. Inspired by talk of a swoop for Dean Saunders, Cottee took control and when Stuart McCall blocked an attempted clearance the little striker rounded Alec Chamberlain and slotted home his 22nd of the season.

The final whistle not only signalled the end of an era, but also brought down the curtain on a mixed season. Optimism still abounded with a generous salute to manager Kendall.

The players trudged off, one or two glancing towards the partisan hordes on the Gwladys Street and clapping, but the vast majority simply heading for the dressing room. Modern players have no sense of theatre. They should have run as one to applaud the fans in all corners of the ground, particularly on this day of days.

Cottee was the only one who broke ranks, jumping onto that hallowed terrace and launching his shin pads into the crowd. "I hope it's not a signal that he's on his way," said one worried fan.

Only time will tell. Cottee's in the team, scoring goals and declaring he is unworried by transfer speculation. On this afternoon, at least, he was man-of-the-match, but the champagne should have been sprayed on the Gwladys Street. It will never quite be the same again.

1992-2001

Manic Mondays

(By Eric Brown, Liverpool Daily Post, May 30, 1992)

Sky's intention to screen matches on a Monday raised concern on Merseyside.

*L*IVERPOOL and Everton have made a joint appeal to the Premier League over Monday night matches. Everton chairman Doctor David Marsh and Liverpool chief executive Peter Robinson have both written to the new league urging a rethink about disrupting the traditional weekend fixtures. Said Dr. Marsh: "I think the whole principle of Monday night football disrupts the social life of British society. We have people coming from far and wide. They won't be able to leave work early on Mondays to travel to the game."

Salmon pink kit shock

(Liverpool Daily Post, June 1, 1992)

*E*VERTON will go back to their roots next season with a salmon and navy change strip – the colours first worn by the famous club.

A century of Goodison glory

(Liverpool Echo, August 25, 1992)

Goodison's centenary was marked by the club.

*E*VERTON recreated history yesterday when chairman Dr. David Marsh led a delegation to the Adelphi Hotel.

Exactly 100 years ago, the Blues used the city centre venue to stage a celebratory dinner prior to the official opening of Goodison Park.

FA stalwart Lord Kinnaird, the hero of five FA Cup finals, proposed the main toast: "Success to the Everton Football Club."

Dr. Marsh repeated the sentiment yesterday under the famous chandeliers in the company of former skipper Brian Labone, who still holds the club appearance record.

The club then presented a copy of 'One Hundred Years Of Goodison Glory' – written by Echo sports writer Ken Rogers – to Adelphi sales executive Sally McCain.

A century ago, the Everton party returned to the brand new Goodison Park in open-topped carriages. Yesterday, they took 21st century transport – a 45-foot American stretch limousine which drew admiring glances all the way.

Ferguson targeted

(By Ken Rogers, Liverpool Echo, January 8, 1993)

The manager's search for striking reinforcements saw him travel north of the border to run the rule over a promising young forward.

HOWARD Kendall's 500-mile round trip to Glasgow this week to take in the Rangers v Dundee United Premier Division clash sparked speculation that he might be about to swoop once more in the transfer market.

The Everton manager was believed to be watching Tannadice striker Duncan Ferguson, but is it realistic to believe that the Goodison outfit could meet the asking price of £2m plus?

Indeed, are any of the leading clubs in a position to break the bank? Even Blackburn Rovers reported a loss this week of £8m, Kenny Dalglish having paid out £3.3m for Alan Shearer, and bought Stuart Ripley, Roy Wegerle and Mike Newell among others for big fees in the chase for Premier League honours.

Everton's most recent balance sheet revealed that the club was £3.6m in the red. Nothing has happened in the interim to improve that situation. Indeed, home attendances have been on a downward trend because of the side's inconsistency, although there are some attractive games to come.

So what would happen if Kendall approached the board and sought backing for another major deal?

Chief executive Jim Greenwood said: "Our situation is no different to the rest of the Premier League with the exception of Blackburn, who have got a rich backer pumping money in.

"We are possibly better placed than most because of the steady improvements made to Goodison in recent years. The expenditure we are facing is reasonable compared to some clubs, but the situation throughout football remains tight.

"This has been highlighted by the lack of transfer movement. Even an experienced player like Kevin Ratcliffe struggled to find a club, even though he was on a free. More players are going to be in the same boat at the end of their contracts. The problem when signing players is that salaries are often bigger than the actual transfer fees. And wages are an on-going expenditure. To try and put it into context, to spend £1.5m on an individual wipes out our season ticket money for an entire season. To pay £3m ties up that income for two years. And then there are the contract arrangements."

The championship of Merseyside

(By Ken Rogers, Liverpool Echo, January 27, 1993)

An early exit from the FA Cup and a mid-table position meant there was little to get travelling fans excited, particularly in midweek – as the Premier League record low attendance indicated.

So you think there is nothing left to play for this season. What about the unofficial championship of Merseyside?

Everton served notice last night that it's a "title" they fully intend to claim. They moved three points clear of rivals Liverpool with a 3-1 revenge victory over Wimbledon. Tony Cottee followed up his double against Leeds with another two-goal haul as the Blues secured their third successive Premier League success, a heady achievement after all that had gone before.'

Wimbledon took just three seconds to commit their first foul. No prizes for guessing who the guilty party was – Vinnie Jones. The Dons launched the ball forward straight from the kick-off for the midfielder to leap clumsily into Matthew Jackson.

The attendance of 3,039 was the lowest ever for a top-flight [Premier League] encounter. Fans are pretty good judges and, in Wimbledon's case, they rebel against a certain type of play. The Dons are a battering ram of a side who refuse to apologise for their uncompromising attitude, but is this really what the new Premier League is meant to be all about?

Wimbledon: Segers, Joseph, Scales, Blackwell, Elkins, Ardley, Jones, Sanchez (Clarke 66), Earle, Fashanu, Cotterill. Subs not used: Sullivan, Talboys.
Everton: Southall, Jackson, Watson, Keown, Ablett, Harper, Snodin, Horne, Preki (Barlow 63), Beardsley, Cottee. Subs not used: Kearton, Kenny.
Referee: Mr. K. Hackett (Sheffield).
Attendance: 3,039.

New Park End given go-ahead

(Liverpool Daily Post, March 25, 1993)

A single-tier Park End was set to be given the thumbs-up.

*E*VERTON have landed a £1.3m grant from the Football Trust to redevelop the Park End of their Goodison stadium.

A new 6,000-seater single tier stand will transform the ground into a 40,500 all-seater stadium by August 1994. The club hopes the new stand – which will probably be built during next season – will help them be chosen as one of the venues for the 1996 European Championships.

Hitman Nev

(By Peter Jardine, Liverpool Daily Post, July 22, 1993)

Neville Southall was back in attack in another Swiss stroll.

*S*IX players shared seven goals as Everton sauntered to another Swiss tour success in Lausanne last night. The Blues routed Swiss Third Division outfit Stade Lausanne in what amounted to an exhibition match. And goalkeeper Neville Southall even managed a five-minute substitute appearance as a striker! Kendall delighted locals and visiting fans alike by sending Southall on for Ward. Even in a brief run-out Southall showed why he is a feared outfield opponent in training.

Kendall quits after Dublin row

(Liverpool Daily Post, December 6, 1993)

Despite inconsistent form, Everton were comfortably in mid-table following a victory over Southampton in front of less than 14,000 at Goodison. Still lacking a physical threat up front, Howard Kendall sought funds when it became apparent a solution could be found at Manchester United.

*T*HE world of soccer was still stunned last night after Howard Kendall quit as manager of Everton FC because of a boardroom row.

Mr Kendall sensationally resigned on Saturday barely an hour after his side's 1-0 win over Southampton at Goodison Park.

His shock departure is understood to have followed a failure by the Everton board to back him in a move to sign Manchester United striker Dion Dublin. The 47-year-old manager had been seeking a striker for months and was willing to pay around £1.5m to get Dublin, for whom Old Trafford manager Alex Ferguson wanted £1.8m.

But Everton's board vetoed the deal which was the final straw for Mr Kendall, who then ended his second spell as manager.

Looking for a light at the end of the tunnel
(By David Prentice, Liverpool Echo, December 22, 1993)

Three games, no goals and only one point meant worries were growing regarding the appointment of a new man.

*E*VERTON'S caretaker-manager Jimmy Gabriel has called for a speedy conclusion to Everton's managerial debate.

The Blues have been without a full-time boss for nearly three weeks and Gabriel said today: "The quicker the whole situation is sorted out the better. Not just for me and Colin Harvey, but for the players and most importantly, the fans.

"It's deadly at the moment. You have me here basically pretending to be a manager, not sure just how far I'm allowed to go with things.

"It's dark and miserable, it doesn't seem to have stopped raining the past two weeks and there's no light yet at the end of the tunnel. We need something to happen soon, just so we all know where we stand."

Enter the silver fox
(By David Prentice, Liverpool Echo, January 8, 1994)

The run had become six defeats in seven winless games by the time Mike Walker was appointed on the eve of an FA Cup third-round tie at Bolton Wanderers.

*C*HAIRMAN Dr. David Marsh introduced Mike Walker as Everton's new manager with a pledge that he could spend – immediately.

Walker signed a three-and-a-half year contract and will watch the Blues at Bolton today. Dr. Marsh indicated funds will be available for Walker to start his rebuilding before the takeover situation is resolved.

Like Howard Kendall before him, Walker breezed into Goodison with a marriage metaphor. "The one thing I like to do is play football in what I call the right way," he explained. "Everton are synonymous with that and it looks, hopefully, like a good marriage."

Responding to the suggestion that he had left a club on the way up for one struggling through a transitional phase, Walker said: "I suppose from the outside you can say that. But I know that if I get things right at this club the sky's the limit and I mean that. I did admire Everton's style years ago, the School of Science, and all that. But I can't honestly say I came here and supported them as a lad. I didn't, but in a sense it's a dream move and the potential is unlimited."

Limpar docks on Merseyside

(By Peter Jardine, Daily Post, March 25, 1994)

A busy transfer-deadline saw two in, with Peter Beagrie moving to Manchester City.

*T*HE boat came in for Anders Limpar yesterday as his ferry to the Mersey finally docked. Seven years after red tape scuppered a possible move to Liverpool, Limpar joined Everton in a £1.6m move from Arsenal. Blues boss Mike Walker completed the first major signing of his Goodison reign, beating Manchester City in a deadline-day swoop.

He also signed 22-year-old Bournemouth midfielder Joe Parkinson in a deal worth £250,000 initially, rising to £700,000 according to appearances. Both players agreed three-year contracts.

Rabbits in the headlights

(Liverpool Daily Post, April 4, 1994)

An embarrassing defeat at Hillsborough saw the Blues slip to 17th.

*I*T was Bob Willis who described England's cricketers as "rabbits caught in the glare of car headlamps" as they slid to Test destruction against the West Indies.

For Caribbean callapso last midweek, read hapless, hopeless Everton frozen in the full beam of relegation at Hillsborough on Saturday.

This was a defeat that came close to being soccer's equivalent of 46 all out – and it takes some doing to capitulate as impressively as the England batting order these days.

Too good to go down? Don't make me cry. Too bad to expect to stay up would be more accurate on the strength of this performance.

Forty years of top-flight soccer is on the line for Everton Football Club, yet the present squad seem transfixed by that dreadful possibility.

Everton have taken one point from the last 15 available, three from 33 on offer away from Goodison Park, and half-time substitute Tony Cottee's consolation goal was Everton's first in more than six hours.

And the fact that title-chasing Blackburn come calling this afternoon, that three of their six remaining matches are away, and that Wimbledon visit Merseyside on the last day of the season and it is no wonder Evertonians are queueing up to ring the Samaritans.

'Biggest game in the club's history'

(Liverpool Daily Post, May 7, 1994)

Everton's captain was insistent on the outcome.

$\mathcal{D}$AVE Watson rallied his team-mates for a Titanic struggle against relegation this afternoon, then pledged his future to Goodison Park, even if, like the doomed ocean-going liner, they do go down. The Everton skipper has been one of the most consistent performers for the Blues in a desperate season – despite two serious head injuries.

Watson has starred for England against Brazil in Rio and in the 1989 all-Merseyside FA Cup final, but admits both pale into insignificance against the appalling possibility of Everton being relegated after four decades in the top flight. Said Watson: "I agree with Mike Walker when he says it is the biggest game in the club's history. Everything is at stake. We simply must win and hope results go our way. It will be the biggest game I've ever been involved in. Big matches aren't just about winning things, they can be about what is to lose as well. Everything is on the line against Wimbledon."

The 32-year-old skipper revealed he will not even consider abandoning ship if Everton's Titanic sinks this afternoon. Added Watson: "If the worst came to the worst my first reaction would be: let's get it right. Otherwise it is a case of getting off the sinking ship which I don't agree with. If you are part of the ship that goes down, I believe you should stick around and get it right."

The Great Escape, part one

(By Peter Jardine, Liverpool Daily Post, May 9, 1994)

Victory – and top-flight survival – was never in doubt.

*P*ETER Johnson must have felt like a gambler in a game of Las Vegas roulette. At 3.20pm on Saturday afternoon, his £10m on Blue seemed like throwing good money after bad. With Everton 2-0 down to a penalty and an own goal there looked like only one jackpot winner – Wimbledon red. By 4.45pm, Johnson's number had come up.

Seven years ago, the Mersey multi-millionaire watched as his investment in Tranmere Rovers went on the line when they beat Exeter to stay in the Football League. It's a game which has gone down in local soccer folklore but Saturday, May 7, 1994, eclipsed even that as the script of legends. Two-nil down, 3-2 ahead and Everton stay up. Shades of the 1966 FA Cup final against Sheffield Wednesday.

Johnson has enjoyed a roller-coaster ride with Tranmere over seven years, involving promotions, play-offs and this year's heroic run to the Coca-Cola Cup semi-final. Yet nothing can surely compare to this 90 minutes – and he doesn't even own Everton yet!

Said Johnson: "It would have been a travesty if they had gone down. It's nice to start in the Premiership instead of the First Division."

He's not kidding. Everton might have sunk without trace with fewer promotion places available next season and their ability to attract players severely hampered (no pun intended) despite Johnson's millions. Instead, by a miracle, they escaped and how Goodison Park loved it.

Hysteria bordering on blind panic giving way to unbridled elation and relief was the crowd's reaction. I wonder how Blues fans watching live on television around the world survived!

Sceptics will occasionally try to convince you that football doesn't mean anything to people. Try telling that to the 10,000 Evertonians who came out of the woodwork on Saturday, and the few dozen who shinned up trees in Stanley Park to glimpse a piece of the action.

Some who were inside possibly still think Tony Cottee scored Everton's winner, as was wrongly announced over the PA system. Cottee was chaired off the pitch later although, in case you don't know yet, Graham Stuart scored the goal that kept Everton up.

Nothing looked more improbable in the fourth minute when Anders Limpar inexplicably handled a Gary Elkins corner and Dean Holdsworth scored the resultant penalty despite the efforts of Neville Southall. Then, after 20 minutes, Everton's 40-year top flight tenure was jeopardised further when Gary Ablett slid the ball into his own net after Andy Clarke took advantage of indecision in the home defence.

It was the latest in a long litany of mistakes by Everton this season but thankfully that was the end of the errors, instead of an era.

Four minutes later Limpar's blatant dive at the feet of Peter Fear conned referee Robbie Hart into awarding a penalty. Limpar's plunge was so theatrical it must have impressed the watching Bill Kenwright, but Stuart scored coolly from the spot-kick with Ablett and Southall the only other would-be penalty takers.

Holdsworth missed a couple of great chances for Wimbledon to extend their lead until Everton clutched at a lifeline. Or rather Barry Horne did. The Welsh midfielder has scored only one goal in his Everton career, on his debut two years ago, and said then with brutal honesty: "Don't hold your breath waiting for the second."

Every Evertonian regarded it as worth the wait when Horne shrugged off Vinnie Jones and lashed home a magnificent 30-yard shot. All the frustrations of Everton's dismal season seemed caught up in his strike and he was rewarded with a bout of back-slapping as ecstatic fans streamed on to the pitch to celebrate.

Yet, as it transpired, a draw would not have been enough for Everton. Horne went close again before, with nine minutes left, Stuart ensured the victory they required. Limpar's pass inside was collected by Stuart and his one-two with Cottee ended with him half-tackling, half-shooting from 20 yards and the ball streaked past Segers into the net.

"I could have saved the third goal," said Dons boss Joe Kinnear later. "I think Segers has a few relatives up here."

The joke will not have gone down well at Sheffield United who had forwarded two crates of champagne to Wimbledon on Friday night in an effort to see Everton relegated. It was a gesture which backfired badly on Dave "He's Down" Bassett.

Stuart's goal gave Everton a victory impartial observers would possibly say they scarcely deserved on chances created. At least here they displayed the passion which if demonstrated more frequently would have ensured survival long before Saturday.

The fans gave them a heroes' welcome before kick-off, yet the truth is for seven seasons the club has been blighted by under-achievement. Call me the voice of treason if you want but years of mismanagement at board and team level took Everton to within nine minutes of relegation and, possibly, disaster. Sheer bottle, and luck, extricated them but let's not forget that a large proportion of Everton's football and results this season have been totally unacceptable.

Mike Walker admitted as much when he said: "I won't be celebrating too much. Staying up is not a big deal, it is more a relief than anything else." But what the almost unprecedented scenes of joy emphasised more than anything was the awesome potential of Everton Football Club. A man like Peter Johnson wouldn't have put in £10m otherwise – and now he might see his investment multiply as do those in Vegas.

Everton: Southall, Snodin, Watson, Unsworth, Ablett, Stuart, Horne, Ebbrell (Barlow 80), Limpar, Cottee, Rideout. Subs not used: Kearton, Angell.
Wimbledon: Segers, Barton, Scales, Blackwell, Elkins, Fear, Jones, Earle, Gayle (Blissett 87), Clarke, Holdsworth. Subs not used: Sullivan, Perry.
Referee: Mr. R. Hart.
Attendance: 31,297.

Hero Stuart on the spot

(Liverpool Echo, May 9, 1994)

Two-goal Graham Stuart revelled in the occasion.

*I*CE-COOL hero Graham Stuart had only taken one penalty before Saturday – and missed by miles! He said: "I took it for Chelsea and blasted that one over the bar but I knew if I could get this one on target I would have half a chance. Neville Southall would have taken it, but I had volunteered and I knew how important it was."

But Stuart didn't see much of his vital winner just eight minutes from time. He said: "Anders played it across and played a one-two with Tony Cottee. I sort of half-tackled the bloke then I just heard the crowd roar. I don't know how it went in. It was an unbelievable day."

"There were plenty of people ready to knock us for not having bottle but you can count the teams who have come back from 2-0 down against Wimbledon on one hand. The boss had a pop at us at half-time which we deserved because it was a ridiculous start. He said if we played controlled football we would get something. The game was drifting a little bit in the second half when Barry cracked a magnificent shot – goal of the season probably – it was for us anyway.

"That was easily the best atmosphere I have heard since I've been here, and that's with one side of the ground down. Who knows what it would be like with 40,000 in there. Because of what we could have lost as a club that was the most important match in the club's history."

Tears, tension and blind panic

(By Paddy Shennan, Liverpool Echo, May 9, 1994)

*D*ON'T let anyone ever tell you again: "It's only a game!" Anyone who was inside Goodison Park at 4.48pm on Saturday afternoon, watching from a tree in Stanley Park, listening on the radio, or watching Ceefax knows it is much more than that.

Even those who hate football must have at least partially understood the significance of the events of Everton by the beaming smiles on the Blue faces of family and friends. It was a roller-coaster day made up of raw tension and the extreme emotions of agony and ecstasy. Tears were flowing before, during and after what was the most incredible 90 minutes of football this famous old stadium has ever witnessed.

There was an air of optimism – mixed with feelings of blind panic – three hours before kick-off as the Blue hordes queued for the non-ticket stands. Such were the numbers in Gwladys Street that I decided to join the lines outside the Bullens Road Paddock to make sure I wasn't locked out – a cruel fate which befell thousands when gates were shut at about 2pm.

The fans began singing in the warm sunshine. I suddenly felt 10ft tall and so proud to be here among such fanatical followers. I realised that, whatever was about to happen on the pitch, Everton's current team and board did not deserve such marvellous support.

At 1.15pm, the gates opened and over in the Gwladys Street End hundreds of youngsters sprinted for the best possible vantage point behind the goal. The chanting began as many held aloft the Echo's 'Good Luck Blues' placards.

An hour later, David Unsworth ran onto the pitch like a man possessed. He charged towards the Gwladys Street clenching his fists, as if to say to the fans: "Come on! Let's win it!" The man standing behind me said: "Just look at that. That man's one of us, a real Evertonian."

As the teams prepared to take the field, it was party time. Blue and white balloons floated over the stands and banners were unfurled, including one which read "EFC in Div One? Do We Not Like That!"

The noise was deafening and the fans' love for the club rolled down the stands onto the pitch. Supporters were on their feet, singing their hearts out. There were tears in my eyes. Feet away, I heard a steward say: "The supporters are doing their bit, now it's up to the players."

The players handed Wimbledon a two-goal lead – and it could have been more. A tannoy announcement – "Could Clare Edwards from High Wycombe please report to the police room" temporarily lifted the gloom. "I wish I was in High Wycombe," said one fan. His friend replied: "Don't worry, we'll be playing them in a couple of years."

The Blues got back into it thanks to Limpar's brilliant dive, but the scores from other grounds ensured a half-time from hell for Evertonians.

As the second half progressed, many seemed resigned to Division One football and began giving their own analysis. "Nev's playing the worst game of his life and Rideout the best," said one. Another shouted: "Come on, Mike. Bring Barlow on for Horne – he's useless!"

Seconds later, the Welshman scored a breathtaking equaliser and his former detractor ran onto the pitch to celebrate. Then the Gwladys Street rose to rewrite Manchester United's famous "Ooh-aah Cantona" chant: "Who needs Cantona when we've got Barry Horne?!"

The crowd was at fever pitch and when Graham Stuart won the game nine minutes from time, Goodison went wild. At 4.48pm, the whistle blew to signal scenes of mass celebration – on the pitch, in the stands and in pubs and houses across Merseyside. Never before have I seen so many happy people in one place and never before have so many perfect strangers embraced each other.

Sunday meant repeated viewings of Match of the Day, packets of throat lozenges and reading the reports in every newspaper, again and again! It may be Monday, but the party will go on for a long time yet. For thousands of people, this was one of the best days of their lives. But please, please, please Everton FC. Don't put us through it again!

Going for a song

(Liverpool Echo, June 14, 1994)

Z Cars was apparently staying as the club anthem – although there didn't appear to be much competition. Simply The Best didn't seem quite right for a side that had just survived the drop.

*E*VERTONIANS have kicked out an idea to change the club's traditional pre-match battle hymn. Blues' fans used the ECHO's "Song for Goodison" poll to urge the club to retain the "Z Cars Theme".

Everton received numerous calls prior to the survival clash with Wimbledon, claiming that "Z Cars" was outdated. Many suggested alternatives, hoping to spark an inspirational response from the faithful. As it turned out, Everton stuck with tradition and our poll suggests it was a wise move. One of the most memorable and emotional afternoon's ever witnessed at Goodison subsequently unfolded from the moment "Z Cars" blasted out. It would now appear a change would have gone against the grain in the eyes of the majority of supporters, according to our poll. A total of 55 per cent backed "Z Cars" compared with 16 per cent for its nearest rival, "Simply The Best."

Forever Everton (11 per cent), Here We Go (8 per cent), We Shall Not Be Moved (5 per cent) and Chariots Of Fire (3 per cent) were the other contenders in our poll. Alternatives suggested in a separate postal vote took care of the remaining two per cent, including Clarence Frogman Henry's fifties classic, "I Don't Know Why I Love You, But I Do!"

Johnson takeover approved

(By Ian Hargraves, Liverpool Echo, July 27, 1994)

Peter Johnson was officially approved as the club's new owner and chairman, with a pledge to bring back the glory days.

*A*FTER more than a year's conflict behind the scenes, all was sweetness and light again at Everton's extraordinary general meeting of shareholders, which welcomed Peter Johnson's takeover yesterday.

The meeting approved by a majority of 1,659 to 22 a resolution to double the existing capital, allow Mr Johnson to take up the unclaimed extra shares and increase the number of directors above the present maximum of seven.

Mr Johnson's election as a director was unanimous, and there was only the faintest opposition by a handful of votes, to the similar election of Bill Kenwright's former consortium partner, Cheshire builder Arthur Abercromby, and the Moores family representative

John Suenson-Taylor. Immediately after the EGM, Mr Johnson was installed as chairman at a special board meeting.

At the same time, two extra directors were co-opted onto the board, both lifelong Evertonians and key figures in Mr Johnson's Park Foods empire. They are Clifford Finch, Park Foods marketing director and finance director, Richard Hughes. Mr Johnson pledged: "I will be passionately committed to returning Everton to its former glory."

Keep it secret

(By David Prentice, Liverpool Echo, August 30, 1994)

Having failed to land a big-name striker, Everton were nearly thwarted in their bid to complete a move for Nigerian international Daniel Amokachi.

$\mathcal{E}$VERTON will slap a "Top Secret" stamp on their next target – after Atletico Madrid tried to steal Daniel Amokachi away from the Blues on Friday night. After the Nigerian's name leaked out through the Press, Atletico president Jesus Gil made a money-no-object bid.

"They came in strongly for him," said chief executive Jim Greenwood. "As a result we will conduct our business in confidence in future."

Amokachi will be introduced to supporters before tonight's game against Nottingham Forest. He will be paraded on the pitch and will even have a banner in the Nigerian national tongue greeting him.

Blues in for Muller

(By Vic Gibson, Liverpool Daily Post, September 10, 1994)

Not satisfied with one forward – Amokachi made his debut that day in a 3-0 defeat – another was said to be joining in the form of Brazilian Muller. An issue related to the payment of tax – the striker was said to have insisted he wouldn't be paying any – scuppered the deal soon after.

$\mathcal{B}$IG-SPENDING Everton are poised to announce the sensational capture of another World Cup star. Brazilian striker Muller is close to agreeing a stunning £2.5m transfer – though a late hitch means he will not watch Everton at Blackburn this afternoon, as originally intended.

Manager Mike Walker said: "It is an exciting prospect. He has good pace and a tremendous pedigree. It would be a mouth-watering prospect if we can link him with Daniel Amokachi."

He would become only the second Brazilian to play in the English league, following Mirandinha's seasons with Newcastle in 1987-89.

Little and Large show

(By David Prentice, Liverpool Echo, October 3, 1994)

Mike Walker continued to seek fresh blood in a bid to find a winning formula.

$\mathcal{G}$LASGOW Rangers' little and large duo arrived at Goodison Park to discuss their moves to Everton. Giant striker Duncan Ferguson and little midfielder Ian Durrant travelled south with Rangers' boss Walter Smith in chairman Peter Johnson's limousine.

Ferguson's availability may only stretch until October 25. That is the date of a court hearing into an alleged head-butting incident with Raith Rovers' John McStay. Ferguson was suspended by the SFA for 12 matches but Rangers appealed and the ban was suspended until after the court case. It could be reactivated after that date.

Toast of the Palace

(By Val Woan, Liverpool Echo, November 2, 1994)

Pressure was building on Mike Walker as his team endured a miserable run of form. A victory did eventually arrive – with Bill Kenwright informed of the good news at the Palace as Gary Ablett's header secured a first win in 13 league games.

$\mathcal{E}$VERTON FC was the toast of Buckingham Palace last night. The right royal blue celebrations began after the team's first victory of the season. Merseyside theatre impresario and Everton director Bill Kenwright had missed the match against West Ham.

He was attending a dinner with other theatre VIPs for the Save the Children Fund, hosted by the Princess Royal. But his hostess made sure that he knew the 1-0 score – by sending a footman to ring Goodison.

Bill said: "The Princess Royal was concerned about our plight at Everton. When I mentioned the match she understood the importance of it and sent a footman to ring the club. There were cheers all round when he came back with the result, and our glasses were raised."

Walker goes. Who next?

(By Ken Rogers, Liverpool Echo, November 10, 1994)

The board finally lost patience with Mike Walker in the wake of a goalless draw at his former club, Norwich City. Ironically the side was enjoying its best run of the season – they had not lost in three games. The Everton captain was confident of success should the right man take charge.

$\mathcal{D}$AVE Watson spoke of the challenge facing Everton – and Mike Walker's successor. The Goodison skipper said: "We need points to get out of trouble. It will be one hell of a battle, but we are up to it and we will work hard for whoever is appointed."

He added: "We need someone who has seen and done it all with a big club. It will be a gamble putting someone in who hasn't managed at the top level. We need someone who can do things quickly."

Royle ascent

(By Ken Rogers, Liverpool Echo, November 10, 1994)

It was confirmed that Joe Royle would be returning home – with Liverpool due to be first up for his first league match.

$\mathcal{J}$OE Royle will be the next manager of Everton Football Club.

The Oldham Athletic boss was meeting Blues chairman Peter Johnson today, who hoped to tie the ends before confirming the deal at tonight's annual meeting at Goodison Park.

Joe Royle today confirmed that he had applied for the Goodison Park job and Latics chairman Ian Stott had given him permission to speak to Everton. The Blues have been keen to make a managerial pairing with former midfielder Peter Reid. But Royle said he believes "arranged marriages" do not work and wants to bring his current number two, Willie Donachie, with him to Goodison.

Joe leads the Blue Army

(Liverpool Echo, November 22 1994)

*A*LRIGHT, be honest. Did anybody, Blue or Red, anticipate a result like this? Liverpool have been vibrant, lively and creative all season – goals popping in to the tune of two or three every match. Everton have been barren.

Robbie Fowler has scored more goals than the Blues' whole team – so it was all the more astonishing that for the fifth Goodison derby in a row the Blues outhustled their more elevated neighbours for a victory only the most churlish of Liverpudlians couldn't say wasn't deserved.

Pre-match, Liverpool were confident to the point of complacency. Anfield legend Tommy Smith predicted a 3-0 hiding. But in recent seasons the inferiority complex Evertonians have harboured going into derbies has given them a decisive edge.

Everton wanted the points more than Liverpool – and once again it was taunts of impending relegation which seemed to light the touchpaper. Chants of "you're going down" were followed by a 56th minute header from Duncan Ferguson that set Goodison alight.

Joe Royle had picked a side that, on paper, looked like a damage limitation exercise. A midfield of Parkinson, Horne, Ebbrell and Hinchcliffe looked little more than a unit selected to suppress Liverpool's own creative flair.

But all four produced thundering performances to out-tackle, outwit and at times even outpass Liverpool as the Blues "went to war" – to use the manager's own words. The quality of Andy Hinchcliffe's crossing from the left was excellent and John Ebbrell looked like he hadn't been away from the first team.

While the midfield pressed Barnes, Molby and McManaman, Ferguson led a brave solo assault in the opening 45 minutes – then was joined after the interval by Rideout and began to threaten a goal.

Loan-ranger Ferguson produced his best display for the club. After six matches without a goal, he rose expertly in the 56th minute to place a deft header past David James from Hinchcliffe's corner.

The pre-match talk had been that Everton possessed the dodgy keeper, but calamity James looked far from comfortable as he stood rooted to the spot. In contrast, Neville Southall produced a save which could have been the turning point of the match. He swooped instantly to his right to block McManaman's shot after the winger had raced clear onto a Barnes through pass just three minutes after half-time.

James was at fault in the final minute, too, when the combination that yielded the first goal clicked again. Hinchcliffe slung in a curving cross from the left, Ferguson challenged James who, panic-stricken, punched the ball against the Everton striker where it dropped into Rideout's path. The substitute slid the ball in from eight yards.

A streaker did his best to steal the headlines – but they had to belong to Joe Royle. He selected a team and motivated them to go out and win a derby, that they were massive underdogs to even draw.

An overdeveloped sense of fun

(By David Prentice, Liverpool Echo, November 28, 1994)

Royle was hopeful of making Duncan Ferguson's loan move permanent – although the deal was unlikely to be straightforward.

DUNCAN Ferguson's Everton future remains clouded despite another outstanding performance by the on-loan Scottish striker.

Ferguson, 22, is due to return to Rangers in January for a court case where he will answer an assault charge. That could activate a 12-game ban from the Scottish FA.

Everton manager Joe Royle admitted the situation was very complicated, but added: "I would like to sign him. There is no doubt about that. You can see he has ability to spare. He is a real handful and he has time on his side. Sometimes he has an overdeveloped sense of fun. I am sure we can sort that out. He is loving it down here. They love their No. 9s at Everton. There is a terrific rapport with him."

Norwich swept aside as momentum builds
(February 18, 1995)

$\mathcal{O}$UT of the relegation zone in the league, the Blues welcomed a Norwich City side in freefall to Goodison Park in the FA Cup fifth round. Everton were ruthless as they secured a 5-0 win, with on-song Duncan Ferguson's run though the middle and arrogant finish off the underside of the bar to make it four was probably the pick of the goals. Anders Limpar, Joe Parkinson, Paul Rideout and Graham Stuart were the other scorers. Limpar commented afterwards: "That was probably the best I have played since I've been at Everton. "

Highland fling
(By Vic Gibson, Liverpool Daily Post, February 27, 1995)

Having signed permanently before the end of 1994, record signing Duncan Ferguson wrote himself into Everton folklore with an iconic celebration against the champions.

$\mathcal{M}$ERSEYSIDE'S biggest crowd of the season saw a single killer blow settle the battle of the Ferguson clans.

Big Duncan hoisted the blue flag over his red cousin Alex's head by bulleting home the only goal after 57 minutes at a packed Goodison.

The Scottish warrior then cavorted bare-chested down the touchline doing a Highland fling towards his namesake on the United bench.

Hopefully Fergie of Everton will wear a blue tartan vest the next time he whips off his shirt. Either that or he gets a sunbed. His exposed torso was almost as dazzling as Everton's brilliant teamwork on a day when they took another massive stride towards Premiership safety. Despite the lengthy loss of top scorer Paul Rideout and his replacement, Graham Stuart, the Blues were able to end United's 13-game unbeaten run and prevent them making it six straight wins since Monsieur Cantona went over the wall.

The dogs of war

(By Vic Gibson, Liverpool Daily Post, February 27, 1995)

An Everton midfielder also had words for critics of the Blues' "Dogs of War".

*W*ELSH terrier Barry Horne helped battling Everton overcome champions Manchester United and snapped: "Don't talk to me about the dogs of war." The 31-year-old midfielder added: "If we hadn't played football we wouldn't have got the result. We don't feel we are playing any different style to Blackburn, Manchester United or AC Milan, if you take it to the extreme.

"There is a horrible side to football and there is an attractive side. You have to combine the two – and I think we did that."

Crowds on the increase

(By David Prentice, Liverpool Echo, April 4, 1995)

The rise in home crowds was recognised.

*E*VERTON'S home gates crashed through the half-million mark on Saturday – for the first time in five years, and with four league matches still to go.

It's a remarkable show of support for the club, who have battled against the spectre of relegation since almost the opening day of the season. The 37,905 who watched the Blues' defeat by Blackburn took Goodison's league aggregate for the season to 520,833 – and the last time that mark was passed was on the last day of the 1989/90 season.

"It's not just the numbers that have been phenomenal this season," said boss Joe Royle, "but the vocal support, too. The fans have made a massive contribution to our very decent home record and we will need them even more in the last four home matches. It's been hard to understand at times, because let's not kid ourselves, the club have been struggling for three years now. On Saturday, when we were behind and chasing the game, you felt that the roof was going to come off."

Club secretary Michael Dunford said: "We have not been out of the bottom six all season, which speaks volumes for the fans' loyalty. I think it's an overspill from last season's Wimbledon match. That game made people realise how vital Premier League football is to the club."

The 40,011 who watched the defeat of champions Manchester United in February was the first time the 40,000 figure had been breached at Goodison since the FA Cup defeat of Liverpool in February 1991.

The last time more than 40,000 watched a league game was also for a derby, in September 1989.

Sorry about the dream final, lads
(April 9, 1995)

*J*OE Royle's "Dogs of War" were expected to roll over at Elland Road (in the FA Cup semi-final) with Tottenham Hotspur set to take their place in a "Dream FA Cup final" with Manchester United.

The Blues were backed by 18,000 Evertonians on three sides of the ground with two giant 80 feet x 40 feet flags, bought by the club, being shown off beforehand while Spurs fans took up the huge East Stand.

Matt Jackson headed the Blues in front early on from a trademark Andy Hinchcliffe corner, and it was one-way traffic with Barry Horne and Joe Parkinson in particular dominant in midfield.

Paul Rideout saw a goal chalked off early in the second half and straight from the free-kick, Everton doubled their advantage through

Graham Stuart. Jurgen Klinsmann fired home from the spot to reduce the arrears but it was to be the day Daniel Amokachi re-ignited his Everton career. Rideout suffered an injury and as he was receiving treatment off the pitch, Amokachi rushed on with the action resuming.

Any panic was soon brushed to one side as the Nigerian netted two goals in the final eight minutes to book Everton's passage to Wembley.

Joe Royle commented: "It was the best substitution I never made." He added: "I shouldn't be here, should I? Sorry about the dream final, lads. We played a lot of good football, which is perhaps surprising to one or two of you having read the previews. So ******s to you. And that's double 'L'. Only joking, lads."

Mystic Meg behind the Blues

(Liverpool Echo Cup Final Special, May 8, 1995)

It was written in the stars – a 3-2 FA Cup final victory.

*E*VERTON will repeat their Wembley heroics of 1966 and win 3-2 in a classic FA Cup final. That's the prediction of National Lottery fortune teller Mystic Meg. Meg's forecast is worth taking seriously. After all, she said Everton would win the cup even before the third-round matches were played back in January.

Mystic Meg also predicts: The Blues' scorers will be Paul Rideout, Daniel Amokachi and David Unsworth (pen) and that Ryan Giggs will score at least one of United's goals plus Neville Southall will save a penalty and a female streaker may run onto the pitch!

Meg explained how she tipped the Blues, saying: "I cast my Rune Stones. This is an ancient alphabet that also has magical powers of prediction. It spelt out a name that looked very like Everton."

Meg's top line shows the letters of the Rune Stones alphabet. The second line reveals how the letters which she cast correspond to the normal alphabet. They spell the name 'EFERTON'. The third lines show's how Meg's Rune Stones fell after Everton beat Tottenham in the semi-final. Mystic Meg said: "This time they give the letters J. R. So it looks like Joe Royle will be celebrating."

Back in January, Meg said that Everton would beat Newcastle at Wembley, a prediction which collapsed when they beat the Geordies 1-0 in the quarter-finals. But Meg now says: "I saw that Newcastle would be Everton's biggest challenge, so I thought this meant that they would meet in the final. The oracles do need interpreting. And, of course, I don't always do this correctly."

Blue nose craze

(Liverpool Echo, May 19, 1995)

The Liverpool Echo's blue noses proved popular.

*H*ÉRE is the nose news. Sorry folks, they've all gone. The good news is there are up to 30,000 of you Blue Noses out there. Our final batch of 5,000 colourful conks arrived this morning. They were snapped up at our Old Hall Street offices by True Blues early today. They ran out yesterday at Everton's Goodison Park Shop.

Duncan Ferguson and 10 nuggets

(By Neville Southall, Liverpool Echo, May 19, 1995)

Everton's veteran goalkeeper was dismissive of his side's chances ahead of the FA Cup final.

*J*UST like our semi-final against Spurs, I suppose we needn't bother turning up at Wembley tomorrow.

Manchester United are the biggest name in world football. They have all the names. We are just Duncan Ferguson and 10 nuggets.

Most of the fans watching around the world won't have heard of half of our players, but luckily for us Wembley seems to be a place for upsets. Ideally I'd like a draw.

We'd have another day out at Wembley to look forward to and it would be a night match, when it will be cooler. A lot depends on our younger lads. I feel a bit jealous of them. The older you get you have to make the most of it because the chance might not come again.'

A couple of old Evertonian friends got in touch this week to wish us all the best for Wembley. Brett Angell popped his head in at Bellefield, which was a nice gesture, and I was delighted when Mike Walker telephoned me during the week to wish me all the best. I always got on well with Mike and it was very good of him to send his best wishes.

Wembley is our national stadium and is steeped in tradition – but I think the atmosphere is better at Cardiff Arms Park. Everyone thinks about Wembley as being some sort of super stadium, which it isn't.

Back in the big league

(By David Prentice, Liverpool Echo, May 22, 1995)

Monday reflections after the Blues had upset the odds on a famous FA Cup day to remember against Manchester United.

*E*VERTON are back among the high rollers of British football once more. The Dixie Dean Trophy Room has been dusted down to make way for the most recognisable piece of silverware in the game.

The club is back in Europe – a stage they graced so sharply 11 years ago. This magnificent old club has travelled an incredible way in six momentous months – and who knows how far they can go now?

The supporters are piling back through the turnstiles in their thousands – and the club's commercial infrastructure has been redesigned with the Big League very much in mind.

But most of all, the players have engendered an indomitable spirit which has carried them to Premiership safety and now FA Cup glory.

Joe Royle has transformed Everton. There were a handful of sceptics when he moved from Oldham back to Goodison back in November – but even they can't doubt that Royle and Everton seem made for each other. In six months he has saved the club's Premiership skin and put silverware back in the trophy cabinet.

He's done it by making players believe in themselves – and more importantly believe in him. Many of the men who overcame Manchester United on Saturday had been written off earlier this season.

Match-winner Paul Rideout had slammed in a transfer request. Now he's desperate to sign a three-year contract – fully aware that Joe Royle wants to bring in new striking blood.

Andy Hinchcliffe was drifting through his career. Now he's one of the most potent attacking threats in the Premiership. And Dave Watson and Neville Southall had been the subject of crowd murmurings that their best days had been and gone. Both enjoyed one of their career best days at Wembley on Saturday.

Southall is an awesome, calming presence at the back. His dash out of his six-yard box in the last minute to barge through a posse of players and collect a cross one-handed, had Evertonians laughing in relief at his audacity.

His two moments of match-winning brilliance had come earlier. First, he arched back-breakingly to touch Brian McClair's header on to the crossbar. Then with 13 minutes remaining he broke United hearts with a superb double-block from Paul Scholes.

That preserved the 1-0 lead given to Everton by Paul Rideout's goal scored at the peak of an Anders Limpar-inspired purple patch. Until he limped off with a hamstring strain, Limpar had lived up to Royle's pre-match boast that the Swede was the most talented man inside Wembley Stadium.

It was his 30-yard dash with the ball from Watson's bold clearance that inspired the match-winner. Limpar switched the ball right to Matt Jackson, he did superbly to cut inside Pallister and set up Stuart. Everton were left holding their heads when his shot crashed back off the crossbar, but Rideout followed up to gloriously get power behind a headed chance that was more difficult than it seemed.

Big Nev celebrates his way

(Liverpool Echo, May 22, 1995)

Neville Southall didn't hang around for the Cup winners banquet.

JOE Royle: "That's Neville for you – nicely awkward. He's not shy, but he is unassuming and he's on his way back to Llandudno. He'd didn't want to know about the banquet. We asked him to stay and he said 'Why?' He's his own man, and I just let him get on with it. I came with an open mind but I'd seen one or two goals on the telly, and people were pointing the finger at Neville. We had a couple of days that were interesting between us. But from the first game he's been magnificent and he's not cost us a goal since I've been at the club. Nothing goes past him without some kind of comment. He has his own abrasive brand of humour but the rest just laugh and get on with it."

Homecoming heroes

(Liverpool Echo, May 22, 1995)

MORE than 300,000 fans welcomed home Joe Royle's conquering Everton team in one of the largest and most joyous turnouts the city has ever seen. The open-topped bus carrying the players, directors and families made its way through the city from Mather Avenue at 3pm, stopping everything in its tracks on its 90-minute journey.

At Liverpool University's playing fields, cricket was delayed as both sides joined in the celebrations.

Nuns wearing blue scarves clapped and cheered outside St Charles Youth and Community Centre in Lark Lane.

Thousands were gathered outside Goodison Park and even Liverpool fans celebrated: one banner read: 'A Red for life – but a Blue for today.'

Manager Joe Royle said: "It's tremendous to see so many happy faces. The fans have been brilliant and we can only say thanks a million to them." Daniel Amokachi said: "Football's like a religion here and I can understand why." And Paul Rideout added: "The fans have been great, supporting us when things weren't going well; today caps it all."

Andrei wings in after record deal

(By Paul Joyce, Evertonian Magazine, August 1995)

Everton broke their transfer record to sign winger Andrei Kanchelskis, although it was to prove a protracted deal.

$\mathcal{A}$NDREI Kanchelskis became Everton's record signing and an elated Joe Royle declared: "I've bought the best right winger in the country." The Blues' boss took his spending past £13m when the 26-year-old agreed a four-year contract. And he was delighted to finally get his £5m man ahead of rivals Middlesbrough and Arsenal.

Royle said: "I first asked Alex Ferguson about him at the end of last season when there were rumours of a rift. Then, when he confirmed he could go, we were straight in. Last year Andrei scored 15 in half a season. We need to score more and he will supply goals, crosses and I am sure, excitement. He will probably be the most exciting player I have ever signed as far as the fans are concerned."

Season-ticket sales are expected to soar past the 20,000 mark to an all-time high as "Kancho" mania hits Goodison.

The Royle curse

(By Richard Tanner, Daily Mirror, November 21, 1996)

Having secured a Premier League-best 6th-place finish in 1995/96, Everton's improving form early in the following season included a 7-1 demolition of Southampton. They travelled to Anfield four days later – where Joe Royle would again come away without defeat.

$\mathcal{L}$IVERPOOL'S hopes of returning to the top of the Premiership were hit by their Royle curse at Anfield. Roy Evans' team had forgotten what it's like to savour the sweet taste of a derby victory since Joe Royle took command of Everton. It's two years today since Royle launched his reign with a shock 2-0 victory over their fierce rivals – and since then he's continued an unbeaten sequence with a win and three draws.

Liverpool were eight minutes away from the win that would have leap-frogged them a point clear at the top after Robbie Fowler headed in his ninth goal of an eight-game hot streak. But it was no great surprise when Gary Speed glanced home an equaliser that stretched their unbeaten league run to seven games.

Southall dropped

(January 28, 1997)

There was shock news regarding Everton's goalkeeping position.

$\mathscr{E}$VERTON legend Neville Southall will be dropped for the first time in 15 years at Newcastle. The last time Southall was missing from an Everton first team for anything other than injury or suspension was in November 1982. Howard Kendall dropped him after Ian Rush had scored four times in a famous 5-0 derby match. He has made a record-breaking 728 appearances for the Blues, is Wales' most capped player and was awarded the MBE for services to football this summer. He is in his 16th consecutive season in the top division.

Everton have leaked eight goals in their last three matches. The job will now fall on £1m summer signing Paul Gerrard to stem the flow.

Kanchelskis departs

(By John Edwards, Daily Mirror, January 30, 1997)

Another player was off to pastures new.

$\mathscr{A}$NDREI Kanchelskis completed a beat-the-deadline £8m move to Fiorentina last night. The Everton winger agreed terms and was on his way to Italy within hours of a fee being thrashed out.

Fiorentina were determined to get their man before the midnight deadline for this weekend's Serie A programme. Goodison boss Joe Royle said: "He had a terrific season for us last year, but he hasn't been right in his mind this time around. He has become unsettled and it was inevitable that he would go sooner or later."

Robson lined up after Royle goes

(By Richard Tanner, Daily Mirror, March 28, 1997)

A run of only two league wins in the calendar year – as well as a shock FA Cup defeat to Bradford City – saw Everton's tag as championship dark horses quickly diminish. The slump in form, not helped by a catalogue of injury problems, led to the departure of Joe Royle. The club were immediately linked with a move for a previous candidate.

*B*OBBY Robson will be offered £1m a year to take over as Everton boss from axed Joe Royle.

I understand Everton chairman Peter Johnson contacted former England manager Robson minutes after Royle's dramatic departure.

Johan Cruyff is also on Johnson's short list. But Robson is No. 1 choice and is expected to be fired by Barcelona this summer after a stormy season.

Johnson wants a high profile international figure and Robson, after enjoying success with England and with clubs in Holland and Portugal, fits the bill.

Royle had been unable to attract world-class players to Everton. He left Goodison by mutual consent yesterday after a row with Johnson following the collapse of a joint £3m deal to buy Norwegian pair Tore Andre Flo and Claus Eftevaag.

I understand Johnson refused to pay the extra £700,000 that Norwegian club SK Brann were demanding to cover Flo's cut of the fee. He also feared an outcry from the fans if Royle went through with his attempt to buy back veteran midfielder Barry Horne.

It left Royle, already under serious pressure because of Everton's poor run of results since Christmas, in an untenable position.

Royle, who was last night unavailable for comment, had 15 months left on his contract and walked out of Goodison with a pay-off of around £200,000.

Gray u-turn stuns Everton

(By Richard Tanner, Daily Mirror, June 24, 1997)

Having stumbled through the latter stages of the 1996/97 season under the caretaker stewardship of skipper Dave Watson, the search continued for a new boss. The Blues thought they had come up with the perfect solution – apparently they hadn't.

*A*NDY Gray last night called for peace as a massive bust-up erupted after his astonishing U-turn on the Everton job.

The Sky TV pundit rejected the Goodison manager's job exactly a week after telling the world how much he coveted the post.

He told Everton chairman Peter Johnson in his interview that it was the one job he would quit Sky for – and even presented Johnson with a list of potential transfer targets.

But Gray stunned the Merseyside club yesterday by deciding to stay at Sky – who have handed him a £3m four-year contract.

An embarrassed Gray tried to defend himself against accusations that he had used Everton by saying: "In my heart I wanted to manage Everton. I would be Everton manager today if chairman Peter Johnson had offered me the job. But he never did.

"Had he pushed a contract under my nose when my heart was ruling my head I would have said 'yes.' But he didn't.

"In many ways joining Everton would have been the realisation of a dream, but increasingly over the weekend my head has been telling me different things.

"I asked myself whether a season as assistant-manager at Aston Villa several years ago was the right grounding for a top job like this. Maybe

I got a little carried away with all the speculation in the media, and to take the job and then let the supporters down would have been too much to bear.

"I expect I will get some stick the first time I return but my head will be held high. I have nothing to hide or regret. I hope my reputation and image as a true Evertonian has not been damaged."

The Sultan of Walton

(By Richard Tanner, Daily Mirror, November 18, 1997)

Howard Kendall was eventually chosen to return for a third spell, although his early transfer dealings suggested that the club's record fee would be safe for the time being. However, there appeared to be hope on the horizon as speculation suggested a takeover.

*T*HE Sultan of Brunei, one of the world's richest men, is planning a sensational £60m bid to buy Everton.

The Sultan is desperate to own a top English football club and the crisis-hit Mersey giants have emerged at the top of his wanted list.

He has also looked at Manchester City, QPR and Crystal Palace – but his advisers believe Everton have all the right credentials and can offer him a Premiership profile.

Former Goodison striker Jim Pearson, who now works as personal sports consultant for the Sultan's family, has alerted them to reports that Everton chairman Peter Johnson is looking to sell his 68 per cent stake in the club.

Johnson's 21,000 shares are now worth £60m, but that is small change to the Sultan, whose personal fortune has been estimated at a mind-blowing £38billion – and who earns £60 every second. He wants to buy a football club as a present for his two soccer-mad teenage sons, Billah and Malik. But his dream is to restore the club its former glories and establish it as a top European force.

The curtain falls on a goalkeeping great

(By Alan Nixon, Daily Mirror, December 10, 1997)

Neville Southall just wanted to play, having made his swansong against Tottenham the previous month – a 2-0 defeat.

*N*EVILLE Southall has told clubs, "Come and get me," as the curtain comes down on his 750-game Everton career. The veteran goalkeeper was told by manager Howard Kendall yesterday that he can go out on loan before his contract expires at the end of the season.

Unbridled joy with a chunk of realism

(By David Prentice, Liverpool Echo, May 11, 1998)

It all came down to the final game. Survival was ensured with a 1-1 draw against Coventry City on a dramatic day at Goodison Park.

*J*UST as Coventry City provided the nadir of Everton's desperate season back in October, so they were present at the zenith.

For the second time in four fraught years Goodison Park rocked to the sound of salvation, as a 1-1 draw proved enough to see off relegation.

Maybe the Everton hierarchy had this in mind all along, when they adopted a paler hue of the famous royal blue jersey. Everton are the new Coventry City – able to preserve their Premiership place by increasingly narrow and unlikely margins. Yesterday's margin was the most desperate yet.

Just five goals separated Everton from Bolton when the season's curtain fell.

Sure, there was unbridled joy at the finish. But there was also a healthy chunk of realism. The wild celebrations which swept Goodison Park when Paul Alcock's final whistle confirmed a 45th consecutive season in the top flight lasted barely 60 seconds.

Fans sprinted ecstatically onto the pitch, mobbed the players unfortunate enough to be caught away from the safety of the tunnel, and cheered manically. But then the cheers of relief and joy transformed into a grim, tribal shout of: "We want Johnson out!"

There has to be a thorough analysis of this most wretched of seasons – and until matters improve Peter Johnson will remain the scapegoat. But for a few hours at least, Evertonians were revelling in the relief of another escape – and there were some memorable moments.

Gareth Farrelly's sugar sweet right-footed drive which flew into the top corner of the net – and the frenzied celebrations which followed. Nick Barmby's heroic performance from midfield – and his heart-stopping penalty miss six minutes from time. And the surreal moment in the 73rd minute when a roar exploded around the stadium to greet a goal 220 miles away.

It was a shattering, primeval roar which rose from the bowels of the earth. The players froze momentarily, turning expectantly to the terraces for confirmation that Chelsea had indeed scored.

All save Michael Ball.

The 18-year-old rookie of just 25 Premiership games turned to his more experienced team-mates, pointed his fingers to his temples and ordered them to concentrate on their own game. Ball's emergence as a defender of class and authority has been one of the few bright spots at Goodison this season.

It was a season which the Goodison faithful almost seemed to have accepted would end in tears even before yesterday's finale. The mood around the ground before kick-off was one of subdued resignation. The arrival of the Everton team coach at 2.30pm sparked a short-lived cheer on Goodison Road. The Coventry team coach's arrival was met with silence. Hardly the intimidating cauldron that worried Wimbledon's players in 1994 – until five minutes to four.

When the first familiar strains of the Z-Cars theme tune heralded the players' arrival in the tunnel, the 40,109 crowd rose for one final effort.

It was an impressive noise.

The sound swept Everton into an energetic and enterprising start.

Madar had already bobbled one shot wide and Barmby been blocked by Breen, when Ferguson headed a hopeful cross back towards the edge of the penalty area.

Gareth Farrelly has been readjusting his sights at the Park End goal all season. This time he lined up his right foot beautifully and the ball soared into the top corner.

For half an hour Everton were undoubtedly in the ascendant. Hedman made an outstanding save from Watson, Nilsson headed off the line from Tiler and Farrelly swept another couple of efforts narrowly wide.

But the second steadying goal never came. Madar exited in a flurry of arms and grimaces and the Blues began to sit deeper and deeper on their lead. Coventry bossed the possession and looked much the likelier scorers – until referee Alcock made a decision quite astonishing in its ineptitude.

Paul Williams' tackle on Cadamarteri was beautifully timed. The defender prodded the ball to safety, but the official ludicrously pointed to the spot. Nick Barmby '98 assumed the Graham Stuart '94 mantle, but Magnus Hedman made a superb save.

If Barmby was distraught in the 84th minute, in the 88th minute he was desolate.

Burrows swung over a cross from the left flank, Dublin rose unimpeded and directed a header which Myhre flapped into the net.

Just one goal from Coventry – or one from Bolton – would have dumped the Blues into Division One.

Instead, the only other goal of an amazing afternoon came from Chelsea. That was enough to bury Bolton.

Everton had survived because of another club's inadequacies rather than their own efforts. It was a grimly fitting way to end a season which has stumbled from one catastrophe to another.

The last time that happened club officials declared: "Never again."

The message this time must be: Never say never again. Whatever it takes, just get it right.

Mid-table mediocrity would be nice for a start.

Third-time unlucky

(By Garry Doolan, Liverpool Echo, June 25, 1998)

Last-gasp survival would not be enough to save Howard Kendall from a third and final departure deep into the close season

*E*VERTON confirmed the decision to part company with Howard Kendall at 2.30pm this afternoon. An official statement said Kendall's contract had been terminated by mutual consent.

Kendall had left Everton's Bellefield training headquarters at lunchtime without making any comment to the posse of assembled press and media. But in the official statement he said he was leaving the club after just 12 months in charge with regrets.

"When I returned to Goodison Park nearly 12 months ago, I genuinely felt I had returned to my footballing roots and fully expected to end my managerial career at the club where I had experienced so many triumphs," said Kendall.

"I leave with regrets, but I know how supporters will understand that a club of this stature demands success. I have no doubt that better times will eventually return."

Kendall also has a message of thanks to the supporters who had largely stood by him during the team's battle for Premiership survival last season. "To the best supporters in the land I say a sincere thank you," he continued. "Evertonians have always been and will always remain close to my heart."

Blue lift-off

(By Garry Doolan, Liverpool Echo, July 2, 1998)

A week later, his replacement was confirmed.

*P*ETER Johnson heralded the arrival of a new era at Everton.

The Blues' embattled chairman insisted the appointment of former

Glasgow Rangers duo Walter Smith and Archie Knox was "the most important day in my Everton career."

And as Johnson unveiled the club's most expensive management team ever at an upbeat Goodison Park press conference, he claimed it would prove a turning point in Everton's recent history.

"I'm delighted we've now got one of the best managers in Britain," he declared. "I'm sure he can do it because he's done it at another big club. There are big club managers and there are small club managers and, as it happens, we have got a well respected name in the game.

"It is difficult to run big clubs like Everton and he's shown he can do it at Ibrox. They don't come much bigger than Rangers. He's handled big names and taken Rangers to the semi-finals of the European Cup.

"I'm just pleased we've got a good manager who has succeeded at the highest level. It could well be the turning point for this club."

Bakayoko fires back

(January 4, 1999)

£4.5m striker Ibrahima Bakayoko, soon nicknamed 'Bak of the Eko', had scored only three times before becoming Everton's two-goal hero at Bristol City in the FA Cup. He had never offered to take a free-kick before his stunning set-piece opener.

*A*FTER a slow start to his Everton career he has now netted four times in four matches and he said after his cup double: "People used to say to me in the street, 'Bakayoko you are no good.'

"But it was difficult to begin with in England. You come to a new country, you do not know the football, you do not know your partner or how your partner plays and Everton do not know how I play. But I feel happier now."

On his free-kick, he commented: "It was nothing special. It was not my best. I have scored lots like that in France and even a backheel. But that is not important. I do not play for me. I play for Everton."

Bill's hopes for the future

(February 15, 1999)

Bill Kenwright, in the midst of an Everton takeover, spoke to Liverpool Echo sports editor Ken Rogers about his plans and hopes for the club.

$\mathcal{B}$ILL Kenwright today gave the clearest hint yet that he is closing in on a deal that will signal a new beginning for Everton Football Club.

The Goodison Park vice-chairman and his advisers have spent the past four months working on a complicated financial plan to try and secure the 68 per cent majority shareholding held by Peter Johnson.

Kenwright said: "I want to make it clear that in no way has Peter Johnson been obstructive to me. He has not asked for hundreds of millions of pounds. He has made me feel confident that he wants me to take over Everton Football Club."

His caution is clearly linked to what happened five years ago when he actually had an agreement in his possession signed by Lady Grantchester of the controlling Moores family which appeared to give him control of the club. Kenwright's elation was shattered when Johnson stepped in at the very last moment. This time around, Kenwright will take nothing for granted. He explained: "If you had said four years ago after my failed takeover bid that I would subsequently be sitting in the vice-chairman's seat with Sir Philip Carter back in his former role as chairman, I would have said you are barking mad.

"The fact that I am even talking about a takeover bid fills me with mixed emotions. On the one hand I am thrilled. On the other I am sad that things have not worked out because it means the club has not progressed the way all Evertonians like myself hoped it would.

"Anyone looking at the Everton situation will have to deal with three key areas. The first – and the one that I have been dealing with – is the complicated challenge of securing the major shareholding. Stage two is to stabilise the club financially. Finally, it is vital that manager Walter Smith is provided with sufficient funds to suit his needs."

Campbell strike gives Blues Anfield joy

(By Ric George, Liverpool Echo, September 28, 1999)

An eventful 1-0 victory at Anfield maintained the Blues' encouraging start.

*L*ET'S get this straight: Everton deserved their win. They were better organised and had better players. Cheaper ones, too. Derbies in the '90s have often gone the way of the Blues because of their greater commitment, but on this occasion they were superior in talent.

Not high on quality, this derby was, nevertheless, a rip-roarer, which combined more than the habitual drama with comic cuts. With three sendings off – there could (should?) have been five – the fans could expect the unexpected in what became a silly second half. By the end, Liverpool were playing with nine men, Everton with 10 and the Reds had an outfield player in goal.

Kevin Campbell's fourth-minute goal set the trend for a first half dominated by Everton, both in effort and in technique. Played onside by Jamie Carragher, the Blues striker gave Francis Jeffers' deft pass the finish it deserved with a thumping shot. Indeed, it was one of many threats posed by the young star who, if he remains level-headed, has the talent to earn global acclaim. But will he?

A mini first-half spat with Sander Westerveld was followed by a 75th minute slap-up where both players traded blows and were expelled for their stupidity. Westerveld was the more responsible.

His side having already made three substitutions, it could not could call on benched keeper Jorgen Nielsen.

Steve Staunton's courage to take up the gloves was commendable, and not unwise because he pulled off a quite superb stoppage time save from Abel Xavier.

Ironically, the Reds threatened most when they had lost their keeper, Everton inexplicably panicking when they had all the advantages. However, when Steven Gerrard received a stoppage time red card for a high tackle on Campbell, Liverpool's hopes were extinguished.

Gazza for Goodison

(By Ken Rogers, Liverpool Echo, July 17, 2000)

The media circus descended on Goodison as the Blues took a chance on a global star.

$\mathcal{E}$VERTON have put their trust in Walter Smith's remarkable personal relationship with Paul Gascoigne, aware of the mixed emotions fans have already expressed about the most unexpected transfer of the summer.

Vice-chairman Bill Kenwright, who spent the weekend with Smith negotiating with Gazza and his agent, explained today: "Once we had secured the players Walter and I had identified to do specific jobs, you begin to wonder about ingredient X.

"The manager felt that with the kind of players he is bringing to Goodison that the time was right and that Paul Gascoigne could fit the bill. Gascoigne is one of the greatest players this country has ever produced. I needed to know that he has the hunger to give it one last major effort."

Guessing game as Duncan waits for nod

(By David Prentice, Liverpool Echo, August 18, 2000)

The return of a Goodison hero...

$\mathcal{D}$UNCAN Ferguson will be kept guessing about the date of his Everton debut, with the season's curtain-raiser at Leeds tomorrow.

The Blues' new number 24 is anxious to make his 134th Everton appearance at Elland Road, after finally completing a Goodison return.

He said: "I have been thinking about Saturday but the manager has his own ideas on the situation, too. I'm 100% match-fit but I'm lacking match-fitness. I'm available for selection anyway."

2002-2012

Vintage Gazza rolls back the years

(Liverpool Echo, January 28, 2002)

A veteran Paul Gascoigne was in inspirational form in an FA Cup fourth-round victory over lower division Leyton Orient at Goodison, setting up three of the four goals in a 4-1 victory. Over 5,000 were estimated to have been locked out with capacity at Goodison having been lowered due to the terms of the club's safety certificate for the game (unreserved tickets were sold for the tie).

WALTER Smith said: "We had a touch of vintage Gascoigne out there. A little bit of the old sharpness and strength may be missing, but he's still capable of doing things that very few footballers can achieve."

Boyhood Everton fan and Leyton Orient midfielder Andy Harris said: "I saw the clock had run up and even though he'd (Gazza) said before the game he'd give me the shirt, I knew it was the one everyone wanted. Maybe I should have got a bit closer to him during the game! But I don't think anyone could get near him, he was that good."

Rooney on the brink

(By David Prentice, Liverpool Echo, March 12, 2002)

Meanwhile a young prospect was beginning to be noticed. Indeed, he would again be on target in victory for the youth side.

WALTER Smith will cast a covetous, but frustrated eye over his talented Youth Cup line-up at Goodison Park tonight.

Focus of his attention will be Wayne Rooney, a 16-year-old striker he would love to add to his goal-shy first-team pool.

The young England Under-17 striker may even have been given his first taste of the Premiership already – but for an FA rule which forbids schoolboys from playing senior football.

Rooney doesn't leave school until Easter, so until then Walter Smith will be forced to watch in admiration from the stands.

The youngster will spearhead Everton's forward line again tonight in an FA Youth Cup quarter-final against Nottingham Forest – just 48 hours after scoring twice for England Under-17s against Lithuania.

"It's asking a lot to expect a player so young to produce another match-winning performance so soon after playing 90 minutes for his country," said coach Colin Harvey, "but Wayne will give everything as he always does."

The youngster scored both goals in the 2-0 defeat of West Bromwich Albion in the fourth round, and added two more against Manchester City in the last round. Another influential show tonight and Walter Smith could be counting the days until Rooney leaves school.

Moyes is the man

(Liverpool Echo, March 13, 2002)

A 3-0 FA Cup quarter-final defeat at Middlesbrough, the club's third defeat at this stage of the competition in four years, piled on the pressure for boss Walter Smith. On the back of the Boro defeat, speculation suggested Walter Smith's spell as Everton manager could be coming to an end and so it proved. Everton moved quickly to find a replacement and made their move for an up-and-coming manager from the lower divisions.

$\mathcal{E}$VERTON today moved for Preston North End boss David Moyes. The Deepdale club have cleared the way for talks as the Blues hunt a successor to sacked boss Walter Smith. And they want the Scot to be in charge at Goodison Park for Saturday's home game with Fulham.

Preston are reluctant to lose Moyes. But they are already talking about what compensation they would want if he joins the Blues.

Walter "very disappointed" to leave

(By David Prentice, Liverpool Echo, March 13, 2002)

*W*ALTER Smith today spoke for the first time about his sacking by Everton. Smith said: "I am very disappointed by the way things have turned out. I wish everybody at the club the best of luck for the rest of the season."

Deputy chairman Bill Kenwright said: "Walter Smith was and is one of the most honest and honourable men in football. He brought a stability and dignity to Everton Football Club when it desperately needed it most. Obviously, today's decision was not taken lightly, but it was felt it was in the best interests of the club as it battles to preserve its Premiership status."

Welcome to the people's club

(By David Prentice, Liverpool Echo, March 15, 2002)

No pressure then on the new manager.

*D*AVID Moyes strode into Goodison Park last night having been compared to Sir Alex Ferguson.

Sir Philip Carter, however, chose to call him the new Howard Kendall. The Blues' chairman dismissed comparisons with the most successful modern manager, preferring to speak of the similarities surrounding the arrival of the most successful manager in Everton's history.

"It is a little like the appointment of Howard from Blackburn Rovers in 1981," explained Sir Philip. "Both are young, passionate managers who have served their managerial apprenticeship at Lancashire clubs outside the top division – and both are very ambitious. I think everyone would be delighted if David could achieve half of what Howard managed, although it should be remembered that even Howard's first few years were difficult ones."

But Sir Philip confirmed that a modest transfer pot would be put at the new manager's disposal. "From the financial point of view we have been putting in place a new financial package recently," he explained. "People seem to think that is simply about introducing a large amount of money into the place. It isn't.

"It is about rebalancing the amount of finance that the club has, some of it changing from one bank to another and so on. But from that point of view I think we are in a stronger position than we have been for some time to actually support David and give him some strength in terms of rebalancing the squad, which may mean that people will be leaving as well as joining."

Moyes met his players for the first time this morning, but he already met some of the club's supporters last night. A small group of Evertonians gathered outside Goodison Park's Park End offices to greet the new boss, and the Scot said it was the fans which convinced him to instantly accept the troubled post.

"The people made me come here," he declared. "I am from a city not unlike Liverpool myself.

"I have been brought up with Glasgow Celtic and Glasgow Rangers and I am now in a city where football means as much as it does up there. I think I am joining a football club which is probably the people's football club in Liverpool.

"The people in the street support Everton and I hope to give them something over the next few years that they can be very proud of.

"You don't get jobs in football management when things are easy and I think we would all be lying here if we said that we didn't think it was a big job. It's been a big job for all the previous managers and it will be no different for me, but it's one which I'm really positive about.

"I have great belief in what can be achieved here, partly because of the people I am working for now, but we are under no illusions it's a difficult task we've got this season.

"I would prefer not to be in this position. I'd rather have the pressure at the top of the league and I hope before too long to be able to say that here."

Young and old shine on opening day

(By David Prentice, Liverpool Echo, August 19, 2002)

It was the generation game on the opening day of 2002/03.

$\mathcal{T}$HE golden oldie nostalgia show was supposed to end at five to three.

Once the wrinkled but familiar faces of yesteryear had taken their bow, it was time for the fresh face of the future to take centre-stage.

Wayne Rooney did his bit. But even if he becomes the most prolific marksman in modern Everton history, he will still struggle to compete with the Goodison record of a striker two decades his senior.

When Les Ferdinand faces Everton, he scores. It's a grim fact of Evertonian life. Like no money, championship-winning teams being broken up by world wars, European trophy winners being banned - and Spurs drawing at Goodison Park.

Saturday's 2-2 stalemate was their fourth in a row . . . since, well since Ferdinand scored a Gwladys Street winner in 1998.

After nine matches which featured a remarkable 40 goals under David Moyes last term, the Blues kicked off with another four-goal entertainer. It was almost as if Everton officials had decreed that the club would kick off its historic hundredth season in the top flight in flashback fashion.

An adventurous 4-3-3 formation hadn't been seen at Goodison since men like Trevor Ross, George Telfer and David Smallman had skipped across the Goodison turf, rather than Saturday's prematch parade when they proudly dragged their slower limbs out there once again.

It was an experiment which might have backfired, but it was a gamble worth taking - and the biggest beneficiary was Tomasz Radzinski.

He used his abundant pace to turn a half-chance into a real one 10 minutes from time, then finished it with supreme ruthlessness. Let's pray it wasn't the exception which will prove a rule.

Evertonians will be hoping the same applies to goalkeeper Richard

Wright. He flopped limply over Ferdinand's hopeful 73rd minute strike, to gift Spurs - temporarily - the prospect of an unlikely away win.

Plenty of other things were different around Goodison on Saturday - including a press box full of excited Chinese journalists.

The object of their attention was midfield international Li Tie. At times the pace of the game caught him out, but for 76 minutes he was composed and controlled, and alongside Gravesen and Pembridge, made for a well balanced midfield unit.

For 45 minutes Gravesen produced his Danish World Cup form. Some of his tight, skilful approach play was among the best football he has produced in an Everton jersey.

The Dane tiptoed superbly through Spurs' covering midfielders to chisel out a chance in the 12th minute which Gary Naysmith's left foot was better placed to convert. Unfortunately Kevin Campbell's eagerness got his left foot to the ball first and Keller saved easily.

Another left-footer gave Everton the lead in the 36th minute, at the end of a move of flowing purpose.

Gravesen swept a pass down the right flank, Radzinski sprinted clear and crossed for Rooney and the youngster suppressed his natural instinct to shoot and swivelled sharply to tee up Pembridge. His finish was fierce, but far from the the only thing he did all afternoon.

Pembridge is the kind of honest, committed star who used to be the norm in English football. It's an attitude which is being replaced by the more technically accomplished but peripheral foreigner, and not necessarily for the best. Until Radzinski's late intervention, all Saturday's goals had surprisingly come from domestic sources.

Matthew Etherington crashed in a 62nd minute equaliser, as Everton's pressing game began to wilt in the heat. Les Ferdinand came on five minutes later for the surprised Teddy Sheringham. No-one was surprised, though, when he scored with his first touch.

Moyes went for broke, replacing a defensive midfielder, Tie, with an attacking one, Rodrigo - and a left foot shot which was blocked in the six-yard box almost repaid his boldness.

But when Kevin Campbell steered a pass into Radzinski's path

10 minutes from time, the Blues grabbed the point their adventure deserved. The significance of the 2002/03 season at Goodison may well be merely historic, but early signs are that it's going to be an entertaining one at least.

Everton: Wright, Hibbert, Weir, Stubbs, Naysmith, Tie (Rodrigo 76), Gravesen, Pembridge, Radzinski (Unsworth 83), Campbell, Rooney (Alexandersson 66).
Subs not used: Linderoth, Simonsen.
Tottenham Hotspur: Keller, Carr (Thatcher 44), Gardner, Richards, Bunjevcevic, Taricco, Davies, Redknapp, Etherington, Sheringham (Ferdinand 71), Iversen (Acimovic 83).
Subs not used: Perry, Sullivan.
Referee: Neale Barry.
Attendance: 40,120.

Rooney the record-breaker

(By David Maddock, Daily Mirror, October 21, 2002)

"Remember the name," implored Clive Tyldesley. Evertonians were already well aware of who he was.

*H*OW fitting that, in Everton's centenary year of top-flight football, they have unearthed a player who will one day be mentioned in the same breath as such legends as Dixie Dean and Tommy Lawton.

Wayne Rooney is the club's youngest goalscorer and is now also the Premiership's youngest scorer. He achieved that against an Arsenal side regarded among the best English football has ever seen.

He did it with an effort that will be a contender for goal of the season, and one which, in the view of Arsene Wenger, would have beaten three keepers all standing on the line.

And what was he doing to celebrate on Saturday night? His manager David Moyes hazarded a guess after the game. "He'll probably be out for a kick-around with his mates, showing them how it's done."

"Rooney really excites me, he is something special – the best young English talent I've seen since I came here as manager, the best player under 20 I have seen in England," Wenger enthused.

"He reminds me of Gazza in a way. He is a similar build, and has the same dribbling ability, but is a striker. I saw Michael Owen at 17, not 16, and Rooney is supposed to still be 16, isn't he?"

That last comment was a reference to the fact that the Everton striker looks anything but a raw kid when he gets out there on the Goodison turf. His goal to win this game, a minute from time, was the sort of thing that maybe only Henry, Van Nistelrooy, Hasselbaink or Fowler would conceive, never mind execute. And – forgive me for repeating this – he is only 16. He won't be 17 until Thursday, and cannot officially sign a professional contract until then.

Leeds hoodoo shattered

(By David Anderson, Daily Mirror, November 4, 2002)

Rooney's brilliance was inspiring an Everton revival.

*B*OY wonder Wayne Rooney celebrated the greatest fortnight of his young life with a dazzling goal that earned Everton their first league win at Elland Road for 51 years.

Everton boss David Moyes, who is determined to shield the 17-year-old from all the hype surrounding him, preferred yesterday's gem to Rooney's strike against Arsenal two weeks ago.

"He will grab all the headlines and he will continue to grab the headlines throughout his career," he said. "This was more the type of goal I want to see him score – I want to see him score more goals in the box, committing defenders."

Moyes voted best coach

(By David Prentice, Liverpool Echo, May 13, 2003)

The Blues' boss went on to win the award again in 2005 and 2009.

*D*AVID Moyes has been named Manager of the Year by his fellow bosses.

Moyes was selected top boss by the managers' union, the League Managers' Association, in recognition of the outstanding progress he has achieved at Everton this season.

He took over in March last year, with the Blues battling to avoid relegation. He kept the club up and with largely the same resources, took them to the brink of European qualification this season.

Moyes said: "When you go into the first major job in your career and see Gascoigne and Ginola in front of you, you realise all your efforts are worthwhile. I feel I have shown those players respect and this trophy shows I have gained their respect."

Rampant Blues stun United

(By Scott McLeod, Liverpool Echo, April 25, 2005)

Despite Wayne Rooney's departure in August 2004, the Blues embarked on their best Premier League campaign to date. A memorable Goodison Park evening saw his new club, Manchester United, vanquished as Duncan Ferguson enjoyed one of his last hurrahs.

SUPERLATIVES cannot do last night justice. Even before you take into consideration the wider context, it equates to one of the most thrilling nights Goodison has witnessed for many years. Bayern Munich, 1985, anyone?

As with that famous night, the mix was perfect. The crowd were rocking, the players were outstanding and the outcome was ridiculously satisfying. All across the city, ears are still ringing and minds are still buzzing.

Victory has rarely tasted so sweet, not just because it has been so long coming against Manchester United but also because there was a young lad from Croxteth on the losing side.

There was even something poetic about the identity of the man who proved Everton's talisman on the evening.

Only Alan Shearer has scored more goals against United since the Premier League came into being than Duncan Ferguson. It was one of those goals which provided Everton with their last league victory against them before last night – way back in 1995.

That was when Ferguson was in his prime. In recent times he has been a shadow of the player who waltzed his way into the hearts of Evertonians all those years ago. But last night he was gargantuan. His monumental frame cast a shadow over the most successful English team of the modern era – and made Rio Ferdinand look more like a £120-a-week player than the £120,000 one his agent claims he should be. Ferguson towered over the England man, winning more air battles than Douglas Bader. And he left Ferdinand in his slipstream for the 55th minute header beyond Tim Howard which secured the victory.

It was as if we were flung back in time to an era when Ferguson was justifiably regarded as one of the finest strikers in the business. Such impressive billing passed him by some years ago. As a result, much of the focus in recent seasons has been on his misdemeanours and on the injury problems which have made him an expensive accoutrement to the Goodison ranks. But last night demonstrated that, when the mood takes him, he can still mix it with the very best.

On paper, Everton have a tougher run-in than either Bolton or Liverpool. But if the rivals for the final Champions League berth were banking on the Blues lamely relinquishing their advantage, this result unequivocally proves otherwise.

David Moyes got his tactics spot on. But, more importantly, he got his players pumped up to the max. They harried United all over the pitch, won every 50/50 and knocked the cup finalists out of their stride. The reward came with a goal which was earned through sheer tenacity. Four times United tried to break free from their own third of the field, only for fearsome challenges to keep them pinned back. The pressure led to frustration, which in turn led to a rash challenge by Cristiano Ronaldo 30 yards from goal. The cross – from Mikel Arteta – and finish were top class but it was the endeavour which earned the set-piece which reflects the story of the game.

Lee Carsley deserves much of the credit for setting such a high tempo. He outshone Roy Keane in the United midfield, charging into challenges and breaking up United's passing game to great effect. Like Carsley, Joseph Yobo and Watson were back in the starting line-up and, like Carsley, they shone. Yobo silenced Ruud van Nistelrooy magnificently, while Watson did such a fine job at left-back you would have thought he had been playing there all his career. Their performances were typical on a night of relentless effort.

As a result, United had to rely on the unerring ability of Wayne Rooney to wrestle some kind of grip on the game. He charged all over the field on a one-man mission to ruin Everton's night, but he couldn't muster anything spectacular.

Gary Neville allowed frustration to spill over 18 minutes from time when he drop-kicked the ball at supporters in the Family Enclosure as he stood on the touchline waiting to take a throw. He couldn't and didn't argue with the red card which followed.

A second red card followed in injury-time, Scholes dismissed after picking up a second caution for a poor challenge on Kilbane. It was a decision which led to a heated exchange on the touchline between Sir Alex Ferguson and Moyes. It was a flash of passion that perfectly summed up the whole evening.

Too often opposition managers are seemingly in awe of Ferguson, just as teams can be in awe of United. It is to Moyes' great credit that he and his players stood tall against their visitors.

There is an unwavering belief that they are more than good enough to keep hold of fourth place. When you couple that with Everton's points advantage, it would be foolhardy to bet against them.

Going fourth into Europe

(By Mike Hornby, Liverpool Echo, May 9, 2005)

With two games to spare, a fourth-placed finish was confirmed.

*J*UBILANT Everton fans were today celebrating the club's return to Europe's elite.

The Toffees secured a fourth-place finish in the Premiership after Liverpool's defeat to Arsenal yesterday, and clinched a Champions League place for next season.

It will be the first time Everton have played in the European Cup since 1971. The 1985 championship-winning team was barred from the competition after the Heysel Stadium Disaster, which saw all English clubs excluded from European football for five years.

Prize money, TV rights, global exposure of the brand, experts say it could generate as much as £10m for the Goodison Park side, but the hard truth is that they will need that money sooner rather than later.

With seven players out of contract, Moyes will need a side capable of performing in two top-flight games a week.

After the match, David Moyes said: "I have been told we wouldn't do it. All credit to the players for sticking at it and proving that they are good players. It feels great. It's been a long, hard season but it's been terrific getting there and I'm delighted. We never said we had the best players. It's a massive achievement for Everton Football Club. At the start of the season I said we were shopping in Marks & Spencer. It's a bit more Dolce & Gabbana now."

Cahill delight at "amazing" season

(By Scott McLeod, Liverpool Echo, May 9, 2005)

The Australian, signed from Millwall for a bargain fee in 2004, took the club to his heart. The fans loved him too.

TIM Cahill, the club's top scorer and the hot favourite to be named player of the year, insists: "We have been fourth since September and it is what we deserve. It is satisfying because it means so much. Every time we have been asked to make a step up we have, regardless of the criticism we have had from other managers, players and football clubs.

"The only thing I imagined when I arrived was that I would be given a chance and I think I have taken it. To be where we are is absolutely amazing especially when you consider where Everton were last season." Cahill also paid tribute to the supporters, adding: "The fans' reaction week in, week out has been fantastic. As long as you work hard, even if you have a bad game, it means a lot to them and it means a lot to us for fans to understand football."

The last of the Corinthians passes away

(Liverpool Echo, April 25, 2006)

Brian Labone died just a couple of hours after he had attended an Everton fans' function. His passing was deeply felt by all in blue.

$\mathcal{J}$T is impossible to put into any meaningful words the sense of shock and sadness at the passing of one of the finest servants football has ever known. Anyone who met Brian Labone – and we're talking thousands on Merseyside alone – felt they had made a friend before he'd finished speaking his first sentence.

What singled out this giant of a man was not the fact he was a ball-playing centre-half of the highest calibre. It was not the fact that he was a born leader, whose charisma and presence meant he didn't need to raise his voice to make his point. No, what singled out this unique man, this complete footballer, was simply his love. His love of life, his love of football, his love of Everton and his love of the supporters.

Everything Everton and Evertonians stand for was captured within the spirit and being of Brian Labone. Up until Saturday he was at Goodison for every home game, meeting, greeting, engaging and enthralling the supporters with his infectious banter, opinions and humour. His footballing friends - and he had them on both sides of Merseyside's football divide - were often hard men. But many were close to tears today on hearing news of his sudden, premature death. Everton Football Club - and all of us - have lost a great player, a great friend and a great man.

Royle's tears for Mr Everton

(By David Prentice, Liverpool Echo, April 25, 2006)

Joe Royle paid a heartfelt tribute to his former captain.

$\mathscr{B}$RIAN Labone was affectionately known as 'Skip' to his former team-mate and friend, Joe Royle. And the current Ipswich manager fought back the tears as he paid tribute to his pal yesterday.

"He was my captain and I loved the man," said Royle. "Myself and Hursty (John Hurst) have been crying down the phone like old fish wives this morning.

"He was a keen wit and hilarious company, but most of all he was Mr Everton. Don't think that's a throwaway phrase. He was, truly, Mr Everton. There haven't been many greater players at Everton."

Labone was an experienced international defender when Royle made his debut as a 16-year-old in 1966, and he helped guide the young striker through the formative years of his career.

"We didn't have youth acadamies then, and the old apprenticeship really was a feudal system. Young players were verbally abused by senior pros, but Brian was never, ever part of that. He was always encouraging, always supportive – and what a player. He never missed a tackle or a header, ever. He was booked only twice in 14 years. Bloody hell! The game was brutal then, and he never shirked a challenge or a tackle, yet he was never sent-off and he was booked only twice.

"He wasn't Harry Catterick's ideal embodiment of a captain because he never rollicked anybody. He was always encouraging his team-mates. But we loved him. He and Westy (Gordon West) made sure I used to go home from training every day with sore jaws from laughing.

"He was such a thoughtful man, too. He always kept in touch and whenever we had a good result here at Ipswich there would always be a text message or a card posted. I first saw him when I was a schoolboy. I was head boy so it was my job to go down to the club every week on the bus to collect the free tickets for the Everton reserve matches.

"We were told then, 'that young centre-half will play for England one day' - and he did. But he was so unassuming that there will be plenty of people around the country who won't know of him. Everyone knows the name Jack Charlton, but Brian was a better player.

"He really was the last of the Corinthians."

Fergie signs off in style

(By Dominic King, Liverpool Echo, May 8, 2006)

The talismanic centre-forward scored an injury-time equaliser in his final game for the club.

*M*IKEL Arteta revealed he happily sacrificed his first Goodison Park goal of the season to allow Duncan Ferguson to end his Everton career in style. Having been given the captain's armband and a guard of honour as he made his way from the pitch following yesterday's 2-2 draw with West Brom, Ferguson signalled he has played his final game for the club.

As he walked around Goodison Park with the rest of the squad at the end, Ferguson − carrying a banner which read 'Once a Blue, Always a Blue, thanks for the memories' − could be seen telling the crowd: "Every one of you is quality."

The 34-year-old, starting for the first time since January 28, gave supporters what they wanted in the final minute when he scored at the Gwladys Street at the second attempt after Tomasz Kuszczak had saved his penalty. Arteta initially went to spot the ball but hastily passed responsibility to Ferguson when James McFadden reminded him that it was the last occasion the former Scotland international would have such an opportunity.

"Everybody would love to have a last day like he has done," said Arteta. "He has been someone special at the club, a special character. All last week, I kept asking Duncan 'what are you doing next season?' but he kept saying 'Micky, I don't know. Maybe I feel like I can keep playing.' So I didn't know. Then we got the penalty and Faddy came running over. He said 'Micky, Micky what are you doing? It's his last game!' I just said 'Fine, here, have it!' That's the way it was. I understand that he wanted to score and I'm very happy for him."

3-0 is enough to make Blue hearts go. . .
(By David Prentice, Liverpool Echo, September 11 2006)

New record-signing Andy Johnson had an immediate impact.

IT was a toss-up who would have the biggest headache on Sunday morning. Unlucky left-back Fabio Aurelio, who twice took booming clearances full in the face during a typically frantic Merseyside derby, or the earnest Evertonian who traced my footsteps the length of Goodison Road and beyond, after leaving one celebratory watering hole in search of another.

"I've waited a lifetime for that," he repeated, like a mantra. "I've waited a lifetime. Make sure you write that. We've waited a lifetime for that."

Not for a derby-day victory, of course, although they have been precious thin on the ground for Evertonians in recent years, but for a scoreline which rubbed Liverpool's noses in it.

The Blues have been made to suffer on more occasions than they would care to recall.

But even on those rare occasions Everton have utterly outplayed their neighbours, they've had to settle for 2-0 triumphs.

Which is why the 93rd minute calamity in Pepe Reina's goalmouth, which made the scoreline 3-0, was so riotously received.

The match was long since won, Everton were comfortably playing out time, but Andrew Johnson's second strike of the day turned an ecstatic afternoon into an historically significant one.

For many Evertonians it had, indeed, been a lifetime since such a one-sided scoreline had been recorded. It was September 19, 1964, when Harry Catterick's emerging young team triumphed 4-0 at Anfield.

It was actually 1909, the last time such a dominant score had been recorded at Goodison Park. So it was easy to understand the elation along Goodison Road afterwards. Everton's young and relatively inexperienced defensive pairing of Joseph Yobo and Joleon Lescott gave monumental performances.

Where Liverpool faltered, they were decisive, where the Reds looked sluggish, they were sharp. A training ground injury to Alan Stubbs ensured David Moyes was left with little option but to pair the two youngsters together. Whether he'd have chosen differently had Stubbs been available is something we'll now never know. But Yobo and Lescott look like a partnership which can grow together.

Everton's only pacy outlet was Johnson but what an option. His willingness to chase lost causes is enough alone to earn him the respect of the Gwladys Street, but when you ally that to a neat touch, a surprisingly physical edge and some better than tidy finishing, you have a new hero in the making.

Johnson's Goodison career could hardly have got off to a better start – a goal on his home debut, another in a first White Hart Lane win for 21 years, then two on his derby debut, make him the most prolific new Blues marksman since Tony Cottee cost a British record transfer fee.

Alan Ball dies

(By David Prentice, Liverpool Echo, April 25, 2007)

Just a day shy of the first anniversary of Brian Labone's death, Evertonians lost another legend.

*W*HAT a crushing irony that it should be Alan Ball's heart which gave out first.

A ceaseless study in perpetual motion – Ball was famed for his energy, his passion and his refusal to quit any battle, no matter how hopeless the odds. Sixty-one is an inordinately early age for such a man to pass away – and the coincidence of his passing coming almost a year to the

day after the death of his skipper and friend Brian Labone, is almost
too awful for Evertonians to bear.

Dixie Dean's place as the greatest footballer in Everton Football
Club's history is unchallenged. Ask a more contemporary fan the
name of the greatest player they've ever witnessed and the answer is
universal: Alan Ball.

He made 249 appearances for Everton, winning 39 of his 72 England
caps whilst a Royal Blue legend, and his heady mixture of delicate skill
and rampant fire branded his name upon Everton hearts.

His appeal is summed up by a story he once told about himself. Ball
was leaving an airport laden with bags, when an eager autograph
hunter demanded a signature. He indicated that he was in a rush and
his hands were full of luggage. Undaunted, and showing a never-say-
die spirit typical of the player himself, the youngster brandished his
book and declared: "Well you're Alan Ball, spit in it!" The youngster
got his autograph.

Ball was a Blackpool player when he conquered the world at the
tender age of 21. But it was only a matter of time before he forged a
relationship with Everton which would endure for the rest of his life.

The youngest member of Alf Ramsey's World Cup squad, he was a
driving force showing maturity beyond his years – and in the energy-
sapping extra-time period in the World Cup Final it was his legs which
continued to pump across the Wembley turf.

Everton signed him for a British record transfer fee of £110,000 just
weeks later. It's not overstating the case to say that Ball transformed
the club. Without his inspiring presence, Everton had lost the 1966
Charity Shield to neighbours Liverpool. That was on August 13.

A fortnight later Ball was in the Royal Blue engine room, Everton
beat Liverpool 3-1 in front of 64,318 ecstatic Evertonians, their new
flame-haired hero scored twice and an idol was born.

Ball ended that first season at Goodison with 17 goals - from midfield
- and never once neglecting his defensive duties. The following season
he scored an astonishing 20 league goals, added 16 more in 1968-69
– then in 1969-70 he was a member of the most cherished midfield

unit in the club's history – Ball, Harvey, Kendall, the Holy Trinity. It was the midfield which took Everton to its seventh league title playing football in the club's cherished School of Science traditions. Ball was both the inspiration and the most idolised player. But it was a two-way love affair.

"Once Everton has touched you nothing will be the same," he later declared – and he continued to champion the Blues throughout his life.

His value to Everton was inestimable. He was a frequent visitor to Merseyside – only last month delivering inspiring speeches to a group of spellbound supporters and former players at the Hall of Fame dinner at the Adelphi Hotel, and then the Crowne Plaza Hotel before the Everton-Barcelona old boys reunion. It's shocking to think that he looked in such rude and robust health.

Former colleagues talk of Alan Ball as one of Everton's finest players of all-time. Few would argue. There wasn't much of Alan Ball physically, but in terms of talent, commitment and inspirational service he was a towering colossus. His legacy will live on forever.

Arteta and Cahill sign new deals

(By Dominic King, Liverpool Echo, June 29, 2007)

Mikel Arteta and Tim Cahill were the two players who most defined Everton during the 'Noughties'.

*E*VERTON wrapped up their first two major signings today as Mikel Arteta and Tim Cahill agreed new five-year deals.

Although the current contracts of both players were not due to expire until June 2010, Everton's hierarchy were anxious to stave off interest from potential suitors in the Premiership and on the continent and reward the contributions they have made in recent seasons.

Talks have been on-going since the end of last season and were conducted in harmony with the midfielders, who have received significant pay increases.

Not only will the news delight Evertonians everywhere, it provides the perfect boost ahead of the squad's return to training next week.

Arteta's decision to spend the best years of his career at Goodison Park will be particularly well received. The current darling of the Gwladys Street has been the club's Player of the Year for the past two seasons and was hugely influential in helping Everton secure a UEFA Cup place.

"We are delighted with how he has done," said Moyes. "He has played really well. We like his skills and ability but he has grown into the team ethic that we have here and I think that has been the reason he has done so well. He has Spanish technique and a British mentality."

Fans' ballot on Kirkby move

(By Dominic King, Liverpool Echo, July 16, 2007)

The Kirkby issue was hugely controversial, and the club allowed the fans to have their say.

$\mathcal{E}$VERTON FC today announced details of a major ballot to gauge reaction to the proposed Kirkby move.

Around 33,000 current and recent season ticket holders, shareholders and members of the club's official fan club Evertonia can vote.

The Blues enlisted the help of the Electoral Reform Society for the ballot in the first week of August, with the results due later that month.

Chief executive Keith Wyness today said the aim of the ballot was "to ascertain the level of support" for the Kirkby plan.

A partnership with Tesco and Knowsley council would see Everton leave Goodison Park, its home since 1892.

Mr Wyness said: "As we promised at our AGM last December we will hold a ballot among our supporter-base to ascertain the level of support for a possible relocation to a new stadium in Kirkby.

"There was never any question of us reneging on that promise. The plan all along was to include as many of our loyal supporters as we could - and we believe we have achieved this. We are confident that a very, very high percentage of those who have historically supported the club will now have the right to have their voices heard.

"Anyone who has held a season ticket in the previous three seasons, along with anyone who has purchased one for the coming campaign, will be eligible, as will any shareholder who has not held a season-ticket since the end of the 2003/04 season.

"In addition all adult members of Evertonia during 2006/07 will also be eligible to participate. Holders of complimentary season tickets are not eligible and anyone who holds more than one season ticket in his or her name will be permitted just one vote, an industry-standard requirement and one supported by the Electoral Reform Society.

"We have worked hard to ensure that as many genuine supporters as is possible will be able to participate and we believe that the final number of supporters who will be eligible will be in excess of 33,000, a figure which roughly corresponds with the number of Evertonians at our Premiership fixtures at Goodison Park. We anticipate that ballot papers will go out in early August which, with a three-week voting period, should provide us with a result towards the end of that month."

Everton will publish plans of the proposed new stadium and reveal the financial implications for the club in the weeks leading up to the ballot. The board of directors will make a final decision on the club's future – guided by the results of the vote – soon after the Electoral Reform Society makes its findings known.

Tribute to Rhys

(By Stephen White, Daily Mirror, August 28, 2007)

The tragic death of young Evertonian Rhys Jones shocked the whole country.

THE players turned out in their famous blue strip yesterday.

But there was no roaring crowd to greet Everton's stars – just a sombre silence as they paid their respects to murdered schoolboy Rhys Jones.

Led by skipper Phil Neville, the multi-million pound squad laid a wreath at a shrine in the pub car park where adoring Toffees fan Rhys, 11, was gunned down. The wreath – in the shape of a blue and white football with the club motto – bore the message: "With deepest sympathy to the family of Rhys from all at Everton Football Club."

England players Neville and Andy Johnson and international stars James McFadden, Tim Cahill and Mikel Arteta laid signed shirts and a pair of boots with the message "Lots of love." Spaniard Arteta's shirt said: "To Rhys, see you in heaven." Another, from defender Joseph Yobo, read: "To Rhys, God bless."

Other players added touching words to shirts and boots at the Fir Tree pub in Liverpool's Croxteth district. Everton's pilgrimage deeply touched Rhys' dad Stephen, who said: "It's really nice for the guys to take time out to go down to the site."

Yak attack

(August 30, 2007)

The record signing of Yakubu signalled Everton's attacking intent.

*D*AVID Moyes believes Ayegbeni Yakubu will prove himself to be an £11.25 million bargain if he maintains his outstanding goals to games record for Everton. The Blues boss smashed the club transfer record for the third time since January 2005 yesterday when the Nigeria international finally completed his move from Middlesbrough.

Having been allotted the most famous jersey in the club's history – number nine – and after signing a five-year deal, Yakubu immediately set his sights on helping Everton make the leap from the top six into the top four by becoming the elusive "20-goal a season man".

Only Thierry Henry has scored more goals in the Premier League during the past four years and if Yakubu shows the form that made him such a success at the Riverside – and for Portsmouth – Moyes feels his transfer fee will become a snip.

Europe invaded by Evertonian army

(By Luke Traynor, Liverpool Echo, October 5, 2007)

After 12 years, the Blues were back in Europe.

*H*UNDREDS of Everton fans painted Kharkiv blue after a rollercoaster night of European football.

Fans descended on the Ukrainian city to roar the Blues into the group stages of the UEFA Cup with a 3-2 win against Metalist.

One fan's witty banner read: "Ukraine, U-saw, U-conquered while another read 'Can someone ask Michael Palin how we get to Kharkiv'.

Members of the Everton London Supporters Club decorated an old Russian tank in the city centre with flags.

Neil Moss, 26, from Formby, said: "At half-time, everyone was shell-shocked and there were loads of lads with their head in their hands.

"There wasn't much time for a drink afterwards as we headed straight for the airport. Let's hope we get teams a bit closer to home in the group stages."

Goodbye Bellefield

(By Dominic King, Liverpool Echo, October 13, 2007)

Everton said goodbye to the venerable old training ground, as they moved to an impressive new facility in Finch Farm, Halewood.

*T*HE gates to one of the most famous training grounds in England closed for the final time this week.

Having been the club's base since 1946, the Bellefield complex has been outgrown and, from now on, a sparkling new facility in Halewood will be the place they call home. But while Everton's players will have every type of fitness machine at their disposal straight away, it is going to take a long time to create the homely atmosphere that was unique to their base of 61 years in West Derby.

Of course, you have to move on in football if you want to be successful but that does not stop nostalgia kicking in – every major win in recent history was plotted behind those walls and there simply isn't enough space on this page to list all the great players who used the pitches.

Bellefield, though, wasn't just about footballers and managers. Far from it. So many characters have helped create an aura that made the place unique, from Big Norman on the gate, Mary and Mo on reception, the manager's PA Sue plus Robbie and his team of groundstaff.

Go back a few years and Mary who ran the kitchens was unfailingly helpful and often offered shelter to paper boys who had been chased to within an inch of their lives by Yogi the guard dog, a beast so ferocious he could have doubled for Stephen King's Cujo. We could go on and on.

Magnificent fans spark Nuremberg victory

(By Dominic King, Liverpool Echo, November 9, 2007)

*E*VERTON'S players had trouble sleeping yesterday afternoon but David Moyes believes the impromptu concert staged outside their hotel provided the spark for them to take control of Group A.

The squad's customary pre-match nap became impossible before the game against Nuremberg as hordes of supporters congregated in the town square and proceed to go through all the Gwladys Street's greatest hits. But far from being upset about the commotion, Moyes was actually overwhelmed and he hopes the 2-0 win in the easyCredit-Stadion was an adequate pay-back for those who had travelled to Germany.

"This is all new to us at Everton really," said Moyes, whose side are now on the brink of qualifying for the last 32. "You could see by the number of fans here how much they have been longing for it.

"There was no motivational speech needed because it was there on the streets of Nuremberg. The fans were a big influence, they were all around the ground and were a credit to the club as well."

Penalty defeat ends UEFA Cup run

(By David Prentice, Liverpool Echo, March 13, 2008)

After a dismal first leg in Florence, Everton fought back magnificently at Goodison, only to succumb in a shoot-out.

*T*HE European adventure is over . . . for now. But Everton have whetted their appetite for the kind of nights which had Goodison Park rocking to its very foundations last night.

And if the Blues are back next season – be it Champions League, UEFA Cup or even the booby prize of the Intertoto Cup – they will be better equipped to make an even bolder impact on the European stage, because Everton were utterly magnificent last night.

They dominated Italy's fourth best team for 120 minutes. They outplayed Fiorentina, they outpassed them, outfought them and outran them. Only goalkeeper Sebastian Frey stood between his team and a rout. And after a 2-0 triumph levelled the aggregate scores, but paid scant service to the level of dominance exercised by Everton, a failure in the lottery of a penalty shoot-out consigned the Blues to an exit they did not deserve.

Thomas Gravesen achieved the unusual feat of scoring with only his second touch of the ball, after he was introduced in the 119th minute for just that purpose. But Yakubu could only chip against a post and when Sebastian Frey spectacularly saved Phil Jagielka's effort Santana only needed to keep his own nerve from 12 yards, which he did.

Everton can hold their heads up high. The Blues started with all the drive, all the purpose and all the conviction which had been so sorely lacking in Italy. Of course, they also had Mikel Arteta and Andrew Johnson in their side.

On the bench in Florence, both were outstanding as Everton ran Fiorentina ragged with a magnificent display of controlled passion.

The early goal Goodison had craved duly arrived after 15 minutes. Steven Pienaar's cross was exceptional, the finish fortunate as the ball squirted up off goalkeeper Frey, hit Johnson in the chest and bounced into the Park End goal. It was the only slice of luck Everton would get all night. They piled forward with fire and resolution and the chances stacked up.

Arteta sliced wide from just 12 yards, although at a prohibitive angle, then saw a free-kick beaten out unconvincingly by Frey.

In the 19th minute the crowd screamed for a penalty as Johnson tumbled, but even as the referee was in the act of waving away appeals Osman followed up to rap a rising drive which was parried.

Jagielka headed over from Arteta's free-kick, Johnson did likewise, then Yakubu twisted and turned in much the same way he opened up Bergen, except this time Frey saved superbly.

Everton continued to carve out opportunities – and this against a side notoriously tight in defence. Fiorentina were buckling, if not cracking, and on the stroke of half-time Goodison erupted when Yakubu looked like he had levelled the aggregate scores from close range.

The noise quickly abated when a linesman's flag ruled an offside decision against Arteta, who had crossed, but seconds later when Mr Braamhaar's whistle sounded again for half-time the crowd rose again to deliver the kind of ovation only usually reserved for full-time victories. The only question which remained was could Everton reproduce the same vigour, drive and purpose in the second 45 minutes. The answer arrived quickly when Yobo's close-range effort was hacked frantically off the line. The second half followed the same pattern as the first – but it clearly needed something very special to break the Italians' resistance. Mikel Arteta provided it – crashing home a laser-guided shot from 25 yards.

Try as they might, Everton couldn't add one more goal. Yakubu went close, then Tim Howard was finally called upon to make a save and did so spectacularly from Pazzini's flying header.

That was an isolated threat as Everton continued to force the pace even throughout a gruelling extra time. Fiorentina survived then ultimately edged through. But the Blues will be back. And on last night's evidence they will be even better for it.

Everton: Howard, Neville, Yobo, Jagielka, Lescott, Arteta, Osman, Carsley, Pienaar (Anichebe 105), Yakubu, Johnson (Gravesen 119).
Subs not used: Wessels, Hibbert, Baines, Valente, Rodwell.
Fiorentina: Frey, Dainelli, Donadel, Gamberini, Osvaldo, Montolivio, Jorgensen (Santana 105), Ujfalusi (Gobbi 90), Kuzmanovic, Pasqual, Vieri (Pazzini 46).
Subs not used: Avramov, Kroldrup, Potenza, Cacia.
Referee: Eric Braamhaar (Holland).
Attendance: 38,026.

The Everton Collection

(By David Prentice, Liverpool Echo, March 18, 2008)

A charitable trust established by the club took possession of an incredible collection of Everton memorabilia.

$\mathcal{T}$HE keys to the past were handed over this week – as the Everton Collection Charitable Trust took possession of the famed David France Collection.

The Trust was established two-and-a-half years ago to acquire the unique collection of football memorabilia collected over a 27-year period by David France, who now lives in British Columbia in Canada.

His collection was described by auction house Sotheby's as the greatest collection of memorabilia they had ever seen relating to one football club, and it will be hereafter called "The Everton Collection".

The deal to acquire the collection was finally agreed in December after a campaign of fundraising by the Everton Collection Charitable Trust culminating in a grant from the Heritage Lottery Fund.

The Trust, set up by Lord Grantchester, grandson of Everton's late chairman Sir John Moores, Blues chief executive Keith Wyness and Everton supporter Tony Tighe, agreed a business plan with the Heritage Lottery Fund.

That plan outlined how the David France Collection would be housed in the Liverpool Record Office where it will be joined together with over 8,000 items of memorabilia from Everton's own archive.

Tighe said: "This is just the beginning of our work. The Everton

Collection now comprises over 18,000 items of memorabilia and it's all here in the Liverpool Record Office.

"We are currently recruiting two permanent archivists through the LRO to work solely on our Collection.

"Their initial task will be to ensure that the Everton Collection is properly conserved, digitised and prepared for the future. This will take a minimum of 12 months. Then we will be in a position to show off our crown jewels. Evertonians and fans worldwide will be able to view the Everton Collection on a special website or in a controlled environment at the Liverpool Record Office."

Fellaini new head boy

(By Dominic King, Liverpool Echo, September 10, 2008)

A new record-signing inspired a craze for wigs at Goodison.

*M*AROUANE Fellaini is ready to become Everton's head boy and ease some of the goalscoring pressure on his new team-mates.

Blues boss David Moyes shattered Everton's transfer record to sign the Belgium international in a £15m deal on deadline day and is in doubt the giant Fellaini will add drive, stature and power to his midfield.

There is, however, more than just energy to the 20-year-old's game and he proved that during his time with Standard Liege; though he can pass and tackle, Fellaini chipped in with a number of goals as Lazslo Boloni's side won the Jupiler League last season.

In total he scored 11 times in 84 appearances for Liege and given that he is 6ft 4ins, it is no surprise to learn that the majority of those strikes came via Fellaini's head from set pieces. Now Fellaini wants to put his height to good use for Everton and with the prospect of Mikel Arteta providing a succession of deliveries from corners and free-kicks, he is determined to become a nuisance in the opposition penalty area.

"I hope I can help the team win games," Fellaini said. "I have scored a lot of my goals with my head but the main thing is that my style of play will help the team and hopefully I will continue to score.

"When I spoke with the manager he said he was looking to bring in quality players to improve the side as well as young players and he said I fit that description. I hope I can take the team forward and help improve the club."

Everton 1 ITV 0

(By Will Payne, Daily Mirror, February 5, 2009)

What happens when televised football goes wrong – during the FA Cup fourth-round replay against Liverpool.

*B*UNGLING ITV chiefs cut to an ad break – and missed Everton's winning goal in last night's FA Cup game against Liverpool.

While midfielder Dan Gosling was scoring a sensational extra-time winner, viewers were treated to a commercial for Volkswagen cars.. and Tic-Tacs.

They couldn't believe their eyes when the match returned – and they were suddenly greeted with pictures of the Everton team in wild celebrations. Fans who had been on the edge of their seats were furious after being denied the key action with just minutes to go.

They deluged ITV with complaints, prompting a grovelling apology from presenter Steve Rider. He blamed "technical problems".

Put the champagne on ice. . .

(By David Maddock, Daily Mirror, April 20, 2009)

On an unforgettable afternoon at Wembley, Everton reached the FA Cup final with a penalty shoot-out victory over Manchester United – and defender Phil Jagielka was able to lay to rest some demons in the process. Unfortunately, despite taking the lead against Chelsea in the final after just 25 seconds, the Blues slipped to a 2-1 defeat.

*P*HIL Jagielka converted the penalty that put Everton into the FA

Cup final and then admitted: "I didn't even want to take it."

The defender – who got away with a foul on Manchester United's Danny Welbeck in the penalty area – ended Sir Alex Ferguson's hopes of a Quintuple by scoring the decisive fifth spot-kick in a shoot-out.

Everton keeper Tim Howard had saved from Rio Ferdinand and Dimitar Berbatov.

But England international Jagielka missed the penalty against Fiorentina last season that cost Everton a place in the UEFA Cup quarter-final and confessed he did not rush to volunteer this time around. "I wasn't exactly at the head of the queue saying, 'Pick me, pick me', and it's fair to say I didn't want to take one, but I'd been practicing them in the week and didn't miss one," Jagielka explained. "So the staff said I should take it.

"When our third penalty went in I was joking with Joleon Lescott on the halfway line that it would be nice if I got the winner, and we were giggling like mad – but I guess that was just nerves. When it came to my turn, it was a hell of a long way from the halfway line to the penalty spot, and by then I didn't even know what was happening. I don't remember how it went in – I had to watch it again afterwards – but it did, and after missing against Fiorentina, this is an incredible feeling."

United swept aside

(By Dominic King, Liverpool Echo, February 22, 2010)

The champions were beaten in style as the Blues' now traditional revival in the second half of the season continued.

𝒟AVID Moyes saluted his best of British chairman on Saturday afternoon, as he reflected on a handsome and deserved 3-1 victory over champions Manchester United.

With one Premier League club faced with closure and others struggling with mountains of debt created by foreign owners, the Blues boss pointed to the shrewd work of Evertonian owner Bill Kenwright.

"The club is certainly getting closer, hopefully, to the great days we had in the 80s," said Moyes. "We know that, strangely enough, it's not just about having a good football team and good players.

"You probably need something else now, and unfortunately it's called cash. But we are going to do it. A lot of people would like to be in Everton's position – and would like to have a chairman like Everton have got. Look at other clubs nowadays. We thought that foreign was all the rage. In fact booking your holidays at home with the chairman you've got. . . that's the type of chairman most clubs would want."

Moyes revealed that there had been a burning pre-match drive to improve the Blues' awful record against Manchester United, by taking the game to the champions. "The players know what I expect and how I want it to be. I think today they took it on. I really wanted to have a go at Manchester United. We wanted to see if we could really go and have a go. Our system meant we were a bit limited in how we could play but I thought we did as much as we possibly could.

"Last night at the team meeting I said 'We're going after Man United tomorrow and we're going to try and get the game won. We always do that, but there was an emphasis this time because we're at that moment, it's mentally where we are. I think Alex Ferguson gives praise where it's due and today he thought we deserved it."

Outstanding victory at City

(Liverpool Echo, March 24, 2010)

Victory at Eastlands made it a Manchester double.

*R*OBERTO Mancini and David Moyes both played down their touchline fracas after Manchester City's clash with Everton ended in explosive fashion tonight.

The rival managers confronted each other as a compelling Barclays Premier League encounter at Eastlands went into injury time with Everton leading 2-0. The remarkable incident was sparked by Moyes, who caught the ball ahead of making a late substitution. Mancini interpreted the Scot's action as time-wasting and went over to remonstrate angrily.

Fourth official Howard Webb intervened and after Mancini had finally been becalmed, referee Peter Walton sent both to the stands.

"I've spoken now with David and if I made a mistake I am sorry," said Mancini, who is under pressure to deliver fourth place and Champions League football.

Moyes defended his actions and cheekily claimed he might even have been doing City a favour. He said: "I caught it because I was making a substitution, I would have thought it would actually have helped him. I was very surprised, I didn't know what I had done wrong. Maybe I held onto the ball a second or two longer than I should have done but I was trying to make a substitution."

Victory provided considerable satisfaction for Moyes after feeling badly treated by City over the transfer of Joleon Lescott at the start of the season. Moyes was highly critical of City as they vigorously pursued the England defender over several weeks and eventually signed him for £22million. Moyes said: "We had a terrible start to the season and a lot of that had to do with Manchester City. I would rather come here tonight and show a bit of dignity with our result. What we should be talking about is the performance of Everton, which was outstanding."

Everton v Everton

(By David Randles, Liverpool Echo, August 4, 2010)

History was made as CD Everton came to Goodison.

*I*F you know your history you will be aware of a special occasion taking place at Goodison Park tonight.

Some 101 years after CD Everton was formed, the Chilean club will finally face their namesakes for the inaugural Brotherhood Cup.

CD Everton were established by a group of exiled Anglo-Chilean football supporters in 1909 in the port of Valparaiso, inspired by Everton's all-conquering tour of South America alongside a travelling Tottenham Hotspur side.

To mark their centenary year, the Vina Del Mar club have been invited to Merseyside to play Everton and arrive as the first Chilean club to play in Europe. It is an honour that delights CD Everton manager Nelson Acosta who says he will be a proud man leading his team out at Goodison.

"This is an historic occasion for Everton Chile and the English Everton," said Acosta. "It is the first time a Chilean team has been invited at club level to come and play anywhere in Europe.

"We will be the first to do it and we are very proud of that.

"Over the years there have been links and similarities between the two clubs. It goes beyond the world of football. We are in the realms of cultural and historic links between the two countries; between our cities. It is a great moment for us."

A game we couldn't lose

(By Greg O'Keeffe, Liverpool Echo, August 5, 2010)

IT must have been an exciting Everton side which embarked on that all-conquering tour of South America back in 1909.

So exciting in fact, that those early 20th Century Toffees inspired a whole new team named in their honour. That club, from the picturesque coast of Vina Del Mar in Chile, made their first ever visit to the land of their forebearers yesterday for a long-planned friendly.

The 171 Chilean fans, more than Fulham brought to Goodison last season, were a lively entourage ensuring the game had a constant samba-style accompaniment with drumming and chanting throughout.

On 51 minutes a slick move eased Moyes' side ahead. Magaye Gueye fired a cross into the area and Jermaine Beckford's emphatic header hit the back of the net.

The incongruities of the night helped make it so memorable. A sense of confusion for a few seconds every time the pitchside announcer declared an Everton substitution and a player sprang from the away dug-out, the unique sight of two Evertons in lights up on the scoreboard and the sound of home and away fans chanting one name at the end.

Everton's second came from another Gueye delivery, this time a corner aimed at Fellaini's towering frame, and Bilyaletdinov capped off his own fine evening by burying a sweetly struck volley. Nelson Acosta's side were well-organised, hard-working and methodical but consistently second best. In the end it was a comfortable win for the blues in a game which, in every sense, Everton really couldn't lose.

Everton: Mucha (Turner, 46), Coleman (Mustafi, 85), Yobo, Jagielka (Arteta, 46), Neville (Hibbert), Rodwell (Gueye, 46), Pienaar (Vaughan, 67), Cahill (Fellaini, 46), Bilyaletdinov (Baxter, 78), Osman (Baines, 46), Beckford. Sub not used: Distin.

Everton: Dalsasso, Blazquez (Oviedo, 83), Arias (Penailillo, 60), Cortes (Bottaro,83), Ramirez, Guevgeozian, Nania (Schwedler, 54), Garipe, Montesinos, Diaz, Saavedra.

Subs not used: Rencoret, Perez, Ceratto.

Referee: Mark Halsey.

Attendance: 25,934.

Spanish magic on the Mersey

(By James Pearce, Liverpool Echo, October 18, 2010)

The fans enjoyed a comfortable victory over the neighbours.

*M*IKEL Arteta was on cloud nine today as he revealed the feelings that followed his first ever goal were better than he dreamed.

The Spanish midfielder's thumping drive early in the second half propelled Everton to a richly deserved 2-0 victory over Liverpool at Goodison Park yesterday.

That strike had added spice as Arteta is best friends with Liverpool keeper Pepe Reina.

It needed all of Arteta's ingenuity to flummox Reina but, at the decisive moment, he showed the class with which he is synonymous to send Everton's fans into raptures.

"I was desperate to score a derby goal and find out how it would feel," he said. "The reaction of the fans was amazing, so to score and to win the game made it even better.

"I was just delighted when I saw the ball hit the back of the net. The ball was coming quite high so I knew the players would be coming at me. So I tried to get an early touch and get it away from my feet as soon as possible. Pepe (Reina) was struggling to see the ball because there were so many players in front of him.

"We'd been talking at half-time about needing the second goal and scoring it made things a lot more difficult for Liverpool."

Tim Cahill is no stranger to netting in derby games and yesterday's strike was his fifth against the old enemy.

As was the case when he fired in at the same end in September 2006, Everton never looked back from that point and Cahill dedicated the victory to Blues everywhere.

"It means everything," said Cahill. "I grew up with Duncan Ferguson and Stubbsy (Alan Stubbs) teaching me all about Everton and knowing what the derby means to the fans.".

Another thrilling win at City

(By Greg O'Keeffe, Liverpool Echo, December 21, 2010)

On a freezing night, Manchester City were beaten again.

*T*IM Howard hailed the "raw emotion" of Everton's return to winning ways after a heroic 10-man performance at the City of Manchester stadium.

The Blues held on for a vital 2-1 win over Manchester City, who were hoping for a victory to send them top of the league, despite seeing Victor Anichebe sent off with half an hour left.

Howard said: "It was a raw reaction at the end. That was pure emotion for us, and we said in the dressing room that it was weird how good that felt. We've beaten a few top teams over the years, but this felt really good. I can't put my finger on it but you saw what it meant to us.

"Maybe it was the cold, maybe because they could have gone top of the league, but you saw what it meant to us. We just seem to do well at certain places and this is one of them. We had that belief here because of past good results and we've only had to come up the road."

Moyes: Cahill my best bit of business

(By Greg O'Keeffe, Liverpool Echo, December 28, 2010)

David Moyes paid tribute to a modern icon.

*T*HE Everton manager turned Joleon Lescott from a £5m Championship player into a £25m England international, put Leighton Baines on a similar trajectory, and took the unfancied Steven Pienaar from Bundesliga anonymity to a highly sought-after inspiration for club and country.

But of all his mega bargains, the Scot insists Tim Cahill is the best piece of business he has ever done. Moyes' capture of Cahill for £1.5m in the same summer that Wayne Rooney left Goodison Park, barely caused a ripple at the time.

But fast forward five years, 65 goals, and countless tub-thumping performances, and the unknown Aussie he took a risk on has become an icon feared and revered in equal measure by opposition throughout the top flight.

"As I've said many times, a lot of our team selection revolves around Tim Cahill," says Moyes. "He scores goals for Everton like Lampard does for Chelsea, not quite in the same quantity, but he has done it over five or six years now. He scores goals every season and has been really vital for us.

"I don't think I'll do a bit of business as good as him again. There will always be business done when you pick someone up from the lower leagues but I don't think that will be done in the English leagues.

"You might do it abroad, but maybe not in England again because it's getting harder and the talent is identified earlier on in the lower leagues these days."

Penalty joy at the Bridge

(By Greg O'Keeffe, Liverpool Echo, February 21, 2011)

There was more joy in an FA Cup penalty shoot-out.

*P*HIL Neville declared that Everton's magnificent FA Cup replay win over Chelsea proves the competition's magic is as strong as ever – as the skipper wrote himself into the royal blue record books.

Neville's winning spot-kick at Stamford Bridge means he is the only Toffees player to have ever scored in three different penalty shoot-outs, after he also found the net against Manchester United and Brentford.

The 34-year-old insists that practise makes perfect, after a week when honing his penalty technique proved a welcoming distraction from being forced to mull over the video nasty of their 2-0 defeat at Bolton.

Neville, who will now lead Everton into the fifth round against Reading next month for the right to travel to either Manchester City or Aston Villa in the last 16, said: "I was confident because I've been practising myself all week.

"We do our homework at Everton and I was really confident stepping up. The fifth penalty is probably the most glamorous one to take. I felt really good. The manager told us just to hit it as hard as we can. My biggest worry was a big divot by the penalty spot.

"Petr Cech looks really big in that goal – but luckily he went the wrong way. I just concentrated on the ball and, as soon as I got back in my stance, I knew I was going to score. Since I came to Everton, I took a penalty against Manchester United in the FA Cup and scored.

"I also scored against Brentford earlier in the season.

"But forget the penalties, the effort we put in and the spirit we showed and the quality we showed meant that we deserved to win the game."

The travelling supporters were in raptures when Neville's kick hit the back of the net and the captain insisted that the FA Cup has most certainly not lost any of its appeal.

"I keep reading that the FA Cup has lost its magic but that's the biggest load of trash ever," he said. "You can't re-create that magic in any other cup competition."

The Toffees were on the brink of exiting the competition with just two minutes of extra time left, until a stunning free-kick goal from Leighton Baines sent the tie to penalties.

"It was a stunning free-kick and a stunning performance," said Neville. "He must have put in 20 or 30 crosses. In all three games we've had against Chelsea he's been man of the match in each of them."

Hibbo the record-breaker

(By Greg O'Keeffe, Liverpool Echo, March 9, 2011)

Shoot...

$\mathcal{I}$F Tony Hibbert runs out under the Goodison floodlights tonight, the defender is likely to set an intriguing and perhaps unwanted Everton record. The 30-year-old will be making his 209th league appearance for the Toffees – and is yet to breaking his scoring duck. That means experienced Hibbert, who has played 278 games in total for the Blues, overtakes John (Jock) McDonald who played a total of 224 games during the 1920s without hitting the back of the net.

Happy return for Pienaar

(By Greg O'Keeffe, Liverpool Echo, February 3, 2012)

After a year away, Steven Pienaar was delighted to be back at Goodison.

$\mathcal{S}$TEVEN Pienaar compared leaving Everton FC to 'walking out of your child's life' – and insists his Goodison Park return felt like coming home. The 29-year-old is excited to be back on loan after Everton beat QPR to his signature, but accepts some supporters could still be angry about his decision to leave for Spurs 12 months ago.

Pienaar, who fought to persuade Tottenham boss Harry Redknapp to sanction his last-minute deadline day switch, said: "In a way it does feel like home.

When I came back the lads welcomed me with open arms, it's a good feeling and like coming back home. I understand (if some fans are still disappointed). It's part of football. One moment you're playing for a club and the next you just walk out. It's like walking out of your child's life. To get the acceptance back you have to work and show that you do deserve to be forgiven." Pienaar is in contention for a return to David Moyes' line-up against Wigan at the DW Stadium tomorrow, but is taking nothing for granted. "To be honest, I feel as if I have to fight for my place," he said. "I still believe I made the right decision (going to Spurs) but in life, things change and I'm happy to be back here. I'm looking forward to making the most of my time here."

One man guaranteed to offer Pienaar a warm reception is Leighton Baines. And Pienaar says the England defender was keen for him to make the move on Tuesday. "Bainsey texted me and asked me if I was coming back home," he said. "I haven't played for a while, but me and him have also had an understanding on and off the field."

Follow the Jelavic road

(By David Anderson, Daily Mirror, March 28, 2012)

It was back to Wembley for another FA Cup semi-final after a Jelavic-inspired Everton dominated Sunderland at the Stadium of Light.

$\mathcal{L}$ONDON is bracing itself for a Scouse invasion on April 14 after Everton won through to make it an all-Merseyside FA Cup semi-final. The capital will be taken over that day as the red and blue hordes head to Wembley for their first showdown there since the 1989 final.

David Moyes immediately began the mind games by installing Kenny Dalglish's side as favourites.

Everton outclassed Martin O'Neill's side to stretch their unbeaten record against the Wearsiders to 17 games since 2001.

Marouane Fellaini was a colossus in midfield, while Leon Osman was a constant nuisance for poor old Sunderland, who just never got going.

Every Everton played performed well and Moyes claimed he saw only men in blue last night. They won thanks to an effort from Nikica Jelavic and a David Vaughan own goal, and that was the least they deserved for their dominance.

Despite arriving at the Stadium of Light just 45 minutes before kick-off, Everton dominated from the first whistle.

Gordon West passes away

(By David Prentice, Liverpool Echo, June 11 2012)

A league champion in 1963 and 1970, Gordon West left us in 2012.

*E*VERTON great Gordon West was a giant of a goalkeeper, with an even bigger personality.

An athletic, ebullient footballer with a bubbly demeanour – he was a hugely popular character at a time when football was sprinkled with larger than life personalities.

Beneath that flamboyant character lay a complex, sensitive man troubled by insecurities. A chapter in his autobiography was headed "Nervous Torture", whilst in the seminal documentary, The Golden Vision, he spoke of being physically sick before going out to play.

But Big Westy overcame those self doubts to establish himself as one of the greatest goalkeepers of his generation. And then, long after he'd hung up his goalkeeping gloves, he became an outstanding ambassador for the Everton Former Players' Foundation, publicly baring his soul to promote the fine work of that charitable organisation.

It was during those nights that Big Westy demonstrated the generosity of spirit. Aided by the Foundation at a time when he needed support himself, he tirelessly publicised the body's activities – and he showed the world that as well as having been a stunningly successful goalkeeper, he was a lovely, lovely man.

His dearest, closest friend was the iconic Brian Labone – and the duo formed Goodison's very own Odd Couple – affectionately berating each other with mock banter. But each barb was always delivered with a glint in Brian's eye and a wink from Gordon. The pair clearly adored each other. Close friends say that Gordon never truly got over the death of his pal in 2006. They were team-mates for more than a decade, each other's best men at their respective weddings and remained firm friends after they had retired from the game.

Gordon left Goodison in 1973 for Tranmere, 18 months after his dear friend's career had been ended by injury – but he left behind a remarkable legacy.

More than 400 appearances, at a time when Everton boasted two of the finest teams the club had ever seen, two league championship medals, an FA Cup winner's medal, an FA Cup runners up medal and England caps that would have numbered more than just three if he hadn't chosen to sidestep the 1970 World Cup finals.

"I'm a family man and I want to be with my family," he explained.'

Cahill departs a modern-day hero

(By Greg O'Keeffe, Liverpool Echo, July 24, 2012)

The Aussie left us with plenty of wonderful memories.

*T*IM Cahill's eight-year Everton FC spell has come to an end after the Goodison hero completed a £1m move to New York Red Bulls.

The Australian international has already been linked with moves to the Middle East and China during the summer, but a switch to one of Major League Soccer's top clubs emerged as his favoured option.

Cahill, 32, was still regarded as a valuable squad member. However, he had to decide between potentially accepting less first team action in the wake of Steven Naismith's arrival, or taking the option of a high-profile move to the USA. The chance to become a star in the USA proved too tempting to resist.

Magnificent Marouane

(By Phil Kirkbride, Liverpool Echo, August 21, 2012)

The plaudits were generous for Marouane Fellaini after his inspirational match-winning performance in the 2012/13 opening-day 1-0 victory over Manchester United at Goodison.

*P*HIL Jagielka has paid tribute to Man of the Match Marouane Fellaini, saying the 6ft 4ins Belgian's performance gave Everton the perfect platform for victory over Manchester United.

"We knew it would be hard against a great team but the big man gave us something to hold on to," said Jagielka. "We were tired at the end but the effort was fantastic and it's great to start with a win. He (Fellaini) is impossible to mark in training so it's great to see him do it in a proper game. We hope this is just the start."

Everton's class shines through

(By Barry Horne, Liverpool Echo, September 22, 2012)

I KNOW that many people, better informed and more eloquent than myself, have written extensively about the pre-match acknowledgement to last week's momentous findings from the Hillsborough Independent Panel. But whilst some people are seeing the panel's findings as an end, it is actually a beginning.

With just about all of the parties involved coming out with unreserved apologies, one would hope that the 'real end' of the tragedy will arrive much more quickly than it has taken to get to this point.

Everton rightly gained acclaim for the arrangements to acknowledge the institutional wrongs that the victims of the disaster have suffered for 23 years. The word that cropped up in many of the articles was 'class', but no-one should have been surprised because Everton is a club which, more than most, does things with class.

Very few commentators mentioned the Gary Speed tribute of 10 months ago, which was similarly moving and fitting. It is easy for occasions such as this to be mawkish and over-sentimental – but Everton on both occasions got the timing, the tone and the content absolutely spot on. Whoever pulled the whole thing together should be congratulated. But the class of Everton Football Club is evident on a daily basis.

The players behave with respect and dignity. They don't throw themselves around every time they are touched, they don't surround referees and they don't complain about decisions.

Players rarely leave the club on bad terms and are rarely, if ever, in the papers for the wrong reasons. Whilst David Moyes will refer to poor refereeing decisions, as he has to, he doesn't use them as excuses or go over the top. He doesn't complain about injury problems either. He just gets on with it.

Transfer dealings are conducted professionally and properly – and this comes from the top – where Bill Kenwright and David Moyes care about the club's reputation. It is something Evertonians should be justifiably and correctly proud of.

... and the final tribute

*T*HIS book will stand forever as a remarkable tribute to the players and backroom staff who have inspired the Everton story for 134 years, 120 of them at Goodison Park. The 'Official Everton Autobiography' also reflects on the words and comment of an army of journalists who have followed the club worldwide to record great moments and hail iconic heroes.

But most of all this book is a massive salute to you, the greatest fans in the world. Having read this major work of royal blue research, you can truly say. . . I know my history!

Ken Rogers